GIGOLOS AND MADAMES BOUNTIFUL
Illusions of Gender, Power, and Intimacy

ADIE NELSON
BARRIE W. ROBINSON

Gigolos
and Madames Bountiful

Illusions of Gender, Power,
and Intimacy

UNIVERSITY OF TORONTO PRESS
Toronto Buffalo London

© University of Toronto Press Incorporated 1994
Toronto Buffalo London
Printed in Canada

ISBN 0-8020-0613-2 (cloth)

Printed on acid-free paper

Canadian Cataloguing in Publication Data

Nelson, Adie, 1958–
  Gigolos and madames bountiful : illusions of gender, power,
  and intimacy

  Includes bibliographical references and index.
  ISBN 0-8020-0613-2

  1. Fortune hunters. I. Robinson, Barrie W. (Barrie William),
  1944– . II. Title.

HQ1090.N45 1994   305.3   C94-931437-4

University of Toronto Press acknowledges the financial assistance to its
publishing program of the Canada Council and the Ontario Arts Council.

Contents

Preface

The writing of this book was a genuinely collaborative effort. When we worked together on a project a few years earlier, the difficulties of coordination on that academic enterprise were, upon reflection, minor and trivial in contrast with those that beset the present effort. Whereas previously our offices were just across a hallway from each other, we were now, respectively, living in Kitchener, Ontario, and Vancouver, British Columbia, approximately 4,500 kilometres (about 2,800 miles for those who are metrically challenged) and three time zones apart. Instead of simply yelling across the hall – 'Hey, come here and see what I've just written' – we were forced to communicate according to Priority Post and first-class mail delivery timetables and frequently via ill-timed telephone connections. Messages invariably crossed in the mail, resulting in incomplete and often subsequently misleading revision directions. 'This is a revision of what was old chapter 3 but is now, I think, chapter 2, on page old-24, new-15 ...' (and a week later) '... I now see by your last letter that old-3, new-2 is now new-new-5 and God only knows what the new-new page numbers are. Help!'

Students of communication are acutely aware of the importance of immediate feedback to maintain a 'loop.' Our system of delayed feedback rivalled that between Mission Control and a headed-for-catastrophe Saturn space flight. That we managed to complete this manuscript without serious damage to any post-office employees, any laying of criminal charges of long-distance telephone harassment, or joint filing for bankruptcy, and still remain civil towards each other at the end is a tribute to either superior genes or modern chemicals.

While this book is a true collaborative effort, each of us will, in private at least, claim credit for every insight and phrasing of note, and blame the other for any errors or omissions that might become apparent to the reader. Therefore, each of us asks all of our readers to please direct all negative commentaries and criticism to the other author.

Acknowledgments

Anchor Books/Bantam Doubleday Dell: extracts from Louise J. Kaplan (1991) *Female Perversions: The Temptations of Emma Bovary.* New York: Anchor/ Doubleday

Arbor House, a Division of William Morrow and Co. Inc.: extracts from Joseph Barry (1990) *French Lovers: From Heloise and Abelard to Beauvoir and Sartre.* New York: Arbor House

Extract from *In Full Flower* by Lois Banner. Copyright © 1992 by Lois Banner. Reprinted by permission of Alfred A. Knopf Inc.

Bantam Books: excerpt from Sam Keen (1991) *Fire in the Belly.* Used by permission of Bantam Books, a division of Bantam Doubleday Dell Publishing Group, Inc.

Carol Publishing Group: extract from Ferdinand Lundberg (1966, 1988) *The Rich and the Super Rich: A Study in the Power of Money Today.* Secaucus, NJ: Lyle Stuart Inc.

Delacorte Press: extracts from Alice-Leone Moats (1977) *The Million Dollar Studs.* New York: Delacorte

Ebury Press: extract from Ann Barr and Peter York (1982) *The Official Sloane Ranger Handbook: The First Guide to What Really Matters in Life.* London: Ebury Press

Edmonton Journal: extracts from Judy Creighton (1992) 'Older Woman, Younger Man.' *Edmonton Journal,* Canadian Associated Press feature, 12 November

Fairfax Publications Limited: Barbara Ehrenreich and Deirdre English (1989) 'Blowing the Whistle on the "Mommy Track."' *Ms.,* July/August

Benjamin Franklin Library and Medical Society: extracts from R.M. Yoder (1955) 'A Way with Women.' *Saturday Evening Post,* 7 May

Reprinted by permission of the Peters Fraser & Dunlop Group and R.I.B. Library, Reed Book Services: extract from Joan Wyndham (1992) *Anything Once*. London: Sinclair-Stevenson

Harlequin Enterprises Limited: extracts from *Harlequin Fun Facts* © 1993 Harlequin Enterprises Limited

Jay Landesman Limited: extracts from Taki/Jeffrey Bernard (1981) *High Life, Low Life*. London: Jay Landesman Limited

Helen Lawrenson, Esquire Magazine, and Hearst Corporation: extracts from Helen Lawrenson (1983, originally published anonymously 1939), 'In Defense of the American Gigolo.' *Esquire*, June

Ellen Levine Literary Agency: extract from Philip Kerr (ed., 1990), 'Introduction,' *The Penguin Book of Lies*. New York: Penguin Books

Hamish Hamilton Limited: extracts from Caroline Moorhead (1980) *Fortune's Hostages: A Study of Kidnapping in the World Today*. London: Hamish Hamilton

Alfred A. Knopf Incorporated: extract from Marquis Boni de Castellane (1924) *How I Discovered America*. New York: Alfred A. Knopf; extract from Carroll Smith-Rosenberg (1985) *Disorderly Conduct: Visions of Gender in Victorian America*. New York: Oxford University Press

Lifetime Books: extracts from Ted Peckham (1955) *Gentlemen for Rent*. New York: Frederick Fell Inc.

Macmillan Publishing Co.: extract from Anne Cumming (1980) *The Love Habit: The Sexual Confessions of an Older Woman*. New York: Penguin Books

McGraw Hill Book Company: extract from Ian Robertson (1980) *Social Problems*. New York: Random House

Money Magazine: extract from C.F. Westoff and Noreen Goldman, 'Figuring the Odds In.' Reprinted from the December 1984 issue of *Money* by special permission; copyright 1984, Time Inc.

Pandora/Harper San Francisco: extract from Starhawk (1992) 'A Men's Movement I Can Trust' in Kay Leigh Hagan (ed.) *Women Respond to the Men's Movement*. San Francisco: Pandora

Penguin USA: excerpts from Brian Ross Duffy (1987) *The Poor Boy's Guide to Marrying a Rich Girl*. Copyright © 1978 by Brian Ross Duffy. Illustrations copyright © 1987 by Viking Penguin Inc. Used by permission of Viking Penguin, a division of Penguin Books USA Inc.

Lynn Ramsey: extracts from Lynn Ramsey (1978) *Gigolos: The World's Best Kept Men*. Englewood Cliffs, NJ: Prentice Hall

Joan Rivière, Heirs of, and *The International Journal of Psycho-Analysis:* extracts from Joan Rivière (1929) 'Womanliness as a Masquerade,' first published in vol. viii (1929) of the *IJPA*

Sidgewick and Jackson: quote from Abby Rockefeller cited by William Davis (1982) *The Rich: A Study of the Species*. London: Sidgewick and Jackson

Thomas Schnurmacher: extract from Thomas Schnurmacher (1985) *The Gold Diggers' Guide: How to Marry Rich*. Montreal: Eden Press

St Martin's Press: extracts from Robert K. Ressler and Tom Shachtman (1992) *Whoever Fights Monsters*. New York: St Martin's Press

Summit Books/Simon and Schuster Inc.: extracts from Marilyn French (1992) *The War against Women*. New York: Summit Books

We wish to thank Steven Wood of the *International Express* and Reena Kreindler for their help with last-minute bibliographic reference checks.

Every attempt has been made to communicate with the owners of copyrighted material quoted in this book. We would appreciate receiving information as to any omission in the acknowledgments.

GIGOLOS AND MADAMES BOUNTIFUL
Illusions of Gender, Power, and Intimacy

Introduction

This work originated as a tangential line of research undertaken by the first author while writing a doctoral dissertation on 'kept women' at the London School of Economics and Political Science in London, England, during the early 1980s. In October 1983, a 'Letter to the Editor' was submitted to every North American and British newspaper with a circulation of more than 100,000 in order to broaden the original research sample. The letter read: 'I am an Assistant Professor of Criminology at Simon Fraser University [in Vancouver, Canada] and am preparing a book on gigolos – men who purposefully seek to be supported by a woman. I invite individuals with personal knowledge of these relationships to contact me. Anonymity and confidentiality are guaranteed.'

At that time, research on gigolos and their Madames Bountiful was generally conceived of as simply a vehicle for the discussion of socially opaque roles in that it exposed a form of 'sexual deviance' in which both the males and the females within such relationships appeared to contravene normative expectations of 'masculinity' and 'femininity.' Although the phenomenon assuredly links the topics of money, power, and sexuality – three subjects guaranteed to invite reader interest – what little that had been published on the relationship seemed somewhat myopic and voyeuristic; the atypicality of such an association preoccupied writers and, as result, attempts to move beyond the prurient seemed frustrated.

Illustrated with photographs of female celebrities or socialites partnered with younger, less 'eligible' men who, although good-looking, lacked independent financial and/or social status, such articles teased the reader to speculate on whether or not the men were 'gigolos,' 'lounge lizards,' 'play-for-pay mates,' 'toy boys,' or 'boy toys,' and implicitly suggested that the women involved were engaging in behaviour that was at least somewhat unseemly. 'Gender-appropriate' behaviour was naïvely viewed as virtually sacrosanct, *as if* transgressions from it were more interesting and informative than the gender roles themselves.

Alternatively, the occasional article in the popular press appeared to be analytically wedded to ideas which presumed that the phenomenon of gigolos and their Madames Bountiful offered a form of validation that was testament to the equal and androgynous social roles that men and women were now playing within modern society, and to the economic mobility of women. These ideas were admittedly tempting. However, upon reflection, we felt the assumptions underlying them were both naïve and overly optimistic. Rather than suggesting a discarding of the tyrannies of gender roles in males and females, roles assumed within gigolo/Madame Bountiful relationships on occasion appeared to us to be pathologies of gender stereotyping. Indeed, at times the gigolo/Bountiful roles seemed grotesque caricatures of gender roles, sheathed in paradox, pathos, and no small measure of absurdity.

While some of the material we collected could have left us with a portrayal of some, perhaps many, Madames Bountiful as victims of various kinds of demographic crunches – a pool of undated, unmated female eligibles who were rejected somehow (no marriage proposals; divorced by, or deserted through the death of, their husbands) – not all of these women could be seen or would view themselves as the 'unfortunates.' Certainly our case-studies would not necessarily confirm such a homogeneous imagery of the women who become involved with gigolos. Similarly, a residual impression of gigolos as nothing more than a group of greedy, parasitic con men who control their partners solely for mercenary and sexual gain and who are easily identifiable as distinct from all other males would be equally misleading. The deeper we probed, the more elusive – and fascinating – the gigolo phenomenon became.

Some time later, while rereading a science fiction novel written by Carl Sagan, one of the authors was struck by the appropriateness of a term to describe the gigolo/Bountiful relationship. One of Sagan's characters stated: 'In classical times, thousands of years ago, when parchment was in short supply, people would write over an old parchment, making what's called a palimpsest. There was writing under writing under writing.' In a sense, an examination of the gigolo/Bountiful relationship reveals an interpersonal palimpsest, with meaning under meaning under meaning. A number of the levels of meaning of this relationship contrast it, but also align it, with its 'traditional' male-female counterparts. Most basically, a study of gigolos and their keepers is about power and sexuality – how they are fused and confused, how people may attempt to use one to gain access to the other – and how people attempt to fulfil their needs – emotional, sexual, and material – within relationships.

We cannot isolate gigolos and Bountifuls from the social context which creates the conditions in which they exist. Rather, we must consider various aspects of the social natures of gender, intimacy and power to see how they influence people in their everyday lives. In the chapters that follow we will be examining the changing context and content of gender that give rise to gigolos and Bountifuls. We will look at social and personal power and how they influence intimate relationships in general, and the gigolo/Bountiful relationship in particular. We will explore changing facets of love, sex, and intimacy, and how the allure and promise of intimacy establish an important, but not exclusive, precondition for the gigolo's existence. We will also illustrate and analyse how the gigolo practises his magic.

Throughout this book we seek to discover how the gigolo engages in his chosen vocation; what motivates the women who employ his services; and what accounts for the emergence, maintenance, and/or dissolution of the gigolo/Bountiful relationship. Finally, as we evaluate various layers of this relationship, we will consider how, within it, power, intimacy, and even gender itself may be illusory in many ways.

MEN FROM ALL SEASONS

'Gigolo' is an umbrella term; it covers many types of men who seek to be supported by a woman. As we explore in more detail in chapter 1, they range from the male stripper who performs cunnilingus on his lady admirers in a car between performances and views his on-stage performance as an audition for the role that brings in the majority of his income; to the professional gigolo who views each woman as interchangeable with those who have kept him in the past and those who will presumably do so in the future; to the 'Sweetheart Swindler' or 'Casanova Con Man' who is less a lover than a manipulator. Between these categories fall various men whose technique seems to consist of ad hoc fumbling around – students who seek out a professional woman to support their university career, men who aspire to the role of pampered lap dog to a wealthy woman and sundry others who are looking for love in all the right places.

Although the aspiring amateur and the professional gigolo may know many of the same people, attend the same watering-holes of the wealthy, and be similarly on the receiving end of a pay packet, in terms of the way they represent themselves and their self-image they differ somewhat. Perhaps the difference is that between involvement and commitment, which can best be explained by utilizing an analogy: that is, think of ham and eggs. The chicken is involved, but the pig is committed. Similarly, when the romantic entrepreneur becomes a professional gigolo, he no longer identifies his role as simply 'having fun' or taking advantage of what the situation and/or the woman offers. His lot is no longer simply that of one who finds that a lucky fate has strewn his path with roses and that his ladyfriend is amenable to supporting him. Rather, he comes to view his role as an occupation and to possess a professional's awareness of what the job demands: how to maximize gains and minimize losses, where to go to meet people who are socially expedient (e.g., Waikiki versus Myrtle Beach; Montpelier versus Wigum) and who offers the best chance of a financially viable relationship.

The following comments of a professional gigolo from London, England, suggest the self-assuredness and polish of one who is committed to his lifestyle:

The appellation 'gigolo,' smacking as it does of the Italian and the unsavoury, I deplore. May I suggest 'Gentleman of Fortune'? So I have considered myself for nine years. It has become my profession, profitable and enjoyable, since for various reasons my teaching career came to a halt nine years ago when I was in my mid-thirties. Suffice to say that I was a bachelor whose only interests were amateur dramatics and European Literature. My financial circumstances were barely adequate and I was unable to obtain suitable employment. It was during a local amateur performance that I realized that life could be pleasant and easy if I used my stage role as my way of life – a young and cultured man whose elderly mother had recently died and who suddenly found himself eyed longingly by ladies in an older age range.

My career began (after two false starts) when I rented a flat – my landlady was a reasonably affluent widow, letting a flat to a professional gentleman partly, I now know, for companionship. I was forced to spend my days at the University Libraries since I professed to being a budding author, engaged on a history of the theatre in the Midlands. Our relationship ripened until the inevitable happened and I provided her with an evening which, I modestly believe, was a revelation to her. My monthly envelope was thereafter returned – would you believe with a chocolate gateau? – and the lady became both obsessed and dependent. I remained for the year and only left when I was loaned 5,500 [pounds sterling] cash to finance a private publication of my non-existent book. The lady could well afford the money and I had amply earned my keep and also the terminal gratuity. After six months, I formed another liaison with a lady in her fifties ... Lord God, she was rich although fifty pounds overweight and somewhat unusual in her sexual demands. I remained for six and a half months with her in her luxury home. One of her peculiarities concerned my clothing and a monthly visit to Paris saw me gaining a remarkable though impractical wardrobe. I left following a final emotional storm on her behalf that verged on madness and left me slightly physically damaged. I took with me a copy of a French Book of Hours that was printed in Paris in 1496. I sold it that very afternoon in London for 2,500 [pounds sterling]! ...

I spent some weeks living as the pet of a divorced lady of considerable proportions who owned a Ladies Outfitters. Unfortunately, I was replaced by a young man and left, disgruntled, with a 200 [pounds sterling] cheque. I have lived, in the last two years, with a sixty-two-year-old spinster, acting for her gratification as her lecherous butler. Upon her sudden death, I had to leave after a certain amount of unpleasantness with the police. I was a beneficiary in her recently made will and her family (who only expressed an interest in her when she had died) made certain vile and honestly untrue allegations. Eventually, the matter was cleared and, upon probate, I received my 50,000 pounds. This kept me for many months ... I am now installed with a horse-faced antique-dealer's widow who allows me to cream the profits from her shop – which I manage superbly – and pays me a superb wage for consoling her in bed. Where I will go from here, I have no idea ...

Similarly, a Canadian real estate agent capitalizes on his job and family connections to meet wealthy widows, divorcées, and women newly separated from their husbands:

I would court one old darling at a time. Inundating them with flowers; spending just enough – but not much – money on them while selling them everything the traffic would bear. So you say this is not Gigoloing? Wait. From one I borrowed the price of a down-payment on my first house – never repaid – and she made my car payments. From another, I manipulated a Hawaiian vacation. From another a Caribbean cruise. From yet another, a comfortable 'alimony' when we both decided it was time to move on. [What do your friends think of your lifestyle?] Oh, they sometimes do ask if I never tire of the Geriatrics. [And do you? What are your relations like with your former lady friends?] Needless to say it creates enemies – perhaps they still care – all were too humiliated to talk. Vancouver's social elite is a relatively small community.

A third man, a bisexual whose 'professionally intimate' partners included both females and males, recently rhapsodized in a letter to the first author (with whom a friendship of more than seven years' duration exists) about his latest lover:

8 Gigolos and Madames Bountiful

As I recall, in my last letter I was rattling on of the musings of bachelorhood and dating life in the big city. I am now a reformed dataholic and have found myself the man of my dreams, my knight in shining armour, my main squeeze if you puh-leeze. His name is Trevor and he is the most kind, generous, affectionate, generous, loving, generous, secure and all those other values which we look for, but rarely find, in a man (and, oh yeah, did I mention he was generous?). We met at a dance in Boston and conversation opened up between us quite naturally considering the less than perfect setting for a quiet tête-à-tête. He was in town with his best friend for the weekend and was visiting from Los Angeles. That night we ended up talking over dessert and coffee latte and neither of us wanted to leave. He was staying at the Bostonian but wouldn't allow me to drop over for the evening. Instead, he made arrangements to meet the next day and the rest is, as they say, history ...

I just got to my seat on the aircraft for my flight back to New York (I was in San Francisco for the weekend) and I had to get out pen and paper to update you even further. As I was saying, Trevor and I have been seeing each other for the last two months now and it's hard to imagine life being any better than it is. We alternate our weekends together (he comes up one weekend, he flies me down the next) and occasionally we slip in a long weekend. This weekend is a little different 'cause I came down on Friday noon and am going back now (Tuesday) and he is coming up to New York on Thursday and leaving on Tuesday so we are able to see one another fairly frequently. Two weeks from now we're meeting in Denver and then going on to London/Paris/Rome for a little holiday. The reason we are able to see each other so frequently is because he is the Chief Executive Officer for a multinational company and owns four of his own travel agencies so getting airline tickets – needless to say – is not a problem ... It sounds quite glamorous but really it becomes kinda tedious after a while. Not being in all these different places but the actual flying itself. Not to mention that it does terrible things to your complexion (God, do I sound like a fag or what?). I know you probably don't have too much sympathy for me and are probably saying 'Fuck Off, Michael,' but it's a rough life and someone's gotta live it! ...

So here's the clincher. Last weekend he asked if I would marry him ... Now, I know it's sudden and it may sound in this letter like I'm being swept off my feet (okay so I am – so what?) but I really have hit the jackpot because he treats me like a king. I'm not just talking about the things he buys for me or eating at the top restaurants, but everyday-little things, like serving me orange juice in the morning as I come out of the shower, or writing me dozens of cards which profess how he feels about me, things like that. He really makes me feel as though I'm the best thing that's ever happened since Kids in the Hall was introduced to HBO (okay, not too funny but how good can you be at 35,000 feet and going 600 miles per hour?). Anyway, I was ecstatic and said that I can think of nothing more fulfilling than spending the rest of my life with him. So, in a week and a half, on Saturday, we're picking up my ring. Trevor is married and the ring that I will wear will be identical to his and will be worn on the right hand (the gay wedding finger). It's very beautiful with about 1.8 carats and is being made at one of San Francisco's shishiest jewellery stores. Trevor thinks it's borderline gaudy but I think it's quite elegant. I know his ring sure caught my eye. It's hilarious because Trevor is a little self-conscious about the ring and he doesn't want to appear pretentious ...

This weekend was yet another exceptional one from start to finish and I'm getting a titch concerned that I'll come to expect my weekends away with Trevor to be as eventful and entertaining as they are now ... We went to a cocktail party at the City Club on Friday night, late morning brunch at the hotel – mixed greens (romaine, arugula, nasturtiums, etc.) with a poppy seed dressing and marinated prawns with saffron rice. Um um. Later, we went to Colossus which, as the name implies, is one of the largest gay nightclubs in the city. On Sunday, we took his Mercedes convertible and toured the Napa Valley, going to several vineyards for their brief tours and wine tastings. We also went to Moët and Chandon which produces champagne. To finish off our day (it was gorgeous, about 80) we went to a fine restaurant called 'Tra Vigne' which is one of the most renowned in northern California. It was like something off of a movie set in terms of the decor, the people, the setting, everything. And the food! Baked garlic with foccacia, caesar salad, swordfish with pasta and sundried tomato garlic sauce, risotto, and gelato for dessert. The finest wines with dinner and Trevor doesn't spare the horses. My God! Unbelievable ...

Last night Trevor and I went to a restaurant called 'Oritalia' in Pacific Heights. The food is a combination of Oriental and Italian and although it sounds a little strange it's quite wonderful. I felt a little out of place because I had just come from swim practice and looked a bit like a drowned rat and the restaurant was on the hoity toity side. The staff made me feel comfortable though, there wasn't any snobbishness of any kind. And the food was incredible. We had calamari, Indonesian marinated chicken sate, angel hair pasta and rosemary basil garlic bread. Quite tasty! Next week I think we'll go to the Caribbean Zone for drinks first then the St. Francis for dinner. They have a little restaurant there called 'La Bella Voce' where members of the San Francisco Opera perform as you're having your dinner. It's not heavy at all but apparently quite entertaining ... The drawback (there is always one isn't there?) is his weight. He's fat. Oh well, God divides ...

A fourth gigolo, an American man, regularly haunts the lounge area of four-star hotels. There he will single out an unattached, middle-aged woman from a group of women; flatter her; inform her that he prefers 'mature women' to silly girls under the age of 45; and proceed to move into her party, affections, bed, life, and pocketbook in no particular order. The man would not be asked to screen-test for any Hollywood movie on gigolos; yet, in the span of one year, three relationships yielded him a profitable $300,000, on which no tax was paid, and enough free dinners, outfits, and holidays to satisfy. The man, at the time, was 55 years old, divorced, 5 foot 9 inches tall and 195 pounds, and had grey hair with a receding hairline. His clothing style he termed 'trendy,' 'avant garde,' although the uncharitable might make remarks of the 'mutton dressed as lamb' variety. Although he was closer in appearance to Dom De Luise than to Tom Cruise, his looks were hardly a bar to a successful career as a Casanova Con Man. He knew what the Hollywood casting directors ostensibly did not.

MOVIES GO TO THE GIGOLO

In 1926, Cecil B. De Mille produced a movie based on Edna Ferber's 1922 short story 'The Gigolo' in which the titular character was portrayed as a villainous despoiler of fair womanhood. Although De Mille had taken licence in expanding and further debauching Ferber's original characterization, the role had not been highly regarded by Ferber herself. The movie persona of the gigolo was that of a rapacious villain replete with a twitching eye and well-greased hair, while both the story and the movie depicted a parable, a morality tale that cautioned the observer about the follies of such behaviour and the ruinous path awaiting men who would find such behaviour appealing.

In her short story, Ferber's gigolo is named Nicholas 'Giddy' Gory, a formerly well-off young American war hero, who found himself, at the end of the war, scarred and destitute in southern France. Unprepared for conventional employment, he became a professional dancer, charming women as he whirled them around a dance floor. The shallow 'glamour' of his existence became apparent and Giddy grew increasingly embittered by his experience. A lost man, he was 'saved' only by his childhood sweetheart who miraculously appeared in his arms as his dance partner. Thus, he was saved by the redeeming power of love. Giving up his debauched lifestyle, Giddy returned with his reclaimed love and her parents to Winnebago, Wisconsin. Whether Ferber intended this to be a fitting punishment or the road to conventional morality is unclear. However, the implicit moral message is stridently clear: the road to happiness is the well-trodden path of conventional gender roles, and no man is worth the money he takes from a woman.

More recent attempts to update social knowledge on the role of the gigolo through popular culture seem similarly underwritten by allegiance to a code of ethics that proclaims the inherent superiority of more conventional modes of behaviour for men and women. Indeed, what distinguishes the more recent renditions of the gigolo in film from their predecessors would seem to be the styles of clothing worn rather than the underlying social message.

The role of the gigolo was, in 1980, the focus of the movie *American Gigolo*; 'Julian Kay,' as portrayed by the American actor Richard Gere, was a devastatingly attractive man who spoke six languages (purposefully learned to increase his eligibility to foreign women), wore beautifully tailored suits, worked out to keep his body trim, and worked out equally arduously in the boudoir to satisfy his lovers. However, the movie plot is no less a morality tale than the earlier portrayal. Julian, framed for a brutal sex-related murder he did not commit, finds himself bereft of friends, benefactors, and protectors; the married woman he was with on the fateful night refuses to corroborate his alibi – that he was with her in bed at her home when the murder was committed. He pleads with both his male and female pimps to assist him and finds himself betrayed by both. Although he beseeches them to help him, offering in exchange to work for meagre payment and to engage in homosexual or 'kinky' sex with their clients, they sneer at him and remain unmoved.

Incarcerated and scheduled to stand trial for the murder, Julian is visited by salvation in the guise of a client, the wife of a senator, who truly loves him. She would willingly become a sacrifice of love, moving from the tyranny of a loveless marriage into the tyranny of adultery. At first, she assists Julian by paying for his legal counsel. When that fails to stem the tide of misfortune that assuredly awaits him, she forfeits her marriage, her good name, and her social status to provide him with an alibi by (falsely) claiming that on the night of the murder, she was in bed with him. Although she has been unable to summon an 'I love you' from him in the past, at the end of the movie he is cognizant and appreciative of at least the solace of love. Behind the glass partition in the prison's visitors' room, Julian drops the telephone through which he has been speaking and presses his hand to hers against the glass. His voice is nevertheless available through the partition as he bows his head and murmurs to her: 'I've waited so long.'

American Gigolo, while suggesting itself as an exposé of 'deviant' social and sexual behaviour, can arguably be seen as a parable in which the banal and the conventional are celebrated and made central. If the female's adultery marks her as a deviant, a subversive force which could signify the decay of the institution of marriage, the shallowness and superficiality of her transgressions against the rules of conventional feminine 'heroes' make her challenge trite and ineffective. Like Julian, whom her husband lambastes as being simply a disposable hanger-on who claims access to people and places through their good graces or benign indifference, the senator's wife has no independent role within the movie and functions only in relation to her affiliation with either man. If Julian has lusted after the fetishistic icons of everyday life – designer clothes, the Mercedes convertible, stereos, antiques – he remains 'masculine' in disavowing the wisdom and desirability of intimacy: he disdains those patrons who would become 'dependent' on him and is unwilling to surrender himself emotionally to any female. His benefactress, true to the fashion of the literary prototypes of female sexual bondage such as Flaubert's Emma Bovary and Tolstoy's Anna Karenina, is willing to sacrifice all for an obsessive love. Why she would wish to do so, and why and how the gigolo became what he is, are left unexplored. Yet once again we find the parable of how a bad man can be saved by a good (although slightly tarnished) woman through the redemptive power of love.

While the lingering image of the gigolo/Bountiful relationship suggested within movie presentations grafts together the ideas of 'man on the make' and 'there's no fool like an old (female) fool,' the stereotypes themselves have been only slightly amended in more recent times.

GIGOLOS COME TO TV

In 1992 the first author was asked to be the 'resident expert' on the topic of 'male escorts' on an American talk show. This television program directs attention to its format of 'reality talk': 'an intelligent alternative to the flood of celebrity- oriented late-night talk shows. Taped before a live studio audience ... [that] will probe behind the headlines to provide substance and context while exploring the issues of the day.' When contacted to appear, the first author was admittedly surprised that the show's production staff had managed to unearth people who would so willingly disclose details of these types of relationships on national television. Our respondents had spoken under the explicit promise of confidentiality and anonymity and, nevertheless, in some cases, it had taken years before a degree of trust had been established whereby individuals would not simply offer somewhat sanitized and sexually aseptic answers in discussions of their relationships ('I really do love her a lot'; 'I only act as a companion to these women, I never sleep with them'; 'The money is only a loan until I get my acting career going/I get my business off the ground/the swallows come back to Capistrano'). Some wariness and a guarded self-disclosure were typical in early meetings; only over time did people redefine their relationships in less socially acceptable terms. Thus, it was somewhat daunting to learn that the interviewing methods of the show's production staff had induced three men and two women, one reputedly a high-status tax attorney and the other a major public relations executive, to disclose details of their intimate lives before several million of their ostensibly nearest and dearest friends.

The show began with three men on set and the voice-over introductory 'tease': 'What kind of a woman would pay a man to wine her, to dine her, and perhaps, even become intimate with her?' The camera then focused on 'Britt,' a lioness with wild red hair, outfitted in a mini-skirt, blazer, and high heels, and 'Shana,' an Oriental beauty with delicate bones and a tiny frame, wearing a tight, sleeveless black mini-dress, and the voice-over continued: 'Shana and Britt weren't satisfied with the men they were meeting. They chose to pay for companionship so they could control exactly what they would get for their money.' The camera then panned to the three gentlemen. The first 'Antoine,' 24 years-old and outfitted in a tuxedo with cummerbund and red rose, was described as a 'professional male escort who charges $50 an hour for his services.' The voice-over proclaimed, 'He says his clients are successful, well-educated business women who want to have a fun, romantic evening ... then forget about him the next day.' The second, 'Rick,' was a mesomorph with greased-back hair tied in a pony-tail, clad in a torn T-shirt, black leather jacket and pants and combat boots. He was described as a 'male escort who says he enjoys fulfilling the fantasies of his clients. At $250 a night, he says he can make any woman feel like a goddess.' The third, the 'high class' escort, was wearing an ul-tra-modern suit, and was billed as affordable only by the most wealthy of women; reputedly 'he charges wealthy women $200 an hour, and the most he ever made was $8,500 for the night.' As if to emphasize this point, this escort had the distracting habit of constantly rubbing the fingers of his left hand together in what is the near-universal gesture for money.

It is assuredly not unusual for talk shows to feature panellists who seem almost overly eager to share their thoughts, foibles, and idiosyncrasies with a network television audience. Perhaps it is in keeping with Andy Warhol's observation that everyone is (or seeks to be) famous for fifteen minutes. Perhaps, as Donald Horton and R. Richard Wohl suggest with regard to 'para-social interaction,' the structure of the talk show itself encourages people to respond to Arsenio, Sally Jesse, Oprah, Donahue, or Geraldo as if they were involved in an ongoing intimate relationship with the 'personality.' For example, in sharing in the celebration of her success at dieting, her chagrin at gaining back weight or her upset over the way she or her boyfriend has been treated by the mass media, Oprah's viewers seem bonded to her by an implicit agreement that the relationship between performer and viewer is not mediated but rather exists as a 'face-to-face' encounter. Whether through the use of direct address, a style of speech that suggests conversing personally and privately with the audience, television-camera pans, or the continuing relationship with the performer functioning as an anticipated and dependable event in the viewer's life, 'in time, the devotee – the "fan" – [may] come to believe that [she or] he "knows" the persona more intimately and profoundly than others do; that [she or] he "understands" his [or her] character and appreciates his [or her] values and motives.' If the devotion of the fan signals only the establishment of a form of relationship in which there is 'a kind of growth without development,' the bond of intimacy may suggest the appropriateness of disclosures between the guest and a 'trusted friend.'

The television talk show, like the soap opera, is a form of mediated interpersonal communication through which we can expand and/or substitute a persona for our emotional involvements with others. Just as soap-opera interaction allows us a temporary visa into a rarefied community in which we may experience much more dramatic and intense relationships than we actually encounter in everyday life – the diabolically sinister business partner, the Hydra-headed passions of the scheming temptress, the beautiful but tormented heiress, or the wealthy but amnesiac hero – the talk show enables us to explore the world of extraordinary persons – the *demi-monde*, the sacred, and the taboo – while insulating ourselves from the potentially polluting taint of physical association with such people. The observer can claim the benefits of interpersonal intimacy without risk, awareness of an unending panoply of human involvements without participating directly, and/or insider knowledge of mysterious persons engaged in 'forbidden' acts without fear of social contagion. However, if we anticipate that the goal of the soap opera is realistic illusion which 'lulls the viewer into a state of obliviousness to the art and craft of production,' 'reality talk' as promoted by the press releases of the television talk show suggests that we may comfortably engage in, to an even greater degree, the willing suspension of disbelief.

If numerous techniques are employed in a deliberate 'coaching of attitudes' which create the illusion that the viewer at home, the host, and the studio audience simultaneously share in the immediacy of the disclosure and respond together, these are not readily apparent. Rather, the talk-show host, as long-term companion, can be seen to offer an implicit pledge that the sanctity of our trust in her or him will not be broached. In the introduction of each notable guest, whether expert, pariah, paragon, or pervert, the tacit assumption is that the guest is duly entitled to occupy that social status. A metaphysical warranty, which suggests that our friend would not betray or beguile us with false pledges about the qualities possessed by the guest, may be seen to accompany each introduction. He or she is vouched for, vetted, and assumed to be a legitimate holder of a particular social status, not an actor purposefully playing a role or an imposter. Similarly, the host's tactic of mingling with his or her studio audience, soliciting questions to be directed to the show's guests suggests the host's ostensible alignment and fellowship with the studio audience and allows for a plausible semblance of intimacy. This tactic additionally can be seen to lend credibility to the supposition that the questions raised and answers garnered are unrehearsed, uncoached, and 'spontaneous.' The answers these questions elicit are viewed as perhaps particularly telling, for an assumption may be made that they successfully eliminate the possibility of deception or collusion. Indeed, disclosures during this time may be seen as if reflective of the guest's 'inner personality,' their comments 'truer confessions' than statements made earlier, precisely because of the unguarded, unrehearsed nature of the questioning.

But, like the cinematic depiction of the gigolo, the talk show as experienced by the first author, also suggested that its presentation of gigolos was similarly structured and rehearsed, offering a stylized depiction of the 'types' of men who allowed themselves to seek money for their services and the 'types' of women who financially supported them. Moreover, it would be naïve to assume that the talk show and the cinematic presentation are essentially dichotomous; one genuine, the other apocryphal, one totally spontaneous, the other ritualistically contrived.

The first male, Antoine, spoke of his role as an escort working for a 'very reputable company' which advertises itself as a 'strictly platonic service providing professionals with reputable men and women for all social occasions.' He professed a distaste for the term escort and stated a preference for the term 'temporary companion,' noting that the agency contract he had to sign strictly forbade any sex or displays of affection, including kisses on the lips, although hand holding and brief hugs were permitted. Although he stated that he was often physically attracted to the women he took out and felt 'electricity' towards them ('You're sitting with this beautiful woman ... moonlight on their faces [*sic*] ... the stars outside ... and you look into her eyes, and want to kiss her, or do something about it'), he maintained that his was an asexual role. When asked which was the 'wildest, sexiest woman' he had taken out, he named a woman who was, 'coincidentally,' the lawyer who was also a guest on the show. He remarked that when he first saw her, 'with her beautiful long hair, blue eyes, awesome body and tight skirt ... I wondered, "Why me?" She could have had anyone.'

His admiration for the attorney was later shown to be reciprocated, and the attorney similarly confessed to feeling a 'sexual electricity' between them, a 'physical chemistry,' noting that if they exceeded five dates they would be allowed by the agency to 'date.' The lawyer leaned close to the man while she talked, her long hair sweeping against his shoulder. The male appendixed her comments with a heart-warming tale of how a couple had met through the agency he worked for and had subsequently married and had nine children. That the agency itself had been in operation for only three years – a rather short time for anyone, even the most fertile, to meet, date, and produce nine children – was overlooked by the escort, the host, and the studio audience. Nevertheless, the escort appeared sincere when he apologized for not remembering to bring pictures of the happy couple and their lovely children. He had, he remarked, intended to do so. The studio audience seemed moved and readily eager to forgive the escort for his lapse in memory; numerous members of the audience stood up during the question period to comment upon what a 'good relationship' the escort and his benefactress 'obviously had' and the 'evident chemistry' between them. Framed as if by a heart-shaped cookie cutter, an illusion was created of the 'young lovers in love' that the audience embraced.

In contrast, Rick appeared as the prototype of mesomorphic villainy. Also featured on the television show was his girlfriend, who admitted to feeling abandoned on those nights when he was with a paying customer, and threatened by the reportedly successful women who employed her lover. However, if the audience had seemed uncomfortable with the bluntness with which Rick admitted the sexual nature of his relationships, and with the pictures shown of Rick that were suggestive of an audition for a *Playgirl* spread, the reception of the studio audience turned from obvious distaste to sheer animosity when he interrupted his girlfriend to assert boldly that if she 'didn't like it she could hit the road.' When he later added that he would not allow her to be an escort because he did not approve of that kind of woman, his words prompted catcalls and loud boos.

The third male, the supposed 'Cadillac' of male escorts, treated the audience to tales of his upper-class background (despite his working-class Liverpudlian accent), his independent wealth, and his supposedly flourishing acting career (despite a lack of credits) and, after prompting by the talk-show host, provided a series of 'cute and comical' tales of his fight to retain his honour when under supposed attack by throngs of wealthy, lecherous, geriatric women. It was clear that there may have been a felt need to 'lighten' the tone of conversation, especially after the audience's reception to Rick, but helium?

Only later did the apparent loquaciousness of the show's panel of participants become understandable. After the show was over, three of the five panel members and the first author talked in the lobby of the hotel in which we had all been housed at the show's expense and wound up chatting through the night. The 'tax attorney' turned out to be an 'escort' from the same agency as one of the males who had appeared on the show. As we sat in the hotel lobby, three men who were with a rock band staying in the same hotel approached her, asking, 'Honey, are you a working girl? Because if you are, you are going to make a whole lot of money tonight!' She laughed, nodded, collected her purse, and flounced merrily off. Strike one.

The second female, billed as a 'public relations executive,' admitted to being a nude dancer who could not afford to wait for reimbursement by the show's production staff for the expenses she had incurred at the hotel and was consequently seeking a 'loan' from the other escorts who had appeared with her. Strike two.

The male escort from the 'reputable platonic agency' was, in fact, the co-owner/operator of the agency with his escort girlfriend. He dismissed the female 'lawyer' escort as a 'stupid bimbo' and asked the first author if she would be his 'agent.' He cheerfully acknowledged that his performance on the talk show had been a 'performance' but was also cheerfully uncontrite. Indeed, he indicated that the tuxedo had been provided by the show and that his role had been to present the 'nice guy,' the platonic innocent who was to stand in stark contrast to the villainous Rick. Strike three.

'Reality talk' thus becomes yet another presentation in which layer upon layer of fantasy and imagery serve to inform and direct social knowledge. Undoubtedly complacency over the accuracy of the image is fostered and promoted by media portrayal of the gigolo/Bountiful relationship. While the topic is bandied about not infrequently on talk shows and/or in magazine articles, rarely is any indication present that the social existence of gigolos and Madames Bountiful is other than 'deviant,' an aberrant social arrangement. There is the presumption of marginality, of the abnormality of both the men and the women in such relationships.

Even if considered evidence of the participants' dysfunctional qualities, the topic of gigolos and their Madames Bountiful nevertheless seems to attract media attention. The reason for its common inclusion? Obviously sex sells. The topic of gigolos, according to a female television producer, is a 'crotch grabber,' and the first author, in turn, was asked to 'dress sexy' for the taping of the television show. Just as the names of perfumes offer a whiff of the exotic and more than a suggestion of immorality – Opium, Poison, My Sin, Obsession – what is on offer to the television audience is clearly temptation, countered by the reaction of the studio audience and mediated by the behind-the-scenes shapers of 'reality.'

PSYCHOBABBLE SCENARIOS

When interviewed by media people on the topic, the first author was asked: 'Were the majority of the women who kept gigolos drug addicts?' and 'Were the majority of men who were kept sexually abused as children?' Repeatedly she was asked to issue snappy profiles of the type of women who would willingly provide financial support for a gigolo and of the men who would allow themselves to be kept. Some interviewers phrased their comments from a viewpoint of armchair psychobabble and suggested that our female respondents must be 'depressive types' who were 'insecure' and/or 'obsessed' with masculine companionship, sexual or otherwise. Others suggested that both the men and the women involved could be 'sex addicts' who were unable to obtain in any one 'normal' relationship the satisfaction they need.

We have noted that a persistent cliché exists which suggests that gigolo relationships are simply exchanges of sexual services/companionship for dollars. However, like all clichés, the description of these relationships as simply mercenary exchanges has the inevitable effect of oversimplifying the circumstances. Not only is understanding of these types of relationships obscured by the prevalence of clichéd descriptions – be it in *Midnight Cowboy*, *Sunset Boulevard*, or any one of a host of Jackie Collins–type sexual fairyland novels – but, as well, perception of the men and women participating in them is distorted by their representation as sexually voracious, greedy men and frivolous, narcissistic women. Alternatively, as we have briefly suggested, the behaviour of the gigolo and his Madame Bountiful may be psychologized and made equally obscure. The gigolo may simply be seen as 'suffering' from some 'affliction' – perhaps, gerontophilia – a condition wherein a young person supposedly prefers a much older sexual partner because of a desire for a parental substitute. Perhaps he is seen as suffering from Don Juanism – named a complex for the legendary Spanish libertine who has become associated with a ruthless seducer who thinks of women as prey – and is insecure and obsessed with the need to prove his masculinity through sexual conquests. Or perhaps he is seen as an addict in thrall to a romantic and/or sexual compulsion – the 'Casanova Complex' – that makes him 'want to ingest' his victims in a cannibalistic rage that stems from fear of and anger towards women.

The woman's behaviour may be subjected to this type of psychological reductionism as well. She may be seen as the pathological one, suffering from the ravages of such conditions as the 'Delilah Syndrome,' which stems from the biblical story in which Delilah, after being controlled and exploited by her father, used seduction to destroy Samson and the Philistines who had dominated her. According to psychoanalytic theory, women who have had unsatisfactory relationships with their fathers may develop a habit of promiscuity with the associated desire to control their male partners and render them weak and helpless.

Perhaps the female's relationship with a gigolo is seen as yet another manifestation of the 'Angry Woman Syndrome' – a personality disorder in which a woman supposedly demonstrates such symptoms as excessive perfectionism, punctuality, neatness, a critical attitude towards others, marital troubles, outbursts of unprovoked anger, and a tendency towards alcohol or drug abuse.

Perhaps the behaviours of both the Madame Bountiful and her gigolo may be linked to Peter Panism – a term often used specifically to refer to the inability of an adult man to commit to a long-term relationship with a woman (just as the adolescent Peter Pan was unable to reciprocate the romantic longings of the young Wendy in Barrie's story) but more generally used to describe a condition wherein a generalized refusal to acknowledge the ageing process is evidenced by such symptoms as dying one's hair, having cosmetic surgery, and the like. Perhaps only the men are seen as suffering from the 'Peter Pan Syndrome' – seeming never to grow up – with the women victims of the 'Wendy Syndrome' – attracted to 'Peter Pans' and characterized by their 'pathological desire' to cure the men somehow.

The point we are trying to make is that it is always possible to attempt to explain human behaviour by identifying mysterious dark forces that allegedly cause people to act in this or that manner. A common tendency exists to assume automatically that 'different' behaviour requires a 'different' explanation. Since gigolos and Madames Bountiful appear, at least on the surface, to be engaging in different behaviour, then, by all means, an explanation must quickly be provided, such as those just presented that emphasize the existence of different underlying forces. The more seemingly bizarre the observable difference, the more bizarre the underlying causes must be, according to many observers.

The danger, however, is that such theories often reduce individuals to robots who are driven only by their pathology or sickness to engage in behaviour. To automatically assume the gigolo is simply a charming psychopath who preys on gullible and deeply disturbed women immediately removes the participants in the relationship from the mainstream of everyday life. We do not believe that such an automatic assumption is justified. There is more to be observed in the role performances of gigolos and Bountifuls than mere manifestations of pathology. It is entirely possible that the players in this social scene are responding to the most basic and ordinary sorts of motives and feelings.

Highlighted in works as divergent as Balzac's *A Harlot High and Low* to Franz Lehar's 1905 operetta *The Merry Widow*, to pop singer David Lee Roth's revival of the 1930s hit song 'Just a Gigolo,' the existence of the gigolo has been hinted at, and alluded to, but he has rarely appeared as other than a stereotype. The role of the gigolo has seldom been the subject of substantive inquiry. Recognition of how social knowledge of this role has been framed largely by the grafting together of layers of illusion acted as the galvanizing agent to spur on the completion of this book. The work will describe a social role that has previously been the subject of salacious description alone or of isolated literary or cinematic accounts.

DEFINING THE FIELD

Whatever the motivating factors that encourage a woman to enter into a relationship with a gigolo, his existence is dependent on a partner who can afford to underwrite the cost of the affair. Keeping a man, like keeping horses, is one of the many things that only the rich can afford to do. Although historically the gigolo was the exclusive property of the aristocrat, the role is now simply associated with wealth or access to it. That is, company expense accounts, cars, apartments, and the like, while not 'real income' or disposable wealth, nevertheless allow the executive their use to provide or support a certain lifestyle. Thus, the costs of an affair may, on occasion, be slipped neatly into the balance sheets under the category of 'entertainment expenses.'

A woman may consider her behaviour in keeping a gigolo simply prudent and perceive that by keeping him she is thus enabled to, at least facilely, retain control of the situation while satisfying her desire for companionship, sex, affection, and/or admiration in a relationship that is a supplement to or a substitute for marriage; however, it is the sort of prudence that only the relatively rich can afford. It may be that for both keeper and kept, money is a larger factor than what it cannot buy. As the adage goes, 'money cannot buy love, but it makes shopping for it a lot easier.' Perhaps, as some have suggested, the single distinction of both the gigolo and his Madame Bountiful within such relationships is merely the unusual degree to which they allow ambition (or self-interest) a free rein.

However, we believe that a study of gigolos is more than a study of narcissism taking an unusual form. One day while flipping through a daily newspaper, one of the authors, who would dispute categorization as a 'Royal watcher,' was nevertheless struck by an excerpt from the well-known Royals biographer Anne Edwards. According to Edwards, the 'House of Windsor began to crumble 45 years ago, when Elizabeth married Philip.' Philip was apparently both penniless and in debt to Lord Mountbatten and thus the 'willing tool to link the Mountbatten name to that of the House of Windsor.' While Elizabeth was apparently in love with Philip, he was apparently 'perhaps more ambitious than adoring.'

A short time after their ... wedding Elizabeth ... learned her husband had a long-time mistress he did not intend to give up ... To the world their marriage seemed ideal, but Philip continued to have an eye for beautiful women ... [A] cool hostility arose between husband and wife and was exacerbated by the lopsided power balance between them. In most matters Philip had to bow to Elizabeth's decree. He had no authority and Elizabeth did not make him prince consort ... nor did she seek his advice. His role was to accompany the Queen on state occasions (always walking a few steps behind) and to make public appearances representing the Crown at special events.

Some have claimed that the Royal Family was an important family role model for a large portion of British subjects – not just an object for emulation but also a symbol of tradition and stability in a rapidly changing world. Based upon events of the recent past, cynics have taken to referring to the Royals as *the* model for a 'dysfunctional' family. Whether this appraisal is valid or not, the trials and tribulations of the moment seem symptomatic of many aspects of family life in many contemporary Western societies. The Royals as microcosm of all families? The question raises yet another question: Prince Philip as a Royal Gigolo, a royally Kept Man? And what about other modern examples? Mr Elizabeth Taylor? Mr Cher?

It has long been a basic tenet of science that a phenomenon without variation, or difference, or change offers the scientist nothing to study or examine fruitfully. If all things, or all people, perform in an unvarying, unchanging way, the behaviour itself becomes almost invisible, so much a part of the taken-for-granted world that it tends to be ignored. One of the enduring aphorisms of science states that the last thing a fish would discover is water – a constant part of its everyday world. The same applies to humans and their behaviour. Some things become noticeable, and therefore a subject worthy of study, only when they change, or appear differently, or are violated, so that we have the opportunity to observe not only the difference itself but also reactions to it. Suddenly all facets of the behaviour in question, and what it is being compared with, can be and must be scrutinized.

It is true that scientists can attempt to manipulate phenomena artificially in carefully controlled laboratory conditions. However, questions always remain as to how well the findings of the lab can be generalized to the reality of everyday life. In the case of gigolos and their keepers, not only do we have a topic for investigation that is fascinating in its own right, but we can observe the real-life situation of an apparent violation, possibly a reversal, of some elements of the male role, the female role, and the relations between males and females. Is it really a reversal? How is it similar to existing male/female relations? How is it different?

Since we are dealing with real people in all of their complexities, living the realities of their everyday lives, we cannot approach our subject with the exactness of the scientist in the controlled environment of the laboratory. Our findings will necessarily be less precise, reflecting our respondents' imprecise worlds. But we can look at and listen to these people carefully and, in the process, raise a fascinating array of questions.

An example of the questioning that almost inevitably evolves as we explore the palimpsest before us has just been provided in the discussion of men married to 'famous' women. At first, these examples appeared to be ludicrous extremes of our basic focal point – gigolos. Further reflection, however, led us to a serious consideration of whether 'gigolos' are necessarily unmarried males. If we chose to restrict our application of the term to the unmarried, we would then have to eliminate from consideration a number of examples we had originally intended to examine. Specifically, 'sweetheart swindlers,' 'marital con men,' and 'marital bounty hunters' – all of whom use legal or illegal marriage as a means of gaining even greater access, for varying lengths of time, to the fortunes of women – would have to be excluded.

Conversely, if we were to expand the limits of our definition of a gigolo to allow us to include the above-mentioned types, we would then be forced to confront the issue of somehow differentiating between acceptably motivated versus unacceptably motivated marital partners. And suddenly the dividing line between the unacceptable deviant and the acceptable model citizen becomes blurred. Seemingly firm ground quickly becomes quicksand. Unfortunately, there are no definitive tests that can easily differentiate 'good' people from 'bad' people – no matter how much we would wish there were.

Eventually we decided that we would, for the purposes of consistency and to further our understanding of the many facets of this phenomenon and its counterparts, have to permit our consideration of gigolos to include both the unmarried and the married. Some of the consequences of that decision will be presented in a later chapter. It is important, at this point, to stress that our objective is to foster understanding of the various dimensions of the phenomena under consideration. We are not on a moralistic crusade of any sort. We are attempting, as much as is humanly possible, to sharpen our powers of observation and analysis. The reader will assess the ultimate success or failure of our efforts.

SOURCES OF INFORMATION AND STYLES OF PRESENTATION

Every method of research contains limitations, and the methods the first author used were no exceptions. It was immediately apparent that standard statistical sampling techniques were inappropriate in researching gigolos and their Madames Bountiful. For example, telephoning every sixteenth number in the London/New York/Los Angeles/Ottawa phone book could arguably result in little more than slammed-down receivers and/or hurled profanities. Since the persons being sought for interviews were not to be located through membership in a particular club or group – there is no Gigolo Society, no Sorority for Madames Bountiful, no 1-800 Gigolo/Bountiful telephone referral service – our methods seemed to provide the only practical way of collecting information.

The original British and European sample members were largely accessed through referrals from friends and acquaintances who knew of the research. This strategy, known as snowball sampling, rests on the assumption that knowledge of certain activities is unequally shared throughout the general populace. Each informant who possesses distinctive knowledge of a social situation is then asked to provide names of, and introductions to, other people who have experience of the same situation. The method is subject to the limitations of respondents' knowledge of a network of like-minded others.

In an attempt to gather an international sample and compensate for those men and women who would drop out, a 'Letter to the Editor,' as noted above, was subsequently sent to North American and British newspapers; newspaper contact was necessarily confined to English-speaking countries to avoid language difficulties.

Soliciting the interest of respondents through newspaper advertisements is not without its own host of problems. Among the hundreds of letters that poured in, we received our share of obvious crank letters, a normal quota from religious fanatics and inmates of prisons – the inevitable 'pen pals' of anyone whose name ever appears in any section of a newspaper other than its obituary column – letters from mothers who believed that their daughters' boyfriends/husbands could qualify for the 'gigolo' label and asked if we could write to their daughters and help them to see the light, and postcards bearing twenty-years-ago-while-on-my-honeymoon-in-Florida-I-saw-this-older-lady-and-her-younger-male-companion-and-I-think-he-may-have-been-a-gigolo-but-I'm-not-sure-Does-this-help? inquiries. Sifting the wheat from the chaff, the first author thanked those who wished to save us, apologized to those who found the Letter to the Editor in itself scurrilous; and answered all seemingly genuine letters, first to ensure that the person existed and was not a purposefully created fiction, and second to begin a correspondence/acquaintanceship or friendship, some of which lasted months or years and on occasion involved face-to-face meetings in locations across Canada, the United States, Europe, and the United Kingdom.

Obviously, some individuals lost interest and/or somehow failed to maintain contact, while others became discredited during the course of the research. For example, if an individual claimed to be an only child in his or her original letter and later claimed that he or she was the youngest of twelve children, reliability became dubious. Although there are perhaps certain differences between our United Kingdom/European sample and the North American sample (largely owing, we suspect, to the reluctance of a 'society gigolo' to do something as *déclassé* as respond to a newspaper advertisement and to the greater reliance on this sampling method in the United States and Canada), the comments of both are fascinating and thought-provoking.

The nature of any relationship with the sample respondents ranged from the most transitory encounter to the in-depth interview and the life-history technique, which involved sustained communication. The average interview took between four and six hours, depending upon the differing topics each subject opened up for possible exploration. Because the interviews were unstructured, comparable questions could not easily be asked of most respondents, a factor which works against any kind of detailed presentation of statistical data on either gigolos or their Madames Bountiful.

With some respondents, however, friendships developed which involved sustained contact for over a decade. As expected, the greater the amount of sustained contact with the respondent, the greater the amount of disclosure, elaboration, and redefinition of his or her situation in socially 'non-acceptable' or 'politically incorrect' terms. Certain respondents spoke of our friendship, rather than of any wish to clarify an ambiguous social role in an academic study, as the impetus to honesty. Similarly, correspondents who replied to newspaper letters often wrote on more than one occasion, inviting questions about the original letter and sending pictures, Christmas cards, and so on. In the earlier work on 'kept women,' a similar pattern of conduct among respondents had been noted; in both cases, it seemed as if becoming 'pen pals' served to reassure respondents that there was a bond that would justify and protect their confidence.

Over a ten-year time span, the first author compiled data from more than 600 gigolos and approximately 100 Madames Bountiful. It was ultimately far easier to obtain a sample of men who identified themselves as gigolos than it was to obtain a sample of women who willingly acknowledged identification as a Madame Bountiful. This imbalance is probably a consequence of the wording of the letter to the newspapers which explicitly emphasized gigolos and not their female partners. Our sample of respondents is also composed of people who are more self-advertising than those who chose to remain silent and not confide in a researcher. Since we can only speculate on the differences that might exist between the two types, we shall refrain from doing so here. Furthermore, as the explicit focus of the research was upon male/female relationships, no attempt was made to solicit interviews with men who performed a Bountiful role with other men.

Although this study cannot presume to be representative of the range of variability which may exist, it does investigate as many divergent groups as possible. While we acknowledge limitations of the sampling method used to obtain information, we nevertheless suggest that the comments and observations of our respondents deserve attention. They offer insights on a type of relationship that has been ignored by academics while being subjected to a host of crude stereotypes within popular fiction and movie treatments.

The men and women in this book are real; they are not composite or fictional characters. However, to protect their anonymity, we have deliberately assigned them fictitious names and altered specific details where the disclosure of such information could possibly lead to their identification. Rather than present summary statistics on, for example, how many of our female respondents sought love, or sex, or revenge – or whatever – as the primary goal in their establishment of a relationship with a gigolo, and how many men were escorts, walkers, or long-term lovers, we thought that the use of interview transcripts would be more enlightening. The words they speak are their own words, written or taped, with only minor editing performed by the authors to eliminate irrelevant or distracting comments. Not every gigolo or Madame Bountiful was equally articulate; for this reason, we have chosen to quote some of our respondents at greater length where the comments seemed especially compelling or revealing.

1

Gigolos

What's in a name? The term 'gigolo' has been variously traced to the Italian, for 'one who smiles' and the French, for 'one who dances.' Both derivations conjure up the imagery of the purposeful sycophant or paid apple-polisher, who 'dances' attendance on a woman for recompense. There are many synonyms, it would seem, for roles linked with, or interchangeable with that of the gigolo. Some terms, such as 'lounge lizard,' 'Casanova,' or 'cicisbeo,' seem somewhat anachronistic; others, like 'adventurer,' 'roué,' 'playboy,' and 'man-about town,' seem dated, if still-engaged-in, euphemisms that suggest a type of sexy Christopher Columbus whose Queen Isabella finances him for more personal than political reasons. Still other terms, such as 'joy toy' and 'toy boy,' are of much more recent origin. Indeed, the lexicographer of contemporary slang Tony Thorne has suggested that the term 'toy boy,' 'a vogue word from 1987 which started as a code term among sophisticates and was eventually popularized by the press ... filled a "lexical gap" in the English language, coinciding with the perceived trend whereby many celebrities of the 1980s were taking up with younger lovers.'

Thorne identified a number of terms throughout his dictionary that may be somewhat interchangeably used to refer to the gigolo. These include 'fanny rat,' 'pants man,' 'stud,' 'sack artist,' 'crumpet man' (used to describe a man who is a womanizer, seducer, or lothario); 'fancy man' (a term used to refer to the adulterous lover of a married woman and 'usually applied disapprovingly and/or enviously'); 'beard' (a show-biz and/or society term used to refer to a 'male escort posing as a boyfriend, lover, husband, etc ... [or] to a lesbian's "official" partner, with whom she is seen in public'); a 'poodle-faker' (a term which emerged in Britain during the second decade of the twentieth century and which was used to describe 'an effete, over-refined or offensively genteel young man in attendance on older ladies. Faker here implies insincerity and poodle the attitude or appearance of a lapdog'); a 'ponce' (used to describe, among other things, a parasitic idler); a 'handbag' (a term 'popular in high society and journalistic circles in the mid 1980s' and used to refer to a 'male escort,' 'a walker ... a decorative appendage to a fashionable lady, often a homosexual male'); and other nouns ranging from the seemingly innocuous ('escort,' 'agreeable companion,' and 'confidante') to the scathing ('bounder,' 'male bimbo,' 'prostitute').

As the reader can see, there is no lack of available terms. Of and in themselves, they are testimony to the varied existence of the phenomenon we will be describing in the following chapters. Most of the words or descriptive phrases obviously form part of the working languages of highly specialized groups of people and reflect their different experiences. Despite the fact that many of our respondents preferred to use self-descriptive words that were morally neutral, we eventually decided to use 'gigolo' as our generic term because it is in general usage and is widely, albeit somewhat poorly, understood.

In contrast to the veritable cornucopia of terms to describe the males, we lack terms to describe the role of the female within such relationships. We did locate somewhat archaic terms such as 'ace of spades,' a nineteenth-century term used by confidence men to describe a 'wealthy and marriageable woman, usually a widow,' but the term itself suggests that the woman is a passive rather than an active participant. Indeed, we observed a singular lack of terminology to describe a woman who *actively* 'keeps' a man, an absence we viewed as in itself significant. On the assumption that our language shapes how we think about our world (this interpretation of language, thought, and society is accounted for in the Sapir-Whorf hypothesis, named after the two linguists who formulated it), reality becomes objectified through the 'habitual grooves of language expression.' This hypothesis proposes that, until a term is constructed for something, it is impossible to think about, communicate about, and fully understand it. The lack of a term to describe the female who keeps a gigolo, in the past or present, may either indicate the lack of female 'keepers' throughout history or represent a studied attempt to ignore them. With apologies to Oscar Wilde, could this female be in yet another form of relationship that dares not speak her name?

Somewhat disbelieving that so copious a nomenclature could exist with reference to the role of the gigolo with not even a single obvious term to describe his female partner, we reviewed hundreds of hours of tape-recorded conversations with our male and female respondents to see if a common or colloquial term emerged. None readily suggested itself. Rather, in our review of conversations with male respondents, it was striking that the terms commonly used to refer to women who kept them were often paradoxically dismissive or discounted their importance. As Simone de Beauvoir once observed, woman was the interchangeable and invisible 'Other'; for our male respondents, their female partners were often simply referred to as 'she' and apparently this device was thought adequate.

Although some men referred to the women who kept them as 'ladies,' others contemptuously referred to women as if they were a menagerie of animals. Thus, they spoke of women as 'fat pigs' or 'cows' who paid to be 'porked' or 'beefed,' 'old nags,' 'sows,' 'chicks,' and/or 'bitches' who 'rabbited on about nothing.' Alternatively, terms such as 'Lady Muck,' 'the Duchess,' 'the Princess,' 'Her Highness,' and 'Her Royal Nibs' were used by various men, typically to mock or disparage the woman's haughtiness or her perceived sense of self-importance rather than to suggest her role as 'keeper.' In a similar vein, some men referred to the women who kept them as *their* 'joy toy' – a curious twist, given that the term itself more obviously refers to the role of the gigolo himself – which suggests yet another way in which language may reflect and refract images of the relative importance of males and females within intimate relationships.

The appellations utilized by our male respondents seemed both offensive and misleading. Thus, to find a common term to adopt to describe these women, we commenced a search of dictionaries – of slang, of clichés, of euphemisms, of the underworld – and canvassed our peers in departments of sociology, history, and English, and still found none. The woman's role as keeper of a gigolo seems distinguished in language only through the absence of a term for it. Somewhat daunted, the first author expressly quizzed several male respondents with whom friendships of long standing had emerged on the term they used for the woman/women who kept them. The males themselves seemed stymied. Although after some contemplation several suggested 'sugar mamma' – to parallel 'sugar daddy,' a man who keeps a woman – the former term sounded forced and contrived. Finally, we concluded that, for the sake of clarity, we would have to coin a term ourselves to describe the role of the female keeper. This task was to prove a greater challenge that we originally anticipated.

In coining a term to describe the woman's role, we considered, tossed between ourselves, and ultimately rejected numerous possibilities. We were engaged in a process of 'naming' (a term and process, familiar within feminism, of rendering visible the previously invisible) a female person and role simultaneously. Thus, the term 'SWELL,' an acronym for 'single woman earning lots of lolly' and 'used by yuppies during the late 1980s to refer to a single woman who was financially well-off,' suggested itself as a promising possibility, but we were forced to discard it as not all our female subjects were single and the reference to 'lolly' – a Britishism for money – might be confusing to a North American audience. Discarding the term 'lover' as inapplicable to certain relationships as it narrowly suggests a sexual relationship and/or a 'beloved' while ignoring the important monetary dimension, we ruminated over the adoption of 'spare,' a term used to refer to 'an unattached, and presumably available female.' However, this term was subsequently rejected because its connotations seemed both old-fashioned and patronizing.

After much equivocation, we settled on 'Madame Bountiful,' believing that it stressed the primary characteristic associated with the female role in these relationships – that is, the capacity to provide financial compensation or support and, from the perspective of the gigolo, to be capable of doing so in as grand a manner as possible. Although the term may sound somewhat stilted, it conveys the idea of the female as an active agent in, among other things, financing a relationship with a kept gigolo. Similarly, it does not implicitly presume that the woman's behaviour stems from a singular motivating force. While, at various times, writers have hinted that single-factor variables such as 'love,' 'sexual voraciousness,' or 'disturbed' thinking may be isolated and serve to explain what women do or do not do, we sought to describe the woman's role as financier within such relationships without prurience, intolerance, or pretentious piety.

After having settled upon the term 'Madame Bountiful' and while conducting further library research, we happened across (twice within the same week) the term 'Lady Bountiful' in two different books, published eight years apart, written by two different authors and seemingly independently of each other. In both instances, the term was used to refer to upper-class women who were known for, and were being described in the context of, their extensive involvement in volunteer or 'charity' work of varying sorts. We rejected substituting 'Lady' for 'Madame' in the present work primarily because the former's connotations hint at royalty and, more importantly, appear to demand a very narrow range of behavioural possibilities. As we shall see later, many of our female respondents would definitely bridle at any restrictive suggestions that they should 'act like a lady.'

Webster's New Collegiate Dictionary defines 'gigolo' as '1: a man living on the earnings of or supported by a woman; 2: a professional dancing partner or male escort.' In defining 'gigolo' as a man who lives on the earnings of or is supported by a woman, there is the implicit recognition that such behaviour is the exception – marginal, deviant, or out of the ordinary. Tacitly, the social injunction upon males to assume the 'good provider' role is made apparent and refurbished. As such, the definition itself may be seen to function at a most basic level to suggest a role of disreputability, of social marginality, and to reiterate what Edna Ferber noted long ago in her 1922 short story 'The Gigolo,' 'the gig is pronounced zhig, and the whole is not a respectable word ... it is a term of utter contempt.'

A role is defined by, among other things, the set of expectations placed upon the incumbent of a given position within a society or community. In part, the purpose of roles is to reduce uncertainty and anxiety over what one is supposed to do in most situations, thus freeing a person to concentrate on other aspects of living. But this liberty of having a cultural 'road map' to follow can at the very same time become a tyranny of constraints in the form of reduced options. As we shall see in this chapter, both females and males have been confined throughout history with regard to 'acceptable' gender-role behaviour. Those who seek to challenge, through either word or deed, the legitimacy of the confinements have usually been punished in various ways ranging from mild ostracism and negative name calling to being cast out of the community via imprisonment, and even death.

In large ways and small, the latest women's movement, of the 1960s to the present, has resensitized us to the subtle and blatant confinements of the female gender role both currently and historically. In the process, feminist scholars and critical analysts have also enabled us to sharpen our understanding of selected aspects of the male gender role. The currently developing men's movement is attempting to further our understanding and awareness of confinements in the present-day male gender role.

While we recognize that the liberation of women is hardly a *fait accompli* and do not dispute the backlash that has emerged in opposition both to feminism as a sociopolitical force and to women who attempt to redefine the boundaries of the female role, we also may note that the traditional definition of masculinity is both restrictive and oppressive. Thus, for example, while the 'sissy' adult male is a target of derision, the 'sissy boy' is included within the bible of the psychological empire, the *Diagnostic and Statistical Manual of Mental Disorders* (the DSM) published by the American Psychiatric Association, as a possible case of 'childhood gender dysphoria.' Tellingly, although compilers of the *DSM III-R* (third edition-revised) manual originally sought to include the 'tomboyish girl' within this category, the National Organization of Women (NOW) and other feminist groups successfully lobbied against a designation of 'pathology' or sickness being attributed to those girls who departed from traditional feminine role behaviour during their early years. No one, it seems, was moved to argue that the young boy who was seemingly not enraptured with a self-definition as one who is made of 'snakes and snails and puppy dog tails' and whose behaviour departed from stereotypical masculinity, should also be permitted to explore, without penalty, his own individualistic preferences.

Similarly, psychologist and leading exponent of women's rights Phyllis Chesler has noted the sinister impact of stereotypes of women in child-custody battles, observing that, in such disputes, 'mothers are routinely punished for having a career or job (she's a "selfish, absentee mother") *or* for staying at home on welfare (she's a "lazy parasite"); for committing heterosexual adultery or for living with a man out-of-wedlock (she's "setting an immoral example") *or* for remarrying (she's trying to "erase the real dad"); or for failing to provide a male role model (she's a "bitter, man-hating lesbian").'

One may, without disputing in any way the validity of and degree of gravity to be accorded Chesler's argument, nevertheless point out that the aftermath of stereotyping is also disadvantageous to males. For example, Norma Wikler has observed that the 'non-traditional' male is also placed in a disadvantaged position within child-custody battles. For example, in the 1987 case *Peterson* v. *Peterson*, an Iowa judge ruled that he would never award custody of a boy to a 'househusband' because having such a male role model would result in the child being 'socially crippled when he is an adult.'

Amid a multiplicity of spectator positions and evaluations of gender-appropriate and inappropriate behaviour, we found the roles of the gigolo and his Madame Bountiful particularly appropriate examples of the difficulties and complexities of male and female roles within society. In this chapter we examine various confinements as well as the insights that can be acquired through consideration of both the apparent gender-role deviations themselves and the responses to them.

THE GIGOLO VERSUS THE PIMP

In modern times, even though the female 'gold-digger' may be to some a mild source of irritation, grudging admiration may still be given to the woman who 'marries well' and seems to have lived out the Cinderella myth of being transformed into a princess after capturing the attention of a prince. Indeed, the massive television audience who watched the coverage of the Royal Weddings (and the subsequent commercial availability of the Royal Weddings on video) would seem, at least in part, to attest to society's willingness to suspend doubt as to the motivations of Cinderellas who marry princes. Similarly, the sociologist Margrit Eichler, in an interesting article on the 'prestige of the occupation housewife,' reported that, when her respondents were asked to assess the prestige of housewives whose husbands were identified, for example, as physicians, she found that the prestige accorded to the wife of a physician was roughly equivalent to that given to a female university professor. As she noted, 'there is some truth to the adage that a woman need not become a doctor, she can marry one.'

However, even if admiration may be given to women who marry advantageously, the role of the gigolo remains socially dubious. Indeed, the comments of knowing friends and family members often suggested their incredulity and/or antipathy to the role of the Madame Bountiful and/or her gigolo.

I tried to tell her, he doesn't love you, he loves your money, but she won't listen. I wish somebody could tell me just what do those kinds of men do to a woman that makes them that crazy? (London, friend of a 64-year-old woman supporting a 31-year-old male)

I find men definitely opportunistic when they sense, or find out, that a woman is career-minded too. I thought men appreciated smart women or ones that could stand on their own two feet. Instead, they want to be looked after or paid for! Most times, of course, all they offer is their mighty phallus! What a shame! (Chicago, 39-year-old woman)

A man who takes money from a woman isn't a man by my standards. I might be old-fashioned, but at least in my generation we knew how to treat women. (Montreal, 53-year-old man)

Best friends are not necessarily close friends. At first I was aghast with his manipulating but never felt it my place to air my disapproval. (Oakland, 44-year-old man)

Regardless of how much he makes getting old gals to pay out money, I pointed out to him that if he'd be a man and work, that with his previous car mechanic work and carpentry work he could clear $30,000 a year easily, that in no way is the old woman going to trust him with enough cash to set himself up. Let's face it, he travels all over the place – the U.S., Canada, Europe with her – but he has to lug her all over, sleep with her, amuse her, etc., etc. What a ridiculously corny situation! I told him, 'Larry, where are your balls man? Act like a man!' (Colorado, 30-year-old man)

Men like that should be lined up and shot. (Chicago, 49-year-old man)

In a similar vein, some time after the first author began gathering her sample of respondents, the following letter arrived in the mail:

Gigolos are only dressed-up pimps. Have you explored the possibility of interviewing a few pimps for your research? I did have the experience of a very nice male 'friend' who turned into 'one of those' when I did some 'work' to make some quick money. He even beat me in the bargain! This fellow although my 'friend' and a college graduate couldn't accept life's responsibilities. I felt sorry for him. He had a phobia – it gave him pay-off sympathy – it justified his bizarre actions (so he said) of searching out women who could pay his way or look after him – sometimes prostitutes. His mother had died when he was really young and he said that it was his need to have a woman take care of him. He had this phobia that women would just leave him – like his mother did – and he wanted 'proof' that she really cared. He created his own hell and because it had a pay-off was unable to accept the responsibility for getting better. (Toronto, 28-year-old woman)

Although the roles of the pimp and the gigolo originally struck us as quite distinct, it is notable that the French suggest only a subtle difference between the two. While the term 'gigolo' is retained for describing those men at the upper end of the hierarchy, the colloquial term 'maquereau' is used to describe a man who 'lives on the avails of a woman' – however her earnings are obtained. 'Maquereau,' which literally translates as 'mackerel,' is also the slang term for a pimp, with the refining phrase 'un grand maquereau' used to distinguish the high-society gigolo from his supposedly plebeian counterpart, 'un petit maquereau' – the street pimp. As the journalist Lynn Ramsey commented in her work, 'The French are so prosaic. To them all gigolos are pimps; it is simply a matter of degree.'

It would seem noteworthy that the conventional definition of a pimp as a man who is 'living on the avails' of prostitution differs from the definition provided of 'gigolo' by Webster's only in its specifying that the woman's source of income be derived from prostitution. Moreover, it is considered not only shameful and socially repugnant for a man to send his female partner off to 'hustle' for his benefit, but criminal as well, as noted by an Alberta provincial court judge who, in sentencing a pimp to a seven-year prison term, stated: 'No one in our society is viewed with more contempt and abhorrence than a pimp, with the possible exception of a child molester.' As John Lowman has argued, such a law 'effectively precludes a prostitute from cohabiting with a mate without that person risking prosecution for living on the avails (especially if they are unemployed).' It is suggestive that sentences for living on the avails of prostitution tend to be more substantial than those imposed upon persons who engage in solicitation in a public place (prostitution) or those who keep a bawdy-house for purposes of prostitution. It would seem that in criminalizing the conduct of the 'pimp,' society seeks to announce its repugnance to and its intolerance for a man who would wittingly allow himself to be supported by a woman, particularly if the monies she earns are obtained through the selling of her body and its sexual services.

Although the laws on 'living on the avails' may be thought to signify society's 'protection' of women from potential male exploiters, such laws seem grounded in at least two broad assumptions which appear to be more misogynistic than avuncular: first, the assumption that women are gullible and easily influenced, and require the law to endorse their selected partner or companion; and, second, the assumption that men who would 'tolerate' and find it acceptable to be partnered with a 'prostitute' must be 'pimps.' We do not dispute that some pimps may be villainous and beat and mistreat their partners. However, husbands have mistreated their wives in the past with legal immunity, and spouses and cohabiters continue to inflict violence upon their partners with less than widespread social intolerance. In criminalizing the conduct of the 'pimp' through legal prohibitions against 'living on the avails,' the law may be seen simultaneously to proscribe and delineate 'acceptable' patterns of conduct for males and females.

Prostitutes may maintain a 'boyfriend,' or 'old man' or 'husband,' but certainly seem eager to distance their lover from the role of a pimp – a distinction that the law itself does not readily appear disposed to endorse. In contrast to other areas within the criminal law wherein the burden is placed on the prosecution to demonstrate 'beyond a reasonable doubt' that the accused is guilty of having committed the act in question, the laws governing 'living on the avails' in Canada require a man so accused to prove himself innocent of the charges against him by furnishing evidence of his independently obtained income. The role of the 'househusband' is seemingly negated rather than endorsed. However, we reasoned, if prostitution is conceived of as an occupational role, is the social intolerance evidenced towards the role of the gigolo really a continuation of the intolerance and scathing remarks directed towards the pimp? Is the distaste evidenced towards the pimp and the gigolo similar – a condemnation of any man who would permit himself to be supported by his female partner's 'hustling' – at any occupation – to furnish him with creature comforts?

GIGOLOS AND PROSTITUTION

In so far as the role of the woman as providing financial support or recompense is central to the definition of a gigolo, an assumption is made, first, that such behaviour violates social standards of 'normalcy' and the taken-for-granted, and, second, that the gigolo is most basically to be disparaged as a prostitute-like being himself. This second assumption itself compels a change of focus from gigolo-as-pimp to gigolo-as-prostitute, a further indication of the elusiveness of grasping the essential characteristics of the gigolo phenomenon. Certainly some would argue that the term 'gigolo' is a euphemism for the word 'prostitute' inasmuch as any sexual activity underwritten by a financial calculation is prostitution. Thus, several of the definitions provided by H. Benjamin and R. Masters would seem implicitly to offer support for the inclusion of the gigolo within the definition of prostitution:

Prostitution starts when the giver becomes a seller. What is love if it isn't a gift? (*Psychoanalysis of the Prostitute* by Maryse Choisy)

Any person is a prostitute who habitually or intermittently has sexual relations more or less promiscuously for money, or other mercenary consideration. (*Prostitution in Europe* by Abraham Flexner)

A prostitute is an individual, male or female, who for some kind of reward, monetary or otherwise, or ... and as part- or whole-time profession, engages in normal or abnormal sexual intercourse with various persons. (*A History of Prostitution* by George Ryley Scott)

Nevertheless, as Edward Glover observed: 'The first difficulty we have to face is that, strictly speaking, there is no such thing as a prostitute type ... It is really absurd to talk of large remedies for prostitution without first establishing a reasonably exact classification of prostitutes. For that part, we might also have to have an accurate survey of allied groups, including, for example, the "enthusiastic amateur" and "gold digger," or the type of individual who marries for money. And if we go so far, we might as well consider the significance of the "dowry" and the "marriage settlement."'

It is not our intention to attempt to employ 'prostitution' as a metaphor and argue that 'all the world's a whorehouse'; rather, we wish to stress that any attempt to decipher its character is fraught with problems. Although these various definitions may not at first appear to be very different from one another, each has a particular emphasis. Prostitution is defined as: (1) a fraudulent display of affection; (2) a professional career in which access to one's body is exchanged for monetary reward; and (3) indiscriminate promiscuity. The plurality of meanings indicates more than a pedantic preoccupation with semantics. The definition of prostitution itself can have moral, ideological, and cultural overtones. For example, consider Seymour-Smith's self-satisfied male definition of the *hetairai* class of ancient Greece: 'In as much as any class of women may be said to be admirable as a whole, they were admirable: they were witty, intelligent, and (so far as we know) good lovers. They performed a useful social function, and were well integrated. They, and not the wife – whose task it was to produce children – were the companions of men. Consider then, in the light of our own time in the West, they were not prostitutes at all.' It is important to recognize that in labelling a person a 'prostitute' one utilizes a term in which an artificial and somewhat arbitrary line is drawn separating with a false rigidity the behaviour of certain individuals from others.

The aspect of the relationship between a gigolo and his Madame Bountiful in which he is 'kept' by her does not lend itself as easily as the prostitute's encounter to analysis as 'simply' an exchange of money for sexual services. The transaction between a 'john' or 'jane' and a prostitute is relatively straightforward. If the client desires a specific sexual position or variation he or she pays the agreed-upon price; if he or she is especially pleased, he or she may leave a tip. The 'exchange' in other social relationships is less precise.

Not many would deny that the relationship of the homemaker wife and her provider husband involves more than sexual partnering and the establishment of financial support. Even if a man marries specifically to ensure himself a steady sex life, and the woman marries in order to be supported, the man and his wife will presumably interact in situations other than the bedroom. The situational context of the encounter with a prostitute may allow the relationship to remain strictly sexual. However, through time itself, the nature of the 'kept' aspect of the relationship may change.

Although we suggest that the role of prostitute is not the only one that can be linked to that of the gigolo, it seems nevertheless telling that, unlike the rich collection of information, both historical and literary, which documents the social presence of the roles of the prostitute or of the kept woman, the role of the gigolo and/or approximations to it have remained somewhat elusive, only occasionally appearing within anthropological or historical literature. In contrast to the voluminous writings on the topic of female prostitution produced by assorted psychologists, psychiatrists, sociologists, criminologists, law reform commissions, medico-theologians, ex-policemen, and practitioners of the world's 'oldest profession' themselves, inquiries that offer thoughtful analyses of the role of the gigolo are notable only by their absence. While the topic of 'male prostitution' does appear as a subheading within library indexes, the male prostitute is rarely if ever discussed as the intended companion of some lonely or sexually frustrated woman. Rather, the male prostitute – heterosexual, homosexual, transvestite, and/or transsexual – is discussed almost exclusively in the context of his providing sexual services for other males.

As William Masters, Virginia Johnson, and Robert Kolodny noted, 'while female prostitution is almost exclusively heterosexual (men paying women), male prostitution is almost exclusively homosexual (men paying men).' There are, to be sure, certain examples of male brothels for women, such as the one which existed in London's posh Chelsea area during the Second World War, and others which currently operate in Holland. However, the very rarity of such agencies is in itself telling. In the past, married women could meet for trysts with their lovers at *maisons de rendezvous*, 'houses of assignation' or 'accommodation houses' which rented rooms by the hour (most typically to prostitutes) and were often strategically located 'in the fashionable West End, over elegant millinery shops or in the back premises [of an] expensive beauty parlor.' However, more typically, the brothel is understood to be composed of female prostitutes engaged in providing sexual services for male patrons. Similarly, the 'kept man' or 'toy boy' role has historically been a social role in which the male 'sugar daddy' features more prominently than the Madame Bountiful.

To explain this gender gap among those who patronize prostitutes or keep sexual partners, some authors have appealed to the supposed existence of a 'natural imbalance' between male and female sexual appetites and the supposedly greater sex drive of men. Reflective of this position,

Donald Symons's work on human sexuality asserted that men are inherently more promiscuous than women. Similarly, in his extensive study of prostitution and the law in England, A.A. Sion commented, 'So long as the average human male is endowed with an imperative sexual urge that cannot be gratuitously satisfied and is economically in a position to provide some material reward in consideration for his sexual release, prostitution will inevitably exist.' This assumption is endorsed by sociobiologists and by others who assume that what has emerged within history reflects a natural order of sexuality that has arisen as a result of some type of evolutionary genetics.

Female prostitution has also often been discussed with reference to its supposed 'functionality' for society. Thus, Kingsley Davis suggested that prostitution existed to satisfy the sexual desires of 'the legions of [male] strangers, perverts, and physically repulsive in our midst.' Similarly, Havelock Ellis suggested support for prostitution's ability to provide a 'catharsis' mechanism through which males who are physically unattractive, socially inept and/or sexually frustrated can fulfil their sexual desires. He suggested that prostitutes exist to satisfy the erotic cravings of married men with frigid wives, those who experience 'a mysterious craving for variety,' or are 'sexually perverted' and seek to indulge fetishes or simply desire to be with sexual partners from a life sphere excitingly different from their own. Female desire for variety, indulgence or perversion is nowhere considered. As Mary McIntosh observed in her article 'Who Needs Prostitutes?,' seldom has there been concern expressed over the provision of a readily available sexual partner for the sexually desirous female.

Alternatively, what can be termed the 'limp penis' theory has been put forward by those who suggest that acts of male prostitution with female patrons are physiologically impossible, or at least highly unlikely. In a 1982 interview with London's *Penthouse* magazine, Madame Claude, the infamous French madam of prostitution's *crème de la crème* noted that 'it is much easier to open your mouth than to lift your arm.' Others similarly have suggested that it is more difficult for a man than a woman to feign sexual excitement.

While on assignment for *The Chelsea Scoop*, and noting that listed within the erotic guidebook *Lusty Europe* was 'Callboy International,' an Amsterdam agency which 'catered for ladies who ... [were] "past the grand climacteric,"' journalist Joan Wyndham interviewed Jan Bik, 'who ran Amsterdam's biggest erotic centre' (of which Callboy International was but a part) and the escorts there, and at 'Sunny Call-Boys,' a like agency. She wrote:

I'd always been interested in the idea of male tarts for women and thought it grossly unfair that men should have access to easy uncomplicated sex, whilst we had only two alternatives – monogamous fidelity or ghastly affairs that nearly always ended in heartbreak. I also liked the idea of being dominant and telling some gorgeous boy to do exactly what I wanted. There was, of course, an obvious snag – the small mechanical difficulty of the man having to get an erection. How did they cope with old, and possibly ugly, women? I was determined to find out, and rang up Jan Bik in Amsterdam ...

Next I roped in my friend Dolly Frankel, as I was far too scared to go alone. Dolly ... [who] was always game for anything, wanted to know if we would actually have to *do* it. No, I said firmly, you'll just talk to the boys and interview their clients – a nice, straightforward piece of investigative journalism ...

J: 'Tell us about this call boy service for women.'
Bik: 'Well, the boys are no problem – I have offers every week. But many of the women play hard to get. They are convinced they can only sleep with a man if they like him – almost *never* will a lady confess she only wants sex just for an hour.'
J: 'But there must be hundreds of frustrated ladies who would happily pay!'
Bik: 'Oh no, if a lady *really* needs sex, she can get it at any time with a wink of the eye in town – for free!'
J: 'What about the really shy ones?'
Bik: 'They'd be too shy to come to me anyway. No, I tell you, it is rather a difficult business – the only boys who make their daily bread from it are the real professional hunters, the playboys who specialise in making a lady fall in love. Then she'll give the boy an apartment, a Porsche, but she doesn't like to give just money. We have tried brothels with boys – never a success! Just an orgasm is not enough for a lady – and in any case how many women are enjoying their orgasm at that age, fifty to sixty?' (Dolly and I exchange amazed looks.)
J: 'As members of that age group we can assure you ...!'
Bik: (Politely) 'You are so old?'
J: 'Fifty-five and -six respectively.'

'Bravo! You look very well on it,' cries Bik, and rings the bell for drinks.

All of these theories, and the thinking behind them, demonstrate numerous examples of gendered confinements of both thinkers and doers in past and present societies. An examination of the theories reveals them to be based upon not only a phallocentric view of sexuality (i.e., one which considers the male perspective and experience, as well as the male phallus, to be central, with the 'limp penis' theory being the most obvious), but also an implicitly coitiocentric one (i.e., a view which considers coitus, or sexual intercourse, to be the central and most meaningful act in its definition of sexuality).

For example, Masters, Johnson, and Kolodny, among many others, offered the following reasons for men seeking out prostitutes: 'some men are temporarily without sexual partners because they are travelling or in military service; others with a physical or personality handicap cannot easily obtain partners ... Some males seek special techniques that their usual partner will not provide; others do not want to invest the time, emotion, and money in an affectional relationship and simply prefer to buy physical sex.' At no point in their discussion do these reputable sex researchers indicate having given any consideration to the possibility that females may seek out male prostitutes (under whatever name) for exactly the same reasons. We have an implicit assumption operating here that men are more driven by their sexuality than are women, and that women either would not or should not express their sexuality for similarly motivated reasons.

We have already noted that 'functionalist' theories do not give consideration to female desire. Furthermore, the 'limp penis' theory assumes that, without an erect penis in evidence somewhere, no sex can occur. Such a limited view does not accord with the sexual facts. Even Madame Claude implicitly noted that it is easier to perform oral sex than coitus, and cunnilingus is more likely to result in female orgasmic satisfaction than is sexual intercourse. Males definitely could perform a paid or unpaid gigolo role, just as females could definitely perform the client role for the same reasons as do males. Clearly there is more to be said in explaining the relative scarcity of gigolos, past and present. The existing theories are hardly an adequate explanation of why history abounds with mistresses and prostitutes, but not with gigolos.

In accounting for this gender gap we should note that:

1 / As we will explore more thoroughly in chapter 2, through socialization, females are taught to prefer men who are older, more successful, and more economically dominant than they themselves. As we will discuss in chapter 3, being in a dominant position in a relationship or indeed, within a sexual position (e.g., female superior) is contrary to the role models which many women have been socialized to find sexually arousing.

2 / Even within contemporary society, women do not generally act as the initiators of the first sexual encounter in heterosexual relationships. Rather, they are more likely to acquiesce to the cultural image of 'women as

pursued, men as pursuers.' However, as we shall see in a later chapter, more women are becoming comfortable with adopting a 'pursuer' role in modern times.

3 / It would seem that men and women react differently to the unavailability of sexual opportunities. Ethel Person has suggested that having sexual opportunities would appear to be more necessary for the maintenance of male self-esteem than for the maintenance of female self-esteem. Thus, when denied a regular sexual partner, a male may seek out a prostitute, one-night stand, etc., as a Band-Aid solution, not only for sexual frustration but for battered self-esteem as well.

4 / While both males and females enjoy physical sexuality in the context of psychological and emotional intimacy, males are much more likely to be able to enjoy sex without that intimacy. In contrast, females prefer sexual activities to be part of an intimate relationship. This may discourage women from seeking out the services of a male prostitute.

5 / Finally, and perhaps most importantly, the relative scarcity of male prostitutes and Madames Bountiful may well reflect an historical legacy and tradition whereby women have infrequently enjoyed the rights, freedoms, or power of men to financially, and/or in socially accepted fashion, indulge their sexual desires.

Historically men have figured larger in the role of gift giver and keeper than as kept, which may reflect their control of goods and services throughout history and across cultures. Above all, keeping a woman or a man signifies wealth and power which are appreciable enough to bring interested parties admiringly around. It can be noted that the many wives of Solomon were thought illustrative of the wealth and power he possessed and not merely of his sexual appetite.

The cross-cultural research of Rosenblatt and Anderson on human sexuality noted: 'The role of gifts in sexual relationships may vary greatly from one society to another, but the apparent commonness of such gifts is intriguing. The gifts may be a symbol of male power, a sign that is common around the world to define male sexual need as somehow greater than female, or a *symbol of relative control of goods cross-culturally* (if males control more goods, they have more goods to give). Gifts may also indicate who is more actively involved, and the initiator of the relationship may feel the greater obligation to provide compensation' (emphasis added).

Throughout history the male prostitute, like his female counterpart, has primarily served as the sexual partner of the male rather than of the female. Males could afford this sexual outlet and were given tacit permission to indulge their premarital or extramarital desires; women could not and were not. Moreover, in a society which has historically followed the social imagery of 'women as pursued, men as pursuers,' the commonality of male, rather than female, gift giving may follow from the social imperative for males to be aggressive within the formation of a relationship and the injunction for females to remain passive.

The comments of a 37-year-old gigolo illustrate the phenomenon of gift giving quite well.

A gigolo must give as well as receive. The difference between winners and losers is knowing that you can't just take all the time, you have to have something to give too. One thing that really works well with women is to give a personalized gift right at the start. It doesn't have to cost much – twenty-five bucks for a key-ring with her name on it ... It lets her know that you've been thinking about her and consider her special. People don't change just because they're rich and *everyone – everyone* likes to get a present. For one lady, I filled up her bathroom with balloons; for another, I sent her seven dozen roses on her fifty-seventh birthday ...

It is obvious in this example that gift giving is not conceived of by this man as simply reflecting generosity of character or some type of fundamental altruism. Rather, it is purposive behaviour undertaken with the supposition that it will advance his attractiveness to his female partner or increase what Hans Zetterburg termed one's 'secret ranking.'

The 'secret ranking' is a somewhat amorphous concept and defines an individual's erotic ranking as 'the secretly kept probability that he can induce an emotional overcomeness among persons of the opposite sex.' Zetterburg suggested that the erotic ranking is only partially based in visible attractiveness; the 'secret ranking' is not precisely a theory of 'sex appeal' as used to describe the allure of the aesthetically beautiful. Thus, he took pains to remind us, a wealthy or successful man who is unattractive need not be rebuffed by a beautiful woman and certainly numerous examples exist of wealthy aged men marrying or being partnered with young glamorous women, corroborating his assertion.

Laura Mulvey's famous formulation of men as the 'bearer of the look,' and women as the object of a spectator's gaze, has suggested that voyeurism, fetishism, and pornography are both cause and consequence of the social structuring of males as active and females as passive. To no lesser degree, the roles of patron and product of sexual consumerism must be linked to a sociocultural analysis of male and female roles.

Earlier we noted our dissatisfaction with the stereotypic depictions summoned up within popular culture of the gigolo/Madame Bountiful relationship. What is especially striking about such depictions is their attempt to focus attention on the man's supposed 'magnetism' or appeal rather than on the woman's ability to 'negotiate from a position of strength' the attainment of a companion. If the woman does possess an independently derived income – as in, for example, Gloria Swanson's role of the aged silent-screen actress Norma Desmond in *Sunset Boulevard* – the presentation is that of a pathological female, tyrannical, despotic, and crazed.

In the movie *Sunset Boulevard*, Swanson plays a 50-year-old suicidal woman who is obsessed with recapturing both her youth and her former glory as a 'star.' She is waited upon and protected by her first (of three) husbands, the director who discovered her and who now functions as her butler and guardian angel, shielding her from the unpleasant task of recognizing the ephemeral nature of stardom – writing her daily fan letters so that she will not realize she has been forgotten; reiterating that she is the greatest star who ever lived; and guarding her mausoleum of a home, a shrine to her former youth and glory, filled with publicity photographs of Desmond as a young actress.

After she has spent twenty years writing the script for a movie on Salome which Desmond believes will return her to the screen, the forces of serendipity bring Joe Gillis, a young writer fleeing collection agents who seek to repossess his car, to her door. She hires him to 'ghost write' her script and becomes besotted and obsessed with him. When her ardour is made unequivocally evident, he leaves and returns to her only upon learning she has attempted suicide by cutting her wrists. Joe's financial insolvency and sympathy-induced sexual behaviour towards Desmond combine with the forces of inertia to make him remain in Desmond's home as her gigolo. His ardour and discomforture in his role are portrayed as increasing proportionally to her possessiveness and generosity. After Desmond criticizes the singularity of his wardrobe, Gillis is taken by her to an expensive men's-wear shop to be outfitted in grand style. Desmond is in her glory, directing the salesman to bring the items she desires Gillis to wear; Joe himself is cast in the role of a mannequin or small child – merely the hanger on which clothes will be placed. When a salesman does direct his comments to Joe himself, he leers at Joe and remarks that, 'since the lady is paying,' Joe should take advantage of the situation and acquire an exceedingly expensive topcoat; Joe's unease and chagrin at the salesman's words are acute. However, Desmond is seemingly oblivious to Joe's advancing self-mortification as she clutches at him possessively, outfits him in expensive clothing, and showers upon him gifts of expensive jewellery and a solid gold cigarette case bearing the inscription 'Mad about the boy.'

Despite the creature comforts he enjoys, Joe evidently finds his existence to be intolerable and emasculating; nightly he sneaks out of Desmond's house in an attempt to co-author a screenplay with Betty, a young woman who is engaged to his close friend. When his friend's fiancée declares her love for him, Joe reveals himself as torn between his selfish desire to possess her, his loyalty to his friend, and his feelings of self-disgust and unworthiness at having allowed himself to become a gigolo for a middle-aged woman. When he overhears Desmond, enveloped in jealousy, telephoning Betty, baiting her with questions as to how well she really knows Joe and the 'type' of man he is, he grabs the telephone from Desmond and invites Betty to come to the home that he shares with Desmond. When she arrives, he is brutal in his depiction of himself as simply a self-indulgent kept man whose actions are dictated solely by a libertine's desire for idle luxury and avarice; he entreats the girl to return to her fiancé and resists her invitation for him to join her and leave. When Betty departs after saying that she cannot bear to look at him after what he has told her, after what he has insisted she hear, Joe goes to his room; returns all the 'gifts' Desmond has bestowed upon him; and, packing his old and meagre possessions in his battered valise, announces to Desmond that he is leaving.

When Desmond reacts with hysteria, crying and beseeching him to remain, Joe attempts to restore her to the world of reality by exposing to her the self-glorifying lies that Desmond has nurtured and that her butler has sustained – the contrived nature of her fan mail and the indifference of the movie studio to her submitted script on Salome – and tells her, 'There's nothing wrong in being fifty as long you don't try to be twenty-five.' He cannot reach her. As he attempts to leave, a crazed Desmond shoots him three times and kills him in her great despair over his departure.

When the police attempt to question her about the murder, Desmond can be summoned out of her silence only by her butler's pretence that the reporters and photographers gathered outside are eagerly waiting to immortalize her 'return' to the movies. Descending her long, elegant staircase in flamboyant style as Salome, Desmond thanks the bemused police officers and assembled media for remaining her loyal fans, promises many more triumphant performances to come, and descends into a close-up of madness ostensibly borne of her obsession in relation to her career.

As Judith Long Laws has suggested, the 'myth of the career woman freak' is, to paraphrase Margaret Mead, that men are unsexed by failure but that women seem to be unsexed by success. In pursuing a career and/or a gigolo, a woman apparently becomes the Frankenstein of her own creation. The moral of the story is that women are misguided if they attempt to adopt masculine attitudes towards work and/or the establishment of an intimate relationship, and ultimately self-defeating.

EARLY PRECURSORS OF THE MODERN GIGOLO

It may be difficult for a female to depart from the feminine role of 'pursued,' even if she enjoys a position of power and wealth. Men's dominant role as the keeper rather than the kept throughout history may also reflect their historic power and their ability to define males' needs as greater than females'. As feminists suggest, women have been kept on leading-strings by father, husband, church and state for centuries, their lives reined in by both formal and informal social controls and their range of expression, expectations, and opportunities limited. The relative absence of the role of witting keeper among women may reflect their curtailed power to acknowledge and/or respond to their needs and interests.

We must bear in mind that throughout most of recorded Western history, the 'institutional family,' as sociologists generally refer to it, was essentially a sociopolitical-economic arrangement, and marriage was basically a functional partnership rather than a romantic relationship. In fact, the concept of an 'intimate relationship' could not be appropriately applied to this family form. Feelings of what we today usually think of as 'affection' for family members were not considered to be essential, or even important, for effective family functioning. The notion of a romantic intimate partnership did not become meaningful until much later in history.

Historically, marriages were largely arranged by parents, operating either independently or in conjunction with some socially acceptable intermediary, working with an eye to establishing the best match, which would maximize the gains for all members of the family groups involved. An important part of this negotiation process for selecting a mate in many cultures involved determining the amount of the *dowry*, either money or property, which would be an essential part of the marital bargain. In cultures where women were considered to be economic liabilities and in need of support, first, by the family they were born into and, later, by the family they married into, a dowry would be paid by the parents of the bride to either the family of the groom or, more usually, the groom himself. At first glance, we would appear to have an atmosphere in which gigolos could flourish, but such was really not the case because, first, the groom's family, or the approved matchmaker, and not the groom himself negotiated the amount of money or property that would be exchanged and, second, the about-to-be-mated had not only relatively little power over the process of selecting their betrothed but also little control over when, during their lifetime, they were to be married.

Throughout most of the past, the institutional family was organized solely around economic production by the members of the family unit to ensure physical survival, close ties with an extended kinship network, and a male-dominated authority structure which gave the male head of the family control of family members and of the family's property. Within the institutional family system, family duty, or what the individual could do for his or her family, was expected to be paramount.

It is noteworthy that those who adopted earlier gigolo-like roles, such as 'walkers,' were often attendants upon women at the express desire of husbands, who were anxious to ensure the sanctity of their property. In accordance with the unwritten social law among wealthy Italians that a woman should never appear in public with her husband but, at the same time, must always have a male companion at her side, the social role of the 'cicisbeo' was created. Thus, the Italian cisisbeo was a male companion paid by a woman's husband to ensure his wife's fidelity. Beginning in Genoa 'circa' 1718, 'cicisbeism' was confined to the upper classes, particularly in northern Italy. It was thought that 'the appearance of the cicisbeo with the lady [was] more *de regle* than that of her husband' and, in consequence, the cicisbeo was charged with serving and entertaining the wife without arousing the ire or the jealousy of her husband. The practice of cicisbeism allowed the woman to have up to four cicisbei, or 'gentlemen-in-waiting,' to cater to her needs: to chatter with her while she dressed; compliment her profusely; exchange gossip; take with her the midday meal; escort her on afternoon visits to her friends, church, and so on; and perform such indispensible tasks as carrying 'her fan, her parsol, or her lapdog.' After the lady had dined alone with her husband in the evening, her cicisbeo or cicisbei would rejoin her as her companion(s) for whatever evening activity – the theatre, opera, etc. – had been planned. As Friedell observed the cicisbeo, 'called in France *petit maître*, in Italy the *cavaliere servente*, who was not infrequently an *abbé*, attended his mistress like a shadow.'

In his work on the history of prostitution, William Sanger suggested that 'originally, there can be very little question that the institution [of cicisbeism] was of an amorous character, and the parties met privately at the Casini, where certain apartments were dedicated to the use of the ladies and their *cavalieri*.' However, even though other historians have suggested that the cicisbeo was more frequently a homosexual companion than a heterosexual lover, the cicisbeo was never intended to provide the woman with a convenient paramour for sexual dalliances; rather, he was to be her companion, her chaperone, one who would negate any possibility that she would be unfaithful to her husband. Lynn Ramsey observes:

Sometimes he was a cleric in the style of the fashionable French abbés. He could also be the younger son of a noble family who would pass through the stage of cicisbeism in order to learn the formalities of polite society. Or he could be an older gentleman with no occupation who was chosen from among poor relations or trusted family friends. For his services, he was well-kept, received a monthly allowance and sometimes even an inheritance. Often the *cicisbeo* or *cicisbei* were named in the marriage contract, and these agreements were binding from fifteen to twenty years. Only the husband could consent to changing the *cicisbeo*. One unhappy lady who wished to dispose of her tiresome escort was informed that such an act would be considered indecent and scandalous

and goes on to comment:

It is not surprising that this extraordinary custom did not survive much beyond the eighteenth century, even without considering the social upheaval of the Revolution. Being a chattering *cicisbeo* was not a highly regarded profession among most Italian men ... Bondi, a Venetian satirist of the time, sympathized with the plight of the *cicisbeo*: 'Supplementary husband during the day, his duty is to stay constantly by the wife of a third party, and by express contract and obligation to be bored by her for days at a time.'

As William Sanger has noted, following the French occupation of 1800, cicisbeism 'became the subject of immoderate raillery and satire.' Men could not be expected to aspire to a role that was not given social validation as one to be respected or admired. Although the term 'cicisbeo' would seem to have become obsolete in present times, Lynn Ramsey maintains that it is still used on occasion to denote in a derogatory manner a man who appears 'effeminate' or less than ruggedly 'masculine.'

Even though historically, women such as the *hetairai*, the educated courtesans of ancient Greece; the 'girl in a green bower' or the diplomatic 'douceurs' of ancient China; and the inhabitants of the large Islamic harem were thought indispensable social necessities to care for the needs of men and, as such, were often socially respected as a 'feminine ideal,' the chattering cicisbeo was never given equivalent status or regard for his role as the companion/confidant of women. Clearly within the gendered confinements of eighteenth-century Italian masculinity, attending to the interpersonal dimensions of intimate relationships represented a devalued departure from the ideal role.

Similarly, in eighteenth-century France, the role of the *chevaliers servants*, or gentlemen-in-waiting, stemmed from a concern with maintaining a fashionable image reflecting privilege and prestige upon the status of a woman's husband. Despite originally being intended as an entertaining companion, the *chevalier servant* could, on occasion, become his mistress's lover, or more often, her partner in intrigue. Nevertheless, the limited power of women remained evident and the power they exerted was largely vicarious. If these gentlemen of the royal French courts seemed happy to flatter the beautiful, the charming, and the rich women of the court, it was with the perception that such associations could furnish a vehicle by which the impoverished nobleman or priest could gain access to fashionable society.

While we are acquainted with the famous mistresses of history – Nell Gwynn and Louise de Keroualle, both mistresses of Charles II; Barbara Villiers, Madame de Pompadour; Madame du Barry; Madame de Maintenon; and others – the anonymity and relative scarcity of world-famous gigolos reflects the historical inability of but a few women to wield the power, status, or independent riches that attract the male gold-digger.

However, as Roderick Phillips has noted, a series of important legal changes occurred throughout Europe and North America between the middle of the nineteenth century and the outbreak of the First World War. Legislation was enacted in one country after another, giving women the right to own and control their own income and property. Prior to this legislation, any money or property earned or inherited by a woman was administered and effectively controlled by her father or husband. While the granting of economic independence in law clearly does not guarantee independence in practice, it does allow for the possibility that a woman of wealth could dispose of what she owned to obtain anything she privately desired. Coupled with other social, legal, and political changes occurring during the early twentieth century, women, some more than others, were gaining a growing sense of empowerment over their own lives.

Another very important transformation took place as all Western societies experienced the Industrial Revolution. Not only was muscle power replaced by machine power, but the location for working with machines was made separate and distinct from the home. Industrialization required the establishment of a centralized workplace, and workers were now expected to leave their homes each day to go to work. Furthermore, with the introduction of a cash economy, work itself became equated with the concept of 'paid labour.' That labour which did not receive monetary recompense, most notably the labours that occurred in the home, came to be socially defined as being of lesser value. The home itself slowly became equated with the family and family activities only, and became increasingly privatized – something which was to be shielded from public view. Over time, as well, 'work' and the 'family' became gendered. The social truisms developed that a woman's place 'was in the home,' while a man's place was 'at work.' Thus, almost all things having to do with the home (such as housework), the family (such as childrearing), and private relationships (such as love) were eventually considered to be part of a woman's sphere or domain. The major exceptions were the areas assigned to a man's sphere or domain: providing financial support for the home and family, and sex (which, while private, was considered to be an area of masculine expertise, based again upon the belief that men were naturally more sexual than women).

These transformations signalled the creation of the *provider* role for men. Social conventions developed which required a man to leave home each day, go to a centralized work location, engage in paid labours, and then bring his pay packet back home, where it would eventually be spent upon provisions necessary to sustain the lives of the workman, his wife, and their children. While it is true that both women and children did labour for wages, especially during the early stages of industrial development, increasingly pressures mounted for the man to be the one family member to perform the 'good provider' role. This notion soon spread throughout all social classes in all Western societies and became entrenched as a central defining element of ideal masculinity – a real man economically provides for his family. In consequence, a man's worth came to be measured by the additional gender constraint of his dollar value. His wife, in contrast, came to be measured by her performance of housewife and mother roles – roles which, it was argued, could not be accorded, or denigrated by assignment of, a dollar value.

The 'institutional' family that was described earlier in this chapter gradually gave way to a new ideal, fashioned during the 1920s, that eventually came to be termed by sociologists the 'companionate' family. Changes in the nature of the industrial economy and in modes of transportation and communication produced increasing social and geographic mobility, which in turn led to significant alterations in the nature of the ties with the extended kinship network. The focus was now upon the nuclear family unit, specifically on companionship relations between husband and wife (still, however, within the framework of male domination), and between parents and their immediate in-home children. Family life became even more private, and the expectation now existed that the family was to be a source of personal satisfaction and individual fulfilment. Marriage in particular was to be based upon continued companionship, love, and affection, and not just upon the satisfaction of economic-survival needs.

To enable men and women to find their 'companion,' a new institution evolved – dating. Beginning late in the previous century, and essentially completed by the 1920s in North America, a shift in the power over mate selection occurred, from parents to those about to be mated themselves. Whether they wanted to or not, parents and parent substitutes gradually lessened their supervisory control over the activities of the young as more single men and women spent more years in schools and universities and various work settings. Modern inventions such as the automobile, the telephone, and the private, dark, cinema provided for greater independence of single people and more opportunities for getting acquainted without having to run the gauntlet of family intermediaries and the old stiff formalities of proper introductions. The increasingly powerful mass media of radio, magazines, and the movies promoted images and models of the new romantic ideals. But these increasing freedoms also brought into focus a new problem: where do you meet other eligible people with whom you could go for a drive, go to the movies, or talk on the telephone? One answer was the dancehall.

THE EMERGENCE OF MODERN-DAY GIGOLOS AND MADAMES BOUNTIFUL

We noted at the beginning of this chapter that the term 'gigolo' has been variously attributed to the French, for one who dances, and to the Italian, for one who smiles. A third view suggests that the term emerged in France during the 1850s and was originally coined to describe the man closer to our contemporary notion of the 'pimp.' At that time, the term 'gigue' denoted a woman of 'sexual looseness' – the 'gigolette' or dancehall pickup. Subsequently, it has been suggested, 'gigolo' came to describe the boyfriend of the dancehall girl or simply a man who frequented dancehalls. While the exact origin of the term gigolo remains somewhat elusive, there can be can be little doubt that the imagery of the swarthy Latin lover remains, facilitated in part, by what can be called the 'Valentino legend.'

The mute idol of the 1920s, Rudolph Valentino began as a professional dancing partner at Maxim's, a New York cabaret, and within the chorus of various musical stage shows. Although the publicists of movie studios wove such a web of myths surrounding his beginnings that even his name at birth remains the subject of speculation, Valentino's career prior to stardom consisted of, among other odd jobs, those of gardener, taxi driver, professional dance partner, and professional 'lounge lizard.'

'The Ladies' Man Supreme' was exotic to his fans, effete to his detractors, and equivocal in his sexual preferences. Although seemingly more comfortable among his close male friends, Valentino married twice. The first marriage ended when his wife reputedly locked him out of their bedroom once and for all on their wedding night; she was later to be described in one of Valentino's obituaries as simply 'one of the many zeros in the arithmetic of life.' The second marriage was to the heiress of the cosmetics manufacturer Richard Hudnut, 'Natacha Rambova,' who dominated him and paraded him around like a jewel for others to covet.

His early conquests had given him tips of five and ten dollars; the dancing establishments, in which he had captivated ladies with his accent and lithe elegance, had simply given him food and drink. Ironically, in 1926, when Valentino, among a group of men prominent in literature, art, and drama, was asked by *Vanity Fair* to define 'The Ideal Woman,' the woman's possession of money was omitted from his list of the 'ten essential elements.' Rather, the stellar qualities that the perfect woman had to possess, according to Valentino, may be seen to iterate many of the traditional 'feminine' virtues:

1. Fidelity.
2. The recognition of the supreme importance of love.
3. Intelligence.
4. Beauty.
5. A sense of humor.
6. Sincerity.
7. An appreciation of good food.
8. A serious interest in some art, trade, or hobby.
9. An old-fashioned and whole-hearted acceptance of monogamy.
10. Courage.

Exquisitely photogenic, Valentino, it has been suggested, largely owed his stardom to the fact that on the screen he appeared to be 'simply the most erotic man in the world.' The presentation of beauty, of elegance, of style and grace has always been perhaps more necessary for the successful gigolo or paid dancing partner/lounge lizard than the actual possession of these qualities themselves. Twenty-five years after his death, *Life* magazine called Valentino 'the symbol of everything wild and wonderful and illicit in nature.' An exalted eulogy indeed for a man who had a cauliflower ear, was a bit cross-eyed and had a slight squint, and was, at the time of his death, decidedly pudgy and balding.

The role of the modern-day gigolo was created early this century in the pre- and postwar dancehalls of Europe and America. Whether the setting was the exclusive Four Hundred Club, The Moulin de la Chanson, The Apollo, New York City's Roseland ballroom, Delmonico's, or Bustanoby's, wherever wealthy women congregated to amuse themselves, the paid male dancing partner appeared. When, on New Year's Day 1919, the Roseland ballroom opened, on hand were 150 hostesses and 25 tuxedo-clad 'huskies,' or male hosts, to aid in the festivities. For ten cents a dance, an elegantly clad male would squire a woman, young or old, around the dance floor. Some sought him simply as a graceful partner; others were reportedly more attracted to his disreputable image. Sheathed in the soft lights of the dancehall, surrounded by the plaintive tones of the music, the male host could find for himself and his paramour a discrete corner in which intimacy could develop. Indeed, it is interesting to note that the director of *Sunset Boulevard*, Billy Wilder, 'had first-hand knowledge' of his subject-matter; reportedly, 'for a time before he achieved career success, he worked in a Berlin dance hall, partnering older women patrons.'

However, if the male dancing partner became the 'pet' of the rich, there were always attempts made by moral vigilantes to protect the honour of women and to do battle for a woman's virtue. In her study of Parisian prostitution in the late 1920s, Maryse Choisy noted:

The dance halls of the Street of the Virtues were all ultravirtuous. The family trade could object to nothing. The prohibitions swung from the rafters in large letters. The signs read:

LADIES – NO SMOKING ALLOWED.
GENTLEMEN – DANCING TOGETHER IS NOT ALLOWED.

What bourgeois morality among the professionally immoral!

Nevertheless, the vision of the older woman (termed a 'flapperdame') who spent the afternoon clutched in embrace by her paid young male dancing partner ('lounge lizard'/'flapper rooster') seem to precipitate consternation and discomfiture. Lynn Ramsey has observed:

American morality could not swallow her dance-hall gigolos, and in 1921 the police blew the whistle on the 25 Roseland hosts. The female 'taxi dancers' continued to partner Roseland's male clientele until 1951, but the women who came to dance had to fend for themselves. The big public dance halls, unlike those in Europe, were constantly being investigated due to pressure from the church and right-wing groups who felt responsible for safeguarding the morality of America. The tango was considered by the latter to be one of the greatest menaces to the country. Among the propaganda was a book called *The Modern Dance*, in which the author testified that the average minister 'knows that moral lapses and spiritual death are traceable too often to the ballroom, and that modern dance is the prolific source of domestic dissatisfaction, and therefore, is the nursery of the divorce court, and that as a social influence it weakens and destroys the best safeguards of virtue and purity.' Meanwhile, however, dancing was thriving in the first-class restaurants and hotels of America ... where glamour queens and society matrons and their daughters could do the 'Boston Dip,' the 'Puppy Snuggle,' the 'Naughty Waltz' and the 'Argentine Ardor' with sleek, sad-eyed gigolos, and nobody dared say a word.

Ramsey noted that, even though there appeared in France after the First World War 'a Parisian dance sensation called the "Gigolo,"' the professional male dancing partner in America was typically regarded as a 'pariah.' Apparently, American society was ready to fight for a woman's honour – even if she herself was not. Moreover, the censure of the male dancing partner may suggest a punishing of male deviations from the accepted norm (i.e., men who are 'employed' by women for a mere ten cents) under the guise of protecting women, which is a more noble, nay chivalrous, socially acceptable undertaking. The underlying motives perhaps become acceptably obscured by an apparent conformity to social convention.

Although dancing or 'tango palaces' exist today to a limited degree in France, and 'tea-time dances' enjoyed a revitalization at places such as London's Waldorf Hotel during the 1980s, there is little of the mass popularity of a venue which originally allowed the gigolo to flourish. While male dancers such as those employed at Chippendale's may provide a form of entertainment that caters primarily to women, and our data suggest that the male 'erotic dancer,' or stripper, may become a primary or secondary career role for the gigolo, the 'dancing *partner*' – who dances *with* a woman rather than gyrates on a table in front of her – would seem to have become something of an anachronism.

Indeed, perhaps the only vestige of the tradition of the readily available and identifiable male dancing partner which remains in North America is in the studios which offer instruction in the various forms of dance. However, should the Terpsichorean 'Monsieur Pierre' desire to seek his fortune as the paid-for companion of a wealthy woman, he may find himself somewhat at a disadvantage. First, his service loses some of its glamour when advertisements beg patronage with the offer of 'seven sessions for $45.' Similarly, the promise of a 'party night' with a DJ, unhosted bar, and other supposed inducements may sound more desperate than enticing. Second, the atmosphere that surrounds the woman and her dancing partner is now sanitized and deodorized; gone are the soft lights, the alcohol, and the continuous hum of other couples talking, which reputedly allowed the woman to 'lose herself' in the romantic atmosphere. Third, it is arguable that, unlike 'ballroom dancing,' contemporary dances do not truly foster intimacy. In the tango, one had the sinuous, languid movements of bodies close together. With the modern exception of 'slam dancing,' whose choreography appears to be borrowed from the mating-supremacy rituals of bighorn sheep, contemporary dances do not really require that one be in the same room as one's partner much less coordinate movements. Finally, if the women we interviewed on occasion identified dating services, health clubs, and escort agencies as facilitating introductions to eligible men, they often seemed dumbfounded when asked if they had ever been tempted to seek a partner from a professional dancing studio. The typical reaction was one of incredulity, and not infrequently included the comment of 'Why? All the men there are gay!'

Deprived of employment furnished within nightclubs and cabarets, aspiring gigolos did not disappear, they simply changed venues; women in the 1930s could still locate gentlemen companions within the employment registries of escort and matrimonial clubs. Ted Peckham's escort service, described in his *Gentlemen for Rent*, was one such remarkable example. He attributed his creation of the escort agency to his observing, while window-shopping along Fifth Avenue, the 'well-dressed women obviously killing time studying the same windows. They, too, were lonely strangers.' J. Paul Getty once observed, 'the successful businessman is one who perceives one of society's needs and fills it.' Peckham's perception was to provide the impetus for his creation of a male escort agency that catered to women. He wrote:

Everywhere I went – movies, hotel lobbies, smart restaurants seen through Venetian blinds – I saw numbers of women without men, reduced to loneliness by an arbitrary social convention. At the same time, I noticed countless attractive young men of apparent education and breeding eating at drugstore counters and in the tea shops which I was also obliged to frequent. These fellows were bored and lonesome too, and their slim budgets, as I knew from my own experience, couldn't accommodate female companionship. The solution seemed obvious ... I would be the connecting link and bring these two desolate and palpitating groups together! All that was needed was a stable of escorts to guide lonely women through the hazards of nighttime New York. I would inaugurate a Guide Escort Service.

Peckham's Guide Escort Service began in the midst of the Great Depression but flourished, despite the fee of ten dollars a night until midnight for the hire of a respectable, well-garbed male of social pedigree and college education. His strategies for obtaining genteel escorts were predicated on the historical association between being a member of the gentility and evidencing a manner commensurate for one of lofty status. In New York, Peckham's first strategy for locating appropriate men was an investigation of the membership of the Yale Club. Promising his first potential 'client' – the Waldorf Astoria – 'a dozen university men, in their twenties, with Social Register backgrounds, perfect manners and reputations, well-dressed and thoroughly presentable, ready to squire any woman you have here wherever she wants to go, and prepared to deliver her back home as her own brother would,' his strategies for recruiting abroad were no less rigorous.

In London he informed the press that he would consider as candidates for his service only those who were graduates of Oxford or Cambridge, who were listed in *Burke's Peerage* or *Debrett's*, although a few assorted dukes and earls would not be unceremoniously received. In Paris, to screen out the *hoi polloi*, all applications were checked in *Tout Paris* as well as in the *Almanach de Gotha* – in effect the Social Register of Paris and the great handbook of European aristocracy. In Rome, although he thought it potentially profitable to provide the reportedly large number of America Catholics who travelled to Rome with young Jesuit novices trained to act as ecclesiastical escorts – guiding tourists through the historical religious spots, churches, shrines, catacombs, and abbeys – this idea failed because of a manpower shortage. Some men, obviously, had callings that differed from the one Peckham envisaged for them.

Regardless of their location, all escorts were required to obey Peckham's rules. These were:

1. Take no more than one drink per hour. Sobriety is essential. If the client gets intoxicated take her home (if you can get her to go).
2. Be polite yet impersonal at all times. Be a good listener. Discuss general subjects but never your personal life. Never mention personal friends or the names of other clients.
3. Don't give out your own telephone number or address. Contact with client must be made through the office.
4. Never enter a client's apartment or room unless other people are present, excluding servants. Say good night at the door or elevator.
5. Under no conditions become personally involved with a client. Any infringement of this means immediate dismissal.
6. Itemize the evening's expenses and return any change to the client. Tip conservatively unless the client wishes otherwise. Repeat business is your best recommendation.
7. Never hint for gifts or tips.
8. Every woman is interesting for at least one evening. Every client must be treated with the same courtesy. If things are dull, it is your own fault.
9. Should a difficult situation arise, contact the office immediately.

As business flourished, the 'professional' codes of behaviour became more stringent, and Peckham augmented his original set of rules with nineteen more which 'had to be read and digested thoroughly by every candidate qualified to achieve listing as a Guide Escort':

1. Don't be late for engagements. In fact, leave home five minutes early to allow for traffic delays.
2. Don't be self-conscious but do everything with a casual air as if you had been doing it for years (this is especially important for the Guide Escort in the exchange of money between him and the lady for the evening).
3. Don't laugh or talk loudly or do anything to be conspicuous. Posing and showing off aren't a manifestation of inherent breeding.
4. Don't dance with your eyes closed or assume peculiar positions on the dance floor.
5. Don't go Broadway in dress. Conservatism in clothes stamps the gentleman. Save your colour for the beach.
6. Don't forget shaves, shoeshines, and clothes-pressing. Your appearance makes the first impression.
7. Don't sprawl your legs all over chairs or forget that there is such a thing as posture and standing straight. It isn't just military – it's a masculine requisite.
8. Don't stretch or yawn publicly.

9. Don't chew gum. Smoking is in order, as few people object to it today (as long as you smoke your own), but watch your ashes and use ash trays.

10. Always carry two immaculate handkerchiefs for emergencies.

11. Don't begin every sentence with 'I.' Be a listener and draw out your companion. You may be surprised to find she has done some interesting things, too.

12. Don't answer with 'sure,' 'yeah,' or 'unh-hunh.' 'Yes' will do. Good diction is important. Don't swear or use slang. The latter is a lazy way out unless it is up to the moment and really expresses the idea. An occasional 'damn' or 'hell' can usually get by.

13. Don't have a line. Use subtle flattery without being over sweet or solicitous.

14. Don't knock anybody. If you can't say something nice, be silent. Anyway, you never know who knows whom, or who your next assignment will be.

15. Don't shout or sneer at waiters or servants, but talk to them civilly. This is only well-bred in the first place and, anyway, there may be a revolution and you'll be on the wrong side.

16. Don't scrape your plate, gulp your food, or make noises at table. Watch your table conversation, as there are certain subjects which inhibit the digestion or spoil the appetite.

17. Don't be a tableware folder or a dish-and-saucer piler. Wait for the waiter to take your plate away and arrange the service.

18. Don't be cheap about tipping. If you expect first-class service, be prepared to pay extra for it – at least fifteen to twenty per cent of the check.

19. Don't overstay. When a lady hints about leaving or retiring, don't insist on one more drink or dance (even if it means another five dollars to you).

Peckham's strategy for obtaining payment from the woman in a discreet manner involved the use of two envelopes: one was to contain the escort's fee (ten dollars until midnight plus five dollars for every two hours of overtime thereafter), while the second was for whatever amount the patron desired to spend on her evening, including tips, cab fares, and so on. At the end of the evening the escort was to place the monies remaining into the second envelope and return it to the patron. From its launching point at New York City's Waldorf Astoria, Peckham's service for unescorted females spread throughout the country. In Peckham's London branch, located at Selfridges' – a major department store – female patrons could simply be billed three pounds ten, the service cost, just as they would be for any other purchase made. In Paris, Vienna, Rome, and Budapest, Peckham's service was enthusiastically welcomed. Indeed, in France, Peckham's service was sponsored by the French government and populated with males of the impoverished nobility. As Palm Beach offered a favourable and hospitable crowd of consumers, Peckham opened a seasonal branch of his business there.

Guardians of female virtue were enraged. In 1939 Peckham's operation, which had seemingly flourished without subterfuge or scandal, was stopped and Peckham was convicted on the technicality that he had failed to obtain a licence for what most basically was an employment agency. When he attempted to apply for such a licence, his application was refused on the grounds that agencies such as his fostered or promoted immorality. Whether women liked it or not, female purity had to be protected.

Throughout the twentieth century, the meagreness of conventional opportunities through which women could locate companionship or develop intimacy with a member of the other sex has been capitalized on by self-styled entrepreneurs, both legitimate and illegitimate. Some, 'lonely-hearts money hunters' like Maurice Paul Holsinger, were con men in search of quick gains, divesting women of money with the promise of an adoring male companion. Others have been bigamists, like Sigmund Engel, the 'twentieth-century Bluebeard of con' who 'married' at least 200 besotted females and divested them of $6 million before his arrest in 1949 at the age of 80. And, still other men have pursued financially viable marriages through serial monogamy.

In her book *Million Dollar Studs*, Alice-Leone Moats devoted considerable space to chronicling the life and 'loves' of Porfirio Rubirosa, the 'big dame hunter,' whose wives included Flor de Oro Trujillo, the seventeen-year-old daughter of the then president of the Dominican Republic; French film actress Danielle Darrieux; dime-store heiress Barbara Hutton; and 'the richest woman in the world,' tobacco heiress Doris Duke. Moats took apparent glee in describing the Mdivanis brothers – Alexis, Serge, and David – who invented royal status for themselves and, by purposeful design, married such women as film actresses Mae Murray, Pola Negri, Louise Van Allen Astor, and Barbara Hutton. Apparently no champion of female emancipation, Moats commented:

American dollars began to go abroad in the form of dollars, of course, long before the First World War, but at that time the parents were doing the purchasing. The socially ambitious started buying foreign titles for their daughters in the last quarter of the nineteenth century when each new wave of millionaires trying to storm the doors of New York's Four Hundred, or their counterparts in other cities, discovered that the doors flew open for the in-laws of dukes and marquesses ...

Still, it must be said for the parents that they at least got something for their money: the titles were genuine, the houses and castles magnificent (even though in need of dollars for repairs), the social position and entree to court circles assured. When the girls chose their own foreign husbands, they usually got men with phoney titles, fictitious family histories, no real estate, a social position so insecure that one of their reasons for marrying heiresses was to use them as rungs on the ladder to the heights occupied by the elite. Those who actually lived up to their reputations as great lovers usually proved averse to wasting their talents at home ...

The studs had an unlimited choice of victims – debutantes, divorcees, widows, film stars. By chance, during the thirty-five years between 1920 and 1955, an extraordinary number of tycoons died young, leaving fortunes to their widows and to daughters who were still under age and, therefore, came into huge fortunes just at the time they were marriageable. The divorcees were equally free to spend the enormous settlements they had received. Movie queens, under contract to the major studios, were earning higher salaries than the heads of corporations, and they too were able to fritter away their money at will.

Nobody could stop the unmarried heiresses from making fools of themselves; the divorcees were in the mood to redistribute the wealth they had obtained from unsatisfactory husbands by spending it to buy others whom they expected to be more satisfactory; many of the widows felt the same way, or were lonely, or ardent or merry; the film stars were vying with each other to acquire the biggest jewels, houses, automobiles - anything that was the biggest. So many moneyed women in search of love and so many lovers in search of money produced a rare condition in which supply equalled demand.

What allies the fortune hunters with the role of the gigolo is the purposive way in which they seek a wealthy woman as a financial and emotional partner; wealth is perceived to be not simply a pleasant by-product but rather the manifest reason for involvement.

As George Saintsbury noted in his preface to Fielding's *Tom Jones*, 'it must be remembered that the point of honour which decrees that a man must not under any circumstances accept money from a woman with whom he is on certain terms, is of very modern growth, and is still tempered by the proviso that he may take as much as he likes or can get from his wife.' Certainly most of us can be said to desire partners who have socially desirable qualities; even if people blithely state that they care not for the superficial qualities of wealth and beauty and simply seek a partner with a 'good personality,' seldom, in reality, are people so indifferent.

While people may be unaware of what features focus their attraction to another or may feel that certain attributes are conventionally approved more than others, rarely does a gigolo or fortune hunter think of a woman's wealth as simply 'a pleasant surprise.' While any person may appreciate it if his or her partner is other than destitute, the gigolo of times past and present views this as a primary factor in focusing his attention and directing his behaviour. As Thomas Schnurmacher commented in *The Gold Diggers' Guide: How to Marry Rich*: 'You can embark on a gold digging expedition without necessarily getting married, but this author believes most strongly in the institution of holy matrimony. Let's face it; it's one thing to swing a few presents and a couple of thousand dollars here and there, but marriage means more. Rich spouses are the gift that keeps on giving.'

Searching for guile-gotten riches, confidence men have played at the role of adventurer, of roué, and of Casanova. The high-society confidence man 'Colonel Novena,' *aka* 'General Alverosa,' 'Count Antonille,' 'Sir Richard Murray' (born Julian Cinquez), portrayed himself as a gentleman with a style and aplomb as if to the manner born, moving in and among the most exalted circles, doting upon the wives and tapping the fortunes of the husbands. Alternatively, confidence men like Allen McArthur, *aka* Ashur McAvoy, have used the role of the 'lover' as a way to make large profits from females. McArthur would eye the lovelorn columns in all the major American cities, checking off likely prospects and writing letters to those who seemed promising. No slouch in the romantic marketplace, McArthur would set up half a dozen women in neighbouring cities and, within a forty-eight-hour period, court and financially defraud his half-dozen victims, one at a time.

Posing as a wealthy businessman, McArthur would travel to meet his wealthy advertiser-for-affection on a Monday. By Tuesday, in the company of his adoring fiancée, McArthur would note, to his chagrin, that his traveller's cheques were missing and he would be unexpectedly beckoned elsewhere by a telegram (that he had sent to himself). The telegram generally stated that his presence was urgently required to complete a million-dollar business deal. Pretending that he was terribly abashed to do so, he accepted the $500 to $1,000 his eager-to-please, eager-to-marry fiancée offered him as a temporary loan for the trip and his expenses – and made his way to the next city and the next female.

In part, the role of the gigolo must, if reluctantly, be traced back to confidence men and women of old who so thoroughly appreciated the magic of bright façades of glittering brocades and equally radiant smiles, and the negotiability of exaggerated or bogus claims to enviable social positions or pedigree. However, there is more to be said.

During the twentieth century, we have seen the demise of one set of standards for ideal family life (the institutional family), the rise and fall of a second set of standards (the companionate family), and the relatively recent development of a third set of standards, a set that we are apparently still grappling with as individuals and as a society.

It was during the transition from the institutional to the companionate family that love and romance became socially defined as essential ingredients for the formation and continuation of intimate relationships. Neither love nor romance was absent in earlier times, but they were not considered to be as important or predominant as they are today. Currently people expect to hear all those involved in an intimate partnership of whatever form state that their 'ties that bind' are of a loving and romantic nature. However, 'falling in love' does not necessarily occur, as the French expression suggests, like *un coup de foudre*; no thunderbolt necessarily strikes from out of the sky. Love and romance may be more pragmatic and selective than is suggested in Barbara Cartland's novels.

It took the social changes of the 1960s and 1970s, referred to by Lillian Rubin as the sexual, gender, and 'therapeutic' or human-potential revolutions, to alter many aspects of the companionate family and give rise to a third new set of family and relationship standards. An emerging emphasis upon the values of gender equality and personal freedom supports more vigorously the right of males and females to seek relationships that will meet their personal needs, and, if a given relationship does not satisfactorily meet those needs, one is justified in seeking alternatives. Within this context of emphasizing self-fulfilment, the issue now becomes one of what the 'family' in general, and intimate partnerships in particular, can do for the individual, and not the other way around. Intimacy has come to be defined as an, if not *the* most, important criterion for initiating or maintaining a relationship. Practical considerations such as political connections or a promising investments portfolio or a great pair of ancestors are supposed to pale by comparison with opportunities for meeting one's intimacy and human-potential needs. In a cold, cruel, impersonal world, the meeting of these personal needs is touted as paramount.

This new set of ideals does not promote the existence of only one legitimate means of meeting intimacy needs, to the exclusion of all others but, both explicitly and implicitly, suggests that satisfaction of individual needs may be found in any number of alternative arrangements: legal marriage; cohabitation; one-career or dual-career families; two-parent or one-parent families; first marriages; reconstituted and bi-nuclear families; heterosexual, gay, or lesbian marriages. In other words, the 'pluralistic' family ideal has emerged to varying degrees of acceptance within modern Western societies. Acceptance or rejection of this plurality underlies some of the fundamental issues of current times as members of societies, business and the courts seek to grapple with new definitions of acceptable and legitimate relationship forms.

Regardless of the form a relationship takes, its ultimate goal is to create an environment that will maximize the ability of each participant to fulfil her or his potentialities as a human being. Family and relationship forms of earlier time periods are now defined as too confining in many ways. Sexuality was constrained to a very narrow range of acceptable motivations and actions. Males and (in particular) females were required to perform roles that, at best, allowed them to become only 'half-persons.' In contrast to psychologies and philosophies of 'human nature' that prevailed in the past and stressed the negative and fearful qualities of humans, which necessitated the creation of constraints, the new ideologies emphasize an inherent basic goodness of men and women that is just waiting to be developed. All that is needed is a combination of a cooperative and nurturing environment and the permission to 'go for it.'

However, some have referred to this rise of the 'therapeutic' or human-potential revolution as signalling a culture of narcissism in which 'self-actualization' could become a buzz-word evidencing little other than an egocentric self-absorption, a 'me-first, me-second, me-third' orientation towards life. Some have castigated this trend as promoting a type of navel-gazing, a mental masturbation that is not only hedonistic but foolhardy. The proliferation of self-help books has been decried by some as suggesting that the 'I'm OK, You're OK' quest for 'self-realization' has become other than truly humanistic; it has evolved, some would suggest, into a stance of 'I'm Dysfunctional, You're Dysfunctional.' Moreover, it has been argued that what we are witnessing is simply a growth of selfishness and self-promotion that paradoxically leads to dissatisfaction and unhappiness. Nevertheless, while the end-product of the therapeutic or human potential revolution can only be guessed at, there can be no doubt that it has suggested to at least some members of contemporary societies that they can 'have it all.' Buttressed with the increasing economic independence of women, the ethos underlying the human-potential movement may suggest itself as encouraging relationships – such as 'keeping a lover' that formerly were considered unseemly, distasteful or simply financially unfeasible, particularly for women.

It is revealing to note that, although the magazine stands at supermarket check-outs routinely feature articles that trumpet such headlines as 'I was JFK's Mistress,' 'JFK and Marilyn,' 'Bobby and Marilyn,' 'My Love Affair with Bill Clinton' and announce the latest in a series of paternity suits filed against males of high social status, such stories have become so common as to be almost innocuous and ho-hum. In contrast, more rarely featured, and perhaps because of this relative rarity, the apparent 'promiscuity' of the well-known woman, particularly those who are married, seems to be much more galvanizing. The 'Diana tapes' and the 'Fergie photos' are two obvious examples of this. Similarly, the coining of 'Camillagate' to refer to a raunchy taped conversation purportedly between His Royal Highness Prince Charles and Camilla Parker Bowles, a married woman friend, suggests that the female, and not the male, is assigned responsibility for maintaining standards of moral and sexual decorum.

Journalist Jim O'Leary made these interesting observations:

Among the unanswered questions in the Prince Charles love-tape scandal is: Why is it being called Camillagate? Think about it. When electronic eavesdroppers caught Diana cooing to her long-time friend James Gilbey, the indiscretion was immediately dubbed Dianagate by the press. Fair enough. Gilbeygate has a pleasant ring to it, but who really cares about the stiff at the other end of the princess's line? ... So why not Charliegate?

Rather than nail the heir to the throne's nameplate on the scandal, news reports tacked Camilla above the door ... Camilla is merely the other woman. Charles is the future king.

It might have been different if Camilla Parker Bowles was some sexy, blonde tart who wiggled by, batted baby blues and dropped a hanky in front of a ga-ga prince. But the only thing the middle-aged mom might have dropped was the phone when Charles moaned one of his smutty propositions ...

Charles is definitely the star of the tape ... Yet, like some Caribbean hurricane, this royal storm has been baptized with a female name.

The inference, of course, is that the other woman, Camilla, is the central figure in the escapade, as if she bears responsibility for somehow leading the prince into this sticky wicket. No one comes right out and says so. But even the normally cheeky tabloids have treated Charles with deference – or is it chauvinism?

When the Diana tapes became public in the fall, the London *Sun* not only published an almost-complete transcript of her suggestive conversation with Gilbey, it also operated a telephone hotline so voyeurs could hear the cooing for themselves. The same paper, however, reacted to the Australian publication of the Charles tapes by printing only some tame snippets of the transcripts. There was no hotline.

A double standard? Of course, but the *Sun* was not alone. No British papers published the transcripts the day after they became public. At least one refused to acknowledge their existence ... The editor of the very downmarket *Daily Star* even went so far to harrumph that he would never 'inflict' such 'terribly offensive' material on his readers. Right ...

One may also note that, despite O'Leary's critical commentary on the appropriateness of the label 'Camillagate,' he did suggest the woman's culpability would have been justifiably greater had she been 'some sexy blonde tart.' However, because Camilla qualifies for the three 'm's' (i.e., married, middle-aged, mom), O'Leary suggested a greater sense of 'male protectiveness' should have prevailed in the media and been extended to her. If surveys on sexual behaviour suggest that extramarital and premarital sexuality are not particularly uncommon for males *or* females, the social evaluation of such behaviours may well still be constructed along gender-specific lines.

It is important to note that when one dominant family ideal gives way to a new form, considerable numbers of people will and do still live within 'older' family and relationship frameworks. Some individuals will prefer to remain with the 'traditional,' while others will adopt the new and different, all depending upon how individuals perceive these forms as being able to meet their acknowledged (or sometimes unacknowledged) needs. Thus, currently, most Western societies have a small number of inhabitants who still exist within an 'institutional' family framework (and are hard pressed to understand all this current fuss over romance and happiness); a sizeable proportion of citizens exist within 'companionate' families (and understand the emphasis upon romance but insist that it can be found only within a 'traditional' heterosexual, life-long, legal marriage); and close to a majority, if not an actual majority of the population, live within some form of a plurality of different and alternative family structures and relationships.

All of the adults within these societies still seek to find a form of family and relationship that will meet their needs. Some therapists refer to this as 'scripting,' with persons seen as attempting to find someone who fits the 'script' – has the right qualities, attributes, or character that define a partner as desirable. But the needs, and more importantly their priority ranking, have changed for a significant portion of the adult population. Safety, security, stability, a sense of commitment – all are important, but the expectations of how best to achieve them have changed. And clearly disagreements exist between different segments of the population over whether the 'new' family and relationship forms are desirable for individuals, all family members, and even society itself.

Currently the 'new' family forms do not enjoy complete support from other social institutions within society, particularly business, the courts, and the political arena. The leaders of these institutions at the moment tend to be males who were mostly raised within the context of the 'companionate' family and who have lived much of their adult lives in a male-dominated, gendered-family-labour environment. These leaders are generally the most vocal among those currently calling for a return to 'traditional family values,' that is, the values that they are most familiar and comfortable with. Tradition, of course, refers to a provider husband and a stay-at-home housewife and mother. Given the trends for the past twenty-five years, this debate promises to continue for some considerable period of time.

THE FIVE BASIC FLAVOURS

The question of what kind of woman can afford a gigolo often presumes that such women have inordinate amounts of discretionary income and/or that the American gigolo, with his designer clothes and European luxury car, is the singular prototype for all gigolos. Both assumptions are false. As we earlier noted, these men assume many roles, and there is often fluidity between the roles, with one type serving as a 'bridging role' for another. Although any attempt to construct a typology of gigolos is difficult, we encountered five broad 'types.'

1 / *The Clydesdale or Golden Boy*: 'Clydesdale' literally refers to an enormously expensive, handsome, hard-working pedigree horse. Although, in the United States, the slang term 'Clydesdale' typically refers to any handsome man, we use it to refer specifically to the highest echelon of gigolos, the pedigreed pal of the upper-class or society woman. A Clydesdale is the pampered playboy and darling of the jet set (and/or 'the international white trash') who has secured his entrée into smart society and who is often better known within it than any individual woman he could be with. His is a type of elegant opportunism. Indeed, the term 'leather' is occasionally used to refer to the skintone and colour of ageing Clydesdales who, fancying themselves as Sun Gods, crave a tanned appearance more than they fear skin cancer.

Mentioned within the gossip/society sections of newspapers or pictured in magazines that pander to those twin passions, the Golden Boy was apt to fancy himself a celebrity of no small stature. Customarily kept by old money, he would disdain affiliation with the *nouveau riche* and the instant millionaire created by a lottery. As one such gigolo commented rather haughtily, 'I'd never give up my quality of life just to improve my standard of living.' This type of gigolo would not deign to be interviewed on a television talk show, however eagerly they courted him; but then, he also would pride himself on disdaining any association with the 'polyester and crimplene crowd.'

2 / *The Lap Dog*: The bourgeoisie of gigolos, these men lack the extensive network linkages that are purposefully pursued by Golden Boys and simply attempt to enter into serial 'marriages of convenience.' Unlike the Golden Boy, who typically prides himself on projecting an aura of personal success and views himself as a somewhat superior type of being, the Lap Dog tends to portray himself as Peter Pan in desperate need of Tinkerbell. As one Madame Bountiful observed of this type of gigolo, 'The trouble with him is that he can't figure out if he wants a lover or a mother.' However, the telling of sad tales from a repertoire of 'unfortunate circumstances' is often used to cajole financial palliatives from his companions.

3 / *The Casanova Con Man or Sweetheart Swindler*: Although the Con Man may seem similar in some ways to the Lap Dog, he is seldom content to simply be kept. Rather, he seeks to acquire independent control of capital from a woman – something that is comparatively rare in the fortunes of gigolos. Whether his design is to pursue a 'matrimonial con' and obtain money from the woman through marriage or through the pledge of it or simply to entice the woman into a bogus business venture while capitalizing on the intimacy the relationship provides, his role as a gigolo is conceived of as being a means to an end, not the end in itself.

4 / *The Walker, Beard or 'Handbag'*: Generally the Walker is a homosexual male and/or one who prefers the term 'committed bachelor,' and it has been suggested that the most important part of a Walker is his elbow. If this is debatable, the role of a Walker is generally restricted to the highest echelons of society. Like that of the cicisbeo in earlier times, the function of a Walker is to amuse and provide the woman with a non-threatening male presence. Our Walkers often provided the woman with a companion who publicly forestalled identification of a more socially unacceptable relationship with a male and/or female lover.

5 / *The Sexpert – Toy Boys/Beach Boys/Escorts, Studs, and Stallions*: Despite the elaborate litany of slang terms used to describe these men, their role is relatively simple. While their wealthier or more socially presentable brothers tend to pursue relationships of variable length, sexperts tend to be only occasional companions purposefully hired for a limited

performance. As is true of his brothers, the vast majority of Sexperts are bisexual (variously referred to as AC-DC, switch-hitters, ambidextrous) and will swing back and forth from females to males, as the occasion requires. Their self-identification as to sexual orientation (i.e., gay, straight, or bisexual) seems more a function of the sex of the person with whom they are engaging in the act at the moment, or who is questioning, than profoundly revealing.

As we noted earlier, while bisexuality was conceived of in the 1980s, at least within certain social circles, as somewhat trendy or fashionable, the current atmosphere (particularly the AIDS concern and worries about having sex with a partner's entire sexual history) may be seen as not conducive to admitting to or claiming bisexuality, as it is not a politically correct or socially enhancing sexual orientation. For respondents interviewed after the mid-1980s, it seemed important to proclaim loudly their heterosexuality with a rigour that was not observed earlier. Men interviewed during the latter part of the 1980s were more likely to announce themselves as resolutely heterosexual than were those who had been interviewed during the early 1980s. Even those respondents who had unabashedly announced their bisexuality when first interviewed during the early 1980s seemed over time to evidence a consciousness that a proclamation of heterosexuality – which appears to be safer – enhanced their eligibility to potential partners.

In the 1990s one of our respondents jokingly noted that, while telling a Bountiful how many women he had been with had formerly been a supposed 'turn on' for the woman, especially 'when you tell her she's the hottest, has the best ass, best tits, is the best lay you've ever had,' he was now routinely claiming to be 'practically a fucking virgin' to new or potential partners. Informing his would-be partner that his previous relationships with women had been 'platonic' friendships, or unconsummated relationships in which 'all we did was lay together in bed and she'd want me to hold her – honest,' he believed that his social and sexual eligibility would be enhanced. When the first author asked the man if this, in fact, was correct, he laughed and said 'C'mon! If you believe that, I've got some great swamp land to sell ...'

Generally adopted by young men (25 and younger, with 30 being fairly old for a toy boy), the Sexpert role may be the launching-pad for the man's entrance into other types of gigolo roles. As in all categories within this typology, there is considerable movement between categories as gigolos age, redefine their expectations of a relationship, and/or are subject to the evaluations – favourable or unfavourable – made by their partners and others.

It is evident that the type of monies needed to indulge in a gigolo relationship can vary enormously. In some ways asking 'how much' it costs to keep a gigolo is like asking how much it costs to buy a car. The answer, somewhat vexingly, is 'It depends.'

In November 1991, Sue Lindsay, of the *Rocky Mountain News*, reported a case involving a bigamist, Gerald Soderquist, who was convicted and sentenced to eight years in prison for 'bilking thousands of dollars' from his fiancée and one of his two alleged wives. Soderquist, who was called by Denver district judge Robert Fullerton a 'chronic liar' and a 'one-man crime wave,' allegedly had no fewer than two wives and seven fiancées at the time of his sentencing. He was additionally sentenced to four years in prison, to run consecutively, for obtaining $1,850 in automotive lighting supplies after forging a fiancée's signature on a credit-card application. One of his fiancées was an employee at a McDonald's restaurant; another lost her life savings – a $30,000 retirement fund; others lost jewellery or money when Soderquist stole from joint accounts and/or would run up charges on the woman's credit cards before he disappeared.

In September 1992, a United Press International story reported on the twenty-four-year prison sentence given to 57-year-old 'Sweetheart Swindler' Alfred Barakett for stealing 'as much as $40,000 US from women.' Barakett had stood accused of taking money from at least thirteen women in ten states after seeking them out through personal ads and singles' groups. Although Barakett claimed that his appeal to women was 'a gift of God' and that the women had simply given him the money because he had treated them 'like queens,' his account of events swayed neither the prosecution nor the judge. Noting that Barakett had used 'hundreds of aliases,' 'prosecutors said that after he had gained his victim's trust, Barakett would ask her to cash a cheque, usually stolen from a previous lover, for him.' Upon his release from prison, Barakett, from Trois-Rivières, Quebec, was to pay $8,940 in restitution to two of his victims and to be returned to Canada.

In January 1992, the *International Express* reported on the conviction of 33-year-old Christopher McFarlane-Grey, a graphic artist and 'Casanova con man' from Tottenham, North London, 'who charmed thousands of pounds out of women.' According to the newspaper article, 'smooth-talking Christopher ... adopted a fake American accent to impress victims. He chatted them up on the Tube, before springing his trap. He convinced the women he was either involved in a string of Hollywood hits or launching into a successful recording career. Then he would claim to lose all his money and ask for sums to tide him over ... The jury unanimously convicted him of four sample charges of dishonestly obtaining 15,800 [pounds sterling] from Amy Jones and 3,060 [pounds sterling] from WPC Hayley Northcliffe.'

As these examples suggest, the stakes need not be astronomical to be judged acceptable pickings by the men or as significant losses by the women involved. For some of our male respondents, $1,000 a night was the going rate, while others drew attention to the $100,000 sports car or the hundreds of thousands of dollars spent on homes and villas they had received from their Madames Bountiful. For others, the stakes were much more modest. Are the former group of gigolos more or less professional? Admirable? Vexatious? To return to our car analogy, does buying a 1986 Lada represent a better purchase than buying a brand-new Mercedes coupe? Again, it depends on who is doing the evaluation and, of course, whether he or she can afford to pay the asking price.

The late film star Bette Davis once complained, 'I was always eager to salt a good stew. The trouble was that I was expected to supply the meat and potatoes as well.' The situation wherein the woman assumes the traditional male role of provider and the man becomes a househusband would seem unacceptable to most people of both sexes because it seems to contradict values, social rules and expectations concerning appropriate gender-role behaviour. If these components are social expectations of male behaviour, the gigolo who purposefully seeks support from a woman as a route to financial and/or material success assuredly acts in a way that is contradictory to expectations of what constitutes the traditional masculine role. Although one can appreciate a man's desire to relinquish the traditional male task of supporting his wife or family financially, one would nevertheless assume that a man would not voluntarily allow himself to be placed in the powerless position of househusband, with its accompanying financial dependence, for any lengthy duration of time. There are few social rewards, it would appear, for being a househusband.

For a woman to become a Madame Bountiful requires not only that she acknowledge her sexuality and be assertive in responding to her sexual needs but, as well, often that she reformulate traditional expectations and conceptions of the feminine role within an intimate relationship. On the surface she must also confront age-old expectations of being provided for as well as the traditional inhibitions against being overtly assertive, even aggressive, in a relationship with a man.

As we have already shown, and will continue to demonstrate, a study of gigolos and their Madames Bountiful should be seen as a type of social history – not a moralistic treatise or a how-to manual. Such an approach locates the social interaction of the gigolo and his partner within a larger tradition of hierarchical divisions between men and women, social roles, and gender expectations. The clichés about the Madame Bountiful and her gigolo have persisted so long and so tenaciously that it becomes compelling to understand what is truly involved in such relationships. We must locate the present-day relationship within the context of contemporary society, for the intimate relationship is not formed, maintained, or dissolved in a vacuum. It exists between two people living within a specific time and in a specific place, and the participants themselves and the relationship they create are influenced both subtly and strongly by the social environment swirling around them. We turn our attention to that larger context in the next chapter.

2

The Quest for Intimacy

We feel compelled to begin this chapter by drawing the reader's attention to the fact that although much of the material here focuses upon women and their quest for intimacy, we are not trying to suggest, either explicitly or implicitly, that the quest is solely or even primarily a 'female problem.' While it is true, as we shall demonstrate in subsequent chapters, that females have been, and to a lesser extent today still are, defined by their relationships to men much more so than the reverse, both males and females seek an intimate partner.

We are also committed to drawing upon the best available material to help make sense of all dimensions of changing intimate relationships within contemporary societies. Much of the research and theorizing about intimate relationships today is still based upon the once seemingly inevitable connection between sexual intimacy and reproduction. Demographers and sociologists have traditionally been concerned with predicting future reproductive patterns and therefore have been concerned with projecting the proportion of females who would most likely be involved in those types of relationships that are most likely to yield children. Given the fact that, strictly from a record-keeping point of view, maternity is virtually always known, but paternity is not always as certain, social scientists, government policy planners, and others have traditionally focused their attention upon females rather than males. And since the vast majority of reproduction occurs within the context of legal marriage, attention has traditionally been focused upon such phenomena as female marriage and divorce patterns.

For a variety of reasons, including the greater availability and use of contraceptives, an increasing rejection of legal marriage as the necessary context for reproduction, decreases in marriage rates, and increases in cohabitation rates, the traditional focus now appears to be too narrow. But we are still forced to draw upon research generated from those traditional sources. The strait-jacket of necessity forces us for the moment to stress the female perspective on the intimacy quest more than that of the male. However, this emphasis is justified, in part, since we do need to understand who is most likely to perform the Madame Bountiful role.

Who keeps gigolos? The stereotype suggests that the woman who does so is somewhat less attractive than the prospect of Arnold Schwarzenegger in drag and is three years younger than God. Similarly, there is the implicit suggestion that the relationship is primarily, or most importantly, sexual. According to the pulp-paperback/quasi-pornographic image of the gigolo/Madame Bountiful relationship, a woman measures the eligibility of a gigolo as proportionate to the size of his genitalia. As Bernie Zilbergeld has observed in his work *Male Sexuality*, through pornography we are told that women crave nothing so much as a penis that can easily be mistaken for a telephone pole.

The penis-with-man-attached image of the gigolo is patently absurd. Nevertheless, it largely constitutes common-sense knowledge of this type of relationship. Similarly, the female June and male December association is, like all stereotypes, valid in part, but tends to create the myth that the woman is suffering from a troublesome menopause and/or that the relationship is a symptom of her senility. In part, ignorance with regard to this social phenomenon may be attributable to its apparent relative rarity when compared with its counterpart: the kept woman/sugar daddy relationship.

Perhaps the more important factor, however, is simply the traditional woman's lack of financial independence from either father or husband. Grocery money does not tend to provide sufficient leeway for the support of a gigolo. For some women, the experience of divorce and/or widowhood entails control over economic resources for the first time; for others, the association between maturer age and the keeping of a lover is similarly linked to cash flow – only when older are many women able to afford the expense. A contributing factor involves the relatively rapid increase in the participation of women in the labour forces of most Western countries. That participation has been the result of a combination of factors, ranging from the ravages of inflation to changes in societal expectations of the female gender role brought about by the growing influence of the women's movement beginning in the late 1960s. Larger and larger proportions of the female population are acquiring independent sources of income along with the independence to use that income in more discretionary ways, for other than the basic necessities of food, shelter, and clothing.

Economics is, however, only one factor that has contributed to the existence of the gigolo/Bountiful liaison. One Washington State woman who at present supports a Canadian man in Victoria, British Columbia, in exchange for fortnightly weekends, punctuated with holidays à deux, asked the first author the rhetorical question: 'Is he [her lover] a "gigolo" in the strict definition of the term? Or is he simply an opportunist that gives value received for work that he does not find unpleasant?' Another woman, a retired university professor, commented: 'There are plenty of women willing to do what I did if they just have the chance and can afford it. My experiences with my peers have pointed up several situations of which you may not be aware. One, there are about six million more older women in the nation than there are men of their age; two, many of these women, approximately half, are widows or have never been married. Last, but not least, it seems to me that quite a number of these women have become quite competitive in seeking out the limited male companionship that is available and are willing to share their resources in order to enhance that competitiveness.'

Despite the existence of popular myths proclaiming that everyone in contemporary society is totally free to seek out the marriage or friendship partner of his or her unique choice, all scientific research clearly indicates that the intimacy quest operates within a series of structurally and personally imposed constraints. As our professor respondent noted, success in finding an intimate partner is, in part, subject to the proportional balance between the number of eligible males and females in the population. The number of these eligibles is influenced by a variety of factors, the major ones of which include the sex ratios of females to males; contemporary attitudes towards marriage and its alternatives, such as singlehood and cohabitation; rates of divorce; differences in mortality rates for the sexes; and social attitudes towards the proper matching of certain personal characteristics of each potential partner.

SEX RATIOS AND MATING GRADIENTS

Perhaps first and foremost among the obstacles encountered on the quest for intimacy is the proportional balance between the number of females and males in the population. In order for everyone to have an intimate partner, there must exist an equal number of potential partners of the other sex, assuming that everyone is interested in a heterosexual relationship (a questionable assumption at best but one that must be made none the less, given the general unreliability of estimates of the gay/lesbian population distributed across different age-sex categories). The proportional balance of females to males in the population is referred to by demographers as the 'sex ratio' and is usually calculated with the following formula:

$$\frac{\text{total number of males in the population of interest}}{\text{total number of females in the population of interest}} \times 100 = \text{sex ratio}$$

A resulting figure larger than 100 indicates an 'excess of males' (e.g., a sex ratio of 105 means that there are 105 males to every 100 females), while a figure below 100 indicates an 'excess of females' (e.g., a sex ratio of 90 means that there are 90 males to every 100 females). The sex ratio within any given society is determined by the combined historical influences of birth rates, death rates, and migration patterns.

The ratio can be calculated for the total population or for only specific segments of it. Calculation of the sex ratio for the population as a whole (known as a 'crude sex ratio') could be misleading since it would include males and females who were not eligible for participation in a quest for intimacy, such as very young children. It is possible to calculate more 're-fined' ratios for certain age-specific segments of the population to reflect those who would truly be eligible for participation in a socially acceptable intimate relationship.

The issue of who is truly and at least minimally *eligible* deserves quick but careful consideration here. This issue has recently been resurrected in a best-selling non-fiction book by Susan Faludi entitled *Backlash* in which she focused a portion of one chapter on the largely media-created 'Man Shortage' or 'Marriage Crunch' controversy. The original controversy grew out of the combination of an unpublished academic study on American female marriage patterns by Neil Bennett, David Bloom, and Patricia Craig (the so-called Harvard–Yale study) that was reported and then further sensationalized in a mass-circulation weekly magazine, and a subsequent unpublished study by Jeane Moorman, a demographer with the U.S. Census Bureau. While both unpublished studies had the goal of predicting female marriage patterns (that is, the proportion of the female population who would be married by specific ages), they differed particularly in the assumptions the researchers made about whether college-educated females would follow the same marriage patterns as females with only a high-school education.

Specifically, Bennett, Bloom, and Craig assumed that college graduates adopt the same patterns, and Moorman assumed that they have established new patterns. Based upon their assumptions, the two groups of researchers used different methods of analysis (with Bennett and colleagues choosing a rather questionable method) which yielded different findings. The Bennett, Bloom, and Craig findings were what could be termed 'pessimistic,' and the Moorman findings were more 'optimistic.' The former study concluded that single females aged 35 or older had only a minuscule chance of ever marrying, while the latter study suggested that the chances for that age group would be significantly higher.

The Harvard–Yale study, the Moorman response, and even Faludi's own contribution to this portion of the controversy, were consistent in one dimension: all of them focused almost exclusively upon the marriage patterns of 'single' females (meaning 'never married' – a meaning that the best-selling book failed to stress), although Faludi did include aged widows in one small portion of her presentation. As we will demonstrate on several occasions in this chapter, the actual eligible population is much larger, especially for certain age groups. In fact, one sociologist has argued that North America has been moving towards a condition of 'permanent availability' in which every adult, outside of the incest taboo, can or will be considered to be potentially eligible as a mate, regardless of current marital status. Being currently married does not necessarily remove one from circulation, as evidenced at the very least by the existence of extramarital affairs, some of which lead to divorce and subsequent marriages with former lovers. However, most research analysts do not include the currently married in their calculations of those eligible for the intimacy quest.

For example, in December 1984, an article entitled 'Figuring the Odds In,' in *Money* magazine, examined the nature of the U.S. marriage market and noted where men were more likely – and unlikely – to be available. The results (shown in tables 1 and 2) are based on marriage statistics and 1980 U.S. Census data; eligibles were defined as those identified by the U.S. Census Bureau as single, divorced, separated, or widowed. Charles Westoff and Noreen Goldman, the authors of this article, noted that, while American women under 25 enjoyed a surplus on the supply side, 'from then on the picture gets bleak.'

Scanning the tables, the reader may quickly recognize those cities where the gigolo/Madame Bountiful relationship is especially likely to flourish in the United States. Table 2 is particularly illuminating in that it reveals the scarcity of eligible elderly men in the various cities of the United States, a

TABLE 1
Where the men are – and aren't
(Number of eligible men for every 100 eligible women)

1.	San Diego	75.1	20.	Dallas	60.4
2.	Houston	73.5	21.	Milwaukee	60.0
3.	San Francisco	73.2	22.	Atlanta	59.5
4.	New Orleans	70.2	23.	Miami	59.4
5.	Los Angeles	69.9	24.	Boston	58.6
6.	San Jose	68.2	25.	Sacramento	58.2
7.	Fort Lauderdale	66.7	26.	Kansas City	57.9
8.	Washington, DC	66.5	27.	Detroit	57.7
9.	Denver	65.6	28.	Philadelphia	57.5
10.	Seattle	64.7	29.	Cincinnati	56.5
11.	Anaheim	63.5	30.	Minneapolis–St Paul	56.5
12.	New York	63.1	31.	Newark	55.6
13.	Baltimore	63.0	32.	Indianapolis	55.4
14.	Tampa–St Petersburg	62.6	33.	San Antonio	54.5
15.	Riverside, CA	62.5	34.	St Louis	54.2
16.	Portland, OR	61.9	35.	Buffalo	54.1
17.	Chicago	61.5	36.	Columbus	52.5
18.	Cleveland	60.7	37.	Pittsburgh	52.2
19.	Phoenix	60.6	38.	Nassau–Suffok counties	49.2

SOURCE: C.F. Westoff and Noreen Goldman, 'Figuring the Odds In,' *Money* magazine, December 1984, p. 33.

subject we shall return to shortly. When table 2 is compared with table 3, which was compiled by Brian Duffy in a how-to guide offering a 'partial list of ... towns, suburbs and cities which have a high rich girl per capita ratio,' one quickly recognizes that, for both Bountifuls and gigolos, factors other than personal desire to become kept or to become a keeper enter into the equation. In this vein, the aspiring gigolo may also wish to consider his chances in terms of the size of the community in which he wishes to ply his trade. While an aspiring gigolo may flourish in a small town or village, the professional gigolo is likely to realize that, when added to a sex-ratio imbalance of females to males, the anonymity of a big city becomes a tactical advantage, allowing him to pursue numerous relationships with limited surveillance, recognition, or detection.

However, more is involved in the quest for intimacy than just the number of potentially eligible partners. Obviously, even if the numbers of potential eligibles of both sexes were perfectly equal, there is no guarantee that all of these eligibles would eventually select each other for a relationship of some kind. Further constraints are imposed upon the selection process by contemporary aspects of our Western dating and courtship

TABLE 2

The marriage market revealed

(The figures indicate the number of 'suitably aged, eligible men for every 100 single women in each age bracket' for the 38 largest metropolitan areas in the United States)

Age	Anaheim	Atlanta	Baltimore	Boston	Buffalo	Chicago	Cincinnati	Cleveland
20–4	135	131	133	123	117	129	122	128
25–9	93	91	84	81	70	85	77	86
30–4	75	74	70	62	54	68	61	68
35–9	57	54	55	47	43	52	48	51
40–4	46	41	48	42	40	44	42	44
45–9	39	33	42	40	38	42	37	39
50–4	34	28	38	38	37	38	33	36
55–9	29	24	34	36	34	34	32	34

Age	Columbus	Dallas	Denver	Detroit	Ft Lauderdale	Houston	Indianapolis	Kansas City
20–4	122	128	137	119	135	149	116	119
25–9	72	87	95	78	97	111	73	80
30–4	55	72	79	63	82	90	60	66
35–9	42	54	59	50	64	68	48	51
40–4	37	43	46	43	50	53	40	44
45–9	33	37	40	40	40	45	38	39
50–4	30	33	36	36	35	37	36	34
55–9	29	29	33	33	31	35	32	30

Age	Los Angeles	Miami	Milwaukee	Minneapolis–St Paul	Nassau–Suffolk counties, NY	Newark	New Orleans	New York
20–4	135	117	120	121	113	119	141	125
25–9	97	78	78	78	66	77	97	90
30–4	82	68	62	62	49	59	83	75
35–9	65	56	50	46	37	44	64	57

Age	Philadelphia	Phoenix	Pittsburgh	Portland, OR	Riverside, CA	Sacramento	San Antonio	San Diego
40–4	54	47	47	39	34	39	53	47
45–9	46	40	45	37	33	37	46	42
50–4	42	36	41	35	31	36	41	36
55–9	37	33	37	34	31	34	37	33

Age	Philadelphia	Phoenix	Pittsburgh	Portland, OR	Riverside, CA	Sacramento	San Antonio	San Diego
20–4	125	128	117	126	130	118	123	179
25–9	78	84	70	86	83	75	70	110
30–4	60	69	54	71	68	62	56	83
35–9	48	54	41	55	53	49	44	62
40–4	43	45	36	44	46	43	38	49
45–9	39	39	35	39	42	40	37	44
50–4	35	35	33	38	40	40	35	39
55–9	32	31	32	36	38	39	33	35

Age	San Francisco	San Jose	Seattle	St Louis	Tampa–St Petersburg	Washington, DC
20–4	136	142	131	119	127	130
25–9	104	100	90	73	82	97
30–4	91	81	74	58	70	82
35–9	73	63	57	45	57	62
40–4	58	51	46	39	49	48
45–9	47	42	42	36	42	42
50–4	41	36	40	33	38	38
55–9	36	31	38	31	36	33

SOURCE: C.F. Westoff and Noreen Goldman, 'Figuring the Odds In,' *Money* magazine, December 1984, pp. 34–5.

Note: In tables 1 and 2, Westoff and Goldman eliminated from the field of eligibles never-married men and women who were 45 and older with the reasoning that 'if a person has not married by the age of 45, the chances of marriage thereafter are almost nil – about 1 in 100.' They further commented, 'under the assumption that similar proportions of would-be lifelong singles exist at all younger ages, we have reduced the total marriage pool at all ages commensurately. The effect of this refinement is a greater reduction in the number of eligible men than in that of available women – a partial confirmation, perhaps, of the widely held view that male homosexuals outnumber female.'

TABLE 3
Places of note

Ardmore, PA	Grosse Pointe, ML	Pasadena, CA
Atherton, CA	Haverford, PA	Pride's Crossing, MA
Barrington Hills, IL	Hillsborough, CA	Princeton, NH
Beacon Hill, MA	Kenilworth, IL	Purchase, NY
Beford, NY	Ladue, MO	Rumson, NJ
Bellevue, WA	La Jolla, CA	Ruston, MD
Beverly Farms, MA	Lake Forest, IL	Santa Barbara, CA
Beverly Hills, CA	Locust Valley, NY	Scarsdale, NY
Birmingham, MI	Lookout Mountain, TN	Scottsdale, AZ
Bloomfield Hills, MI	Los Gatos, CA	Shaker Heights, OH
Bryn Mawr, PA	McLean, VA	Southport, CT
Burlingame,CA	Manchester, MA	Tiburon, CA
Chevy Chase, MD	Mercer Island, WA	Tuxedo Park, NY
Clayton, MO	Metairie, LA	Tyler, TX
Darien, CT	Midland, TX	Victoria, TX
Dunwoody, GA	Minnetonka, MN	Wayzata, MN
Far Hills, NJ	Mission Hills, KN	Wellesley, MA
Fox Chapel, PA	New Canaan, CT	Winston–Salem, NC
Germantown, TN	Newport Beach, CA	Woodside, CA
Greenwich, CT	North Oak, MN	

SOURCE: Adapted from Brian Ross Duffy, *The Poor Boy's Guide to Marrying a Rich Girl* (New York: Penguin, 1987), pp. 17–27.

norms. These norms or rules exert social pressures on questers to select partners from what are deemed appropriate social categories. One set of rules comprise what may be called the 'dating differential' or, depending upon the desired outcomes, the 'marriage gradient.' For the sake of simplicity we shall refer to this set as the *mating gradient*.

Regardless of what our most cherished values may tell us, all people are not equal. They vary at the very least in age, physical size, educational attainment, intelligence, and current and/or potential income, and therefore we can and – even if we don't wish to admit it – do rank-order males and females from high to low along a continuum in terms of their possession of these characteristics. When it comes to selecting a potential intimate partner, the rules in Western societies are quite simple – men are supposed to select 'down,' whereas women are supposed to select 'up.' If the resulting outcome is marriage, then the phenomenon, from the female perspective, is referred to as *hypergamy*.

In other words, women are taught from an early age to select a partner who is somewhat older, bigger, and in possession of more education, intelligence, and income (real or potential). Conversely, men are taught to prefer a partner who is somewhat younger, physically smaller, and in possession of less education, intelligence, and income (real or potential). It must be stressed that the differences in desirable characteristics being sought after are not large. The 'Cinderella–Prince Charming' myth is just that – a myth. Reality emphasizes relatively smaller, but still notable, differences between potential partners. In this regard, and as an indicator of our changing times, Scott South found, in a random sample of Americans aged 19 to 35, that men now report being generally unwilling to marry a woman who does not now have, or is unlikely to have in the near future, steady employment. So, what we have here is not a difference between some income and no income, but rather a relative difference in income.

One of the immediate consequences of these rules of Western society is that, assuming everyone performed according to expectation, we would have two very different groups of unselected males and females. The unselected males would be those who possessed the lowest desired qualities (except for age at certain periods in the life span) because they would not be able to find females of lower quality. In contrast, the unselected females would be those who possessed the highest qualities (again, except for age at certain portions of the life span). This phenomenon of the mating gradient helps to explain, at least in part, why unmarried women in our society are often from relatively higher-status populations than are unmarried men of the same age.

E. Spreitzer and L. Riley noted that higher levels of intelligence, education, and occupation are associated with singleness among women. According to a recent survey conducted by Britain's Institute of Management, 33 per cent of female managers were unmarried, as opposed to only 8 per cent of male managers. Similarly, Marshall's study of Canadian women in male-dominated professions noted that these women were 'more likely than women in other occupations to have never married, or if married, to have had fewer children or to be childless.' The research of D. Nagnur and O. Adams observed that 'highly educated women typically marry later, if they marry at all. The longer women postpone marriage, the more likely they are to remain single for life.' They observed that about one-half of single, 30-year-old women and two-thirds of single, 35-year old women will never marry.

Elizabeth Haven has suggested that Nagnur and Adams's finding may be the outcome desired by such women; that high-achieving women tend to consider marriage too confining and thus elect to remain single. Although some women within our own sample desired to remain single and unattached, a substantial portion of respondents did seek the intimacy of long-term relationship (although not necessarily marriage). These women a frequently could not find anyone of the other sex who possessed the higher sought-after characteristics, and their equals on the other-sex continuum appeared to find such females too intimidating.

Obviously the imbalance of desired characteristics has, as one of its consequences, the reinforcing of power differentials in traditional relationships between men and women within our society. A balancing of those characteristics, or even an imbalance wherein the female possesses more of the higher qualities, would upset the traditional power structure. Despite the general appeals over the past twenty-five years for a redressing of power imbalances in private relationships, such imbalances currently appear to be too threatening, according to the available scientifically documented evidence for mate selection. For the moment, the different compositions of the undated and unmated pools of males and females, and the generally typical power imbalance within relationships, appear to be the products of societies which have not yet fully embraced the principles and practices of true equality between the sexes.

If we focus upon the issue of age, the dating/mating norms of Western societies suggest that the most desirable relationship would be one between a younger woman and a slightly older man. In terms of marriage, data this century from Canada, the United States, and England and Wales indicate that the average age difference between males and females at first marriage has consistently been around one to three years. Unfortunately, it is impossible to obtain any reliable information on the average age differential between intimate, but not married, partners; however, it is assumed that such relationships generally follow the same pattern, at least among younger age groups. Using this information it is possible to calculate more refined sex ratios for eligible males and females in a population. Table 4 shows some recent calculations for selected age groups of eligibles (never married + widowed + divorced) based upon estimates (which are usually very reliable) of the Canadian population for 1991 and actual figures for 1981.

We can see from table 4 that, at the younger ages, basically under age 35, we currently have in Canada an excess of men. As noted by Susan Faludi, among others, this situation also exists in the United States, with more eligible men than women for the younger age groups. These conditions stand in stark contrast to the situation of twenty-five to thirty years ago where females who were born on the leading edge of the 'baby boom' immediately following the Second World War and into the early 1950s were, in their late teens and early twenties, looking for potential partners from among the male birth cohort born prior to the baby boom. These males comprised a very small birth cohort, and the females in question

TABLE 4
Sex ratios for marital eligibles, selected age groups, Canada: 1981 and 1991

Age (in years)		Ratio	
Females	Males	1981 (actual)	1991 (est.)
15	17	117.4	102.4
16	18	107.7	104.6
17	19	100.0	110.1
18	20	100.0	113.8
19	21	98.1	111.4
20	22	94.6	102.2
21	23	95.2	101.8
22	24	97.4	107.4
23	25	97.4	116.0
24	26	101.3	127.3
25	27	103.4	127.5
26	28	98.9	119.6
27	29	101.8	114.7
28	30	100.6	117.7
29	31	98.3	116.8
30	32	97.9	109.8
31	33	99.0	108.3
32	34	99.1	108.1
33	35	80.6	103.1
34	36	70.0	99.6
35	37	84.4	97.9
36	38	86.6	92.3
37	39	81.6	89.0
38	40	80.6	89.0
39	41	81.7	88.0
40	42	80.5	85.6
41	43	80.8	85.3
42	44	80.2	84.1

SOURCE: Adapted from Warren E. Kalbach and Wayne W. McVey, *Canadian Population* (Toronto: Nelson, forthcoming).
Note: Eligibles = never married + divorced + widowed
Ratios = number of eligible men for every 100 eligible women

were confronted by what family sociologists and demographers of that time called 'the marriage squeeze.' These women faced the demographic reality of an excess of younger women of marriageable age and deficit of older men of the appropriate age for marriage, and were therefore literally squeezed out of the marriage market. Their younger sisters met a different reality when they reached the age of seeking suitable partners, as the baby boom, and the 'baby bust' that followed eventually resulted in an excess of males among the younger age groups.

Returning to table 4, we can also note that, from about age 29 in 1981 and age 34 onwards in 1991, women face a deficit of males. In general we find a greater imbalance with increasing age. It is notable that the ages of the women who kept gigolos in our sample fell within two predominant age clusters: 35–44 and over 55 (although we attempt to present the largest age array here in our case-study material in order to provide readers with the greatest range of illustrative experiences).

The reader may question whether individual members of a society are actually cognizant of the excess or deficit numbers of one sex or the other. Although most individuals are unaware of the precise sex-ratio statistics for any given year, they are likely to have a general impression of the ratio of available males and females in their particular community and the implications for competition, or lack thereof, for establishing relationships with members of the other sex. Such statistics might simply be recognized in statements such as: 'Where have all the good men gone?' or be perceived, as our respondent quoted earlier suggested, as necessitating that certain 'concessions' be made in the quest for intimacy.

As we saw earlier, the issue of the number of available men varies across the age structure at any one period in history. In the 1960s and 1970s the younger female in her early twenties faced a deficit of men. By the 1980s females in their thirties began wondering where the men were, assuming the females were interested in looking for them. This assumption – that *all* females, as well as *all* males, are actively involved in the pursuit of intimacy – is difficult to prove. A certain portion of the population may be, and probably are, completely uninterested in forming intimate partnerships. Since the actual as opposed to the estimated size of this population segment is unknown, with all due respect to our American colleagues Westoff and Goodman, the uninterested cannot accurately be taken into consideration when developing eligibles estimates for various portions of the population. An additional number of those who are potentially eligible, according to official statistics, have essentially removed themselves from contention through cohabitation. For the remaining thirtysomething-or-older age category who are seeking intimacy, an additional population segment contributes to an expansion of the pool of eligibles – namely, divorced men and women (they were not a significant factor for earlier age groups or time periods). Since the mid-1960s, divorce rates have increased significantly in Canada, the United States, and England and Wales. Indeed, the United States has the highest divorce rate in the world, while Canada and England and Wales have about the same yearly rates. All of these countries have basically doubled their rates since the early 1960s.

With increasing age, another factor begins to affect the number and social characteristics of the eligibles – namely, that of mortality and survivorship. For example, available data indicate that females born in Canada in 1986 can expect to live 79.7 years. Males born in 1986 can expect to live 73.0 years. If the typical age difference at first marriage holds for these newborns, and assuming their marriage lasts until the death of one of the partners, we would then expect that these females will be widows for approximately nine years (the difference in age at marriage of two years plus the difference in life expectancy of almost seven years). Currently, 60-year-old females in Canada in 1986 can expect to live for another 23.2 years (average life expectancy increases the longer one has lived, up to a certain limit). Sixty-year-old males in 1986 could expect to live another 18.4 years. The 'life-expectancy gap' exists and creates problems for those who wish to share their life with a relational/romantic partner.

Similarly, according to the U.S. Department of Commerce, Bureau of the Census, in 1981 a preliminary 'guesstimate' of the life expectancy for a male was 70.3 years, and for a female 77.9 years. At age 40, a male could expect to live an additional 34.0 years, a female an additional 40.1 years. At age 65, a male could expect to live an additional 14.2 years, and a female an additional 18.5 years.

This pattern would seem to exist as well in the United Kingdom. John Craig, in a 1983 discussion of the growth of the United Kingdom's elderly population, noted that 'women with their greater life expectancy now outnumber men at all ages higher than about 50, and the proportion of women in the population therefore increases with age ... Generally, two-thirds of people over the retirement age are women.'

Regardless of whether one examines the 1960s, the 1980s, or even the early 1990s, a group of females exists for whom the problem has always been one of an imbalance between the eligible sexes – namely, females over 55. Given the already-referred-to expectation, and practice, of women marrying older men, older divorced, widowed, and never-married females are at a distinct demographic disadvantage. Table 5 provides an example of some sex ratios calculated for certain age categories of marital eligibles for Canada, based upon 1991 census data. The two-year age differential used to construct table 4 is no longer applicable since the age dif-

TABLE 5

Sex ratios for marital eligibles, selected age groups, Canada, 1991

Age (in years)	Sex ratio	Age (in years)	Sex ratio
45–9	78	60–4	49
50–4	70	65–9	37
55–9	60	70–4	29

SOURCE: Calculations based on Table 3 'Population by Marital Status and Sex showing Five-year Age Groups, for Canada, Provinces, Territories, and Census Metropolitan Areas, 1986 and 1991 – 100% Data,' in *Age, Sex and Marital Status: The Nation*, Catalogue 93-310 (Ottawa: Minister of Industry, Science and Technology 1992).

Note: Eligibles = never married + divorced + widowed

TABLE 6

Sex ratios of marital eligibles for selected ages, census metropolitan areas, Canada, 1991

CMA	Ages 20–69	Ages 20–44	Ages 45–69
Thunder Bay	108	128	65
Calgary	107	126	54
Edmonton	107	124	60
Oshawa	105	127	52
Vancouver	104	122	61
Kitchener	104	126	48
Hamilton	98	120	51
Windsor	97	119	52
Winnipeg	96	117	51
Toronto	96	115	48
Sudbury	96	113	58
Chicoutimi–Jonquière	95	127	48
Ottawa–Hull	95	114	49
St Catharines–Niagara	95	121	48
Regina	95	110	54
Victoria	94	118	48
Montreal	92	116	51
Halifax	91	106	51
Saskatoon	90	106	48
Saint John	89	107	53
St John's	89	102	50
Quebec City	88	112	49
London	88	107	44
Trois-Rivières	88	115	50
Sherbrooke	85	107	48

SOURCE: Calculations based on Table 3, 'Population by Marital Status and Sex, Showing Five-year Age Groups, for Canada, Provinces, Territories and Census Metropolitan Areas, 1986 and 1991 – 100% Data,' in *Age, Sex and Marital Status: The Nation*, Catalogue 93-310 (Ottawa: Minister of Industry, Science and Technology 1992).

Note: Marital eligibles = single, never married + widowed + divorced ferential between partners who form their relationship at older ages tends to be greater in comparison with those who form relationships during their teenage or twentysomething years. As we can see from table 5, the sex ratio continues to decline dramatically with increasing age and demonstrates a combination of differential mortality (particularly at the oldest ages) and the greater propensity of divorced and widowed men to remarry, thereby taking themselves out of eligible circulation. Here females, seeking intimate partners, who ask 'Where have all the good men gone?' must confront the answer: 'They are confirmed bachelors, gay, currently in relationships of some form, or dead.'

As indicated in table 6, these sentiments will be heard with greater or lesser frequency depending also upon one's geographical location. Table 6 represents a Canadian counterpart to U.S. data shown in table 2. In table 6 we focus upon the largest major urban centres whose combined numbers of inhabitants accounted for a little over 61 per cent of the total Canadian population in 1991. Since research has indicated that the most basic factor influencing the possibilities of establishing a relationship is propinquity, or simply having physical access to eligibles, geographic location is another variable that must be acknowledged.

TRADE-OFFS AND COMPARISON LEVELS

Thus far we have focused upon some of the most basic structural constraints influencing whether one will be likely to achieve initial success in the quest for intimacy. But focusing upon sex ratios, mating gradients, and geographical location by no means paints the complete picture. Operating within this broad framework are a number of other factors. While all of us develop, sometime during our lives, a picture of our 'ideal mate,' the average person typically does not expect to find the perfect intimate partner. Most of us discover ourselves in the situation described by Elaine Walster and William Walster wherein 'our selection of a mate appears to be a delicate compromise between our desire to capture an ideal partner and our realization that we must eventually settle for what we deserve.'

We often find that we must compromise our ideals. Typically we find ourselves attracted to a person who possesses sufficient or even more-than-sufficient quantities of one desired characteristic but insufficient quantities of another. We then frequently decide (sometimes consciously, sometimes not) that we can live with this combination. In other words, we 'trade off' the lower quality for the higher quality. Such trade-offs are more common than we often would wish to admit. One person will trade off less-than-desirable age for high income in a potential partner. Another will trade off a less-than-desired intelligence level for striking physical attractiveness. Usually, we have some point below which we will be unwilling to make a trade-off, but rarely can we easily describe that 'cut-off' point in words (particularly at 2:00 a.m. in a bar). And not everyone shares the same cut-off points (leading to the often remarked, 'What does he/she see in that geek/turkey/loser anyway?'). As we will see, the notion of trade-offs becomes an important explanatory device for understanding many gigolo/Madame Bountiful relationships.

In response to the original 'Letter to the Editor,' an American woman wrote:

Your identification as a criminologist implies that exploitation of women by gigolos is criminal in nature. I question this assumption ... [K]eep in mind that my reference group is older persons, both male and female. I have seen very little, if any, June and December associations ... I have known the woman in this case approximately 50 years; her husband worked with my husband, the two couples were close friends. The husband of this woman died ten years ago and I think the wife welcomed her freedom from an association that had never really given her a great deal of joy. She had grown up in a small town, the daughter of a businessman and subject to the inhibitions that prevailed in the early part of this century. Her life was very proper, very prosaic, but she, I think, still envisioned herself as the adventuresome girl who had never really had the chance to do all of the things she would like to do. Her widowhood provided freedom. She was financially secure, her income steady and large, her home paid for and no outstanding obligations. She has only one daughter whose home is 3,000 miles distant and since she was still involved in rearing her own family as well as being employed at the time of her father's death, she did not feel that her mother had too many worries to overcome.

About two years after this woman's husband died, she met a man at one of the social gathering programs for older folk and she brought him to visit my husband and I, introducing him as 'a good bridge partner' she had met. Their association ripened rapidly and although we distrusted him from the outset (he was about 25 years her junior) she seemed so utterly happy that we were hesitant to raise any real questions. The same type of reasoning applied to the daughter's assessment of the situation. First, the daughter does not need the estate held by the mother and would much prefer that it be spent by the mother rather than hoarded for inheritance. Second, the man in the case was attentive. For eight years he helped keep her home repaired, he escorted the woman dozens of places; he provided daily companionship. He saw that her medical appointments were kept, he introduced her to dancing and took her to 'senior citizen dances' five nights a week; he made her very happy. We all knew that she was supporting him but the other considerations outweighed the financial one.

A second woman, a 29-year-old New Yorker, wrote:

It may seem unusual for a woman to pay for a man and although I can feel resentful, I feel that women are trained to be giving – perhaps too giving, in relationships ... And when a woman has financial independence, that can become the currency of the relationship as well, rather than offering the traditional gifts of beauty or virginity or culinary expertise ...

I was the youngest daughter of two daughters raised in a fairly traditional home; my mother quit working before she had my sister and never went back. She didn't have to. My father is very well-off and, among their generation, if your wife worked it implied something negative about your ability to be a good husband ...

My sister was from childhood a China-doll type of beauty, blonde hair, blue eyes, and as she grew to an adult height of 4'10", was always considered the beauty of our family. Tiny, perfect Dolly Parton–type body ... When she'd introduce me to her friends as her 'little sister' they would always guffaw and say 'you're little sister?' because by 14 I was 5'5", 160 pounds. I hated that and felt she did it deliberately to draw attention to my bulk next to her petiteness.

It didn't help my feelings of inadequacy either that I had a mass of superfluous facial hair – I used to hold my hand over my upper lip when I talked, hoping people wouldn't notice but, of course, they did and I was taunted by comments of 'you need a shave' throughout high school ...

From an early age I learned to compensate for my perceived unattractiveness by being very giving although perhaps that's not really being fair to myself. Let's say I was sensitized to how people could be hurt by thoughtless behaviour and was over-sensitive to being liked. I wanted everyone to like me ...

After years of electrolysis, dieting I became, to my surprise, this 'sexy chick.' Although I never grew into the hour-glass type of woman, I could wear the size 3 designer clothes and know, objectively, that people find me very attractive. Even my sister's husband has come-on to me – a shocking event! – that I didn't take up on – because to me she still was the standard I measured myself against ...

Somewhere along the line however, giving things to be liked to simply lessen the chances of being hurt, forestalling the nasty remark because of bribery, I kept on giving. If I had little money, I'd still give, now that I've got lots, the gifts have become bigger ...

My friends tell me that I attract the wrong sorts of guys because of my nature and make men into gigolos. They may be right but I don't really care. Beauty, sex, money – all women buy love and affection and money is less fleeting than beauty ...

It may seem strange that I still buy into a relationship when I don't have to but I'm still more comfortable in the role of giver rather than taker. I know how to soothe hurt feelings and, as well, how to get a man to jump to attention. At the same time that there's something very open and giving in such relationships, there is simultaneously a good measure of cynicism and Machiavellian control ...

'In giving one receives' – that may sound blasphemous but it's not untrue. I rarely have illusions about relationships. I've recognized long ago how much people measure others by superficial qualities. There's a saying how people who are beautiful have people who love them for no reason and how people who are ugly have people hate them for no reason ...

Part second nature, part deep-seeded feelings of unattractiveness, part desire for control – all enter into why I keep my lovers.

Jon, a 42-year-old bisexual man, commented on his Madame Bountiful:

Margo is very kind-hearted and exceedingly generous. She is very giving to all her friends – not just to me. I think she has a real need to give things to others because she's so insecure. She has a very high position in government and is extremely intelligent but doesn't feel she is attractive because of her weight and needs lots of attention and emotional support. It can be very hard on me sometimes because she is a very demanding sort of woman ...

She is very self-conscious about her body and, although she tries very hard to please me, she tries to cover up her body in bed and won't let me try to please her because she's so conscious about having these enormous rolls of fat ... I'd like to please her and make her come ... but she won't let me go down on her because she thinks she's too exposed in that position ... Maybe she's afraid she smells or something ... She'd rather have more false climaxes than a Beethoven symphony than relax in bed ...

I have helped her enormously but it's very, very, exhausting for me ... She used to wear only dark clothes when I met her but now I've got her to the point where she'll wear bright colours and go swimming with me in public ...

It sometimes is very embarrassing to me because I can't go into a store with her and say that I like something without her going and buying it for me.

[Do you buy her things as well?] I'd like to, but right now things are exceedingly difficult for me and I really can't afford to. Also, it's very difficult to buy anything for her because she can afford things of a much better quality than I can afford to give her, so I feel it would almost be an *insult* to give her something I could pay for.

Jon justified his serial involvements with a number of rather overly large middle-aged ladies as almost altruistic behaviour. An antique dealer by trade, Jon always seemed to find himself unhappily in the red at month's end. A break-in by a discriminating burglar who relieved Jon of his most expensive pieces; an untimely audit by the tax department; a vengeful ex-lover who had stored several *objets d'art* for him at her home and would now not return his possessions because of her anger at being scorned; a child from an early marriage requiring costly dental treatment – as troubles befell him, Jon would present his woesome news to his latest paramour with the apparent stoicism of a cow standing in the rain. His lovers almost always would offer to alleviate his economic distress.

It would appear that the first Madame Bountiful discussed by our respondent traded off her gigolo's much younger age for the many attentive acts he performed for her. In our second example, the trade-off factor itself seemed based on a perceived deficit quality or characteristic within the Bountiful. It would seem noteworthy that the woman's perceived failure to live up to some elusive ideal of feminine beauty was thought a sufficient impetus to offer up a trade-off: acceptance and tolerance of her deficits for the more tangible benefits of her (financial) assets. Indeed, the comments of Jon, our respondent gigolo who appears to have traded off his Bountiful's physical appearance for her wealth, suggest such trade-offs may be common.

The trade-off factor itself applies to those qualities and characteristics which exist within a partner. However, we often make relationship decisions based on factors which exist outside of the other person.

When we expand our focus beyond the partner, we take into consideration what is known in scientific circles as one's 'comparative level of alternatives.' In other words, 'What other choices have you got?' Not only do questers have to examine a potential intimacy partner's 'résumé' to see if he or she can meet or beat a cut-off point, but they also have to evaluate the present possibility in comparison with whatever else appears to be available both now and in the foreseeable future. People find themselves selecting a partner from among what they perceive to be a limited number of available choices. Outsiders may not understand the selection of an apparent 'runt of the litter,' and don't always appreciate that one may see the partner as being not all that bad, considering the alternatives.

Lara, a 33-year-old American, was a senior manager in private industry. She had supported a highly pampered gigolo, aged 42, for the past eight years and had financed his return to school. The man appeared to be somewhat of an academic dilettante; after eight years' attendance at a university, he had yet to obtain his general arts degree. The woman had a reputation in industry of being terribly ruthless and utterly shrewd. Yet, when one saw her interacting with her gigolo, it was similar to viewing Disney's Bambi and Thumper. Surely, her friends asked of the first author, she could see through his simpering and fawning performance? Surely, her brother suggested, if she would only *look* for another man she could find one more worthy of her. She commented:

I realize that many other people don't understand why I'd let myself be 'used.' My friends either politely refrain from acknowledging that I'm the provider – playing a male role, if you will, in the relationship – or throw the fact in my face – as if I hadn't noticed, was too stupid or 'blind with love' to notice. Of course, I know this reality and certainly, at times, it upsets me ... I once tried to get my father to like Curt more by lying and saying that Curt and I share all expenses 50-50. My dad wasn't impressed. He asked me, 'What about the good old days when a man would support a woman totally?' I told my father that I didn't want that, that I really enjoy my work and would always want to work regardless of whether my partner was wealthy or not. It's true but – I'll admit – there's nothing anyone can tell me that I haven't already told myself. At any rate, I've made my own bed and I know he's more company than a cat ... I've tried – or at least I've *looked* for someone 'better' but there's lots of prize jerks about, married men happy to have an affair but no-commitment-please, guys with two ex-wives, three kids and four bank loans ... I'm tired of looking and don't need the hassle of the single's scene.

The late heiress Christina Onassis remarked, 'My most fervent wish is that I shall meet a man who loves me for myself and not my money.' All wealthy women – or men – must inevitably confront the uncertainty whether they are loved for themselves or for their money or, more likely, whether their wealth has been traded off against many or most of their more personal qualities. The ultimate test, of course, consists of cutting off funding or the expectation of funding at a later date. One of our respondents, the daughter of a fabulously wealthy British family, informed the first author that, whenever she faced this dilemma, she simply informed her boyfriend that her family was so opposed to her liaison with him that they had instituted legal proceedings to disown her. She smiled somewhat wistfully when she noted that few had stayed around longer than to ensure that her parents would not have a change of heart; none was blithely indifferent to her fabricated news. A variation of this test could come in the form of a prenuptial agreement, a legal document which generally says 'what's mine is mine and will always be mine and you can't have it.' Of course, this agreement usually does not preclude any sharing of 'what's mine' for the duration of a relationship and may not therefore be as effective a test as the one used by our British respondent.

In the nineteenth century, Henrietta Green, the 'richest woman in the world,' attempted to follow the stalwart advice given to her by her father, who directed her to 'Never ... give anyone anything, not even a kindness.'

True to her training, she boarded in tawdry hotels, subsisted on rice and other odd scraps, and never, ever, tipped a waiter ... 'They say I am cranky or insane because I dress plainly and do not spend a fortune on my gowns,' shrugged the nation's worst-dressed moneylender. 'Plainly,' however, was putting it politely; her garments actually grew green with age before she discarded them, and by her own admissions, she saved a significant sum by laundering only the bottom layer of her petticoats ...

Even in the bosom of her family, it seems, the unfashionable usurer found it necessary to maintain a vigilant guard against greed. Husband Edward signed a prenuptial waiver of any claim to her fortune, but was nonetheless banished from her bed when he went bankrupt in 1885. ('My husband is of no use to me,' she was subsequently heard to complain. 'I wish I did not have him.') Son Ned hobbled through life with only one leg due to Mama's miserly ways: Green refused to pay for medical care after an unfortunate sledding accident, with the eventual result that the limb had be amputated. Only her dog Dewey, in fact, saw the softer side of the coldhearted capitalist. 'He loves me,' she explained, 'and he doesn't know how rich I am.'

Some of the wealthy women we interviewed had attempted to bypass the dilemma posed by their possessing money by safely electing to pursue the marital choice their parents had made for them and simply keeping a lover on the side. Some wealthy women had an uneasy perception that everyone around them, particularly men, thought they were 'marks' and would attempt to 'exploit them' or 'play them for a fool.' As F. Scott Fitzgerald noted of the rich in his short story 'The Rich Boy': 'they possess and enjoy early, and it does something to them, makes them soft where we are hard, and cynical where we are trustful.'

To forestall the possibility of an alliance driven by exloitation, women often chose a suitable marital partner with the same grim pragmatism that characterized shopping for footwear for mountain climbing; style and decorous embellishments such as love and sexual attraction were viewed as superfluous. In such cases, marriage often took the form of a corporate merger, with a young and promising man acceding into a responsible position within the family firm. Often this formula was termed the 'European style' of marriage and praised for its 'sensible' and 'civilized' approach that provided for a 'successful' husband for status, security, and the siring of children, and, it was hoped, a 'fascinating lover' for whatever else was desired. Having an 'arrangement' supposedly allowed these women the opportunity to 'have your cake and eat it too.'

Case-Study: Vanna

Vanna, a wealthy Madame Bountiful, recounted that, for much of her relationship with Raymond, her 'protégé' and paid gigolo, she felt a sense of the unreasonable happiness that precedes disaster, and described her relationship with her gigolo as 'crazy making.' A pale blonde who looked like Grace Kelly and appeared to be in her thirties, though in her fifties, Vanna spoke at her manorial home in a marble-floored room decorated with embossed Italian wallpaper and magnificent artworks, caressing an antique silk quilt that carefully graced the back of a white loveseat. The room featured numerous ceiling-to-floor windows, and one was struck by the silence and remoteness of the property; a maid quietly brought a silver tea service and quietly left. Married to a wealthy executive with whom she had two now-teenage sons, she talked about the 'emptiness' of her life despite its opulence and noted the 'insane risks' she took with her lover. When asked why, she stated that it made her feel 'alive' and that she had run out of 'busy work.'

When the boys were small, she had chauffeured them to and from their private schools, even though there was no manifest need for her to do so and in spite of the fact that this task had taken up several hours each day during the school term. Not 'in spite of the fact,' she corrected herself, but 'because of the fact.' She had redecorated the house numerous times, commented that she had herself sewn the valances for the windows in the room in which she was seated, had gone on numerous shopping sprees to London to buy knickknacks at Asprey's and attend art auctions at Sotheby's, and volunteered herself to run errands in her Mercedes jeep.

According to Vanna, she had married young and had 'worshipped' her dazzling, successful husband. She pointed out the statues depicting mother and child that he had given her on the occasion of each son's birth, and characterized him as a 'wonderful man' whom she 'would not hurt for the world.' She boasted of his accomplishments: his degree from Harvard, his business acumen, his largesse in indulging her spending habits – but also noted his frequent absences, his disinclination to do things that were of interest to her and his somewhat unsatisfying sexual technique. It was not that he was unwilling to do 'anything,' she stressed, to please her. In fact, she commented, he wanted to do things like perform cunnilingus upon her; it was she who declined. Sex with her husband had become routine by her choice, something to be done with as quickly as possible. She laughed somewhat grimly and commented that her lover, who had little to recommend him, sexually or otherwise, was more exciting to her in and out of bed. In contrast to her attractive, well-groomed husband, her lover, whom she described as subject to premature ejaculation, somewhat balding, having a host of 'neurotic ideas' about his body and bodily functions, and reportedly professing himself to be 'gross,' 'hairy,' and totally undeserving of both her affections and her financial support, she found a compelling partner. By her own account, she 'ministered' to him.

Raymond, as described by his lover, did not seem terribly appealing; part waif, part nebbish, he sounded like a character out of a Woody Allen film. She recounted how at first he had apologized when they made love for 'sweating' on her, stammering that she was so pure and perfect and that he was just so 'bestial.' In telling how he had admitted to her that he felt 'too shy' to use the bathroom in the hotel room they shared for their first sexual liaison for fear of 'disgusting' her, she laughed and ascribed this 'endearing' testimony to his 'innocence' and 'charm.' Indeed, it seemed that each self-deprecation uttered by Raymond, each avowed neurosis and each unveiling of feet of clay, made him a more desirable lover to our Madame Bountiful. She stressed his fine qualities – for example, he was reputedly much more concerned that their relationship remain clandestine than she herself. She recounted an incident in which they had gone for a long walk in a nature retreat and she became strongly desirous of making love with him. He had demurred, stressing that he felt the need to 'protect' her. Similarly, on occasion when she had voiced a tentative desire to simply leave her husband and begin a new life with him, Raymond had reportedly become saddened, 'blaming himself' for causing a rift in her marriage, emphasizing that he should not have 'ruined things' and entreating her not to do anything precipitous. That was Raymond, she commented, always unselfish and sensitive to what was best for her.

Even though a different interpretation could be placed on Raymond's actions, her perceptions allowed her to provide an image of both Raymond and the relationship that was intimate, warm, and charming. Our Madame Bountiful tried to impress upon us how sensitive and witty, and what a brilliant pianist, Raymond was; according to her he just lacked confidence in himself and had been browbeaten by life's circumstances. She recounted the biography he had presented: a scathing and critical mother who had 'driven away' his father and had been unable to show any emotional warmth to her children; a father who was ineffectual with his wife but 'brutal' in relation to his children, particularly Raymond; the selection of a career that had been governed by a desire to extricate himself from his home as quickly as possible rather than to provide any intrinsic joy and which, in consequence, had been abandoned; and now, life with his mistress who was supporting him, who allowed him the time and space to 'find himself' studying piano at a university with all expenses paid, and who seemed to revel in her role as the 'ministering angel.'

In describing her role, Vanna likened herself to famous patrons of the arts, telling with evident familiarity the story of how Tchaikovsky had had a patron, Madame de Scholt, who had made it a condition of her sponsorship that he never contact her in any form and then abruptly, for no apparent reason, had broken off sponsorship of him. She paused, musing that some writers speculated that the reason for her rescinding patronage was her discovery that Tchaikovsky was a homosexual, at a time when homosexuality was a criminal offence. She talked about George Sand and Chopin, about a richly born countess who had given up everything for the love of Liszt, about Madame Bock who had founded the Courtis Institute of Music in Philadelphia, and of how Beethoven had been sponsored by the nobility. While one of Raymond's friends was to comment wryly at a later date that 'if you want to be an artist you have to develop less artistic tastes' than Raymond possessed, the elegant quality of her relationship as Raymond's patron and mentor did not seem unappealing to his Madame Bountiful.

At first glance, Raymond appeared to be hopelessly miscast as a gigolo; his body, which his lover had rhapsodized over, commenting on his 'muscular legs' and 'masculine build,' seemed simply dumpy and undistinguished. He was an accomplished though not brilliant pianist who favoured the romantic composers – Chopin, Schumann, Brahms – the type of performer who might have won local music competitions in his youth but was unlikely to win further acclaim. Although Raymond came across as somewhat more effete and evasive than 'poetic' and 'sensitive,' his lover apparently did not share these interpretations of his behaviour. The self-effacing quality that his lover found so endearing and his timid manner were notable; he commented that his favourite pianist had been Dino Lipatti, and his lover later was to comment on the profound congruence of this preference. Lipatti had often sought work as an accompanist rather than as a performer in his own right and had died early of leukaemia. The poignancy of his choice of heroes did not seem lost upon his lover.

In the first conversation in the presence of his lover, Raymond tended to deflect specific questions, countering with his own, such as 'What courses do you teach at the university? Your job sounds fascinating.' When the first author responded with cynicism, commenting that he surely was not interested in learning precisely what she lectured on, he opened his eyes wide in the manner of a incredulous ingenue as if amazed that one would think him other than sincere, and he gently insisted that he was truly interested. Indeed, in his lover's presence, Raymond presented himself, with the whimsical sadness of a man who has suffered, as a mildly animated form of road kill. He commented that his real joy lay in composing, and he mentioned, somewhat wistfully, how he that day had tried out an electronic grand piano that could so facilitate his endeavours. His lover asked him how much the piano cost and he protested, stating that he could not even think of asking her to buy it for him, that she had been so kind and tolerant already. He expounded on the kindness of his lover, the vast reservoirs of emotional support she provided him ...

The next time the first author saw Raymond, at a party thrown by his lover and at which he played, he was asked how he enjoyed his new piano. He seemed somewhat flustered, and said it was wonderful but stressed that he had not asked for it. His lover was simply such a generous, giving person.

If the portrait Raymond painted of himself was timorous and humble, there was another side to him. Simultaneously kept by two other women, each of whom believed her position unique, Raymond was perhaps the most despotic and misogynistic of all the men interviewed. For example, when one of his lovers was hospitalized after attempting suicide, Raymond showed his devotion by going off on a skiing trip with his long-time friend Jerry, an extremely rich surgeon. When the woman later told him that she had been very hurt that he had not come to visit or sent flowers, he stated that he had spent many nights at the hospital but had 'restrained' himself from coming up to see her, afraid of upsetting her by his presence. Similarly, although he maintained to all three of his 'patrons' that he was the epitome of discretion and had not told even his best friend about the sexual nature of their relationship, this, in fact, was not the case. Rather, the sexual and financial escapades of Raymond and his Bountifuls served as the topics of numerous conversations in which the women's gullibility and 'obsession' with him were ridiculed and his 'embarrassment' – with them and for them – given emphasis.

Raymond was a 'pet' or a 'pet hobby' for Vanna. Being his patron engaged her in pseudo-voluntarism, a program of socially gratifying, time-consuming 'work' that was more enjoyable than onerous. However, it may be noted that, in contemplating her role, she self-flatteringly likened it to the role of patrons of musicians in former times – not to the role of a star-crossed lover or a heroine caught up in some cataclysmic love affair. Vanna described the joy of Raymond in a way which made the sensation he aroused seem more akin to consumer satisfaction.

Michael Apter, who frequently writes on the topic of excitement, coined the term 'parapathic' to refer to the type of emotion that is aroused when, for example, one is watching a horror movie, or a 'weepy' movie, from the comfortable vantage point of a familiar setting. The emotion that is aroused is real enough, but the circumstances allow one to experience the feelings of arousal from within a 'protective frame' that is comforting and provides for feelings of security and safety. Vanna's excitement with her gigolo seemed to arise from the fact that having an adulterous relationship was an 'escape route' which facilitated freedom while closing no doors behind her. Although she acknowledged that she had, upon occasion, contemplated leaving her husband for Raymond, she certainly disavowed any desire to wash Raymond's socks and engage in the plodding jog trot of daily companionship. If 'familiarity breeds contempt' – or at least indifference – an affair may, because of the curtailed nature of the involvement with a lover, promote the heightened arousal and excitement – sexual and other – that made Raymond a walk on the wild side. For Vanna, Raymond was a lion in a cage.

Watching a lion tamer put a number of lions through various manoeuvres within the space of a relatively small and confining cage allows the audience to revel in the majestic quality of the animals – the strength they embody, the elegance of their movements – while simultaneously congratulating themselves on not being the lion tamer. There is a consciousness of danger, that the animals being admired are not Aunt Bertha's friendly declawed tabby, but that same quality of danger would seem to attract rather than repel the viewer. The lions are wild, primitive, untamed. Yet, while the feelings aroused by the lions may be powerful, it is the presence of the cage that allows the experience to be defined as pleasurable and unthreatening. The cage not only provides protection, but allows diffuse feelings of arousal, danger, excitement, and fear to be translated into something pleasurable.

The reader may note that Vanna acknowledged a lack of sexual desire for her husband in contrast with the heightened sexual excitement associated with having sex with Raymond. In part, her comments may reflect a more general observation made by sex therapists who note that this lack of sexual desire for one's partner is the 'most widespread sexual problem' among couples who live together. However, Raymond's caged-lion quality would simply not seem to apply to a heightened sexual response. Indeed, in recounting her pleasure with Raymond sexually, Vanna's repeating of his comments about her graceful, ethereal loveliness and his being a 'rough beast' suggests she had not overlooked an opportunity for self-promotion.

Love in a garret may be poetic, but Vanna certainly had no desire to experience it. If her relationship could be described as offering exhilarating feelings equivalent to those experienced by a skydiver, it was still that of a professional in possession of a fully functioning parachute.

GENDER ROLES IN TRANSITION

An important element of the intimacy quest that cannot be ignored is the constellation of thoughts, feelings, and behaviours that comprise gender roles. All of us are familiar with the intense re-examination and transformation processes the female gender role has undergone since the mid-1960s. The male gender role has undergone significantly less intense examination, but, since the mid-1980s in particular, the intensity level has been going up. At the moment, the term that most accurately describes the situation is simple – confusion.

Flooding the print media and the airwaves, scientists, journalists, therapists, social commentators, official spokespersons, and speaker wannabes armed with studies, articles, books – some scientific, most not – have all given testimony, and frequently impetus, to the current confusing state of male/female affairs, or lack thereof.

The confusion seems to take two basic forms. On the one hand, many males and females are personally confused about what they want and expect from a member of the other sex, as well as what they themselves should be thinking, feeling, and doing in any and all forms of relating to that other sex. On the other hand, many people have very definite opinions regarding the one and only proper form of gender behaviour, but these people cannot agree. Consequently, both males and females from the 1970s to the present day have been, and still are, sending out contradictory and confusing messages to each other about the requirements of a desirable mate and about how to conduct themselves in their quest for one.

To become a Madame Bountiful, a woman must often reformulate traditional expectations and conceptions of the feminine role within an intimate relationship. This is not always a simple or straightforward task. As one 36-year-old Canadian woman said of her relationship with her 29-year-old divorced lover:

At the start I disguised the reality to myself. I wanted the house, the dog, the white picket fence and I tried to make our relationship over into something that it wasn't, that I knew deep down it could never be. He was a divorced man with a kid and from the onset he had told me that he was experiencing financial difficulties with child support, a loan on the house he had bought for his wife, his rent for his apartment and I thought, well, that's fine. My supporting him will just be a temporary thing. He'll sell his bloody home and then we'll have an egalitarian relationship – I might have to help him out on occasion but, once he's on his feet, he'll appreciate what I've done for him and make it up somehow. Only it doesn't work like that.

Considering the fact that I was paying all his bills, including money for child support, you'd think that he'd try and make it up to me by helping out with housework, doing laundry – anything. It didn't happen. To 'save money' I bought a house that set me back almost $400,000 and, of course, he moved in. When I had just let him stay over before, I had rationalized his lack of helping out with finances, groceries, doing the simple task of loading the dishwasher as, well, he doesn't feel at ease, he's not totally comfortable and anyhow, it's my place, I should bear all the expenses. However, that's probably one of the big reasons I bought the house – 'our house' – what a sick joke.

If anything, he turned into a bigger chauvinist than he had ever let himself be before. And the situation was so bizarre. I'd be doing the liberated, independent career woman all day and then I'd be running home, feverishly making dinner so that His Royal Nibs wouldn't be pissed off with me. He'd sit there and eat it, complaining that I had cooked too much and was trying to get him fat – this after, of course, I had gone out to do the grocery shopping and carted the stuff home by myself – and then just leave the dishes on the table. Once in a while he'd make the big concession of actually carrying the dishes to the sink but in all our time together I never saw him stack or unload the dishwasher. This guy puts on the big show about how he's a 'real man,' how he's so great with anything mechanical, and he can't figure out how to load a stupid dishwasher …

But it's not just the dirty dishes that got to me. It was the 24-hour-a-day drudge of playing out this hypocritic show, this façade, to everyone who saw it. When we'd go out to dinner, we'd take my car and I'd give him the money for supper in advance – so his precious male pride wouldn't be hurt. It all looked so lovely on the surface. There I am, pulling up in a $60,000 car – mine, with my elegantly dressed lover – whose clothes I paid for, going to a top restaurant – which I paid for, and then going for a scenic car drive up to Whistler – on my gas. The memory of just little things now is enough to make me cringe. I remember that I'd give him, say $250 for paying for dinner, drinks and a tip and the bill was only $175. I'd never get the rest back from him. Of course, I didn't say anything. That wouldn't do; I'd just wait and do a slow burn wondering when and if I was going to get my money back. I could be so assertive and dominant at work but whenever I dealt with him I just couldn't get the words out.

Our last big fight before I told him I'd had it and he could get the hell out started off pretty oddly. He was giving me his bullshit about how he was saving money up for a diamond ring for me – an old song – and how, although he had said that he'd be able to buy it for me by September (this was March) he'd seen an even nicer one – but I'd have to wait for another eight months or so because he couldn't afford it right now. This was such garbage. He'd been telling me about some bullshit necklace or ring for the entire two years we were together and the only thing he ever bought during the whole time were a bunch of lousy flowers. Twice. Anyhow, I just got quiet and he asked me what was wrong, was I mad at him? I said, maybe I'm just mad at myself for trying to be a sweetheart all the time and never tell you what I'm feeling. He said, 'That's crap, I could believe that of anyone but you. You have no trouble expressing yourself – you always get what you want.' I couldn't believe it. After all the stuff I tried to do for him, tried to be for him, not only didn't he appreciate it, he couldn't even see that it had taken some effort on my part. It's as if I had a money bush growing in the garden – my work didn't count. I didn't have to go out and hustle the way everyone else does who wants to succeed ...

He saw I was getting mad so he tried to write off what I had said by telling me I was just tired, that I was working too hard. I love that. Whenever I was upset with him he'd always try to take this hard line and give me shit that I was 'neglecting' him and was a 'workaholic' – that I took too much work on, didn't have time to relax and go on vacation with him and what I needed was – aside from a good screw of course – was a holiday. 'Why don't we take off on vacation and go to the Seychelles? You always love the Seychelles.' [Was that a vacation he was offering to pay for?] Of course not – he was basically telling me as he always did that since I needed to relax, he and I should go on a vacation which I would pay for – this is supposed to make me forget that what upset me in the first place is the fact that I'm supporting him, acting like a charwoman in addition to the cook, housekeeper, babysitter whenever his brat comes over, sex kitten, and financier to boot!

[How did you handle his suggestion?] I told him that it was over between us and that I was fed up with him and wanted a man who would support me once in a while. He got all self-righteous and told me that I was no better than my friends who were married to rich men, that all I wanted to do was find a rich guy and that I didn't care about the important things that we had together, that he loved me, could never respect anybody more than he did me, that he didn't want us to break up, didn't want to go. It's hard watching a bank walk away. I just told him that perhaps I wasn't as liberated as I thought I was ...

While some males still adhere to the traditional notions of wanting their desirable female to possess only homemaking and people-nurturing skills, most males now seem to want a female who is economically capable and psychologically stronger in public life, but also one who will defer in private life and still largely take responsibility for managing the home, children, and husband – a sort of super-cuddly Superwoman who can not only take care of business but also channel considerable energies to making and sustaining relationships. On the other side of the coin, Wendy Dennis has suggested that men are now being directed to 'transform' themselves 'from dull but dutiful breadwinner, in the Ozzie Nelson mold, to androgynous danger-boy, in the Mick Jagger mold, to caring-sharing-and-relating soul-mate, in the Phil Donahue mold, to risk-taker with a vulnerable heart, in the Bruce Willis mold, to sensitive but sexy man-boy, in the Kevin Costner mold' – in other words, a super-cuddly Superman who still takes care of business but also sustains a relationship with his partner in all of the desired dimensions. Consider, for example, one other writer's answer to the question of 'what women really want': 'We dream of a world full of men who could be passionate lovers, grounded in their own bodies, capable of profound loves and deep sorrows, strong allies of women, sensitive nurturers, fearless defenders of all people's liberation, unbound by stifling conventions yet respectful of their own and others' boundaries, serious without being humorless, stable without being dull, disciplined without being rigid, sweet without being spineless, proud without being insufferably egotistical, fierce without being violent, wild without being, well, assholes.'

Again, we must bear in mind that these prescriptions are not universally shared.

As further evidence of the transitions and confusions of our times, the directions being provided in the last examples are primarily, but not exclusively, from women to men. But, at this very moment, we are also witnessing the generation and development of a new groundswell men's movement that is, in large part, predicated upon a rejection of what may be termed 'women-defined men,' and in favour of trying to create a new image of 'men-defined men.' Whether it be in search of 'Wild Men,' or 'Warriors,' all with 'fire in their bellies,' increasing numbers of men are investing in books, seminars, and weekend retreats designed to promote the creation of a new alternative to the modern male – an alternative that is supposed to be generated from within and not imposed from outside. At the very least, this current process and goal reinforce the theme of 'independence' that has long been a part of the major underpinnings of the male role in Western societies. It also promises to clash eventually in many ways with the demands being made upon men, from both male and female sources, that they be more 'relational-oriented.' Considerable work remains to be done before the independent and autonomous Wild Man can also become a loving and nurturing relational partner.

It is important to stress that we are not witnessing battle lines being drawn between the sexes, with all males on one side and all females on the other. Rather, males and females array themselves along both sides of these designs for ideal gender roles and ideal intimate partners. That alignment, in large part, contributes to the existing turmoil of the day. Confusing and competing messages are being directed towards the individual male and female, of whatever age, to be this or to be that, either to adopt whole-heartedly the total package being proffered from one source or another – or to create, on one's own, some blend from the vast cafeteria of choices on offer. While a smorgasbord of choice initially appeals to a sense of freedom, it can in many cases become daunting, even immobilizing, to the chooser. And it can also lead to a nostalgia for the supposedly 'good old days, when men were men and women were women' and everybody knew the difference and was supposedly content to perform a prescribed role. Nostalgia tends to be very selective, and yet seductive and comforting, in its reduction of complexity into apparent simplicity. As we show throughout this book, various combinations of choices have produced gender-role performances that are somewhat different from and, simultaneously, somewhat similar to traditional expectations.

At the moment, both sexes are succumbing to a set of rising expectations and drafting intimate-partner 'job descriptions' for which few could realistically qualify. One result is a reduction of the marriage rate, a reduction which is the consequence of many factors, of which those expectations are only a part (for example, the increasing cohabitation rate). But as a result, many women are making a deliberate and active choice not to commit to a relationship that they feel will not meet their needs. This freedom is now possible because of the increasing economic independence, but not necessarily affluence, of women and the consequent lessening of their financial dependence upon men.

Concurrently expectations exist that reinforce the notion of a 'couples' society. This Noah's Ark mentality that expects all things to be in 'two by two' formation makes the single person in a social situation a discomforting oddity to all persons concerned. The dominant etiquette still demands that one should have an escort/companion for many social functions, partly for appearance's sake, partly for protection against unwanted advances from members of the other sex (particularly, obviously, men). The 'couples' society sends its own socialization messages which insist that, since everyone is basically incomplete in and of him or herself, an intimate partner is necessary for a sense of completion or wholeness – a message that we can trace back to Plato.

CONTRADICTORY ALTERNATIVES

We thus have two seemingly contradictory situations. On the one hand, we have slowly been developing an acceptable social environment for the existence of single-by-choice (i.e., more proactively motivated) individuals. On the other hand, the pressures to have an appendage that walks and talks independently is *de rigueur* for most, or at least many, social situations. While these pressures are experienced by both males and females, it would appear that societal messages, both subtle and blatant, stressing the importance of a relationship for both public and private identity, have been and still are directed much more towards females than towards males. Interestingly, these contradictory situations were forecast by the late demographer Marcia Guttentag and her husband, Paul Secord, a social psychologist, in a provocative book on the sex ratio issue published in 1983. They noted that, with men in 'short supply,' in combination with the fact that men typically control the basic legal, political, and economic institutions within societies, two contradictory sets of pressures producing two different outcomes for females and for female social roles will result.

A real or perceived deficit of men and a reduced likelihood of commitment from those males, given that men have access to a larger number of potential partners, would produce pressures towards an increasing independence of females since male support, of both the economic and the emotional varieties, could no longer be counted upon. We have witnessed a vast number of books, articles, and television and radio talk shows devoted to the supposed male 'fear of commitment,' although it has never been made exactly clear whether the issue was a generalized fear among most males towards all females or a particular male's reluctance to commit to a future with a particular female. Underlying these media presentations is the theme that males cannot be counted upon, and therefore females are best advised to strike out on their own. While some commentators continue to blame women for making dumb choices of men under these conditions, many have suggested channelling energies towards changing those conditions. Efforts should be directed towards increasing female power over the structure of a society, particularly in the arenas of government, business, and the law; to increase independence rather than dependence upon men; to develop female-centred values as opposed to values based upon what males want females to be; and to develop independent identities. In other words, the range of options for females beyond marriage and motherhood must be increased and acted upon, according to proponents of this point of view.

The Bountiful alternative is not totally out of the question, as we can observe from the comments of some of our respondents which demonstrate many of the processes and options we have been referring to here. Indeed, this alternative was anticipated in 1976 by Constantina Safilios-Rothschild: 'As the sex stratification system changes more women gain high social status and power ... Experience will have enriched women as persons and status will give them a special power, as well as improved self-confidence and self-image. Such women, particularly during middle age or after, will often become attractive and attracted to younger men ... Many of these women can be expected to actively pursue the men they find attractive. Some of the men they pursue, particularly the younger ones, will most often have not only less money but also less status and power, and this power differential may be exploited by some women.'

As we mentioned earlier in this chapter, some of our female respondents felt marriage, especially in its traditional forms was too confining; they spoke of the perception that they would be 'suffocated' in a traditional wife/mother/housekeeper role. In contrast, the role of a Madame Bountiful allowed them the semblance of an ordered, intimate romantic/sexual life which satisfied their needs for companionship, affection, an escort, and so on, but did not engulf them totally.

One 39-year-old woman from Berkeley, California, wrote: 'It strikes me that we are probably an aberrant example, even among such inherently "aberrant" relationships, but that, in fact, is probably why I am writing to you. I am very happy in this relationship and would like it to be known, if only statistically, that such a relationship can provide personal satisfaction. Of course, my personal satisfaction may be attributable to the idiosyncrasies of my personality as an individual, but it exists nevertheless.'

As one 34-year-old woman from Philadelphia remarked:

Did you ever watch 'All in the Family' where the wife was constantly told to 'stifle' herself? I never could understand why people always laughed at that but they did. Or, did you ever watch the old reruns of 'The Honeymooners' where Jackie Gleason was always threatening to punch his wife with 'To the moon, Alice, to the moon'? So much for the golden age of television. I get mad when people laugh at things like that because it's not funny and it does happen. My ex-husband was rich but he was a cheat and a very brutal man. When he'd drink there wasn't a great deal of difference between him and Ralph Cramden [the character played by Jackie Gleason in 'The Honeymooners'] ...

I've made myself a life now that I enjoy. Work is very important to me. Unlike a relationship, when you put a lot of energy and care into a career, what you get out is generally what you put in. In my job [a stock broker] I meet a lot of men but I've made it a rule to keep my personal life and my professional life strictly private. I don't want my personal life to affect my job or my concentration and distract me from getting ahead. What I want is a sail and not an anchor. With Les [her gigolo] things are great, because it's on my terms. I see him when I want to, it's simple, it's uncomplicated and it's all I have time for right now. It's nice to go out and have someone you can relax with ...I don't need a husband, I need a 'wife'! ...

It's often struck me as unfair that men and women in our society are treated so differently. My mother still tells me of her friends' rich son and how they're *dying* to meet me and when I tell her that I never want to be married again she gets totally choked and says 'Oh dear, oh dear.' If I was a 34-year-old male, nobody would be after me to marry especially since I've already done that trip once, and they would think it's great that I'm well known in my job, making an excellent salary, able to buy what I want, go where I want. Instead, I'm made to feel as if I'm letting everyone down, taking a dagger and stabbing at the heart of Motherhood and Apple pie. I like my life – if it offends somebody in Smalltown, U.S.A., sorry ... I'm not out to please anybody any more. It suits me.

Concurrently, that very same deficit of men, according to Guttentag and Secord, would also lead to other pressures being placed upon women to increase their positive appeal to men in order to obtain commitment and support from them. Thus females would also receive messages in a variety of forms stressing the 'traditional factors': the importance to men of physical attractiveness; housekeeping and homemaking skills; a positive orientation towards motherhood; and the ability to provide a strong 'supportive' role for the men in their lives, as opposed to doing anything that might be perceived as 'threatening.'

Jean Jacques Rousseau said women should be educated to please men; unfortunately, the behaviour, actions, and attitudes of certain women who unwittingly drift into the role of Madame Bountiful suggests that there still are women who are simply trying to please men. It is evidently very difficult for some women to behave as though equality of the sexes exists when so much of our society assumes that it does not.

In the past decade we have witnessed a strong backlash throughout the media, and even political parties and pressure groups, attempting to reassert the dominance and importance of 'traditional family values.' The messages are primarily directed towards, and demand change of, females and much less so towards, and of, males. Implicitly, if not explicitly, these messages also reinforce the importance of 'independence' as a dominant theme of masculinity, regardless of what the existing reality actually is.

THE OPTIONS

For females of certain ages, both now and in the recent past, the available options appear to be somewhat limited and confusing at the same time. One could seek out and find a mate to marry or cohabit with. One could choose to opt for the status of permanent singlehood with or without the required 'walking' appendage for social functions. One could choose to create a lifestyle revolving solely around other females, which may or may not include a sexual dimension. At younger ages one could choose to maintain high expectations for a desirable mate and, failing to find one initially, wait until later for the next cohort of males being recycled through divorce, and perhaps find one 'the second time around.' During the interim, and as part of an important element of one's lifestyle and continuing identity, one can establish and maintain the independent economic and career foundations of life.

As we noted at the end of the last chapter, the pluralistic family institution today recognizes that human needs may be met within a number of relational forms. Individuals are grudgingly being granted permission to construct the relationship that will work to the benefit of both partners. Consequently, another option one could take involves ignoring the traditional age constraints of the marriage gradient surrounding appropriate relationship partners and select a much older – or younger – intimate partner. This latter option obviously appealed to a sizeable minority of women during the 1980s. Thus, as Lois Banner has observed of the older woman–younger man phenomenon:

Many of my own middle-aged women friends have formed such relationships. They are joined in this behavior by well-known entertainment figures like Mary Tyler Moore and Olivia Newton-John, whose relationships with younger husbands and lovers have been emblazoned in gossip sheets and family magazines alike. For a time several years ago hardly a week went by without a story on the phenomenon in some mass-circulation magazine or on some television talk show. Popular writers cite statistics showing that cross-age relationships between older woman and younger men are on the increase. Thus, for example, of the marriages that took place in 1983, more than 30 percent of the women aged twenty-five to thirty-four married younger men. In that year, among women aged thirty-five to forty-four, nearly 40 percent married younger men.

In an interview publicizing her 1992 how-to guide, *The Older Woman's Guide to Younger Men*, 53-year-old Valerie Gibson, a veteran of five marriages currently married to a man in his thirties, argued that since the age of 40, when she began dating younger men, her 'research into the subject' has her convinced to say that 'many older women in the 1990s will be choosing youth and virility over maturity' in selecting their partners. The article pointedly noted that actress Elizabeth Taylor at the age of 60 selected a 40-year-old man to be her eighth husband, that mystery writer Agatha Christie was married to a man twelve years her junior, that 'Catherine the Great couldn't resist young soldiers and the first Queen Liz had a similar predilection.' Gibson is quoted as stating: 'I think many older men today are stale and weary ... Most are so wrapped up with their ex-wives, their careers and the pursuit of making money that all the joyful things of life with them are often lost.' Although she noted the lack of acceptance accorded such relationships – from society generally ('Many people believe the older woman is either a raging nymphomaniac or the young man is after her money'), and from the man's mother particularly ('That problem is obvious. You are often either her age or close to it. What is more, you're certainly not who they would choose for their son'), Gibson was adamant that many men are attracted to older women for other than financial reasons.

According to interviewer Judy Creighton of the Canadian Press:

Gibson, a small, red-haired woman with a throaty English accent, says the young men she interviewed often find that women their own age have nothing to say and no life experience. 'Young men say that younger women think they are in love after the first date. They want to get married immediately or they want to know what kind of car the young man is driving and if he has a good job.' On the other hand,

Gibson says young men tell her that older women are more worldly, independent and stimulating. 'And what women may want at this point in their social and emotional life just happens to match up with what many young men want,' she says. 'That means a good time with someone who is not necessarily destined to be a lifetime partner but who is fun to be with, interesting to talk to, good to look at and makes you feel special.'

American data apparently indicate, according to Susan Faludi, that in 1986 'nearly one-fourth of [all] brides were older than their grooms, up from 16 percent in 1970.' Unfortunately, general statistics such as those provided by Banner and Faludi give us no indication of how much 'younger' than their brides these grooms actually were.

A more precise recalculation of marriage data published by Statistics Canada for the year 1991 for each five-year age group between 25 and 29 and 70 and 74 and the years 1985 and 1989 for each five-year age group between 25 and 29 and 45 and 49 (all women and men over the age of 49 in 1985 and 1989 and over 74 in 1991 are lumped into one category and are therefore not suitable for any meaningful analysis), finds that the percentage of women marrying grooms from younger age groups ranges from 11 to 33 per cent. The highest incidence in all three years is found among women in the 35–9 age range, closely followed by those aged 40–4. While these figures are interestingly high, it must stressed that at least 67 to almost 90 per cent of women marrying in these years selected men from either the same or an older age group. This basic fact is typically ignored by the media (and some writers) since it is simply part of the taken-for-granted normalcy of everyday life and does not lend itself to sensationalistic claims.

Further examination and analysis of the Canadian data indicate that 50 percent or more of the women in all five-year age groups who married younger men in all three years chose mates from the adjacent age group, that is, men who were from one to five years younger. However, with increasing age up to age 49, the percentage choosing from this adjacent age group decreased. In 1991, for example, among females aged 25–9 who married younger males, 99 percent selected a husband one to five years younger. Among females aged 45–9 who married younger males, 55 per cent chose a husband one to five years younger, 26 per cent selected one six to ten years younger, 14 per cent one eleven to fifteen years younger, and 4 per cent one sixteen to twenty years younger. In other words, among women (up to age 49) who marry younger men, the older the woman, the greater the likelihood she will select a much younger mate.

Among older age groups, beginning with ages 55–9, the proportion of women selecting a marriage mate from the adjacent younger age group begins to increase. In the absence of any systematically gathered information to the contrary, we can only assume that such age differences are also characteristic of liaisons occurring outside marriage.

The reader must bear in mind several important facts in attempting to interpret these findings. First, these marriage data do not distinguish between first, second, or subsequent marriages. In general, age differences between brides and grooms tend to be greater with each subsequent marriage. Second, and closely related, the age differences reported here are in large part attributable to the fact that a wider range of alternatives is available to older women. Obviously a woman of 25 cannot marry a man fifteen years her junior, but a woman of 45 can marry a 30-year-old man. So, opportunity is an important consideration here. Up to a point, older people simply have a wider range of possibilities to select from. Third, older people tend to feel less constrained by age expectations than do younger people. As mentioned previously, the lowest percentages of women marrying younger men are found to occur in the 25–9 age category. We find greater conformity among these younger women in meeting the social expectations that they will marrying someone of an appropriate age. It appears that, with increasing age, there is less concern with 'what people would think.' Fourth, and finally, the statistical information available to us indicates only the ages of the marital partners and nothing else. We know nothing about social factors, such as the participants' education, income, and social class, or personal factors, such as their physical attractiveness or perceived alternatives for intimate relationships. We have absolutely no information here regarding possible comparison levels and trade-offs that may or may not have occurred as these partnerships were negotiated and formalized.

All we do know from such information is that men are not the only ones who select a younger marital partner. Of course, as we have already noted, the mass media, and especially the popular gossip magazines, sensationalistic 'newspapers,' and television talk shows, are quick to provide details about the marriages of older celebrity women and their younger men. But these details probably cannot be generalized to fit the circumstances surrounding the marriages of most women to their younger men. For our purposes here, it must be sufficient to note that, while still in a relatively small statistical minority, marriages between older women and younger men are not exceptional or completely outside of the range of available options.

Of course, for those who either cannot or simply do not want to be married to an intimate partner, another option would be to establish a 'part-time lover' relationship – that is, either become someone's mistress or become the Madame Bountiful to a paid gentleman companion. Regardless of which type of intimate partnership is entered into, each of the participants must confront certain elements common to any relationship. We turn now to a consideration of some of the most basic of these.

3

Eroticism and Love
in Intimate Relationships

Intimate relationships contain many dimensions, central among which are eroticism, love, and a distribution of power between the partners. This chapter focuses on eroticism and love, while various aspects of power are considered in chapter 4. Each of these dimensions is considered separately even though they are obviously intertwined. As we will soon see, during the past twenty-five years women in general have been working through socially induced inhibitions in acknowledging their own sexuality and in negotiating for more 'love' from, and a greater share of power with, males in intimate relationships.

In the process of researching and writing this book, we sought a new word to describe an active process of being sexual or erotic. We have a verb – 'to love' – that functions as an umbrella term for a number of general and specific thoughts, feelings, and behaviours. But there is no accepted verb, such as 'to sex,' that covers to sexual thoughts, feelings, and behaviours. 'To sex' does apply to the process of determining the biological sex of, for example, rabbits – a function that must be acknowledged as useful for the purposes of a rabbit breeder, – but does not help in our quest for an appropriate word to convey precisely what we mean.

Initially, one of us suggested the term 'eroticide.' However, we realized that if 'homicide' means 'to kill a member of the species *Homo sapiens*,' and 'infanticide' means 'to kill an infant,' then logically 'eroticide' would have to mean 'to kill eroticism.' While that definition would make this term useful for commenting upon the many things that both males and females do to the erotic mood of the moment, it makes the term inappropriate for our intended purpose. 'Erotary?' That suggested a cross between a power tool and a sexual aid – a vibrator that featured prerecorded Michael

Bolton songs. 'Eroticy' (as in 'larceny, and 'idiocy') sounded equally unappealing.

We began to develop empathy for the eminent psycho-medical researcher John Money, who devoted a number of pages in the introduction to his book *Gay, Straight and In-Between: The Sexology of Erotic Orientation* to the difficulties involved in settling on a title that would capture the entire field he was currently exploring. He noted that it would be nice to have a 'word like fuckology ... to signify the science of what it is that people actually do under the cover of polite expressions like making love or having sex.' After exhausting both modern and old English, plus a number of other languages, he gave up in frustration and decided to make do with the less precise words of his subtitle.

Lloyd Saxton confronted the same dilemma in the sixth edition of his family sociology textbook. After rejecting the usual euphemisms ('making love,' 'sleeping with') and the 'Middle-English term fuck,' which was 'precise, explicit, and grammatically flexible, but ... usually regarded as vulgar,' he decided upon 'copulation' because it too was precise, explicit, and grammatically flexible ('copulating, copulated, would have copulated, will copulate, and so on'), *and* socially acceptable. However, Saxton used this term only in the context of penile-vaginal insertion and was forced to rely upon 'erotic behaviour' as his general term. Alas, after considerable further thought, and more confirmation that the paucity of adequate and acceptable terms in the English language reflects our traditional antisexual heritage, we found ourselves turning to the less-than-satisfactory 'eroticism' as our all-purpose term. While there is no verb 'to erotic,' one could at least theoretically 'commit an eroticism' in thought, feeling, or deed.

EROTICISM SCRIPTS: CHANGES AND DIFFERENCES

As we will soon see, the history of changes over the past century and a half in sexual values, attitudes, and behaviours in Western societies is largely a history of changes in female erotic patterns. The female erotic script has undergone the most significant alterations over time, while the male script has remained basically, but not totally, unchanged. Despite a commonly held belief that performing sexually is nothing more than 'doing what comes naturally,' accumulated scientific evidence over the past fifty years clearly indicates that many, if not virtually all, of our heterosexual thoughts, feelings, and behaviours follow socially constructed guidelines. As Mary McIntosh noted: 'We often take ... everyday beliefs

and experiences as evidence about the eternal nature of differences between the sexes. Sex, after all, is something we think of as very "natural"
– you do it with little or no equipment and with no clothes on. But nothing could be further from the truth. There *may* be a generic "sex" drive
that is natural, but the specific ways in which it will be expressed, and
indeed whether these will be recognizably 'sexual' at all, depends upon
the way in which the individual handles the general culture and the specific life-experiences she confronts' (emphasis added).

Beginning early in childhood, males and females receive continuous direct and indirect (mainly the latter) messages that inform them of socially
acceptable and unacceptable ways to be sexual and to recognize what is
sexual about their beings. However, as we will see, the new changes have
been overlaid upon old beliefs, attitudes, and values, resulting in a, at
times, confusing and contradictory admixture of bold new expressions
and vestiges of the old. Some individuals exemplify a new eroticism and
stand in sharp contrast to their neighbours who embody the traditional.
Other individuals contain within themselves a personally constructed
combination of both the new and the old elements. Needless to say, the
contents of these scripts vary over historical time and differ in important
ways for males and females.

From the nineteenth century onwards, the medical empire of general
practitioners, gynaecologists, obstetricians, mental health professionals,
and asylum workers defined female sexuality in a way that affected the
lives and liberties of women in everyday life. As 'experts,' their opinions
served to legitimate the suppression of women and their eroticism by viewing any behaviour which contradicted the norms of chastity or marital
fidelity as indicative of sickness, of mental ill-health. For example, the
prominent British medico-theologian William Acton's 1857 treatise *The
Functions and Disorders of the Reproductive Organs* ... broadly defined
'nymphomania' as a 'condition' of sexual looseness and 'depravity' which
amounted to unchaste behaviour and/or masturbation in women. No
equivalent 'condition' was identified in men, even though a 'Casanova'
and 'nymphomaniac' engage in virtually indistinguishable behaviour.
However, the terms used to define the behaviour in males and females
suggest very different interpretations and evaluations. The former, one
would imagine, is simply thought of as 'lucky'; the latter, as one who is
mentally ill, unstable, and possibly dangerous – if not to others, then to
herself.

Similarly, G.H. Savage's 1884 work, *Insanity and Allied Neuroses*, described the female psychological malady of 'simple hysterical mania.' Its

symptoms? Supposedly women evidencing this pathological condition could be identified through their socially aberrant behaviour. Savage advised: 'They rapidly become less and less conventional. Thus, a lady will smoke, talk slang, or be extravagant in dress; and will declare her intention of doing as she likes. At this stage love affairs, and the like complications are common.' For a woman to evidence anything other than passivity in the sexual realm – to give evidence of sexual interest, desire, activity, or aggressiveness – was viewed as indicative of mental and/or physical ill-health.

Of course, there were always women who defied social conventions. For example, Autumn Stephens's *Wild Women: Crusaders, Curmudgeons and Completely Corsetless Ladies in the Otherwise Virtuous Victorian Era* cited the Californian railroad heiress and 'professional flirt' Aimee Crocker for the unconventionality of her lifestyle. Crocker, whose autobiography was entitled *And I'd Do It Again*, possessed the income that allowed her to act in a unrepentantly individualistic manner that was discordant with the Victorian ideal of female piety and purity. Stephens observed:

'Flirtation ... can be the most fascinating pastime in the world,' gushed ... Crocker. By the age of sixteen, the voluptuary vixen had already tumbled for a German prince 'who had the most romantic saber scars,' and a Spanish toreador ('his touch left scars on my soul'). To the great relief of San Francisco society columnists, Crocker's wounds healed quickly and she went on to hula a deux with King Kalakaua of Hawaii, jitterbug through the jungles of Borneo with a bona fide headhunter, and hootchy-kootchy her way into the harem of the Rajah of Shikapur.

Nor did adventurous Aimee, five times a bride, feel compelled to curtail her bed hopping during bouts of matrimony. Consequently, her marriages tended toward the rather abbreviated variety. It is one thing, after all, for a sophisticated spouse to shut his eyes to a love triangle; altogether another to overlook a veritable polytetrahedron of passions. Even the most peripheral paramour, however, seldom proved completely problem free – particularly the type who naively featured himself as leading man rather than best supporting actor. Ah well, that was simply the gaucheness of youth ...

As to whether her quintet of unfortunate grooms (including a Russian prince almost forty years her junior) who wed the wealthy wanderlust-victim ever got over *her*, Crocker wasn't much concerned. 'Husbands, at best, have little to do with "people,"' she sniffed. 'I know, because I have had a certain number of them.'

Based on their content analysis of 'marriage manuals,' Michael Gordon and Penelope Shankweiler documented a change in the opinions and beliefs of the medical profession in particular, beginning around the turn of the twentieth century. Slowly, good and virtuous women were 'granted' by these professional experts, in a simultaneously sincere and condescending fashion, a right to be sexual so long as it was confined within the institution of legal marriage. This new female sexuality was believed to be characterized by two major qualities: monogamy and dormancy. Females were believed to be monogamous by nature and therefore saved their sexuality for one man and one man only – namely, their husbands. Men, in contrast, were not considered to possess this monogamous quality, thus providing an apparent justification for a double standard of expectations for male and female sexuality. In addition, it was also widely believed and prescribed that female sexuality was essentially dormant, quietly residing under the surface, until awakened in true Sleeping Beauty fashion by a man – again, a husband. In contrast to the prevailing view in previous centuries, a 'good' woman could now be sexual and enjoy erotic interest, desire, activity, and perhaps occasional aggressiveness in her marital bed.

While these official revelations appear to have had a notable liberating impact on both marital and non-marital eroticism of the time, during the next significant change, which occurred with the mid-1960s 'sexual revolution,' the supposedly monogamous character of female sexuality was altered further by numerous scientists and social critics to permit, even advocate, premarital sexual experiences without the previously necessary justifying context of marriage, or the promise thereof. Dozens of studies conducted mainly upon those in the vanguard of change, college and university students, documented the steady increase in the proportion of the female population in particular who were experiencing eroticism (not only sexual intercourse, but also oral and even anal sex) while still unmarried and typically with no intentions of entering into marriage with their current sexual partner.

While the changes in sexual behaviour have often been attributed to the invention of oral contraceptives (or 'The Pill'), various forms of contraception were available and used in the past, and obviously, an inert object – a pill – cannot by itself, bring about significant changes in behaviour. Behaviour itself must change first – including, at the very minimum, a willingness to take The Pill. Among the many other changes occurring during this time were women's growing financial independence from men and a growing female sense of empowerment that has continued to this day. As Ira Reiss noted: 'the greater the power of one gender, the greater that gender's sexual rights in that society.' A growing economic independence, coupled with a more effective form of contraception that permitted greater control over reproduction, further weakened the previously inviolate link between sexuality and legal marriage.

What now constitutes an 'appropriate' context for sexual encounters has become increasingly problematic for eligible partners of all ages. Attitude research has indicated that the most acceptable context is now one of a 'stable, affectionate' relationship. But what constitutes 'stable' and 'affectionate'? For the past twenty years, we have also experienced a significant decline in the traditional (since the 1930s and 1940s) dating continuum, with its discernible and sequential stages of commitment ranging from 'casual dating' to 'going steady,' to being 'informally' or 'formally' engaged, and so on. Only the 'engagement' stage was once considered an acceptable context for erotic intimacies if couples couldn't wait until marriage itself. But now the term 'dating' itself has become obsolete, and the stage descriptors have been replaced with phrases such as 'seeing' and 'hanging out with' and 'going out with' someone, although it is completely unclear, even to the participants themselves, as to when 'seeing' or 'hanging out with' changes to 'going out with.' Even more unclear, and thus left to the individual participants for negotiation, is the issue of which of these conditions is stable and affectionate enough to warrant eroticism of any and all kinds.

The most dramatic increases in female premarital sexual behaviour occurred during the period from the mid-1960s through the 1970s. By the mid-1980s the rates of increase began to slow down, a phenomenon that was attributed by some observers in both Canada and the United States to what they hoped and believed was a newly developing 'trend towards conservatism,' or a 'resurgence in traditional family values.' However, recently Ira Robinson and colleagues have suggested that the rates of increase slowed during the 1980s simply because we had reached a 'ceiling effect.' In other words, we had reached a level at which all, or at least the vast majority of, those who might possibly be interested in sexual experimentation prior to marriage were engaging in it. Those who had not done so were what the authors refer to as the 'committed virgins' who, for one reason or another, prefer to wait until marriage before experiencing sexual intercourse and who will probably constitute about 15 per cent of the younger population. National survey data collected from American teenagers has also found the same trend: a dramatic increase in the proportion of females experiencing sex during their teenage years during the 1970s and the levelling off of the rates of increase during the early 1980s. This research also noted that the age at which people become sexually active continues to decrease.

What we have been witnessing is a trend towards convergence in the sexual behaviour patterns of young unmarried males and females. Statistical equality of experience has not yet been reached, but movement towards that end-point continues, albeit at a reduced pace. The overall trend is one whereby increasingly permission is being granted to both males and females to act upon their sexuality – and at earlier and earlier ages.

But it is not only premarital sexuality that has been changing. We have also been witnessing a simultaneous 'trend towards convergence' in extramarital sexuality, brought about again by increases in female erotic behaviour. The 1981 *Cosmo Report*, based on a questionnaire contained in *Cosmopolitan* magazine, found that 54 per cent of their married female respondents had had at least one extramarital affair and that 61 per cent of their 10,000 female respondents reported that they had had at least one affair with a married man (almost double the percentages reported for female adultery in the famous Kinsey surveys on sexual behaviour published in the late 1940s and early 1950s). The available evidence suggests that the frequency of affairs decreases with age for husbands but increases, up to a point, with age for wives. Husbands tend to have their first affair within the first five years of marriage, whereas wives indulge in extramarital sex later in the marriage. In addition, husbands generally claim they are looking for sexual novelty, but wives claim that it is the qualities of tenderness, caring, and sensitivity that they find appealing in their new sexual partners.

Among our respondents, a 37-year-old married woman from New York commented:

Explaining how I came to be involved in an affair seems incredibly complicated. First of all, I should explain that there's a pretty big age difference between my husband and myself; I was eighteen when I met him and he was thirty-nine. It didn't seem such a big deal then because he had everything going for him. He didn't look thirty-nine; he was rail-thin, fantastic dresser, great car, lots of money and I find money can be an incredible turn-on! ... I was starting to do some modelling but that went nowhere ... I didn't really care because I thought who needs to work anyhow! ... He was always a gentleman about my past. He assumed I'd had lovers before him – who doesn't nowadays? – but he didn't ask and I didn't tell him ...

Like most men I find, he has a double standard. He'd want me to perform oral sex on him, but wouldn't think of reciprocating ... The biggest mistake I ever made with him was telling him I thought his friend Ken was good-looking. That night he wanted me to let him have anal sex with me. What is with men? I told my girlfriend about it and she said that nowadays all guys suddenly want anal sex. I let him have it his way but I tell you, I thought to myself, 'You bastard, looking for virgin ground?' I felt it was just a control thing, you know, Tarzan and 'you're my woman and don't you forget it' type of crap ...

After having three daughters in seven years, I wasn't really that interested in having more kids even though I think my husband wanted to keep trying for a son. I finally told him, 'Look, I'm over thirty, I smoke, either I get fixed, you get fixed or we start using condoms because I'm going off the pill.' For a week he wouldn't use a condom and then when I wouldn't put out ... have you ever smelled burning rubber? [Laughs]. Anyhow, he used them but didn't like it ...

I told him if he didn't like it he could get a vasectomy, after all, it's no big deal – it's not like what a woman has to go through – in a hospital, aesthetic – just into a doctor's office, snip snip and here's an icepack ... Sure enough, I got pregnant right away because he'd only put on the condom right before he was ready to blow. I told him I could get pregnant just with the pre-cum but he wouldn't believe me. I had a miscarriage in my second trimester and I thought, that's it. One way or the other ...

In many ways it was my husband's cowardice to get a vasectomy as much as anything that led to my taking lovers.When he wouldn't go in to get fixed, I finally had it and told him, 'fine, I'll do it.' Its funny – if I were still afraid of getting pregnant, I don't think I'd have cheated on him ...

Don't get me wrong, I wouldn't say sex is the biggest thing involved in my affair. *Everyone* has affairs. It's not just me. I was a late bloomer ... It's, I don't know. Let's say every morning for over ten years you have coffee and a muffin for breakfast. It doesn't matter how good that muffin is, you're going to get bored with it. Give me toast! Corn flakes! Anything ... Sex [with a husband] becomes so routine you're going through the motions and trying to bring him off as quick as you can just to get the damn thing over with ...

I know I'm attractive but I need that reinforcement, I want to feel like a woman not just a wife. Shawn [her lover] can be crazy and it's fun. I'm cautious still – with the AIDS thing you'd have to be crazy to be into one-night stands – shit, I'd rather masturbate till my hand fell off – so I have him wear a condom, just in case, you know? I don't want to sleep with all his ex-lovers. Anyhow, the last time we slept together, after he had come, he took off the condom, dropped it on my foot and said, 'Here, now you can tell [your husband] you were late because a safe fell on you.' He's a total fool but lots of fun ...

In a way, supporting a lover is my protection. You know the saying about how you only value what you pay for? Well, it works both ways ... I don't think Shawn is stupid enough to fool around while I'm supporting him. He's got too much at stake. At least, he'd make sure to be very, very, careful because if I got so much as an itch, he knows he'd be history.

However, while we note the changes in acceptable scripts for female sexuality in particular, we are not suggesting that earlier held ideas have simply dropped out of sight and are no longer with us in any form. Vestiges of earlier scripts and stereotypes still exist – not only in the professional attitudes and behaviour of experts but also in both the conscious and the unconscious attitudes that some men and women maintain and which continue to inform, direct, and restrict female sexuality.

A 42-year-old woman commented:

They say that women reach their peak sexually in their thirties while men reach their peak when they're around nineteen. That spells trouble doesn't it? If I was young now I don't know if I would have lived my life differently or not. My daughter went through sheer hell being a teenager; all her friends were on the 'pill' by the time they were thirteen or fourteen years old. Sex is a lot to handle for a girl that young – not just the physical part and the risks of getting pregnant – it's the mind games that go along with sex. Its hard to take at my age, forget about when you're thirteen years old ...

I always thought Erica Jong and her 'zipless fuck' were pure garbage. As long as women can get pregnant and are still called 'sluts,' there's no such thing as a zipless fuck except for men ... I wonder about women like Erica Jong. Are they so wrapped up in their fantasies that they don't know that the majority of women don't live in Hollywood? It's great if you're Madonna and you can earn the big bucks doing things like masturbating in a church, but it's just a gimmick to shock people, not real life ...

Yes, I keep a lover, and some people might think me a hypocrite but it's not really a fair comment. My lover is my best friend – not just my lover – and what I do is private and I keep it that way. If this were an ideal world, my lover would be my husband; I don't even think my husband would be a friend. Maybe an acquaintance ...

I'm not out to shock or offend anyone. If my marriage and family weren't important to me I'd be single again and the kids would be living with their dad. But I'm not.

In focusing attention on the importance she attaches to her family and marriage, this woman stresses the ways in which her behaviour may be seen as conforming to social ideals and expectations of traditional femininity (e.g., the disparagement of promiscuity, the aspersions cast upon women whose actions seemed to her to be calculated to 'shock' or 'offend'), *despite* her unconventional act of keeping a lover in an adulterous relationship.

INITIATING EROTICISM

The cultural script of 'men as pursuers, women as pursued' is still widely held as an ideal and still reiterates the notion of female sexual passivity. While women appear to be more knowledgeable than men in the strategic use of flirtation, well-versed in the subtle attempts by which one can suggest or signal sexual interest and receptivity, men would still appear to be the principal architects of sexual relationships. Thus even today it is more often the man who asks a woman out on a date than vice versa; similarly, it is more frequently the male, rather than the female, who initiates sexual activity and directs its type and frequency. One major exception appears to occur in the case of a dating couple who decide to abstain from sexual activity; in this situation it is typically the woman's veto that constitutes the major restraining influence. Thus, in accordance with older scripts, males hold the basic power of observable initiation while females ideally hold the power of refusal, a power which is manifestly ignored in cases of rape.

Obviously sexuality has long been an important part of the masculinity equation in Western societies, or as Sam Keen so eloquently stated: 'a boy's penis becomes the pole around which his consciousness revolves.' As we noted in an earlier chapter, traditional stereotypes held that males possessed a more powerful sexual 'drive' than did females. Consistent with that belief, males received a series of socialization messages that, as often as not, emphasized an aggressive, quantitative, orientation towards erotic encounters. Sex was often portrayed as something that males took from females, and the greater the number of 'takes,' or the higher the 'scores,' the more masculine the performer. Although men and women in contemporary society may be attempting to become sexually liberated and reaching – at least in theory – towards an androgynous ideal, there is still some way to go.

As Carol Tavris noted in her survey of 28,000 men and women in the United States, cultural stereotypes as to what is seen to constitute a truly 'feminine' woman and a 'real man' are tenacious and affect both men and women. Thus, she noted that females are *more* likely than males to stress that a 'real man' must be a skilled lover (48 per cent of females versus 38 per cent of males). Although the most recent *Psychology Today* survey did not provide a directly comparable question, its findings did suggest that for these high-income, highly educated respondents, the 'new ideal man' still sees women as 'less aggressive in bed and less aggressive in general.'

However, some modifications to this traditional script are becoming apparent. In his latest book *The New Male Sexuality*, Bernie Zilbergeld noted that a new element has been added: 'an important change in men's view of their role in sex in the last twenty-five years or so. It used to be that scoring was all that mattered ... But now we are much more focused on the pleasure of our partners. You can't consider yourself a good lover unless you give your partner an earthshaking experience.' Sexual technique, as a cure for sexual illiteracy, becomes a deadly serious concern in so far as real men are supposed to be knowledgeable and competent in the mechanics of sex, super-cuddly sexual Supermen who are able to orchestrate orgasms in their partners that cause them to metaphorically leap tall buildings in a single bound. Perhaps this new dimension explains somewhat our male respondents' claims to inordinate sex-making ability.

You can't learn how to be a gigolo from a book; you've got to get first-hand experience. Everybody develops their own style and has to figure out what will work for them ... I've had more than two hundred lovers and it's taken me that many to perfect my style. [Which is?] I talk sexy with women and I'm very sensual. To me it doesn't matter what a woman looks like, she can look like a fat slob but it's okay because whenever I'm screwing her I can always be screwing whoever I want in my own mind. [Don't you ever have trouble becoming sexually aroused with a woman who is physically unattractive to you?] No, or if I do, I encourage her to go down on me and give me a blow job. [And if she won't?] Well, I suggest 69 – that way she'll usually go for it. Women love being eaten, but if she's got hang-ups about oral sex, it calms her down to be giving me a blow-job while I'm eating her. If she gives good head and if she lets me come that way, I think it's great, but a lot of women don't like me to come in their mouths.

[Is that your favourite sexual position?] Definitely. It may be the old macho thing. Here's this rich chick and she's got her mouth around my dick and is licking away like it's ice-cream or maybe it's the ass-backwards aspect – you have this woman on her knees getting you off – but I love getting head. [And giving it?] Yeah, I don't mind that either. When I get a woman really aroused and she gets all wet it's a real turn-on for me. Give me a woman whose husband has never eaten her out and she's mine for life. You don't need a pecker like Long Dong Silver for something [a clitoris] that's not even half an inch long ...

Jayne [his present lover] has a nice-enough looking face but her body is grossly overweight. She's got great tits though so I concentrate on her tits when I'm screwing her ... [Do you find that sexual aids are necessary?] Not really. I've used them on occasion – I bought a vibrator to use on Jayne because she has a real problem coming, but she didn't like it much.

I find that a lot of women don't care whether they come or not – they just like the feeling of making love. Jayne always comes when I eat her out but half the time she'll just want straight sex because she's more comfortable that way. Hell, she's paying for it ...

At the beginning it would bother me a lot if my woman didn't come and I would spend hours each time trying to make her come. Now, I realize that for Jayne at least, half the reason she likes sex is because she thinks its naughty. I've screwed her in the toilet of an airplane, she's given me a blow job in the first-class compartment of a plane, hotel elevators, in the driver seat of a Lamborghini Countach at the side of the highway, in the kitchen while a black tie affair is going on, in a hot tub party with her friends not even knowing, I got three fingers up her that gave it to her. It takes around five minutes and I don't think she comes all the time but she tells me how sexy it makes her feel. (Los Angeles, 32-year-old gigolo)

Despite the timidity of this respondent's Madame Bountiful, evidence exists as to the increasing incidence of female initiation of heterosexual relationships. The classic large-scale study of 'American couples' conducted by Philip Blumstein and Pepper Schwartz found that, among heterosexual married and cohabiting couples, the man was the initiator of sexual encounters in more than twice as many couples than was the woman.

One of their male respondents commented: 'We have sex four times a week. Sometimes I initiate it; sometimes she does. Used to be more often for me. She's catching up ... a little self-confidence.' Interestingly enough, even when both married partners were interviewed as to who was more likely to initiate sex (self, partner, or both equally), agreement between partner responses was close, but not unanimous. Whereas 51 per cent of husbands indicated themselves as more likely to be the initiator, only 48 per cent of the wives indicated that it was their male partner. Wives thought they were most likely to be the initiator in 12 per cent of the couples, while husbands estimate that the percentage was larger – namely, 16 per cent. Finally, 33 percent of husbands thought it was about equal, while 40 per cent of wives thought initiation was equal. These discrepancies, although not large, do illustrate that identifying the initiator is subject to interpretation as to what constitutes the 'opening gambit' in the chess match of sex.

Cohabiters were a little closer in agreement; 39 per cent of couples were in complete agreement regarding male initiation. However, 19 per cent of male cohabiters attributed initiation to their partners, while only 15 per cent of the females indicated that they themselves took the lead. Forty-two per cent of the males, and 46 per cent of the females, thought initiation was equal. Aside from the similar pattern of a lack of complete agreement, particularly regarding equality and female initiation, it is worth noting more cohabiters than married couples perceived initiation to be undertaken by the woman or by both partners equally.

Blumstein and Schwartz suggested that female cohabiters were more likely to experiment with the female role, break with tradition, and seek equality with their men than were married women. The authors also found that older cohabiting men were more likely than younger men to resent women taking the initiative in sexual matters. Apparently these older male cohabiters were willing to break with tradition with regard to formal marriage, but not with regard to the male erotic role. As one of their female respondents said of her male cohabitation partner: 'He is ... of an older generation, where women don't use explicit language or swear or push themselves too much ... I think it would insult him if I were to be the more sexually forward person ... He enjoys some interest and enthusiasm on my part ... but being responsive is different from being overbearing ...' Furthermore, the authors suggested that male initiation was in keeping with the idea that a male has a greater sexual appetite than does a female. A woman who initiates sex conveys the image of having a greater sexual appetite, an image that could be threatening to many men, particularly those who have accepted the cultural dictum that they, like a well-known battery, must be ever ready.

One other finding of this study is informative. The data indicated that couples who initiate and refuse sex on an essentially equal basis report more satisfying sex lives and even happier relationship lives and, particularly in the case of equal rights of refusal, more frequent sex. Thus there would appear to be certain benefits from greater female use of power for both initiation and refusal of sex within relationships.

The recent major sex survey, *The Janus Report*, reveals that 67 per cent of female and 54 per cent of male respondents disagreed with the statement 'I always prefer that my sex partner initiate sexual activity.' While the extreme wording of the statement probably contributed to the high figures, the results are none the less suggestive of an increasing acceptance among both men and women adults of more female initiative in sexual activities. Two-thirds of the women in this nationally representative sample asserted a claim to initiating erotic encounters based upon their own desires and not always passively waiting upon their partners' desires. Just over half of the male respondents indicated not being content if their female partner 'always' initiated sex, but they clearly were not objecting to their partners taking the lead at least some of the time. These male responses may be indicative of a desire for an equitable balance between male and female initiation.

N. Brown and A. Auerback, in a limited study of fifty married couples, found that female initiation of marital sex increases with the passage of time, reaching an upper limit of 40 per cent of the time. As we can see, male initiation predominates. Furthermore, Kathryn Kelley and Beverly Rolker-Dolinsky found, among university undergraduates, that female-initiated dates tended not to lead to relationships lasting beyond the third date. However, in an unpublished study, Kelley also found that about 90 per cent of a small sample of undergraduate males reported having been asked for a date by a female. It would therefore appear that the incidence of female initiation is increasing both inside and outside of the bounds of marriage. Still, as Sharon Brehm found in her review of the research literature on social power: 'Even today, female dominance in a heterosexual relationship is less acceptable to *both partners* than is male dominance' (emphasis in original). These studies and reviews indicate that 'dominance' of one partner by the other is becoming unacceptable. The trend towards equality of initiation and refusal is being increasingly endorsed in both word and deed. However, the traditional script of 'men as pursuers and women as pursued' clearly has not yet been laid to rest, and likely is still predominant.

Consistent with the traditional cultural inhibition of female sexuality, contraception has typically been seen as the female's responsibility. In part this view is attributable to the obvious fact that the female most directly suffers from an unwanted pregnancy; however, it is also a reflection of the commonly held belief that female sexuality is not as powerful as that of males. As a consequence, females were, and are, believed to be capable of more rational thinking regarding things sexual. Within this setting inhibitors still exist for a female acknowledging her participation in sexual activities. In the past, the failure of adolescent females to use contraception was not infrequently attributed to the fact that, in order to obtain most methods, they had to acknowledge their 'bad' behaviour to strangers and/or those in positions of authority over them (parents, doctors, pharmacists, clinical personnel, and so on). Since, in our society, some women still attempt to conceal the 'indelicate' matter of menstruation, deflecting attention from their purchases of tampons or sanitary napkins with a shopping cart full of toilet tissue, cosmetics, magazines, toothpaste and hand soaps, one can potentially appreciate the discomfort and chagrin some women experience in acknowledging their sexual activity through obtaining contraception.

The contraceptive times are changing, however. The most recent research on a representative sample of American women 15–44 years of age noted that the vast majority of those women who had experienced intercourse in the three months prior to the date of the study did use some form of contraception with 'The Pill' by far the leading method. Moreover, research indicates that condom use significantly increased among teenagers and never-married women between 1982 and 1988, with Wendy Dennis claiming that, in 1988, 'industry estimates indicated that women represented some 40 percent of the ... American condom market.' Indeed, Dennis reported that, in recent years manufacturers have targeted the female market with 'whisper-thin condoms, rose-petal-embossed condoms, mint-flavoured condoms and condoms in tasteful carrying cases' Reputedly, 'cinnamon, licorice, and chocolate, market research indicates, are the preferred choices.'

While actual purchase of condoms no longer appears to be as traumatic as in earlier times, introducing the topic of contraceptives in a sexual encounter is still not without its difficulties regarding present motivation and the extensiveness of erotic histories. Clearly, the magnitude of these problems is somewhat lessened when oral contraception is being used.

To some degree, reliance on oral contracpetion may effectively cloak one's desire for or participation in sexual activity, hiding it not only from others but from oneself. A woman need not admit being or intending to be sexually active in seeking or taking 'The Pill' as it is possible to misrepresent its function as simply being the desire to regulate one's menstruation or to alleviate its attendant abdominal cramps. However, such misrepresentations may fall on deaf male ears. Lillian Rubin quoted one of her 18-year-old male respondents as saying 'You always know the bad girls; they're on the Pill ... It means they're always ready for sex; that's why they're taking it.'

In terms of more specific behaviours, sexologists have suggested that to achieve orgasm a woman – or man – must be willing to act in a 'sexually selfish manner,' taking an active responsibility for her or his own pleasure, asking for and going after the sexual stimulation she or he needs. Women who take an active and responsible role in their own sexuality tend to experience orgasm and/or be multi-orgasmic more often than women who do not. The research of Masters and Johnson noted that there is an increased likelihood of female orgasm when the woman takes the female-superior position in intercourse as that position increases clitoral pressure and sexual stimulation. However, many women reportedly view such behaviours or positionings as 'masculine' or inappropriate for a 'nice girl' and modify their behaviour to accord with what they feel is more role appropriate. Indeed, research conducted by Allgeier and Fogel revealed that, when unmarried college students were asked to give their opinions of couples who were having sexual intercourse in various positions, women, but not men, gave evidence of a real distaste for the couple in the female superior position. They rated the woman as 'dirtier, less respectable, less moral, less good, less desirable as a wife, and less desirable as a mother when she is on top than when she is beneath the man during intercourse.' These negative judgments may reflect negative attributions given to someone who engages in what appears, according to the new Kinsey report on sex, to simply be a less frequently used position in the United States. But they could also indicate discomfort with apparent female 'dominance' in a sexual encounter that respondents fear will 'spill over' to non-sexual areas of life.

Statistics compiled by Kinsey and colleagues in the 1950s and by Fisher in the 1970s suggested that approximately 60 per cent of North American women never or very rarely had orgasms during intercourse. If, as Masters and Johnson suggested, non-orgasmic women tend to be 'spectators' of their own sexuality, passively watching their sexual experiences unfold before them like a cinema patron rather than behaving like an active participant, becoming orgasmic will not simply be the result of a change of position in intercourse, but rather will require an alteration of the nature of their attitude towards sexuality, and challenging the stereotypes of femininity itself. Some evidence for such changes may be evident in the findings of Lillian Rubin, who, after claiming that 'most experts agree that a woman's ability to be orgasmic is related to her comfort about her sexuality,' noted that about one-third of her sample of 15-year-old girls who were having sex reported that they were orgasmic most of the time, although which factors (e.g., erotic identity, sexual position, other simultaneously engaged in erotic acts such as digital manipulation) contributed to this phenomenon were not indicated.

Mounting evidence exists that even women who were raised on traditional scripts frequently modify their eroticism behaviour over their lifetimes. Researchers and therapists have noted that, with age, married women gradually develop a more genital focus for their own eroticism.

Not that they necessarily lose their previously socialized interest in the interpersonal components, but women do learn to become more comfortable with their sexual bodies and with asserting a right to engage in erotically pleasing activities. As Hilary Lips stated: 'In women ... there is an early appreciation of the sensual and emotional aspects of sexuality, but the genital response is often limited and inconsistent in adolescence and young adulthood ... [I]t is only in later adulthood that women develop a capacity for intense genital pleasure.'

BOUNTIFUL BENEFITS

As some of our women respondents noted, benefits can be gained from the role of the Madame Bountiful. First, there is more power in courtship for females if they allow themselves the freedom to be the aggressor in the relationship, asking someone out, rather than passively waiting by the phone. Research undertaken by R.D. Clark and Elaine Hatfield at a university in the southern United States reported that college males enthusiastically welcomed females taking the sexual initiative. In this study, women students approached male students who were strangers to them with the comment 'I have been noticing you around campus. I find you very attractive.' The authors of this study reported that, after delivering this line, most of their women confederates were extremely successful in getting verbal compliance from males with requests that they go out on a date, go to the woman's apartment or, especially, go to bed with her, although the experiment stopped short of actual bedroom doors.

Second, dominant and extroverted people typically report engaging in more frequent and varied sexual behaviour than do submissive or introverted people. For the woman who takes on the support of a gigolo with the intent of supplementing her marital sex life or satiating her desire for sex without marriage, the knowledge that she is powerful financially may engender the perception in a woman that she is 'in control' and can dictate the direction and scope of sexual activities. Thus, one of our female respondents, a 32-year-old woman who owned her own business, spoke of her 'kept lover' as simply providing a 'service.' He was described as 'functional' rather than a beloved. She commented:

Laurie fills a need that I have and that's it. He fills the tank when it gets low – nothing more, nothing less. Sex for me is a great way of just getting away from everyday worries – frees you up and lets me be in my body instead of my mind all the time. You're looking at me like you don't know what I'm talking about! Look, there's two kinds of people. People who live in their mind and people who live in their body. People who live in their bodies are sensual people, they feel comfortable with their body, appreciate the sensations of sex. enjoy their bodies. People who live in their minds are usually fat, hung up about sex, can't relax, smoke too much, drink too much, eat too much. To those kind of people, their body is uncomfortable, they can't just put on a leotard, stretch out, and enjoy the feeling their body gives them ...

In business you have to be focused in your mind and you can't let yourself be too much in your body because, if you're a female and in your body, you won't be taken seriously. But after work you need that physical energy. Sex can be like meditation or a long hot scented bath, something you do to make yourself feel better. I could masturbate but I don't really like to. It's too much work! That's Laurie's job ...

If I need my hair coloured, I go to a professional. Why start messing around with a do-it-at-home jobbie? Everyone has a job and needs some money. Let's just say I'm helping out the economy and giving Laurie a job that provides – for me – an essential service.

Third, the ability to be a Madame Bountiful, the financial independence that makes the role viable, may negate somewhat the double standard of ageing that women face in our society. In as much as a man's greying hair may be thought distinguished, the lines on his face to bestow character, and his power and status to be the principal determinants of his value as a sexual partner, a man's sexual value may be less affected by the ageing process than a woman's. Although actors such as Paul Newman, Clint Eastwood, Charles Bronson, and Sean Connery remain romantic leads, 'blonde bombshells' once 'past their prime,' such as Brigitte Bardot, Kim Novak, Elke Summer, Diana Dors, and the Gabor sisters, seem to feature only as game-show celebrities and on television/motion picture awards nights when the lighting is soft and the sighs for nostalgia are in the air. Within contemporary society, women are not typically seen to become more attractive with age. Rather, they are simply seen to become older.

In her discussion of the phenomenon of older women and younger men, Lois Banner suggested how, historically, material advantage functioned to increase a woman's attractiveness:

Elizabeth I of England and Catherine the Great of Russia had a series of younger companions as they aged. Germaine de Stael, the famed early-nineteenth-century writer who brought German romanticism to France, had a long and eventually unhappy relationship with the younger writer Benjamin Constant. She spent the last years of her life happily with the young, adoring John Rocca. George Eliot married her younger secretary, John Cross, after Henry Lewes, her longtime companion, died. The American Margaret Fuller, journalist, feminist, and friend of New England transcendentalists, when thirty-six journeyed to Italy and there met and married Count Giovanni Angel Ossoli, ten years younger ...

This phenomenon of relationships between aging women and younger men in European regions was not confined to the elite. Especially in the early modern era, such associations could be found throughout the class structure. They existed in notable percentages among the peasantry and the working class, who usually formed families for economic reasons rather than romantic ones. Through inheritance as widows or through savings, some women possessed monetary resources; thus they became attractive marital prospects. In preindustrial Europe for aging women peasant proprietors to marry their laborers or for widows who had inherited businesses under the guild system to marry their workers was not peculiar.

There are women who will attempt to hide the ageing process by engaging in vigorous aerobics workouts and adopting judicious eating habits. Others will seek out the skills of top plastic surgeons to supposedly turn back the clock. A well-known California plastic surgeon was revered by one of our female respondents who, in 1985, rattled off how much she had paid for her various 'lifts': for a facelift – $6,000; for rhinoplasty (to reshape what she felt was an 'obviously Jewish nose') $3,000; for lifting her lower and upper eyelids – $3,000; for having her buttocks and thighs 'resculptured' – somewhat more than $5,000. While certain women may attempt to disguise the ageing process with plastic surgery, not all felt tummy tucks and face lifts necessary or sufficient. Some viewed the companionship of a younger man as not only invigorating but fitting, given their levels of energy and vitality.

Felicity Mason, *aka* Anne Cumming, *aka* Britain's 'randy Granny,' observes:

Many of my friends have asked me why my lovers are so young, so I have begun to ask myself the same question. I think the answer is habit, and, as with many habits, I fell into it by mistake. I enjoyed it, and so I continued it. It seems to me harmless, and often beneficial, to both parties ... I have sometimes asked myself, 'Is it worth it?' Perhaps the young men themselves should answer this ... I myself regret nothing and no one ... [As Alex Comfort has noted] 'The first step in preserving your sexuality, which for many people is deeply important in preserving your personhood, is to realize that sexuality can be, and normally is, lifelong in both sexes.' Sex is a highly undangerous activity. Stopping it unwillingly is far more dangerous to health than a little exertion.

A 61-year-old female respondent remarked:

I'm certainly aware that many people, perhaps most, find the idea of an older woman being interested in sex somewhat jarring – disgusting even – and I think for the most part it goes back to when we're kids and can't imagine our parents actually making love.

When I was twenty, I thought that people in their thirties were 'old.' In my thirties, I thought that people in their forties were 'middle aged.' When I became forty, I pushed back my idea of when middle age started because believing yourself to be even middle aged sounded like you were over halfway dead ... When I was fifty I remembered something my mother had told me when she was around the same age. She told me, 'Well, I've escaped the prospect of ever dying young.' I'm not ready for death yet – I haven't lived yet. Not really ...

When you have a young family, you give, give, give. There's no time for yourself. My husband was very involved in his work ... Children – there's always things happening when you have kids and even now, my kids get on me for paying for Dan, but, at the same time, they always seem to need money themselves and they come running to me to provide. It's selfish of them but, as my mother used to say, 'Parents can support ten children but ten children will never provide for one parent.' With the time I have left I feel I'm entitled to support whom I want ...

When we first married, I was willing to accept my husband's rules because he was the one with the money so he called the shots. That doesn't make for a very satisfying relationship. Sexually he wasn't a satisfying partner. He neglected himself. He didn't go to the dentist or brush his teeth and his breath stank, wouldn't wear deodorant – thought that was for homosexuals, had bad eczema. He wasn't a well man, and sex with him was just plain unpleasant ...

My first affair – there were several before my husband died – was a joy to me because the man was just so clean. He always smelled of cologne – to this day, if a man is wearing that same cologne I think of him ... My husband knew the man but never knew I was involved with him. He couldn't stand him, called him a 'dandy,' a 'womanizer,' but then my husband was like that – very critical of everyone, no one was as smart as he was and he had a talent for cutting people down. A master at finding fault with people. This one was this and this one was that ...

I like people. I like having friends and going out. I could never do that when my husband was alive ... I think children can be very selfish and my kids need to grow up quite a bit before they realize that I'm not just their mother. I have needs too.

According to family therapists, one of the most difficult tasks human beings experience is achieving a deeply intimate relationship with another while maintaining a separate and independent identity. Similarly, it has been suggested that while males, by and large, have the easiest time establishing an independent identity, they have difficulty achieving closeness to others. For women, the opposite holds true. Thus, women may care so intensely about achieving emotional closeness with their partner, seeking 'oneness' or 'we-ness' in a relationship and fearing rejection, they neglect their own needs for a sense of self, personal freedom and autonomy, and sexual fulfilment.

In her writings on women's sexual fantasies, Nancy Friday took pains to remind us of the prohibitions against female sexual freedom and self-pleasure – the Nice Girl rules which direct that a woman waits passively for a man to make his approach and declare his love before her sexual arousal is triggered. Similarly, Naomi Wolf suggested that even today, women may define their sexual desire as a reflection of someone else's desire for them. While females learn to act and look sexy, Wolf argued, there is no necessary accompanying knowledge given to them on how to feel sexy independent of male desire.

Susan Brownmiller has commented: 'Love confirms the feminine psyche. A celebrated difference between men and women (either woman's weakness or women's strength, depending on one's values), is the obstinate reluctance, the emotional inability of women to separate sex from love. Understandably 'love makes the world go round,' and women are supposed to get dizzy – to rise, to fall, to feel alive in every pore, to be undone. In place of a suitable attachment, an unlikely or inaccessible one may have to do.'

For Nancy Friday, 'sex is an energy, a source of life to be felt, enjoyed, and also used to fuel and feed all the other areas of our lifes.' She suggested that the practice of sexual freedom grants power along with pleasure, allows women to discover and accept their bodies and, ultimately, to separate out 'sex' and 'love.' This separation of the sex drive from the confinements of love Friday considers essential. Indeed, there is the implicit suggestion that if women were more sexually fulfilled they might also be less emotionally needy.

However, if some would judge the relationship between the gigolo and his Madame Bountiful as unsuitable, the relationship need not be catastrophic. Woman and gigolo may be bound together by ties of financial dependence but ties of sex, affection, tenderness, even genuine understanding, are possible as well. A woman may welcome a relationship in which she is, at least theoretically, the dominant partner by virtue of the power that possession of money gives her.

A 44-year-old female respondent from Toronto, Canada, commented:

I've read or heard all the comments about how women if they're not married must be sickos, or lesbians, or – whatever. I've had my spinster badge for a long time now so it's no new surprise to me when I come across it. That's okay. I can live with it. My – shall we call him a boyfriend? Pet project? – is an artist and he's one of life's luxuries I can afford – within reason. It's nice, comfortable, but I could live without him. I'm a generally positive person and I get along very well on my own. He's a little extra indulgence I give myself, but he's less important to me than I am. There's no competition there. He's strictly minor league, and if he thinks differently well that's his problem ... I know my keeping a man might give some people a good attack of the giggles – 'Hey Martha, don't that beat all?' – but the joke's on them. They're more likely than not the ones in a go-no-where, do-nothing relationship. 'It's Saturday, time to get a pizza and get a video honey.' That's living?

Not surprisingly, our gigolos and Madames Bountiful demonstrate some variations in the thoughts, deeds, and feelings of their erotic experiences. As we have seen, some of our Bountifuls are very forthright about the importance of eroticism in the relationships with their gigolos. However, in general, our women respondents do not talk or write as much about this dimension as do the men. In confronting this difference, we face an age-old issue that has plagued sex researchers. Does this mean that eroticism is less meaningful for our female respondents, or is it generally too embarrassing or private a topic for them to discuss with strangers? The latter explanation would seem inappropriate here for at least two reasons.

First, given the changes of the past twenty-five years, where sex has come out of the bedroom and into modified sex education courses in preschool (as part of 'streetproofing' children against sexual abuse), it is unlikely that a reluctance to talk about it, even in euphemisms, is the answer. That may have been a major problem many years ago, but not now. Second, since these respondents are not only engaging in a socially different relationship, but are willing to discuss it with a relative stranger, it is unlikely that they would be hesitant about disclosing all the dimensions of what is a meaningful part of their lives. We are led to conclude therefore that, while eroticism has a place in their lives, it is not first place. In other words, eroticism is just not as central to the life experiences of our women as it is to our men. In still other words, our respondents are not very different with regard to this point from the general female population.

Neither are the men. We have already noted earlier in this chapter that sexuality or eroticism has long been a central defining dimension of the masculinity equation in Western societies. In light of certain changes in our cultural definitions of masculinity, to be mentioned briefly here and elaborated later, it can be argued that eroticism has assumed an even more central location. As Sam Keen has suggested: 'A "real" man proved himself by impregnating a woman, protecting her against enemies, and providing for his family. Currently, easily available birth control and the desire for small families or childless marriages have removed the fertility test; unpopular wars and nuclear arms have eroded the conviction that we are being protected by the military; and two-career families have taken away the male role of being the provider. As a consequence, men seem enormously invested in pleasing and performing for women. For many men the erogenous zones seem to have replaced the battlefield as the arena for the testing of manhood.'

As noted in chapter 1 and earlier in this chapter, depictions of sexual prowess (either real or alleged) are featured meaningfully by our gigolos in both their discussions and writings. Our men are neither providers nor impregnators. As we will see later, they do offer some measure of protection in certain circumstances. But, of all the dimensions mentioned by Keen, eroticism remains as a central means for most gigolos of demonstrating some semblance of masculinity.

LOVE, ROMANCE, AND INTIMACY

Before we examine women and men in relation to love, romance and intimacy, we should first pause and briefly examine the terms we have been treating quite casually thus far. As every lover can readily attest, 'love' is one of the most difficult of all emotions to articulate or express in simple words. The ancient Greeks did not have just one word for 'love,' but instead distinguished between three different states: *philos*, which referred to a deep abiding friendship and is the derivation for 'platonic' love; *agape*, which referred to an undemanding and self-sacrificing type of love, where the well-being of the other person is more important than one's own, and is the derivation for 'altruistic' love; and *eros*, which referred to a passionate and highly sexualized love. Sociologists generally agree that, when referring to the love between men and women in contemporary society, the preferred term is 'romantic love,' which refers to an admixture of all three.

Romantic love itself is a modern derivative of courtly love, which originated in twelfth-century Europe. Courtly love in its ideal form was both non-sexual and extramarital. By the Victorian era of the nineteenth century, expectations had evolved to the point where it was believed that marriages should be forged more upon the basis of romantic attraction than on that of practical economic or political considerations, and thus love and marriage were united. But the Victorians were still characterized by an essentially antisexual orientation, particularly with regard to 'good women,' and therefore sex in marriage was still considered more in terms of duty rather than pleasure. As we saw in an earlier segment of this chapter, it was not until the present century that eroticism gradually became integrated as a desired and vital component of the idealized romantic love equation within marriage. Lloyd Saxton suggested: 'Contemporary romantic love is visionary, idyllic, imaginative, and adventurous. It is the idealization of beauty, grace, and charm in the woman and strength, courage and sacrifice in the man ... The principal role that each person plays in romantic love is to fulfill the other person's ideal expectations ... They label their emotions as "romantic" and then feel and behave in accordance with "romantic" expectations. Not only does each person idealize the other, but each also tries to fulfill the ideal of the other.'

In keeping with even more recent social changes, and with the recognition that love need not be present within marriage or may be present in the absence of a marital relationship, social scientists and members of the therapeutic community have broadened their focus to elaborate the concepts of 'intimacy' and 'intimate relationships.' Daniel Perlman and Beverley Fehr, in their review of research on and theories of intimacy, concluded that the major characteristics involve a sense of closeness and interdependence between the partners, an experience of warmth and affection towards and with each other, and (perhaps most important) self-disclosure of thoughts and feelings to a level significantly beyond what occurs in everyday casual relations.

Thus, true intimacy blends eroticism, love, and a mutual vulnerability to yield a relatively enduring interdependency between the partners as they play out their roles. This intimacy script provides a basic framework for the relationship between the gigolo and his Madame Bountiful. However, given the fact that this relationship involves a departure from the script in many ways, the participants themselves must negotiate several changes both within and between themselves.

Acting, thinking, and/or feeling in a loving way is closely connected to gender roles in Western societies. As research has noted, males in our society are reared in a way which purposefully encourages the development of competitiveness, independence, and achievement, which are essential for their future occupational success. Attributes such as nurturance, relatedness, obedience, and responsiveness are stressed in the socialization of females. Whereas men are expected to derive their greatest sense of self-esteem from their occupations, women are expected to derive their self-esteem from how well they function in the building and maintaining of heterosexual relationships.

Research has determined that many current common-sense beliefs about gender differences in love do not conform to established fact. For example, while women are often believed and expected to be more idealistic and naïve about the power of love – after a childhood overdose of exposure to the Prince Charming/Sleeping Beauty/Cinderella fairy tales, which stress the importance of love and romance, particularly for women, and promote the belief that once love is found 'they all lived happily ever after' – virtually all of the research which has examined 'romantic idealism' concludes that men are in fact generally more idealistic (and perhaps naïve) than are women. Perhaps *because* of the traditional expectations for females to find success, upward mobility, companionship – in short: everything – within a relationship, women would seem to be more practical and analytical in their approach to love than are men.

According to various studies, men typically fall in love earlier in a relationship than do women – although they may not admit this to their partner until much later – and after the ending of a marital or non-marital relationship, and regardless of who the terminator was, men experience more symptoms of 'lovesickness,' such as loneliness, suicidal thoughts, apathy, alcoholism and other substance abuse, depressions, and other psychological disorders, for longer periods of time. Women are more likely to recover in a shorter period of time than are men. Women are also much more likely to closely monitor an ongoing relationship and to formally end the relationship. In contrast, men are typically unaware that something is drastically wrong in the relationship until they realize they are hearing the weight-challenged lady sing.

Under the sociocultural umbrella of romantic love, numerous psychologists, therapists, counsellors and other clinicians have attempted to differentiate between what may be termed 'healthy' love and 'unhealthy' love. Necessarily mired in value judgments, for there are no objective standards available here, the goal of such attempts has been to differentiate between underlying motivational needs and a kind of love that would contribute to a person's well-being as opposed to one which would ultimately yield negative results to one or both of the participants. Essentially each of these types of love, and their related motivations, has been explicitly or implicitly derived from the theoretical foundation established by Abraham Maslow in his distinction between D- (for deficiency) and B- (for being) love.

In D-love, the individual operates out of a sense of strong need, and seeks a partner who will fill in or compensate for his or her deficiencies. In other words, the search is on for someone to make one whole. But, ultimately, the needs cannot be met by another person, and the needy one exists as, in Maslow's words, an 'empty hole' that can never be filled. In contrast, the 'being' lover is already whole and simply seeks someone with whom to share that wholeness. In very simplistic terms, the difference here is between someone who operates out of a sense of weakness and someone who operates from a position of strength.

A person operating from a motivational condition of deficiency needs would readily accept the cultural dictum that everyone is incomplete of and in themselves, and further that 'everybody needs somebody,' as a once-popular singer used to proclaim. In contrast, a person operating out of 'being' motivation would reject this philosophy and simply seek and/or experience an enjoyable intimate relationship whenever the opportunity presented itself. In Maslow's words: 'B-lovers are more independent of each other, more autonomous, less jealous or threatened, less needful, more individual, more disinterested, but also simultaneously more eager to help the other toward self-actualization, more proud of his [sic] triumphs, more altruistic, generous and fostering.' Maslow himself admitted that the distinction between two types was somewhat artificial and that most people operated out of both sets of needs. What was crucial was the proportional balance between the two. However, this distinction is important for us in so far as it reflects the differing motivations of our Madames Bountiful, particularly in seeking a partner for a relationship of some sort. Those who seek someone to make them whole will approach any potential relationship in a condition of strong need. Those who don't 'need' anyone in that sense of the term will approach potential relationships with a very different agenda. Failing to find a perfect mate will not be viewed as a disaster, nor will any inner pressure be experienced to attempt to recast the imperfect as idealistically perfect. We shall see the consequences of these two different motivational states in chapter 5.

For the moment we can note the example of Charis, a 37-year-old woman who held an important post in the cosmetics industry on the West Coast of the United States and was keeping Larry, a 31-year-old gigolo originally from Vancouver, Canada. Larry would be extremely attractive were it not for his 'pothead' eyes, which seemed chronically red and watery from his continual use of marijuana and hashish. The daughter of a senior executive in private industry; educated in the Netherlands, England, and America; fluent in German, French, Spanish and English, Charis was exceedingly beautiful; when the first author told her that she looked like the actress Jane Seymour she laughed, and remarked that many people told her that.

My first relationship from age eighteen to age twenty-six was with an older married man whom I met in London. I still love him to this day, but I realize it will never work out. He was supposed to come to see me in L.A. about a year ago and like always, he didn't even phone to say what had happened 'till three days later. For three days I hung around the apartment, smoking a cigarette, brushing my teeth, reapplying my lipstick, smoking a cigarette, brushing my teeth, reapplying my lipstick. When he called he told me that his father-in-law had died and for the first time I thought, 'I'm *not* going to say I understand, I come last.' I told him, 'Fuck you, fuck your wife, fuck your father-in-law and fuck this relationship.' No more ...

When I met Larry I could see right through him, but I didn't really mind. So he's a user – so what's new about that? He can't get through to me because I've become as hard as steel. I even know that while he wants to stay with me and marry me, deep down he really resents the fact that I'm supporting him for he tries to play power-sex games with me.

[Power-sex games?] Well, for example, let's say I'm working on a promotional campaign and I won't get home until 4 or 5 in the morning. Haven't eaten all day, just coffee and three packs of cigarettes. Larry will want to screw me when I get home – it doesn't matter if I'm into sex or not – it's like conquering a country. I've been out of his jurisdiction, he has to reclaim me. Or, just before he's ready to come, he always gets on top and pins my hands down with his hands – it's almost a necessity if he's going to be able to come.

Sometimes I'll get so mad but I'll just think to myself, 'Larry, you dumb prick. You really think you've landed the goose that laid that golden egg, don't you? You *think*.' There's no way I'd ever marry that jerk – I'm just biding my time. I wrecked my life with one creep and now it's hard to find a guy who is not married ... But Larry is just an interim step. For a long time I didn't have the courage to break it off with my first lover. I tried once and went back and told him that 'Half of you is better than none of you' and asked if we could get back together again. I'd see him whenever he'd want to see me. This relationship is on *my* terms.

Approximately four months after this conversation took place, the first author had a telephone call from Charis. The relationship with Larry was over.

He would phone me at work when I was working late, whining ... how he missed me and why didn't I make more time for him, that he was lonely blah, blah. I don't need that crap – *I'm* working and he's not, so I want encouragement ... I just was steaming. When I got home there he was, all big sad puppy dog eyes ... That was it.

I told him, 'Look, I'm the one who's working so don't give me this crap about how I should feel sorry for you.' He started doing this old routine about how he felt bad that his writing wasn't going well but that he couldn't write when he got depressed. I had it. I told him, 'Pack your bag loser, you're history.'

[How did he respond?] I couldn't believe it. He said, 'But I thought you loved me. You couldn't have loved me as much as I love you. What happened? I thought everything was all settled' – and get this – 'you were going to take care of me and *worship* me.' And *then* the jerk has the gall to say, 'I guess that means you're not going to give me the C and C 36 [a type of boat] that you promised me for my birthday.' Can you believe the nerve of the man?

In their exposition of a then-new theory of male adult development, Daniel Levinson and his co-researchers introduced the concept of 'the Dream,' which referred to a mental construct created during early adulthood that had the 'quality of a vision, an imagined possibility' and contained 'an imagined self having a variety of goals, aspirations and values, conscious as well as unconscious, and pursuing his quest within a certain kind of world. A man's Dream is his personal *myth.*' This Dream becomes a kind of guiding beacon for structuring and eventually measuring the success of one's adult life.

In her book *Women and Love,* Shere Hite also referred to 'the Dream,' in which a large majority of her female respondents indicated that they believed that love should be the most important part of their lives even though a significantly large majority also indicated that their current love relationship was no longer the centre of their lives, essentially because their vital needs were not being met by their partners, a point we shall explore shortly. Most respondents in Hite's study, regardless of their current marital status, also indicated that 'they have not yet found the love they are looking for, that they hope their greatest love is yet to come.'

In the search for an intimacy partner to complete the Dream, women appear to focus upon certain desired behaviours of men. In addition to the relevant status characteristics that are part of the mating gradient, the focus of the moment here is more upon the matter and manner of personal style. A number of researchers in recent years have noted that women and men are most comfortable with, and prefer to engage in, different kinds of loving actions. Indeed, the sexes even differ in terms of what they consider to be loving behaviours.

In general, female lovestyles emphasize the following: self-disclosure of one's innermost thoughts and feelings (especially intense feelings such as love, fear, sadness); expressions of affection (especially verbal intimate-talk); active listening (not just listening but also giving feedback to let the speaker know he or she has been heard); being mutually vulnerable (trusting each other enough to risk being reciprocally disclosing of fears, weaknesses, and anxieties – a consequence of being non-judgmental regarding what one hears).

Males, in contrast, generally prefer doing things together (shared physical activities, but not including housework); spending time together (just being in each other's presence, as in watching TV together); providing things (advice, financial support, fixing things around the house); and sex (giving and receiving). With regard to sex, it is not surprising to observe that sexuality – a multidimensional phenomenon – is associated with multiple layers of meaning. In addition to being an enjoyable physical release and an instrument of power and control, sexuality also provides males with a means of expressing love, affection, and a sense of close intimacy. For those men who feel uncomfortable with verbal terms of endearment, eroticism provides a behavioural mechanism for them to demonstrate their love.

The different lovestyles reflect stereotypical expectations of traditional gender roles, with the female style being more 'expressive' and the male style being more 'instrumental.' In more colloquial terms, it has often been suggested that female intimacy is of the 'face-to-face' variety, while male intimacy is of the 'side-by-side' type.

Sociologists have noted that women rather than men are apt to be assigned responsibility for the caretaking and monitoring of relationships not only within intimate relationships but also within both the private and public sectors of their employment. They 'mother' – soothing and restoring hurt feelings, keeping conversations going with a minimum of interruption; and anticipating and responding to the emotions of anxious/unruly/disruptive family members, relatives, customers, and clients.

The male style conforms to the general male-role expectations which stress being independent, autonomous, and in control of themselves. This style also complements general social expectations for males to perform the provider role. Providing things implicitly suggests that the 'providee' (stereotypically the female), and not the 'provider,' is more needy and somehow dependent, not able to function independently. There is little risk of appearing to be interpersonally vulnerable when being a provider for others. The two lovestyles thus reinforce power differentials between the sexes. They do so, of course, by ignoring the many things women provide for men in the context of an intimate relationship.

During the 1940s, 1950s, and 1960s, social scientists of all persuasions were almost unanimously in agreement that these two lovestyles (although they were not referred to as such) were complementary and even sufficient for a relationship to function smoothly. We had an apparent division of labour of love which somehow implied that such a 'division' was essentially equally and mutually beneficial for both intimate partners. Such benefits were mainly assumed, not empirically tested. But a more recent and growing body of research findings has indicated that such a division is particularly problematic when each partner expects the other to reciprocate in kind.

In studies such as Shere Hite's, we find respondents giving eloquent expression to female dissatisfaction with a lack of reciprocity from their male partners. While it is unclear whether the dissatisfactions themselves or the giving voice to them is relatively new, women have been sustained in their search for the Dream of reciprocated love by the therapeutic revolution which, unwittingly, endorses the female lovestyle as the ideal style of intimate relationship. As we will see in stark detail in a later chapter, one of the keys to the success of the gigolo lies in his ability to reciprocate that desired feminine lovestyle. The gigolo, at least in the initial stages of the relationship, focuses great attention – whether sincere or feigned – on his partner; talks with her; listens to her; and is affectionate and disclosing of his fears, anxieties, and wants (especially economic). But, as we shall see, he offers – and demands – much more.

A 53-year-old married grandmother observed:

I find that, in today's society, people realize that they have a right to certain basic things – like happiness, and love and a compatible sexual partner – and it's not just the luck of the draw. When I was a girl, if you married a man who was a total disaster, you were expected to stay with him – even if he beat you – because, after all, you were his wife. As a young married woman, one of my neighbours was a lovely woman married to an eminent lawyer, and our two families would get together, our children played together – we were fairly close. One day their daughter told mine that she didn't want to go home, that her daddy was hitting her mother and she was scared. My daughter came to me and told me and I really didn't know what to do. I didn't know what to do. These people were our friends – successful people – not the type you associate with this kind of thing. To believe it meant that I should do something and I really didn't know what I could do. Nowadays there's places women can go, but in those days, what could you do? Ask her to move in? That wouldn't wear very well with my husband and I didn't really have any evidence that he *had* hit her. Just my daughter telling me that her friend had said ...

I think women now feel that they are entitled to be happy, to take charge of their lives. More so than before at any rate ... Sex with my husband had never been, shall we say, 'exciting'? It's like eating for him, something that he feels a need for but there's no real finesse or sensuality involved. He's hungry so he eats. A sandwich. He isn't about to go into the kitchen and whip up a souffle ... He is a good man but not the type of man who you can sit down and discuss things with. He doesn't want to know ...

When the kids were small, I'd get so lonely with him gone all day and no one but the kids to talk to. I'm sure there's a law of the universe that states that whenever a mother of young children gets on the phone to talk, that's when her kids suddenly have to be right there. On the spot. Screaming. So I talked to no one ... And if there were problems during the day, I couldn't talk to him when he came home. He was tired and would start screaming at me that he couldn't take it, he was tired and he had bigger things to worry about. 'Deal with it' he'd tell me. Well I had 'dealt with it.' I just needed someone to talk to. And who else are you supposed to tell? ... I don't know for sure if he's had affairs in the past, but I wouldn't doubt it. I don't particularly care if he did ...

I don't accept this idea that marriage has to be based on having sex *only* with one man for a whole lifetime. Why? At my age I don't think I have to worry about getting pregnant. Why think of sex as like drawing water from a bucket where after you take a cup there's less left to enjoy? It's more like drawing water from a well – if there's a steady source supplying the well, there's more water ...

I married at 21, which was late – god, my mother was sure I'd be a spinster! – but I'm not the same woman now as I was then. I've grown and what I want now is not the same as I wanted then. I'm a woman now not a 21-year-old girl, and the things that are important to me are just that – important. Why shouldn't I take care of my needs? I'm important too. I think women hurt themselves when they just dedicate their whole life to their families. Kids grow up and move away and unless you stake a claim for your own happiness, you have nothing in the end. Just bitterness. Kids need a healthy mother and a man loves a healthy wife. In my case – and I'm not speaking for all women – having a lover keeps me healthy. And sane. It can't be helped ...

When I was 20 I never liked getting my picture taken, I just took pictures of the kids. I always thought my hair wasn't combed well enough or I wasn't dressed right ... Sometime in my late thirties it hit me, well, this is it. I'm not going to look any better than I do now, what am I waiting for? Not only was I shying away from the camera but from life itself. It was a start of a new era for me ...

I won't pretend that all of my relationships have been wonderful. Some have been total disasters ... Men like having relationships with married women because it's safe in a number of ways. You can't demand much and they give even less! But that's okay if you enter into a relationship with your eyes open ...

I'm comfortable with my husband. We've had our ups and downs but I would never leave him. Where would I go? We share a beautiful home, children, grand-children – there's a lot of memories there, good and bad memories, but memories that we share in common. And that's part of my life but not all of it ... My first lover was a young man I met at a political rally. He was beautiful in a classic way, fine-boned, sensitive face. We started talking and I felt myself drawn to him for his spiritual qualities as well as his looks. He was obviously a great reader, and the things he talked about – religion, philosophy, man's relationship with nature, the meaning of genius – they were mesmerizing. What a contrast. When the man opened his mouth and talked, I couldn't help but fall in love with him. He talked *to* me. Not at me. Not across me. Not 'Do you want me to pick up the kids?' or 'Where would you like to go for holidays this year?' My husband is supposed to be one of the most financially astute men in his field but, when he talks about his work, it's all gibberish to me. I appreciate that he has the Midas touch for making money, but when he talks about business I find myself plastering a smile on my face and just nodding every so often. I'm just not interested ...

When I first met him [her lover] he smoked and when I told him I was allergic to smoke, he put out his cigarette and apologized. That was before smoking was a social no-no. To this day my husband smokes in the house and tells me 'It's my home too' ...

When he [her lover] asked me if I wanted to go for a coffee or lunch sometime I felt I was entering into something dangerous, that if I said yes, it would mean saying yes to a lot more than a coffee ... On our fourth meeting, we arranged to meet at a mall – he didn't even own a car – and I felt like a girl when he saw my car, waved, and ran over. That was the first time we kissed and what a kiss! It started out as just a peck on the cheek, but as he drew back, he smiled, very gently took my face in the palm of his hands, and it became a beautiful, thrilling kiss. I felt like I couldn't think, hear – like the world had stopped and the only thing that was real and alive was what was happening right inside my own car ...

[What did the man do for a living?] Live off women. *You're* surprised? So was I! I think he did actually have some sort of training though I'm not sure what it was in. I *think* it was fashion marketing or something like that. Designing jewellery. I did talk my husband into giving him a fairly large amount of money to open up an art gallery but that capsized fairly quickly. He had no talent for business – just for giving women the business ... Sometime in the past he had worked as a private fashion consultant, helping women put together their wardrobe for a new season. I'm not sure exactly how that works but anything is possible. I gave him a small fortune by 'hiring' him to redecorate several rooms in our house. That was totally nonsense but it gave us an excuse to spend a lot of time together without my husband wondering too much about certain cheques ...

His background? The story changed so much that I didn't really see any point in trying to pin him down. For what purpose? ... When I've had the doldrums I've been to counselling and there's really only two things I got out of it. One: that you can't be responsible for other people changing. You can't help them or change them. You can only figure out what makes you happy and help yourself. And two: that in this day and age, if you want someone to talk to you, you have to be willing to pay for it. He was giving me what I wanted – best marriage counsellor I've ever been to ...

CINDERELLAS, CINDERFELLAS, AND LOVE

Implicitly, all gigolos recognize the utility of the model of courtly love and the legacy of the courtier or troubadour in enacting their role. Although fundamentally adulterous in conception, the ideal of courtly love attempted to reconcile spirituality with sensuality. Essentially the term 'Mistress' as used by the troubadours referred to the exalted Lady who was the wife of some high-born man. At least theoretically the term did not signify a sexual relationship; rather, it was used synonymously with terms such as 'My Lord' and testified only to the man's adoration. In seeking to win the Lady's approval the troubadours wrote poems, and the knights fought battles in her honour. By requiring that men be faithful in their love, and content to love without hope, the religion of courtly love offered a model of courtesy to women that Chaucer depicted as a distinguishing quality of *gentillesse*.

However, gentility to women, like any social gesture tried and found effective, became a social expedient. Adoration had the potential of becoming glib flattery, and attentiveness inconsequential gestures done simply out of a concern for form. Thus, the letters of Lord Chesterfield to his son offered the paternal wisdom that women were simply 'children of a larger growth' and that 'a man of sense only trifles with them, plays with them, humours and flatters them as he does with a sprightly, forward child.' Similarly, he advocated the strategic use of flattery: 'Nature has hardly formed a woman ugly enough to be insensible to flattery upon her person ... An undoubted, uncontested beauty is, of all women, the least sensitive of flattery upon that head; ... she must be flattered upon her understanding.' Lying as gentlemanly conduct?

In a essay entitled 'The Rolling Spheres of Falsehood,' Oliver Wendell Holmes depicted 'truth' as a cube of stainless ivory, and a 'lie' as a sphere. He noted that 'the spheres are the most convenient things in the world; they roll with the least possible impulse,' while 'the cubes will not roll at all; they have a great talent for standing still, and always keep right side up.' According to Holmes, the dictates of timidity, good nature, and polite behaviour conspire in their insistence 'that truth must roll, or nobody can do anything with it': 'and so the first with her coarse rasp, the second with her broad file, and the third with her silken sleeve, do so round off and smooth and polish the snow-white cubes of truth, that, when they have got a little dingy by use, it becomes hard to tell them from the rolling spheres of falsehood.' While Holmes suggested that timidity, good nature, and the rules of polite behaviour encourage the creative reshaping of truth, Tennessee Williams bleakly observed that, in contemporary society, 'Mendacity is a system that we live in. Liquor is one way out an' death's the other.'

Philip Kerr, editor of *The Penguin Book of Lies*, argued:

In all walks of life we are exposed to lies to a degree unparalleled in our history. Millions of people watch television shows like 'Dallas' and 'Dynasty', whose families would rival the Borgias with their lying. Our best-selling newspapers – the *Sun* and the *National Inquirer* – have made a cult not just of the tall story (this would be forgivable if it were merely lying for lying's sake), but of the lie that is intended to sell more newspapers. The proliferation of electronic media means that not only politicians, but advertisers are able to lie to more of us, more powerfully than ever before ...

Ethics, honesty and truth are no longer perceived to be of such fundamental importance in public life because they are not perceived to be of much importance in private life either. Our sensitivity to lying has decreased in inverse proportion to our greater greed and selfishness, because that's the kind of society we have. It may even be the kind that we want.

Whether or not one agrees with Kerr's markedly pessimistic view that lying can be seen as a more universal language than Esperanto, the 'little white lie' that lubricates social interchanges ('Have you lost weight? You've gained? No!'; 'You're Methuselah's mother? I would have sworn you were his sister!') can become an all-encompassing whitewash when painted with the purposeful brush of the gigolo.

It would seem that the culture of romance itself not only allows for but promotes fraudulent misrepresentation as to both the nature and the intensity of the emotions felt by persons within an intimate relationship. If one is at loss for words – if 'raunchy,' 'suggestive,' 'amorous,' 'apologetic' won't do – one can always buy someone else's and send them in the form of a greeting card. In general, Western culture is deluged with books, magazines, movies, and media communiqués which extol love as either a palliative to all life's trials or a utopian panacea. If one's partner is a music lover, send her the appropriate compact disc – there are songs to fall in love to, be seduced to, despair to and commit suicide to if and when one's 'baby' does not love one any more. If nowhere else, the lover can always find a commiserating reference group in stereophonic sound.

Although the tendency in romantic relationships may be to privatize emotions and gestures, creating inside jokes with hidden meanings and coining private terms to refer to each other's anatomical parts, the props of a love affair are seldom unique to a particular relationship, and gestures of love can become clichés of romance. There is no polygraph or lie-detector test to determine the truth of a loving remark, of the sincerity of a gesture within an intimate relationship. While the florist's advertisements direct us to 'Say it with flowers,' the meaning of what exactly is being said is negotiable. If red roses are interpreted as an intrinsic symbol for romance and love, the symbols could simply be emotionally empty gestures. Indeed, it often seemed that gigolos within our sample who prided themselves on 'understanding women' or 'knowing what women want' simply evidenced knowledgeability in wielding the props of romance.

Peter, a 29-year-old bisexual gigolo, commented:

I first met her [his current Bountiful] while working out of an escort agency in California. The hours were good, lots of time to be on the beach ... She phoned up the agency and wanted someone to go with her to this party where her ex-husband would be with his new wife. After that, we started to go out for all her friends to see me and I decided that I could do better on my own than with the agency ...

[How do things typically proceed?] On the first date I'll tell them I'm a graduate student and not just an escort – that I'm just doing this to make ends meet, dividing up a package of hot dogs, two a day, so I'll have enough to eat all week without starving – that will make a woman open her purse pretty fast. When I take her back to my place, it looks the part – books around the room. I read a lot and tell her I'm housesitting a friend's place, or staying with a friend till I get enough money to find my own place. It usually works. Then I'll take her to bed and give her the thrill of her life. Kiss her everywhere, tell her how beautiful she is, give her the best head she's ever had ...

If she doesn't want to go to bed, I tell her I'd like to give her a massage or just have a bath with her. I'll bring candles into the bathroom, a bottle of wine, nice glasses and I'll just caress her. I don't have a huge cock, just six and a half inches, but I can do more with my talking than other guys can do with nine inches ...

While most discussions of pornography note the varied and sundry ways in which it misinforms and fetishizes the nature of sexual relationships, such discussions are limited to male pornography – the varied and sundry 'men's magazines' that run the gamut of explicitness: *Playboy*, *Penthouse*, *Hustler*, *Screw*, *Fuck*, and the like. There is, however, as Robert Stoller observed, 'a pornography just for women' – modern-day romance novels – and it would seem that these assuredly also create a fantasyland of sexual illusions that provide fertile ground for enhancing the effective manoeuvrings of the gigolo.

Ira Reiss noted that the dominant theme of male-oriented erotica is 'a fantasy story of women who are sexually insatiable and are thus incapable of resisting any type of male sexual advance.' This combination of strong female erotic desire, coupled with a lack of resistance, precludes the possibility of a male's sexual advances being rejected. In contrast, female-oriented erotica features a male who is ultimately romantically obsessed. It is 'love or attraction of an intense personal sort which in this female fantasy renders the male helpless to resist. He must pursue her, give her what she desires, and treat her properly.' One notes that even if the male protagonist is ultimately incapable of being rejecting, he is none the less still performing the active role of pursuer.

In her 1982 book, *Loving with a Vengeance*, Tania Modleski observed: 'The success of Harlequin Enterprises, Ltd. [a publisher that is typically credited with being the originator of the mass-market romance series concept] ... has been extraordinary. Since 1958 when the first Harlequin Romance was published, over 2,300 titles have appeared. In 1977, Harlequin had 10 per cent of the paperback market in North America, selling 100 million books on this continent and 50 million more in countries like Israel, Germany and Holland ... The novels are now translated into sixteen languages. The readership is, apparently, entirely female and comprised of women of all ages.' According to *The Harlequin Story: Harlequin Fun Facts*, Harlequin romances were published in more than a hundred countries in twenty-one languages by 1988. 'If all the words of all the Harlequin books sold last year were laid end to end, they would stretch 1,000 times around the earth or 93 times to the moon. That's a distance of one quarter of the way to the sun.' Reportedly Harlequin books are so popular in Japan that a Japanese dictionary of modern language defines 'harlequin' as 'a word describing romantic sensations.' The average reader was female, between 25 and 49; 40 per cent of female readers were college graduates and typically willing to spend thirty dollars per month on romance novels.

In the beginning years, Harlequin Romances were simply updated versions of the classic fairy tales for women: the stories of Snow White, Cinderella, and Sleeping Beauty revisited. In their conclusions they are interchangeable – the beautiful maiden is rescued from a dismal fate by a handsome prince. The prince on a white horse may be replaced by a successful doctor in a Mercedes, but the prototypically tall, dark, and handsome stranger rescuing the beautiful girl, and the happily-ever-after ending, were the trademark formula of the Harlequin romance. Such novels were, avowedly, 'clean, easy to read love stories about contemporary people, set in exciting foreign places.'

Over the last two decades, the range of Harlequin romantic fantasies has expanded. Although incest, adultery, and abortion remain taboo, there is now an assortment of 'bodice rippers,' as they are termed in the publishing industry, to appeal to differing female erotic tastes. As Louise Kaplan commented, Harlequin is now capable of 'providing loyal readers with an inviting assortment of romantic delights.' She elaborated:

The basic Romance series stresses a clean, fresh approach to sex, where heroines are virtually innocent to start with and metaphorically so after the seduction; sexual tensions are subdued and passionate language kept to a minimum. Moving a tiny notch up the scale of erotic tension, another Harlequin series prides itself on realism, 'in which the sensual scenes evolve naturally and reflect shared feelings and desires central to the characters' sexual involvement.' With Superromance we begin to encounter mature heroes and heroines who appeal to the more 'passionate reader.' Another series depicts current values and thus high levels of sensuality and very aggressive heroines; yet another 'delivers suspense and romance in perfect harmony.' A highly sensuous group of romances written for 'today's woman' dispenses 'the promise of love – the guarantee of satisfaction.' The Special Editions series recognizes the seamier side of erotic life and bravely 'tackles sensitive issues' while simultaneously embracing the traditional 'romantic ideal that love can, indeed, conquer all.' And not to neglect women who still need to have their romance ribboned by traditional values, there is a series that brings 'the reader all the wonder and magic of the heroine's discovery of a love that lasts a lifetime.'

While the traditional Harlequin-based story outline continues to reinforce traditional power imbalances within relationships, the general trend among all erotic romance novels over the 1970s and 1980s has shifted towards the depiction of a more balanced power alignment and the development of more self-motivated and autonomous female central characters. These females are increasingly portrayed as successfully asserting their needs and desires economically, erotically, and romantically.

More recently, romance novelists and publishers have begun addressing the needs and fantasies of aging baby boomers. Indicative of this new trend, *The Bridges of Madison County*, a romantic tale of 'no-fault adultery' whose central characters are in their mid-forties and beyond, has already sold approximately three million hardbound copies – signalling the presence of a large audience who want to believe in, and read about, the sexy romantic activities of the middle-aged. Leading authorities in the print and electronic media predict that more books, and movies, will soon be generated to tap into this new market. Love and romance are clearly not the exclusive province of the young.

As Carol Thurston noted of all erotic romance novels: 'If a large dose of autonomy, equality, cooperation, and compromise, as well as love and respect, are now integrated into the ideal male-female relationships portrayed in these stories, it is largely because readers have demanded it. And even if some or all of that is still a fantasy in their lives rather than a reality, it is indicative of their aspirations.' Still, at the end of the story, Harlequin and other erotic romances provide the female with a husband. The imagery and importance of the message for women – namely, the need for an intimate relationship – remain constant.

We would not suggest that all of our female respondents desired that a husband emerge from a kept-lover relationship, but the construction of illusions through the maintenance of such a relationship did seem important.

Some of our women desired a gigolo as a life-support system to resuscitate or make comfortable an existing marriage, an 'erotic comradeship' – to use the phrase Barbara Denning adopts – in which unfulfilled needs can be satisfied without having to leave the existing marriage. For some married women, the relationship allowed them to seemingly obtain revenge on a husband who could be having an affair or was inattentive or seemingly indifferent. Yet others felt that they could and were entitled to 'have it all.'

Similarly, the reasons that single women kept gigolos varied. Some felt their behaviour prudent, maintaining that they did not have sufficient time or interest to devote to a relationship or to invest in seeking out a desirable man through more conventional means. For some women it seemed that one of the pleasures of the Madame Bountiful role was that it allowed the woman to be more wife than a girlfriend but less wife than a wife. Others subscribed to the traditional notion that a woman is incomplete without a man and were timid about attending parties or engaging in activities on their own. Some wanted sex; others a status prop – the gigolo as the latest in a succession of disposable commodities designed to impress; The latter group conspicuously spent and conspicuously consumed. And, of course, there were those who steadfastly denied that their lover was a gigolo (although the man had blithely identified himself as such in our interviews), insisting to others and to themselves that he was simply a decent, caring fellow down on his luck, who would lead them, the moment he got back on his feet, into the fairy-tale romance they had dreamt of.

As George Orwell noted long ago, 'human beings don't only want comfort, safety, short working-hours, hygiene, birth-control and, in general, common sense; they also, at least intermittently, want struggle and self-sacrifice, not to mention drums, flags and loyalty parades.' The Dream is variable; accordingly, the gigolo as performer must be flexible enough to generate a wide variety of interpretational frames for his actions and for the development of a relationship, able to impose interpretations or definitions of events onto his behaviour, and dramatically shape the meanings the effects he helps to create have for the viewer. In short, he must read his audience's emotional state and be able to integrate his actions to align with his audience's point of view.

As one of our gigolo respondents commented, 'She must come to see me as unique, worth more to her than her mother, father, children ... What I have to do is find the right button to push. All the rest happens in her own mind.'

But, can he pull it off? Can a man really be empathetic? Aren't women the sole possessors of 'women's intuition'? And what exactly is 'intuition'? Social scientists conceive of intuition as an example of empathy, and conceive of empathy as a quality of being sensitive to, and capable of experiencing, the *feelings* of others. Research findings on the subject are somewhat mixed, with the results seeming to depend upon the type of study used to obtain results. About the only trait which has found consistent support for female superiority is being sensitive to non-verbal cues in real-life situations. Women in general are superior to men in general in picking up and correctly interpreting the meaning of such things as body and facial language from the person they are relating to. Assuming that this is an accurate example of empathy, we are now faced with the task of explaining why.

Some scientists have suggested that women are 'naturally' more empathetic than men, while others, like Nancy Chodorow, attributed the supposed gender difference in empathetic skills to the difference in gender socialization. Chodorow argued that because females remain connected to their mothers, while males must separate from their mothers in order to establish an independent identity, girls emerge 'with a basis for "empathy" built into their primary definition of self in a way that boys do not ... with a stronger basis for experiencing another's needs or feelings as one's own (or of thinking that one is so experiencing another's needs and feelings).'

However, even if the demonstration of empathy is more customarily assigned to females, all human beings have this capacity. As Carol Tavris has argued, there is little evidence to suggest that differences in empathy are the result of innate or biological predispositions. Research has demonstrated that 'men who were training for or working in occupations that required nurturance or sensitivity were as good as women at decoding nonverbally expressed emotions. Whether this finding can be attributed to the effects of practice or to the self-selection of unusually sensitive men for such occupations is difficult to know.' Even if the men were unusually sensitive before entering training, the fact remains that men *can* be as empathetic as women. Whether they choose to be, or need to be, is another matter. The evidence would suggest that most men don't.

Tavris stressed that empathy should be considered a learned trait that demonstrates not a 'female' skill but a 'self-protective' skill that is characteristic of subordinates or those who have lesser amounts of power. In an original and interesting study, Sara Snodgrass paired women and men in work teams, randomly assigning a man or a woman to be the leader. Her findings reported that the person in the role of subordinate or follower was more sensitive to the non-verbal signals provided by the leader than vice versa, regardless of whether a woman or a man occupied the role of leader or follower. This observation led Snodgrass to conclude that phrases such as 'women's intuition' should more fittingly be termed 'subordinate's intuition.' As Tavris commented, 'Men, like women, manage to develop empathetic skills when they need to read a boss's temper and intentions for their own security and advantage.'

Because his position, at least in the initial or inception stages of a relationship, places the professional gigolo in the role of the subordinate who must attempt to 'read' and interpret the behaviour of his potential partner, he cannot afford to ignore the woman's behaviour, proximal cues, and so on. Rather, he must engage in an active attempt to decipher them so as to understand and predict the potential behaviour of his desired partner.

A Californian gigolo who lives in a Marina del Ray condominium given to him by a past lover noted: 'I express interest in *them*. I ask for *their* opinions, about *their* kids, about *their* phlebitis, how *they* feel, what *they* want to do. Most women don't care to talk about sports or politics – if they do, fine, we talk about it, but most women would rather just talk about themselves.'

Similarly, the following letter from a woman who became tangentially involved on the sidelines of a gigolo/Bountiful relationship suggests that, even when partnered by one Bountiful, a gigolo is never truly out of circulation.

Two years ago in June, my husband and I met a 72-year-old woman and her 35-year old male companion. They had parked their travel van in the camping grounds of —— Beach (near us), and it was when the elderly woman was out walking on the Saturday evening that we met. To cut this part of the story short, my husband can get too friendly and hospitable at times and he invited the couple back to our home. They stayed 3 nights. In fact, my husband insisted they could use the downstairs guest suite. At the time, I never gave it much thought that the pair slept together.

At the end of June this year, I wrote to the Florida couple an innocent, sweet type of letter saying that I meant to have sent them a Christmas card but had temporarily misplaced their address. I was absolutely amazed to receive a telephone call in August from the woman while visiting nearby telling me that she and Gordon would like to visit us during September.

In mid-September, I received a telephone call from the fellow. They arrived at our home around 10:00 a.m. It was while on this 12-day stay that I really got to know Gordon (the gigolo) and Delores.

Apparently, Delores is a 74-year-old widow (been widowed for 5 years) and well-off financially. She met Gordon 4 years ago in Florida. Delores used to sit out on her verandah most mornings doing her handicrafts. Many times Gordon would walk past her place on his way to work and casually say, 'Good morning – nice day,' and that was that. Then one day he walked up to her, got acquainted and asked if she had a room for rent. Anyhow he rented a room, then shortly after she went to Ohio to visit her sister and was gone for three months. It was on her return that one thing led to another and from there on, they slept together. She bought a nice, roomy travel van as he got her interested in the travelling bug.

It seems to be their lifestyle – travelling many months of the year all over the U.S.A. and Canada and going home for Christmas so she can entertain her bridge club lady friends.

Gordon and I became very attracted to one another by the second day of their visit. Let's face it, he is most handsome with his curly black hair, dark brown eyes, gorgeous tan, beautiful body (he doesn't work out) *but* it was his wonderful personality and the way he expressed himself and told such funny stories of his adventures that won me over. Of course my being a married woman with three sons meant I had to face reality. Nevertheless, Delores was very jealous of Gordon and I because we had such a lot in common.

During their stay it didn't take me long to realize how Delores operated. Regardless of her wealth, I considered her cheap the way she sat back, preferring anyone but her to pick up the tab. She would give Gordon his daily beer money, and money for his film to be developed. Somehow he got the old gal to pay out $2,500 for camera, lenses, etc ... The old biddy kept complaining to me how Gordon is supposed to be going through all her money, using her credit cards and how broke she was getting. So the night before they left, Gordon approached me in the kitchen and showed me close to $15,000 in uncashed traveller's cheques. He said, 'Ilse, you call that broke! She's $!#$?! cheap!!!'

Gordon and I had some lengthy talks together as the old gal generally went to bed by 11:00 p.m. She was usually mad at me because Gordon preferred to night owl with me. We became incredibly close ... He admitted that she doesn't cook him meals on a regular basis ... From what he said, he would be taking Delores back to Florida (the van is in joint, he managed to get her to do that) then he wants to head back to Wisconsin to pick up the remains of his life – getting a job – so at least his self-respect can return.

I had to tell him that if the roles were reversed – that if I were with an old man – *IN NO WAY* would I let an old buzzard use his money as a power ...

I'm telling you how it is. I felt sorry for Gordon at times because he couldn't even sneak out to the van to read a book. She wouldn't let him out of her sight.

Anyhow, I found Gordon to be quite honest in every way. I was touched when he packed our kitchen cupboards full of canned crab, sardines, wild rice, etc., etc. In his own way, he knew how Delores' cheapness irritated him. He took beautiful close-up photos of all our children, which I'll treasure forever.

Likewise, I felt very moved by Gordon when he telephoned me on the Wednesday afternoon (the day they left) asking me to meet him at the school where I picked up my oldest son. He wanted to say goodbye to all my children (I had the other two children in my car) and he gave them $5.00 each. Gordon was in tears, and I too joined him that way.

He's a divorced man with two teenage offspring. It's unfortunate his wife won't let him see his kids ... No matter what Gordon is, we will continue to be close friends. He gave me his address in care of his mom in Wisconsin and we both intend to communicate.

Pointing to Delores's 'stinginess' and ignoring the fact that Gordon had 'somehow managed' to obtain joint ownership of the van, a $2,500 camera, to stock her larder with goods presumably paid for by Delores, this correspondent demonstrates the self-imposed myopia that sometimes is the result of believing in the reality created by a gigolo. Certainly her claims that Gordon was never allowed even the privacy to read a book does not mesh with her claims of late nights spent 'night owling' with him, or with his ability to absent himself to meet for a final goodbye with her and her children. However, whether or not his claim of being forcibly 'estranged' from his children by his ex-wife is real or contrived, Gordon certainly seemed to demonstrate awareness of what our correspondent would define as admirable and/or thoughtful.

Empathy and emotion work (the ability to manipulate one's emotions) become role prerequisites within the professional skills of the gigolo. Even if at a later date these qualities may be discarded as no longer useful or necessary and/or are viewed as somewhat superfluous – as is most obviously the case in the role of the Sweetheart Swindler – they are viewed as essential in the initial stages of a relationship. Even if the empathy is deliberately cultivated and contrived, the demonstration of it would seem to be integral in reading the target's dream and in attempting to fulfil it.

Thus we appear to have conflicting and contradictory pressures operating upon our gigolos and Madames Bountiful simultaneously. On the one hand, females in general are less idealistic and naïve than males in evaluating their intimate relationships. On the other hand, the mass media are filled with romantic images designed to keep the ideal Dream alive and well. These images would appear to establish a state of expectation that perhaps '*he* is the one,' and could provide, as we stated before, fertile ground to be exploited by the gigolo. As we will see in chapters 5 and 6, that expectation appears to allow for at least the initial success of gigolos, but does not necessarily mean that the success will be maintained over a long period of time with all Madames Bountiful.

Males in general have been found to be more naïve and idealistic about love but are also generally found to be lacking when it comes to providing the kinds of loving behaviours that will meet the romance expectations of females. Yet, we know that males can meet those expectations, when the situation demands it, and our gigolos appear to have learned their lessons well. In doing so, however, they find themselves acting in ways that do not currently meet existing masculine ideals, which appears to exert pressures within the gigolos to exert their masculinity in other ways. We shall explore some of those ways in subsequent chapters.

4

Access to Power: Conventional and Unconventional Channels

In the 1969 film *Midnight Cowboy*, actor Jon Voight played the role of 'Joe Buck,' a handsome and somewhat simple young man who travels from Texas to New York with the intent of satisfying the myriad wealthy women who are supposedly 'begging for it.' His background is only hinted at through the flashbacks of memories he has while travelling in the magical coach of the Cinderfella, the inter-state bus. Unlike Cinderella, who, the story goes, was the daughter of a wealthy man and who was only rendered destitute upon her father's death as a result of the greed and jealousy of her stepmother, Joe Buck has in his background neither any association with wealth or access to it. Rather, fragments of reminiscences suggest a licentious 'grandmother' who took him into her bed with or without her various new beaus, who gleefully administered enemas to him, and who left him positioned in front of the television set with a TV dinner in the oven when she would go out on dates. Perhaps the greatest tragedy revealed by Buck's reminiscences is the fact that his relationship with his grandmother, squalid as it was, seems to be fondly recalled.

Claiming 'I'm not a real cowboy but I'm one helluva stud!' to various people he desires to impress, Joe Buck obviously believes in the American Dream of freedom of opportunity. Adorned with a black cowboy hat, fringed leather jacket, and cowboy boots, he parades up and down the streets of smart shopping areas, asking well-clad women for directions to the Statue of Liberty. His strategy proves to be markedly unsuccessful. Despite his belief that he will make enormous sums of money and become the sought-after plaything of rich women, he instead finds himself a street hustler servicing whichever male or female selects him. Living in a condemned building until it, like his dreams, is razed to the ground, selling his blood and stealing to supplement his meagre earnings, he believes himself to be on the road to success after receiving $20 for his services from a wealthy woman he meets at a Greenwich Village party and then being referred by her to one of her friends. However, his ambition to achieve success as a 'stud' is not to be fulfilled; he forfeits his chance and murders a homosexual 'trick' for the paltry sum of the $57.60, what it will cost him to take his dying friend to Florida by bus.

Although, to the best of our knowledge, none of our respondents had committed a homicidal act, by and large it would seem that in our world today there are many more 'Joe Bucks' than there are 'Julian Kays.' While many of our respondents embarked on the road to supposed riches with aspirations of finding a Princess Charming, access to wealth and power for fortune hunters is still constructed along class lines. While it is relatively easy for a man to become a 'Sexpert,' the role of a Clydesdale – typically aspired to by the vast majority of our male respondents – proves more elusive.

We noted in an earlier chapter that the female 'gold-digger' would seem to be less of a social pariah than the male 'fortune hunter.' Indeed, it is interesting to note that in his earnest tome, *The Gold Diggers' Guide: How to Marry Rich* earlier referred to, Thomas Schnurmacher pointedly acknowledged that 'the larger portion of this book is intended for women who want to marry rich' and was eager to name a gilded laundry list of eligible bachelors – including, 'out of respect,' Haroldson Lafyette Hunt who had passed away eleven years before the book was published. In contrast, Schnurmacher asserted that 'men who want to find rich women ... are a vanishing breed,' devoted a scant three-quarters of a page to the topic of 'gigolos,' and largely restricted his commentary to noting that gigolos rarely looked like Richard Gere and that the women who keep them rarely looked like Lauren Hutton (who played the role of the senator's wife in the film *American Gigolo*).

Despite his presumption that gigolos were 'a vanishing breed,' we may note that Schnurmacher seemed to contradict himself by his apparent eagerness to identify certain men such as Philippe Junot as simply 'a Parisian social-climber ... [who] charmed his way right into the Royal Family of Monaco to marry Princess Caroline ... [and whose name since their divorce] has been linked with such notables as Cornelia Guest, the debutante Darling of the New York society columns.' Nevertheless, Schnurmacher informed his reader – male or female – who 'must want to marry rich or you would not be reading this book' that, 'first of all, in order to marry rich, you must locate yourself in areas where the rich tend to congregate. It is easier for a stewardess to marry someone in first class than it is for anyone travelling economy to attract her attention. Not everyone can be a stewardess of course. That is why it is essential to familiarize yourself with the natural habitats of the wealthy and powerful.'

Much of Schnurmacher's book was devoted to gossipy details of mind-numbing trivia. For example, he breathlessly rhapsodized about the benefits to be obtained by positioning oneself backstage at rock concerts: 'If you think that hanging around backstage hoping to meet your rock idol is likely to work, you're absolutely right. That's how Jerry landed Mick. It also worked for Linda Eastman who bagged Paul, and Patti Hanson who bagged Rolling Stones' Keith Richards. Ditto to Alana Hamilton and Kelly Emberg, both of whom shacked up with Rod Stewart ...' Although he devoted almost three pages to a tourist's guide to the 'foreign bar scene' where millionaires may be found – for example, the Member's Club in Caracas, Club 29 in Istanbul, and 'Diana's, located in the fabulous Oriental Hotel,' in Bangkok – Schnurmacher seemed undaunted by the fact that all the places he recommended are private, members-only clubs. Apparently, after having managed to find their way to Bahia, Brazil, his stout-hearted readers will undoubtedly find some method to wangle their way into the Hippopotamus club.

Is finding a wealthy patron as easy as Schnurmacher would suggest? We noted in a previous chapter that the family has undergone a number of transformations over the sweep of history, particularly from the 'institutional' to the 'companionship,' and more recently to the 'pluralistic,' family forms. Researchers contend that the family changes have been and are experienced unequally across all class segments of societies. In general, the most fertile ground for change tends to be found in the middle classes. The upper classes, considered today to comprise the top 1 to 5 per cent of the population (depending upon the researcher) in terms of social, political, and economic power, have generally been most resistant to change. Within the upper classes we continually find a strong emphasis being placed upon extended kinship ties to the point where the classes themselves come to resemble a modified extended family.

By and large, living individuals are simply considered to be the current embodiments of the family and the guardians of all that the family represents. They carry the name, refurbish the reputation of the family itself in the social circles that matter, and maintain or improve upon the material wealth. Joseph Kahl suggested that the upper class is characterized by 'graceful living.' Depending upon geographical location, a distinction may be made within the upper class between two important subcategories –

literally an 'upper-upper' and a 'lower-upper' class. In everyday terms, these distinctions are approximated by the phrases 'old money' and 'new money,' or the 'nouveau riche.' The terms themselves are inadequate to encapsulate all of the distinctions that are important. In particular, they tend to emphasize money itself and imply that the crucial factor here is to be calculated in terms of amounts of material assets when, in fact, the emphasis should be placed upon the descriptors 'old' and 'new.'

Many publications have reprinted a portion of an account written during the early 1950s by an anonymous 'inside' author and first included in a textbook by Ruth Shonle Cavan:

Every family is proud of its heritage and talks freely about its ancestors. In almost every home on the wall in a prominent position is the family tree, appropriately framed. Many families have a crest, which is also framed and which is used on stationery, rings and so forth. The *Social Register*, a book containing only the names of people who are considered upper-upper class, is used as the telephone directory. Very seldom does anyone in the family find it necessary to use the regular telephone directory. Outsiders are made to see that they are not wanted. Money has *nothing* to do with getting into the *Social Register*. The criterion used is the family background. If the family dates back for many generations, if the members belong to exclusive clubs, and the daughters have always made their debut, the family is considered upper-class. 'Outsiders' who suddenly make a lot of money are not readily accepted. The family background is what is important and you can't change that – you either have a good family background or you don't.

The 'many generations' referred to in the quotation varies from country to country and from community to community. In all cases, however, 'old money' comes from 'old families' who have been living in, and frequently provided leadership for, the community for usually at least four or five generations. This passage of time allows for the development of a family history and the traditions which living family members are expected to uphold. 'New money' families, who may in fact possess more material wealth but have no history to draw upon, are frequently engaged in activities designed to manufacture traditions to be passed along to future generations. Some of these activities include conspicuous and ostentatious consumption, designed to publicly display wealth and announce 'we have arrived.' Such 'gold-carded' or purposive displays of wealth are considered to be quite vulgar and pretentious by those in higher and lower positions in the status hierarchy.

Things are either 'U' (upper class) or ferociously 'non-U' to their upper-class social evaluators. Indeed, terms such as 'Sloane Ranger' (which uses as a reference point the posh location of Sloane Square in Chelsea, London), 'county set,' 'preppie,' and 'BCBG' ('Bon Chic, Bon Genre') convey a sense of the identifiable and privileged sameness or commonality among those of the upper class. Thus, that inimitable guide to social snobbery, *The Official Sloane Ranger's Handbook*, relegates the 'non-U' to a position of scorn as a walking gaffe or *faux pas*. By transgressing the sacred taboos by word (referring to 'horse riding' instead of 'riding') or deed ('The man who threw a snowball at St Moritz'; 'The man who asked for a second helping at the Lord Mayor's Banquet'; 'The man who coughed at the first night'), the *nouveau riche* supposedly identify their ineligibility for inclusion. Indeed, the *Handbook* notes that Sloane speech is in itself 'codified, archaic and a trap to the unwary' and that one of its 'paramount' principles is élitism, 'they shall not pass.'

The society columnist and millionaire playboy Taki commented on the differences between the rich and the *nouveau riche*:

The behaviour of the truly rich has no parallels with that of the merely rich. An aged, but accurate, story has the late Duke of Marlborough descending the stairway of a country house one morning, waving his toothbrush in the air, and complaining that 'The damn thing doesn't foam.' It happened that the Duke's manservant had recently died and the new one was unaware of the fact that toothpaste had to be smeared on the brush before his grace used it.

The merely rich buy art; the truly rich buy artists ...

The British upper-class code term 'p.l.u.' ('people like us') serves to indicate social discrimination and approbation among the highest echelons of society, where consideration of background, breeding, blood, and bloodstock are rarely ignored. As *The Official Sloane Ranger's Handbook* (which identifies Princess Diana as a 'supersloane') observes in its discussion of 'WRM' ('what really matters'): 'Rangers are "we" people, not "me" people. Background means a lot to a Ranger. They want to establish it – name, rank and number – when they meet someone ... Family/school/university/job/connections should all be made clear; ambiguities are worrying to the highly tuned. Hence the eternal Ranger queries: "You live in Shropshire ... do you know the Sloane Rangers?" or more politely "You live in Shropshire ... you must know the Sloane Rangers." ... *Family* is a magic word (as in Royal); it means more than the sum of individuals' (emphasis in original).

As George Orwell suggested long ago, if all men are created equal, some are thought more obviously equal than others. Finding a wealthy potential patron may be as easy as Schnurmacher suggests; however, making her acquaintance and then becoming her financially supported lover involves overcoming substantial social-class and other related obstacles. But as we shall see, surmounting them is possible if one understands the social terrain.

PEDIGREE CHUMS

While both money and power often provide or purchase freedom, such freedom in the upper class does not automatically extend to the selection of an intimate partner. In an earlier chapter, we introduced the reader to the 'mating gradient' which attempts to dictate, or at least shape, the mate-selection process in modern Western societies. The underlying theme of that gradient is an expectation that intimate mates will be unequal in many ways. While the gradient applies within most of the social-class hierarchy, it does not apply with equal force within the upper class (although it may apply in a limited form in those areas which contain the two upper-class subgroups). Within the upper class, the dominant expectation is that mates will be of relatively equal status. Today, as in the past, marriage within the upper class more so than any other class involves the union not of two individuals, but of two families, or more accurately, the incorporation of a new member into the fold of one family.

Upper-class families, then and now, still tend to believe that the family has a strong vested interest in intimate relationships formed by one of their members. Such relationships potentially have great possible repercussions for a family's standing in the community or society and for family wealth. In consequence, the upper class would seem to exercise far more control, supervision, and regulation of dating activities than do other classes. Much of that control is expressed in physically placing adolescents and young adults in locations such as schools, clubs, and work settings where they will meet 'the right kind of people.' Even older adults are subjected to close scrutiny and attempted manipulation of emerging relationships, and the participants themselves typically sense a restriction of freedom of choice of their intimate associates.

Once again, Britain's Royal Family serves as a prototypical example of these pressures and of the second-guessing that occurs when a family member appears to go outside of what is considered to be an appropriately preselected pool of eligibles. The abdication of King Edward VIII to marry the American divorcée Wallis Simpson is perhaps the most obvious example of selecting a partner considered to be unsuitable and the social ramifications of putting pleasure before duty.

In the 1950s, the relationship between Princess Margaret and Group-Captain Peter Townsend caused consternation because of the fact that 'Townsend was ... a divorcee and in the 1950s a divorcee simply couldn't consider marriage with a princess of the blood, especially when the Princess's sister was titular head of the Church of England.' On 31 October 1955, the famous statement of Princess Margaret was issued: 'I would like it to be known that I have decided not to marry Group-Captain Peter Townsend. I have been aware that, subject to my renouncing my rights of succession, it might have been possible for me to contract a civil marriage. But mindful of the church's teachings that Christian marriage is indissoluble, and conscious of my duty to the Commonwealth, I have resolved to put these considerations before any others.' Her action would seem to attest to the importance within the upper class of placing duty before pleasure in the selection of a marital partner. In contrast to the Edward VIII/Simpson situation, Margaret's action suggests concern with family honour, with self-denial as the means by which a higher ideal is pursued.

Similarly, some have suggested that, in the United States, the Kennedy family are considered the equivalent to British royalty. The scathing condemnation of Jacqueline Kennedy, the widow of assassinated president John F. Kennedy, for her decision to marry Aristotle Onassis is telling. Despite the fortune possessed by Onassis, he was considered to be less than a suitable partner for the widow whose husband had ruled Camelot. Many observers clearly did not agree with the apparent trade-offs Jacqueline Kennedy made in evaluating Mr Onassis as a suitor. Outside observers, however, may never know what alternatives she felt existed at that time.

The Prince of Wales once commented, 'I've fallen love with all sorts of girls – and I fully intend to go on doing so. It's very important to find the right partner. In my position, obviously, the last thing I could possibly entertain is getting divorced.' Prince Charles recognized that his marriage was to serve not his own interests but rather those of what was referred to as the 'family firm.'

Throughout the 1980s and 1990s, an enormous amount of scrutiny, both public and private, was afforded the 'woman who would be Queen,' Diana, and to a lesser extent, the 'woman who wouldn't,' Sarah. In these and like situations, it would once again seem that more is considered than simply whether or not a potential companion makes the individual happy. Rather, the overarching issue is obviously one of whether the 'outsider' will fit in and exemplify and ultimately pass on the family traditions unsullied.

With a divorce and two separations among the Queen's children in one '*horribilus*' calendar year, some have begun to question exactly what those family traditions are. Ruth Shonle Cavan noted that, because of differences in gender longevity, the ultimate head of an upper-class modified extended family is usually a woman – literally, a matriarch – to whom family members defer in cases of major family decisions regarding descendent members such as the 'type and place of education, occupation and selection of the spouse.' One would not wish that the selection of a prospective mate result in the matriarch echoing Queen Victoria's famous remark that 'we are not amused.' Once again, we must stress that the Royals are being profiled here simply because they provide highly visible and well-known examples of many of the issues facing families located among the upper strata of any Western society.

ELEGANT OPPORTUNISM

Marriage across the invisible but potent class lines may be possible in an attempt to either purchase a 'family history,' or to maintain a financially impoverished one. The desired outcomes, however, may not always be realized by all parties. Thus the 1897 marriage of Anna Gould, heiress and daughter of financier Jay Gould, to Comte Paul Ernest Boniface de Castellane seemed precipitated by the social snobbery of the bride's family, eager to capture the social coup of the year by marrying their daughter to a French (impoverished) nobleman, and the mercenary calculation of the groom who assuredly recognized a financial windfall in marrying the heiress. In the five years of his marriage, Castellane went through Anna's $3-million yearly income and created a debt of $4.5 million; however, in his autobiography, Castellane asserts:

In justice to myself, I can honestly affirm that Miss Gould's fortune played a secondary part in her attraction for me. She was, in many respects, unusual – and the unusual has always fascinated me! I was never a fortune-hunter, and although I shall probably be given the lie, I can only repeat, and urge in my defence, what is perfectly true, that during the twelve years of my married life I never attempted to feather my nest at the expense of my wife. True, I spent her millions, but ... I have actually represented a more than profitable investment for her ...

Neither Anna Gould nor myself reckoned with the serious difference between our nationalities and our upbringing ... There is no doubt that the sudden possession of great wealth awoke in me the prodigality inseparable from most of the old nobility, whilst in Anna it only seemed to develop the economic Scotch instincts ...

When I married Anna Gould, I laid the world and its possibilities at her feet. When she divorced me, she kicked them inconsequently away!

His critics, however, are less admiring of Castellane than he was of himself. Thus, Lynn Ramsey has remarked: 'Boni's infidelities, well-known in Paris, were only part of his cruel treatment of his wife. He made her suffer for the 'sacrifice' of having married a woman he considered ugly. It was said that he made Anna pin a $1,000 bill to the bed curtains everytime he made love to her.' Whether 'fortune's prize' or 'fortune-hunter,' Castellane recognized that his desirability centred on his ability to furnish the Goulds with an entrée into European society. And, after his marriage to Anna faltered, he once again capitalized on this asset with other wealthy American women.

Although Castellane's title was genuine, con men – and women – have long known the snob appeal of aristocratic titles and self-professed ties to the rich and well known of high society. As the father of the 'marrying Mdivanis,' three brothers who became notorious for marrying heiresses (one heiress, Louise Astor Van Allen, married two of the brothers in sequence), bemusedly remarked, 'I'm the only man who ever inherited a title from his children.' The Mdivanis invented for themselves a background as Russian princes in exile after the Russian Revolution who, as the story went, had lost splendiferous estates, palaces, and jewels. However, their claims and the strategy itself were hardly original.

In the 1870s the French peasant woman Thérèse Davignac acquired $14 million by falsely claiming that at 'a later date' she was to be the heir of $20 million supposedly left to her by the American industrialist Robert Henry Crawford; in the early 1900s Cassie Chadwick replicated Davignac's earlier con and enjoyed millions, buying diamonds by the carton and hosting $100,000 dinners by claiming that she, supposedly Andrew Carnegie's illegitimate daughter, stood to inherit $2 million. Indeed, the hapless Jay Gould had earlier been victimized by his awe of aristocracy when 'Lord Glencairn,' *aka* 'Lord Gordon-Gordon,' duped him out of half a million dollars. Informing the wealthy, but uneducated, Gould of his close relationship with Queen Victoria, the daring missions he had performed on her request as her supposed confidant, and the undying gratitude and favour with which the monarch subsequently viewed him, Gordon-Gordon contrived a splendid past which overwhelmed Gould and made him an easy victim. After all, the word of a gentleman should be security enough – shouldn't it? – for any person approached to merge financially and/or emotionally with him.

Within this same vein, the 'gilded prostitution' of transatlantic marriages, which typically involved American heiresses and impoverished but titled British gentlemen between roughly 1870 and 1920, offers a fascinating area of exploration for it suggests both the difficulties experienced by high-status women in seeking relational partners and the social judgments made as to the gender-appropriateness of the women's and men's conduct. The term 'gilded prostitution' was coined by William Stead, a journalist and self-appointed moral vigilante, who was best known for exposing the white-slave traffic between Britain and the Continent. In his book, *The Americanization of the World*, he noted: 'it was rather a degradation of the idea of American womanhood to regard the American girl as a means of replenishing the exhausted exchequer, a kind of financial resource, like the Income Tax. Indeed, it is not too much to say that when there is no love in the matter, it is only gilded prostitution, infinitely more culpable from a moral point of view than the ordinary vice in which women are often driven by sheer lack of break.'

Although it seems as if Stead's manifest intent was to denounce the exploitation of American women, he implicitly denounces them – and not the men they married – as the prostitutes. As Maureen Montgomery noted in her study of status, money, and transatlantic marriages: 'the absence of a love relationship and the presence, instead, of crude social ambition meant that the more extreme critics of Americans would have regarded them [the women] as 'gilded prostitutes.' In contrast it seems that the peers who entered upon these marriages were better able to retain their reputation, possibly because they were seen to be sacrificing their personal interests for the sake of salvaging their estates.'

Stead's disparagement of these women as prostitutes would seem to tell us more about the values and concerns of society at the time of his writing than about the character of the women and men who entered into these types of marriages. As Montgomery suggested, the social intolerance indicated may be seen to reflect censorious attitudes towards women and the perceived threat such wealthy Americans posed to the patriarchal order. Moreover, it also suggests that, for certain well-bred men who may claim only their social pedigree as a negotiable asset, effort expended towards 'marrying well' may be of strategic importance in advancing or solidifying their social position.

Within contemporary society, it would seem that the mystique of a title still retains a potent appeal, at least for some individuals. According to *Luxury Lifestyles: The Riches of Royalty*, a magazine which panders to 'royal watchers,' titles are a 'marketable commodity.' The magazine instructs its readers that

anyone who wasn't born into nobility can still become royalty – if they have enough cash to buy a title and the savvy to avoid scams. Expensive German titles have been offered for sale by Christophe Paikert, a Munich stockbroker, who arranges brief marriages between nobles in need of money and people willing to pay to become an aristocrat. He set the cost of becoming a prince or princess at $1 million, while the title of count or countess was $100,000. British titles, however, can be had for much less, from $10,000 to around $150,000. The average price of British royal titles, which are routinely sold at London auctions, is about $18,000.

But buyers should beware of scams involving phoney titles. A recently exposed scheme involved a mail offer from someone claiming to be an Albanian trading attache selling the titles of count, duke and prince. 'It's baloney,' said a real Albanian minister. 'We don't have dukes."

Another danger is that people may talk – and you might not like what they're saying. That's what happened to the Countess Henrietta de Heornle, who ruled the social scene of ritzy Boca Raton, Fla., when the town newspaper reported that she and her husband, Count Adolphe, bought their titles for $20,000. The miffed countess threatened to cut $22 million in charitable donations out of her will, but changed her mind after townspeople staged a public rally to show their support.

However, should the allure of a title be great, one need not be brazen about it – one may, like the transatlantic bride, acquire it through more subtle measures. As Taki observed in his 'Living Well Is the Best Revenge': 'The truly rich never pay for anything, as somebody else is always happy to do that chore. And as everyone knows the super rich never carry money with them ... Nor are the truly rich ever lonely, even when widowed. In the case of truly rich women, losing a husband usually means picking up a European title. There are thousands of noble prospective bridegrooms waiting in the wings ...'

Within the constraints of the upper classes, a woman may have inherited wealth and the splendid paraphernalia of the extremely rich and still not realize herself, or have validated by persons significant in her life, that a role other than that of being a dutiful wife and gracious hostess awaits her. This type of assumption seems echoed in the comments of Ferdinand Lundberg in his 1968 work *The Rich and the Super Rich*. Commenting on the importance of inheritance as a primary factor in becoming part of the super rich, he observed:

Great wealth ... is no longer ordinarily gained by the input of some effort, legal or illegal, useful or mischievous, but comes from being named an heir. Almost every single wealth-holder of the upper half of 1 percent arrived by this route ... 40 per cent of the top wealth-holders are women. Now, while some women have garnered big money by their own efforts ... few women have been even modest fortune builders. Women simply do not occupy the money-making positions in finance, industry and politics. But they have been heirs ...

Women, owing to their inexperience with financial affairs, are generally poor estate managers, Hetty Green [who transformed a $10-million inheritance into an estate worth ten times that amount during the late 1800s] notwithstanding. They are more easily victimized by specious schemes, fail to take advantage of obvious opportunities, and so tend to drop out of the group and to be under-represented. Men are usually financially more capable and their greater staying power entitles them statistically to a larger representation among the heirs than women.

While Lundberg's assumptions about women's cupidity and gullibility are less salient in today's society, they may have been applicable in the not-so-distant past.

It was Barbara Hutton, granddaughter of the Woolworth-chain founder, who was first called a 'poor little rich girl,' and there assuredly have been numerous others since. Despite her being a bright, forthright girl who might have become successful in her own right, the option of independent endeavour for her did not apparently occur to anyone. After all, young ladies of impeccable breeding did not dirty their hands with business. Rather, upon inheriting $42 million on her twenty-first birthday, Hutton was introduced into New York society, rushed from one fashionable soirée to another, and married a succession of seven husbands, 'the worst assortment of men this side of a police line-up,' the majority of whom were enthusiastic about spending as much of her money as possible during the short period in which they were around. Schnurmacher directed us to:

Take Barbara's first husband. Prince Alexis Mdvani had a family tradition of marrying well ... On her wedding day, she wore diamonds and pearls worth more than a million dollars. But the Mdvani affair cost Barbara about two million dollars, which was a lot of scratch in the mid-thirties.

Barbara married her second husband a year later, proclaiming that her search had ended. She described her romance with Count Kurt Reventlow as 'safe and sure.' This romance cost Barbara over four million dollars before it finally petered out ...

Barbara married husband number three, Cary Grant, because she was impressed that he actually enjoyed working for a living ... [A]las ... Barbara and Cary were divorced. For the first and last time in her matrimonial life no money changed hands.

Ignor Troubetzkoy, a Lithuanian royal was husband number four. That marriage didn't work and neither did marriage number five, to the enormously talented Porfirio Rubirosa. This Dominican playboy stayed married to Barbara for less than three months before he returned to the arms of Zsa Zsa Gabor. Rubirosa did, however, receive a two-million-dollar settlement from Barbara ...

Her sixth husband, Baron Gottfried Von Cramm, used Babs' money to fluff up some castles. His divorce settlement: two million dollars.

Husband number seven was the last one for Barbara. His name was Prince Duan Vinh Ha Champassak. The [sic] were married for some two years. Duan was a master of understatement. He once said 'Barbara gave me more than four million dollars. She gave me love.' Oh, please!

More recently, Abby Rockefeller, daughter of David Rockefeller, re-called her reaction when her father informed her that she would one day inherit $25 million: 'When he was finished, I said that I thought that I would prefer not to have it. I said that what I did not like was the idea of it hanging over me, affecting my future and my present, affecting my re-lations with people, and affecting my relations with him. I said that it was just bad for relations. I thought we had enough to deal with between us without this sort of thing.'

As Cyndi Lauper sang in the 1980s, 'money changes everything.' Nev-ertheless, few find great wealth an alarming-enough prospect to impel them to forfeit their chances to obtain it. Rather, the obverse would seem to be true.

In a short story entitled 'The Secret of Success,' published in *Smart Set* magazine in 1922, David Ogden Stewart addressed himself to examining the various strategies adopted to achieve career success. In this story, his young hero read all the how-to-achieve-success manuals, worked hard, was the first to arrive at the office in the morning and the last to leave at night, reviewed his work in his free time and still failed to better his po-sition. However, he did eventually become president of the firm – by mar-rying the president's ugly daughter. This unusual story of the path to suc-cess suggests that, despite the changing times, for some, marriage was still more pragmatic than romantic in its origins.

The question then, as now, might be: how does one translate fiction into fact? We may note that Schnurmacher's book truly offers little more than a telephone directory of expensive-jewellery appraisers, art galleries, butler and chauffeur agencies, plastic surgeons, make-up artists, hairdressers, health clubs, high-priced hotels, and investment brokers; halfway through his book, as if dazzled by his topic, Schnurmacher seemed to ignore the fact that his readers had yet to capture the goose that would lay for them the proverbial golden egg. However, for the eager wannabes of today, never fear, a self-help book has arrived in the form of *The Poor Boy's Guide to Marrying a Rich Girl* by one Brian Ross Duffy.

THE POOR BOY'S GUIDE TO BIG-DAME HUNTING

Announcing one's desire to embark on a career as a gigolo or fortune hunter may precipitate a host of contrasting reactions, ranging from amusement to antipathy; within the world of self-help, the desire for information – on whatever topic – is rendered legitimate. As an 'explicit instruction manual for achieving health, wealth and happiness,' the self-help guide offers readily accessible advice for the interested, bemused, or simply curious, while making the search for information as unproblematic as possible. The self-help book 'attempts to communicate in a lively, interesting, readable and simplified manner' knowledge that purports itself to be of 'immediate and practical use to the reader.'

In her 1978 book *How to Get Whatever You Want Out of Life*, Dr Joyce Brothers devoted an entire chapter to 'How to Make People Do What You Want.' The secret to becoming a 'power person'? Manipulation through the 'most effective psychological tools' – 'flattery, rewards, guilt, and fear – in that order.' 'The ability to manipulate effectively is the key to power,' Brothers, ever the humanist, unabashedly trumpeted. Exploit your connections: 'It's whom [sic] you know that counts.' Behave like the most obsequious of apple-polishers: 'Everyone has an inferiority complex … zero in on those areas of real concern to the person being flattered … bolster his ego in areas where he may feel unsure.' If that fails, Brothers advised, 'It is relatively easy to manipulate people through guilt.' Practise the art of 'sensitive listening techniques.' Be scientific about it – utilize Brothers's 'Quick List Technique.' Create your own 'manipulative handbook' on how to gain power, friends, and success through the fine art of manipulation.

The guide for the beer-budget boy with champagne tastes is yet another in the self-help genre and, like all self-help books, *The Poor Boy's Guide to Marrying a Rich Girl* is clearly addressed to the lay reader. The author, Brian Ross Duffy, was described as a 'graduate of the University of Virginia ... an M.B.A. from the Harvard Business School' and an investment banker in New York City. These background features would seem important in documenting Duffy's credentials as an expert big-dame hunter. Indeed, Duffy conspicuously acknowledged in his preface such notables as Cornelia Guest, Patty Hearst, Cosima von Bülow, and Caroline Kennedy, gave 'special thanks to Princess Stephanie of Monaco and her charming sister Princess Caroline' as well as 'other rich girls (too numerous to name).' According to Duffy, each female referred to (a veritable who's who of rich girl–dom) 'was a constant and considerable source of information and inspiration.' That Duffy himself was not married to a rich girl, or to anyone else for that matter, would seem a somewhat jarring commentary on the viability of his method; however, he excused this seeming disqualification with a claim about his own extreme fastidiousness, 'Regrettably, I haven't found the right rich girl yet, although I've come close on many, many occasions. I have, in fact, always been extraordinarily difficult to please ...'

Unabashed by his singlehood, Duffy took pains to emphasize that wishing, hoping, and apple-polishing your way to the status of pampered housecat is a viable and practicable strategy. He was eager to pepper his how-to book with the names of men who, supposedly, had lived out the dream and included an 'Honour Roll' of 'success stories' containing such notables as Prince Philip; Charles Spittal Robb (the husband of Lynda Bird Johnson, former president Lyndon Johnson's daughter); Claus von Bülow; Stephen E. Smith (husband of Jean Kennedy and father of headline-attracting accused rapist William Smith); Bernard Shaw (the ex-policeman and bodyguard who married Patricia 'Patty' Hearst two months after her release from prison); and Rafael Lopez Sanchez (who married Paloma Sphynx Picasso, daughter of Pablo Picasso). Ever helpful, Duffy even included the addresses of the men who appear on his Honour Roll (Prince Philip c/o Buckingham Palace, Buckingham Palace Road, London SW1, England) in the event, one muses, that the aspiring poor boy desires to go directly to the source to solicit additional help. Prince Philip as Agony Auntie? One can only speculate on how many aspirants flooded the palace mailbags seeking personal answers to how to find a woman and make her keep you.

For those still unconvinced that they may travel through the golden arches and not simply arrive at McDonald's, Duffy also included a section on women who are/were 'legends' for 'their generosity towards poor boys.' As in his section on the Honour Roll, famous names flowed easily from Duffy's pen as he identified such women as Barbara 'Babs' Hutton, 'whose seven husbands ("the magnificent seven") were typically the beneficiaries of both generous dowries and settlements'; Doris 'Dee-Dee' Duke, who 'married twice, both times to well known playboys'; Marguerite 'Peggy' Guggenheim, who according to Duffy was 'addicted to poor (albeit artistic) boys' and who 'managed to have warm and sharing relationships with dozens of poor boys, including painters Yves Tanguy and Max Ernst, and writer Samuel Beckett ... ending his writer's block once and for all'; and Christina Onassis, who had 'the private resources to make even the poorest boy happy.'

Duffy offered strategic pointers on such essentials as the major events in a rich girl's life, sources of introductions, and identifying a rich girl's probable major while at college, and stressed the importance of positive thinking and a spirit of iconoclastic improvisation. For example, Duffy stressed the value of attending horse shows and pointedly noted that Captain Mark Phillips's interest in horses 'led directly to his meeting, courting, and marrying Princess Anne of the United Kingdom.' According to Duffy, 'Mark [Duffy was nothing if not familiar] lived by the motto that "the horse is the poor boy's best friend."' Similarly, benefits for cultural organizations (the ballet, symphony, or opera), special causes (runaway youth, homeless persons), and, most important, benefits for 'the rich girl's favourite diseases' were pointed to as profitable spawning grounds where the lowly frog may be transformed into a prince. Duffy was evidently knowledgeable about the importance of propinquity in the establishment of relationships.

Echoing the importance of 'Sloane speech,' referred to earlier, the poor boy's guide additionally furnished such helpful measures as a dictionary of terms likely to be bandied about the world of the wealthy, which, he suggested, could potentially frustrate the wannabe's attempts to fit in. How else could a poor boy deconstruct the meaning of such rarefied terms as 'Mummy,' 'nanny,' and 'philanthropist'?

Enjoined to emulate the 'Jermyn Street look' of the 'society boy' – 'tailored suits, velvet dinner jackets, emblemed blazers, ascots, silk fourcade ties and many, many scarves,' the wannabe was also instructed to analyse, synthesize, and integrate Duffy's assorted 'rules of behaviour.'

For example, when 'building a close and enduring relationship' with the targeted female's 'mummy,' the neophyte was cautioned to

(1) Never challenge Mummy. In many a rich girl's house, Mummy knows best.

(2) Display honour and respect for Mummy and Mummy's many friends
(3) Constantly compliment Mummy:
    'Silk taffeta was made for you.'
    'I love your chest.' (Not *her* chest, the Regency chest.)
    'The Cancer Ball was a great success.'
    'I enjoyed meeting Halston.'
    'You photograph so well.'
    'Maybe you should be a decorator.'
(4) When visiting always bring a house present, however small.
(5) Mummy is committed to appearances. Always be neat, well groomed, and well dressed.
(6) Never swear in front of Mummy.
(7) Always praise Mummy's food (she may not have cooked it, but she probably chose the menu, the chef, or the caterer).
(8) Always be prepared to discuss her varied interests, whether they include horse breeding, decorating, or the newest disease.
(9) Dance with Mummy whenever you can, but *don't* hold her too close.
(10) Never interrupt Mummy. When Mummy speaks, everyone listens.

Finally, Duffy provided an identifying list of one hundred surnames 'synonymous with wealth' (for example, Harriman – descendants of the robber barons; Ford, DuPont – the 'first true American industrialists'; Hearst, Pulitzer – publishing; Cargill – grain; Land – invention; Packard – ingenuity; Getty, Hunt – natural resources, typically oil; Morgan – 'merchant families that trade money'; Coors, Busch, Bronfman, Stroh, Kennedy – beer and alcohol) with the caveat given to the 'serious reader' that 'the list is not designed to be all-inclusive. The serious reader will want to undertake his own research.'

If Duffy's work sounds reminiscent of Ted Peckham's strategies, presented in chapter 1, this should not be all that surprising. Knowingly or not, both prescribe a code of conduct modelled on Oscar Wilde's famous dictum: 'Take care of the luxuries and the necessities will take care of themselves.'

A 32-year-old man, formerly a model, talked to the first author over coffee at London's Richoux restaurant:

You can trade titles for money but it's very difficult to find a woman with both. On the one hand, if a woman is titled, she can introduce you to a better class of people and that is always useful. On the other, if she has money, who was it that said money can buy a lot of love but love can't buy money? ... Arab women, no, they aren't good because they're chaperoned and under the control of their husband. If they're not Arab and just married to a Saudi prince, they're not going to take the chance of throwing it all away unless they're very stupid ... [Who would be] The perfect lover? Soraya Khashoggi [ex-wife of Adnan Khashoggi who received the world's largest divorce settlement of over one billion British pounds]. No breeding unfortunately, and a total slag, but she moves in the right circles.

A Canadian gigolo from Toronto rued the dearth of 'eligible women' he was meeting:

There's two types of women who can afford me. The first type is old money, good background, knows the right people. The drawback with that type is that she's probably old. If she's young she's not going to pay for a gigolo and anyhow her parents will get in the way. [How?] Jacques, for example. His girlfriend's father told her that if she went on holidays with him, she could wave any money they had goodbye. As well, young, really rich girls are incredibly stuck up. Unless they're trying to get back at their parents, they won't give anything worth giving ... The second type of woman is one who saves her money under her mattress and buys Canada Savings Bonds for her old age. If she lets me teach her how to enjoy life and have a good time, we can have a lot of fun. Chances are she's *nouveau riche* and doesn't have any social connections, has never even stepped into Holt Renfrew, thinks Sears is a great place to shop and her idea of a big holiday is a trip across to Buffalo to visit her sister. That she has to change. No way am I going to waste time on a polyester princess driving a Pony with those spongy curlers in her hair.

For some gigolos who prided themselves on pandering to 'high society,' life was to be lived in accordance with an invisible how-to-guide of social snobbery. One gigolo gushed over his preferred haunts:

In St Martin [in the Caribbean] Las Samanna is the place to stay – that's where Mick Jagger and his crowd stay. Or, the 'Rock resorts' – they're hotels owned by the Rockefellers, Little Dix Bay; there's gorgeous places in Senegal and Corsica -very exclusive of course, the Relais resorts or the Romantic Inns – all are quite splendid. In Europe? Well, the George V and the Ritz of course are good places to meet women – you can go for an elegant meal at Focquet's – that's still popular – or Michael Miecer's, Jamin's isn't bad. In London, I love Claridge's, but you won't find any English women there ... Spain – the Castillo de Santa Catalina in Jaen or the Conde de Gondomar are nice; the Conde de Gondomar is my favourite in Spain because it's convenient if you're yachting ... My favourite is Le Club in the Mediterranean – oh, where is it? You know – it's just down the coast from where Brigitte Bardot is ... (London, 27-year-old gigolo)

Eager to relay the details of golf in Augusta, summers in Southhampton, and weekend house parties in aristocratic society, such men could commit to memory an amazing collection of social trivia and rules of etiquette: a gentleman may stir his drinks with his finger; a gentleman always lights a lady's cigarette first, or if he is lighting a man's cigarette, lights his own first and then the other man's; a gentleman always stands when a lady comes to the table; a gentleman always wears boxer shorts not briefs; a gentleman uses the toe of his shoe to grind out his cigarette and not his heel; a gentleman always wears socks with his shoes but not with his loafers; a gentleman does not button the bottom button of his vest; a gentleman never comes to bed nude, he must wear at least his pajama bottoms; a gentleman always takes his weight on his elbows. All these and similar rules of stylized conduct could be adopted not simply as signalling standards of etiquette, but as techniques that would allow a man to negotiate from a position of strength. That is, the creation and sustenance of self-flattering images were thought to promote acceptance by a better class of potential Bountifuls.

TO THE MANNER MADE OR BORN

Earlier in this work we suggested that 'gigolo' was basically an umbrella term that covered a plurality of roles and we identified some of the forms these roles could assume. As we noted, to suggest that the types are discrete would be misleading. Although we posited a typology of gigolo roles, we do not wish to suggest that it resolves itself into a moral hierarchy with househusbands married to career women at one end and Count Gigolas preying on hapless virgins at the other. Social life is rarely that obligingly simple.

Is there a distinct type of man who becomes a gigolo? Even though Coco Chanel suggested that 'there's not a man alive who won't take money from a woman,' the traditional stereotype of gigolo does suggest a singular type of being: a handsome, sexy Latin man with the 'equipment' of a porn star and the scruples of an alley cat. Our research would dispute the presumption of a monolithic gigolo type characterized by a certain appearance or moral code. However, we did observe some factors among our sample of male respondents which seemed to be significant as background variables. These were: (1) a history of childhood sexual victimization; (2) a marginality of career or employment opportunities; (3) a background that facilitated the man undertaking the role of the upper-class dilettante.

'SEDUCTION,' 'INITIATION,' OR 'ABUSE'?

Between a quarter to a third of our male respondents referred to some form of childhood sexual contact with an adult. One bisexual gigolo, summarizing his history, stated:

I was born an only child in Holland, middle-class family and was spoiled rotten. I went to a private Catholic school and was a straight 'A' student … I was sexually aware at age 11 and did the usual as all kids do, masturbate with buddies and general fooling around. Being from a strict Catholic home my allowance was small and in early high school I took a paper route to make more money. This is how it all started.

I found out soon enough on the paper route that they were sex starved ladies and gentlemen. When I collected my paper money there was always a bonus and I caught on quick. From then on I charged on the spot for every sex encounter. Being young, somewhat naïve, I learned everything, blowjobs, screwing, S & M, etc. you name it, I learned it. Mind you, I was 14 years old, horny and willing. I made about 1,000 guilders a month. So my parents would not know, most of the money went into a private savings account. I gave up my paper route but continued with my private house calls. At age 16 I graduated and had about 3,000 in the bank, which seemed a lot at the time. I went to the University of Nijmegan and soon found out where I could make money …

In Nijmegan I met a widow, she was about 40, wealthy and fat. We agreed on 1,000 guilders a month plus a private apartment. She wined and dined me; study was always easy for me so all this activity sexwise (at that age) did not get in the way.

During semester break my lady friend and I went to Paris. Being a student in French, I loved it. We stayed for a week and I made up my mind to move there as soon as I could.

Approximately six months later I took all my money out of the bank, packed my clothes, and took the train to Paris. I found a room, tried to enrol at the Sorbonne, but was told that there was a waiting time for foreign students. So, I enrolled for the time being at the Alliance Française.

After two months I was accepted at the Sorbonne University. During this time (two months) I had no sex but I did scout the places to make money. Since I had my savings, there was no need to hook. Study was hard and soon money was low.

So, here I went. Soon enough I met a man who paid my rent and university fees, later an American lady who just paid cash. Between these two people I went to bed with scores of people. Funny enough I met guys and girls in the same trade; also funny, of this crowd, I was the only one going to school. Drugs and booze were very, very popular; as of this day, drugs I have not used, booze yes! The people I ran around with knew the trade, where to hang out, etc. Suddenly I found myself being involved in this weird group, but I was making '$$' [money] so, at that age, who cares, who cares! The Dutch care. I was drafted and low and behold I became a Marine. I was stationed in the Dutch town of Den Helder (close to Amsterdam). The salary was low so weekend trips to Amsterdam were rewarding to say the least. Then I was sent to Aruba, then Dutch territory. I must have been the wealthiest Dutch marine there because I fucked my brains out for lots of cash. In Aruba I met a schoolteacher, who wanted to sponsor me to come to the U.S.A. ...

I went back to Holland, discharged and then back to Paris. Spent the summer in St Tropez and made a bomb [bundle].

The day I graduated, I packed and moved. I checked the paper and – male escorts wanted. I applied and got the job. I've worked for two years. I now live happily supported by a man 28 years older than me. Nice flat, elegant neighbourhood – sex-starved man but lots of money. Of course, I am no dummy, and went back to school. I hate to brag, but I am very advanced and got him to pay for my school fees at the L.S.E. [London School of Economics]. I accepted this older man's persistence, although sex is limited as my sex drive is very low – with him. [Do you have any plans in the event he leaves you?] As you can see, I'm somewhat of a gypsy. If he moves on it's likely that I would too. If he dies – I hope that he leaves me his car.

These men themselves typically did not define their partner as an assailant, or themselves as the 'victim' of abusive conduct – particularly when the adult involved, as was not uncommonly the case, was a female. For example, one male respondent currently in his early thirties and kept by a woman in her late fifties, casually remarked that, as a young male in Italy, he had been 'initiated' into heterosexual intercourse by his father's mistress at his father's bequest. He commented that, after his teenage brother had acknowledged being homosexual, his father had felt it essential to ensure his other son was given an early indoctrination into rigorously heterosexual activity; at the time of his sexual encounter with his father's mistress he was reportedly 10 years old. Similarly, in a casual way, the man mentioned being 'seduced' by a much older female cousin as well as by the family nanny, who, at the time was reportedly in her mid-forties. The man commented that the nanny had claimed that her fondling of the boy's penis and performance of fellatio would encourage it to 'grow' to impressive dimensions and make him into a 'man.'

Although we are wary of putting forward a type of reductionist account and stress that we *cannot* assume that this event had causal significance in the man's decision to become a gigolo, this finding does warrant further discussion for several reasons.

First, it may be that such early sexual contact 'eroticizes' or 'sexualizes' encounters between males and females for these men, with the result that all subsequent male-female relationships tend to be perceived through a 'sexualized' filter as well. Thus, the men's chronicling of sexual trivia that resulted in hours of tape-recorded 'oral sex' might be explained with reference to this early introductory experience, and their assumption that vigilance while engaging in such behaviour with the goal of then being able to regale others with tales of their actions was admirable, desirable, and emulatory.

Second, research on childhood sexual abuse has noted a gender difference in the victim's response to victimization; whereas females typically turn their anger into themselves and, in partial consequence, become re-victimized in myriad other ways (such as becoming prostitutes, remaining with violent male partners in later relationships, and being statistically more likely to be the mother of a child who is sexually abused), males typically turn their anger at being victimized outwards and, in turn, victimize others. As such, the actions of some of our respondents may suggest a type of behaviour which, in 'incorporating the aggressor' – or coming to identify with and model their own behaviour on the role of the powerful adult who abused them when they were powerless – explains why certain men entered into these relationships.

Third, it was notable that various men within our sample were either runaways or 'throwaways' at the time they entered into their first 'kept' relationships. The definition of a first relationship as being, for example, of a paedophilic 'chicken/chicken hawk' nature, in which they were sexually abused, is ours, and not necessarily theirs. For these men, their patron was often conceived of as simply the 'good friend' who 'saved' them from living on the street or financing themselves through an admixture of hustling, selling drugs, or doing break and enters. Lacking any other marketable skills and finding being 'kept' a profitable venue, particularly at an early age, such men may neglect or abandon conventional career channels and serve an unwitting apprenticeship as a gigolo.

Fourth, the finding that adult females frequently figured in the early childhood/young adulthood sexual experiences of some of our respondents was unexpected, if only because the gender of both victim and assailant ran contrary to the typical reported cases of child sexual abuse in Western societies. It has been repeatedly noted that childhood sexual abuse is a common antecedent in the lives of prostitutes and that there are very obvious gender dimensions to the phenomenon of child sexual abuse, with males being disproportionately represented as assailants and females as victims.

However, various academics and others have suggested that the 'dark figure' of female sexual abuse of children may be much larger than previously anticipated. Nicholas Groth has argued that the incidence of sexual offences against children perpetrated by adult women is much greater than would be suspected from the rare instances reported in crime statistics, and suggests that women offenders may not be recognized as such because it is 'relatively easy' to get away with abusive behaviour under the 'guise of child care.' Extrapolating from her study of ninety-three women and nine men sexually abused by their mothers, Kathy Evert, herself a reported victim of child sexual abuse at the hands of her mother, asserted that 'no one ... knows the extent of sexual abuse by females, especially mothers.'

Ken Plummer has argued that 'there is a considerable degree of female-child sexuality' and that the stereotype of the paedophile as a male is both false and naïve. He maintains that the sexual offences committed by females against children remain hidden 'because of the expectations of the female role which simultaneously expect a degree of bodily contact between women and children and deny the existence of sexuality in women.'

The view that negates the possibility of a female committing an aggressive sexual act, not on the basis of evidence but rather in spite of it, and the suggestion that when a female sexually victimizes a child, particularly a male, no harm is done, reflect and refract images of gender roles in our society. Although we stress that our data show only a correlation between child-adult sexual contact and becoming a gigolo and that we cannot assign causal significance to this factor, it does suggest one of several possible pathways to entering a gigolo career.

THE INNOVATOR

In the 1930s Robert Merton noted that, in North American society, a disproportionate emphasis was placed on the attainment of the goal of 'success' and far less importance placed on the means through which it was to be obtained. If the traditional or conventional means through which to achieve success (ambition, deferred gratification, drive, self-discipline, hard work, education) were unavailable or not seen as capable of fulfilling one's aspirations, deviant or illegitimate means may be pursued in so far as they may bring the individual access to desired goals.

Merton developed this observation to suggest that the overarching importance placed on success might account for the reason certain individuals became criminal, with criminality serving to indicate an act of 'overconformity' to rather than defiance of social values and goals. That is, if having the mansion, the foreign cars, and the bulging wallet is sufficient to mark one as 'having arrived,' persons may ignore the conventional means and believe that the attainment of the goal is all-important. Thus it is noteworthy that, despite his infamous route to success, in his time Al Capone was able to gain acceptance among the best social circles. Put simply, and in relation to our focus of interest here, the gigolo may redefine the acceptability of his actions by the inversion of a popular dictum; that is, it's whether you win or lose, and *not* how you play the game, that counts.

Although this is very much a simplification of Merton's theory, his idea of the non-conformist as an 'innovator,' one who accepts the social goals as desirable but uses deviant routes to attain them, does seem apt in describing this pathway to becoming a gigolo. These men wholeheartedly embraced the idea of living well and the spirit of private enterprise. We never met a gigolo who was a Marxist, Trotskyite, socialist, or communist; 'Karl,' to our gigolos, could only refer to Lagerfeld.

Although a highly placed occupational or educational background in and of itself would be unlikely to prove to be a barrier to a man assuming the role of the gigolo, it was telling that the vast majority of our male respondents did not have an occupation or education that afforded them, through convention, an independently derived high social status. These men were not doctors, lawyers, judges, or rocket scientists. They could possess a certain quasi-celebrity status for their individual accomplishments (such as for having won a relatively prestigious golf or tennis tournament, for having been a child prodigy on the piano or violin, for having been a 'regular' in a minor role on a television soap opera or a B-actor in a number of unspectacular and somewhat unremarkable films, for having been featured in a photo spread or advertisement in a high-fashion magazine, for having published the occasional short story or magazine article), but, by and large, 'fame and fortune,' that elusive state of nirvana that these men ostensibly craved, had eluded them. They were more typically the wannabes who sought elevation of their social standing in a somewhat vicarious manner, believing that conspicuous consumption and purposeful affiliation with the wealthy and/or powerful were, in themselves, socially uplifting.

Where the men did possess some form of independent career, it was typically the type that afforded a certain amount of elasticity in its pursuit;

for example, the real estate agent who bragged about the 'killing' he could make through a few strategic commerical property sales but who seemed content to let his 'killer instinct' abate while he was being kept and who re-entered his licensed profession only when circumstances (the termination of a relationship or a Bountiful's displeasure with him in some facet of his role) suggested it would be an opportune or strategic move. Similarly, the number of 'writers' who seemingly wrote their epic novels, histories, biographies, and assorted tortured masterpieces in invisible ink was truly amazing. Granted the gestation period for any work of art may be long, but, for many of our respondents, the 'screenplay' that was never written, the 'biography' that was being 'researched,' the 'symphony' that lay 'deep within' their souls but required an excavation crew to extract was more common than the one that appeared in hard copy, as were musicians who seemed to play their Bountifuls more artfully than their instruments. Nevertheless, such masterpieces as were prophesied by gigolos often required the investment of capital by the man's Bountiful for their creation, long stays in various sites to conduct research, expensive computer systems to facilitate the creation and retention of breathless prose, and instruments and recording systems to translate the man's true virtuosity.

The types of (additional) careers the gigolo most typically elected to pursue were those which did not offer a rigorously standardized 'career ladder' or sequence through which success would be obtained. Unlike becoming a medical doctor, a process in which the movement towards recognition and validation is standardized, requiring a university education, the completion of specific courses and examinations, a period of internship or residency, and so on, becoming the Great Actor, Writer, or Musician may be seen to follow a somewhat nebulous path. The possession of a degree in English at even a Master's or Doctoral level does not guarantee that its possessor will be regarded as the successor to Shakespeare or Yeats, nor will attendance at the Royal Academy of Dramatic Art necessarily impel others to regard the man as a Barrymore or Olivier. Where success within the preferred profession was viewed as more capricious, attributable to 'who you know,' 'being in the right place at the right time,' 'Lady Luck,' or simply 'fate,' gigolos seemed capable of justifying to both themselves and others, the vagaries of their accomplishments and their becoming kept.

However, it would be inaccurate to assume that all of the men interviewed were content with the ephemeral status of glorified hanger-on. Some did parlay their being kept into a independent career that was exceedingly profitable. One man's career ambitions were facilitated through financing and advice provided by his Bountiful's network of friends, and he succeeded in launching an enormously lucrative career in real estate; a second, who married his partner, used her father's financial support to establish a contracting firm that would make him exceedingly wealthy. Curiously, however, once gigolos had achieved a marked degree of success on their 'own,' their association with Bountifuls seemed likely to be severed at the men's initiative.

While various men sought to give additional grounding to the legitimacy or inevitability of their becoming a professional gigolo by referring to unfavourable economic conditions – the recession, high rates of unemployment and bankruptcies, the 'hundreds of PhDs who are driving cabs' – on occasion some would go farther and lambaste government schemes such as Affirmative Action and Employment Equity for engaging in 'reverse discrimination' that supposedly prevented white males from attaining job positions or promotions. 'What else can a guy do?' one gigolo rhetorically queried. 'Nowadays all the good jobs are going to the blacks and to women. A white guy like me doesn't even have a hope in hell of getting ahead of the game any more.' However, in pointing to the material symbols of success – the creature comforts that enveloped them, the Who's Who guide of people they knew; the number of their friends that had graced the covers of *Newsweek*, *People*, *Paris Match*, *Stern*; the epicurean delights they had feasted on during a meal that had cost more for a party of four than a salesclerk earned in an entire month, winning – or losing – large amounts of money in Las Vegas, Atlantic City, Monte Carlo; travelling in the private jet, the yacht, the top-of-the-line Mercedes-Benz with all the extras, the Rolls-Royce – the gigolos basked in the reflected glory of their luxurious surroundings.

And the benefits may be considerable. For some of our male respondents, the financial rewards of being a gigolo allowed them to acquire properties, stocks and investments, antiques, cars, and a sizeable bank account. However, for others, despite being given a paid-for condo in which to live, a luxury car to drive, and a yearly income that could amount to hundreds of thousands of dollars, money was discarded on non-negotiable luxury items designed to impress, which resulted in negligible savings or capital. Tipping lavishly to impress waitresses and car valets; giving extravagant presents or wining and dining extracurricular girlfriends/boyfriends and/or potential Bountifuls; dressing to make grandstanding entrances and flamboyant exits; consuming drugs with the voraciousness of a bulimic on a binge; saving money by having a friend of a friend who worked at a Donut shop do maintenance on the car and, consequently, spending large sums to repair the additional damage – all could collectively dwindle the man's monies into non-existence.

To the extent that the man assigned importance to demonstrating to others that he had 'arrived,' he would pursue parallel relationships or subsequent ones with a fierceness only partially born out of economic need. After all, his material possessions, as evaluated by the giver of the gifts, would not necessarily result in the Bountiful seeing *him* as someone independently worthy of admiration; rather, it might be thought that the extravagances enjoyed by the man simply reflected well on *her* ability to afford an expensive 'pet.' In consequence, if the man desired to revel in wielding designer goods and social props, he needed an audience that was unaware of the origins of his apparent wealth. Only in the initial stages of courtship with a new partner, or by having a girlfriend/boyfriend on the side, could the man portray his lifestyle in a manner which focused attention on his goal – and not in the strategies he had used in pursuit – of living well.

Finally, some gigolos, while focused on the enjoyments of the present, knowingly evaded the issue of an uncertain future. A society gigolo, originally from Argentina but living in France at the time of the interview, commented:

I may exasperate women but I never bore them. From one woman I go to the next, we remain friends and they still adore me. Just last week I was told by a beautiful woman who was a lesbian that, were she to go back to men, it would only be worthwhile with a man like me ... Women find me a challenge. I never commit myself to one woman. I will be her escort, her lover ... I would not let myself become her wife. If she desires to meet the most clever and charming people on the continent, she will meet them. I will play with her all night and make love to her like she's never been made love to before. I will teach her how to dress, how to walk, how to talk ... She will become the finest lady of all she meets. But I will not be her puppet, I have standards that must be met. [Such as?] She must be generous and anticipate my needs and those of my friends ... She must have an open hand ...

[Do you see yourself doing this for a much longer period?] What do you mean? [Do you want to be a kept man when you are 60 years old?] If it suits me. I don't think so far into the future. You are too practical ... You think like an accountant, 'This year I will work, next year I will work twice as hard and when I am old I will have a nice pension.' Why do you worry so much about the future? It will come ... What will *you* do when you are sixty? Keep a gigolo?

To paraphrase Dorothy Parker, the love affair that goes on between the gigolo and himself is often the prettiest one of all he relays.

THE DILETTANTE

The theme of the historical 'initiation novel' suggested a supposedly prototypical sequencing of events through which a young, impoverished male acquired social graces, skills, and access to a *grand tableau* of people, places, and events through affiliation with an older wealthy woman. However, despite this stereotype, the background of the gigolo is not uniformly a plebeian one. Indeed, it was occasionally the gigolo's ability to furnish his Bountiful and others with evidence of his social eligibility by having attended at the 'right schools,' by demonstrating that he was 'a man of breeding' or that he 'came from a moneyed family' that promoted and crystallized his success. While, on occasion, these qualities could be feigned, or were more apparent than real, for others the 'syndrome of the second son' seemed an appropriate designation by which to describe the man's movement from 'Hooray Henry' or 'deb's delight' into the role of the gigolo.

Historically, the role of the second son, the 'spare' who, should something disastrous befall the 'heir,' would accede to the position of authority within the upper-class family, could be viewed with envy. If his position relegated him to somewhat inferior status with regard to the family fortune, it also demanded less onerous duties of him and made his options less bridled than the heir who would take over the family firm. In terms of access to glory, his role was undoubtedly inferior; displaced by the ordinal position of his birth, he could never aspire, except by accident or exceptional circumstance, to attain the position of his older sibling. However, as the classical definition of 'school' meant 'leisure' and the eventually emergent definition of 'education' suggested 'preparation for absolutely nothing' (as befitting a member of the upper class who was the traditional recipient of education throughout much of Western history), our dilettante would appear to fit that dated educational bill.

In today's society, such factors as death duties, the high cost of taxation, and the rapidly increasing level of technological expertise necessary within industry have lessened the extent to which having supped off a silver spoon may function as the singular prerequisite for a continued lifestyle of those 'to the manner born.' While the continuing importance of nepotism and family ties in furthering upward mobility through both enterprise and marriage is not disputed, being the 'second son' or simply being able to boast of attending Trinity College, Oxford (which is somewhat known for its taking of inferior but well-bred students), or an upper-class university may be a cause for less veneration than it was in the past. Thus, the late 1980's British acronym 'lombard' ('lots of [family] money but a real dickhead') is a distinctly pejorative term; similarly, the term 'Hooray Henry' conjures up the imagery of P.G. Wodehouse's famous character, the vacuous but eminently well-bred Bertie Wooster, who needed the inscrutable Jeeves, as much nursemaid as butler, to take care of him.

For the displaced well bred who have little else to recommend them, the role of the gigolo was often particularly fortuitous inasmuch as their background furnished them not only an entrance into smart society and access to potential Bountifuls, but an advantage over others in being the group most likely to enter into marriage with a particularly well-placed Bountiful. Despite their lack of independent means and in spite of their motivation for marrying, their affiliation with a Bountiful could be integrated as unproblematic and would be viewed as simply a typical example of 'wealth marrying wealth.' For the upper-class Alex in Wonderland, the chase after the White Rabbit could be conducted with the leisurely stride of the stranger in paradise who is comfortable in his setting and has, at minimum, a rough map to follow. He knows the names of the fashion designers that bespeak success – Lacroix, Oldham, Sui, Versace – does not gasp when his lover spends over five hundred dollars on a cable-knit bra, thousands for a new outfit, or tens of thousands for a 'nice' piece of jewellery. If he prefers to drive a six-year old car, it is part of his quixotic appeal and is seen to attest to the fact that, to him, 'money doesn't really matter.'

While his less-well-bred brothers may feel the need to work out in the front window of a Los Angeles gym to call attention to themselves, the dilettante often seemed more confident of his continuing appeal, even as his hair thinned and his stomache protruded. Thus, while one Bountiful jumped, bounced, rowed, and had herself personally trained to an enviable figure, her well-born gigolo disavowed any interest in 'going Lycra.' He disdained the diet of 'rabbit food' she swore by, and went for coffee and cakes while waiting for the woman to return from her herbal or mud bath, mineral wrap, and assorted beauty treatments. Claiming that 'man is a carnivore' and requires daily fuelling with meat, the man encouraged his Bountiful's efforts to stay thin and profusely complimented her on her appearance but felt little need to work out or diet himself. Privately he commented that the woman's expending of energies simply attested to her need to 'prove herself' and rather grandly acknowledged that the standards for female beauty were more exacting than those placed upon men. However, 'it is still, after all, a man's world,' he remarked. 'If women want to play with the big boys, they shouldn't complain.'

THE WEALTHY, THE JET SET, AND THE GLITTERATI

The late Andy Warhol, in his book *Andy Warhol's Exposures*, noted that many inhabitants of the world of glamour suffered from what he termed 'Social Disease.' Although his definition of 'social disease' is not that which may spring to mind (a sexually transmitted illness), he cautioned that it was highly infectious. Its symptoms?

You want to go out every night because you're afraid if you stay at home you might miss something. You choose your friends according to whether or not they have a limousine. You prefer exhilaration to conversation unless the subject is gossip. You judge a party by how many celebrities are there – if they serve caviar they don't have to have celebrities. When you wake up in the morning, the first thing you do is read the society columns. If your name is actually mentioned your day is made. Publicity is the ultimate symptom of Social Disease.

But you know it's really fatal when you don't want to get rid of it. You couldn't anyway.

How do you catch Social Disease? By kissing someone on both cheeks.

The gigolo/Madame Bountiful relationship frequently has a style which identifies its strong association with wealth. The playgrounds of the rich, such as Gstaad, St Moritz, Cannes; and the residences of the rich, such as Chestnut Hill (Philadelphia), Carnegie Hill/Locust Valley/Tuxedo Park (New York), Beverly Hills/Hillsborough/La Jolla/Newport Beach (California), Greenwich/Southport (Connecticut), Grosse Pointe (Michigan), Philadelphia's Main Line; Chelsea/Knightsbridge (London), can be seen to provide a setting wherein people seek to be known as rich. Similarly, knowing what sports, activities, and places are fashionable is part of the superficial gentility of any 'kept' relationship.

What makes a particular commodity fashionable is difficult to ascertain, but it seems that, in part, such qualities as novelty, cost, exclusivity or rarity, and capacity to attract notice are involved. In illustration, the element of novelty was suggested by the comment of several of our male respondents that a 'foreign accent' was a marketable commodity which was thought to enhance their particular appeal to women. For example, a British accent among North Americans and an American accent in Britain, real or contrived, were thought to single the man out as unique, out of the ordinary, and consequently more desirable.

One gigolo born in Morocco noted that his ability to speak French and his 'French' accent were favourably viewed by many women. While being from Morocco may be thought 'exotic,' the man felt that it did not adequately convey the sense of 'sophistication, *panache*' he wished to evoke. Eager to extend his appeal, he typically embellished his background to his would-be patrons with the claim that he was French (rather than Moroccan), that he had studied at the Sorbonne, and that his family had a manoral home located on the Champs-Élysées. 'A house on the Champs-Élysées?' the first author queried him. He then admitted that, never having travelled to France, he had a second-hand familiarity only with the city of Paris; in like fashion, the Champs-Élysées was the only street in Paris that he had heard of and was aware of it from having viewed the movie *Moulin Rouge*. In any event, he commented, his supposed biography seemed to satisfy the majority of his North American interlocutors, and apparently few sought greater specifity about or corroboration of his origins.

In similar fashion, there were British men with East End Cockney accents who would lay claim to being Oxbridge educated and landed gentry to their American partners; English men who claimed to their English patrons to be from Texas, spouting 'ma'ams,' 'y'awls,' and an affected way of speaking that accrued more from viewing *Dallas* than from having lived there; American men who feigned British accents and sounded as credible as Englishmen as Dick Van Dyke did in *Mary Poppins* (not very); the 'Spaniard' who could not speak Spanish; and the man from Montreal whose Semitic looks allowed him to shift his origins between Israel and Egypt as the situation seemed to demand. Obviously, in creating a bogus biography, one always runs the danger of detection – of meeting a potential patron whose knowledge of foreign languages, accents, and geography is profound rather than superficial – and, in consequence, of losing credibility as a potentially desirable companion. However, while acknowledging such risks, these men were conscious of a 'snob appeal' that affixed itself to things that were unique or out of the ordinary.

Knowing where to eat, where to go on holiday, where to gamble, and what to pay distinguishes the rich and reveals the circles in which they move. The fashionable is esoteric; knowing what is fashionable and being able to afford its pursuit allow the gigolo to proclaim himself as someone who 'has arrived.'

Allan is a 27-year-old gigolo based in New York. Beautifully tanned from a vacation at the Cable Beach Hotel in the Bahamas, he talked to the first author while walking down the Madison Mile of smart shops and restaurants. Like Paris's Faubourg St Honoré, Milan's Via Montenapoleone, and London's Brompton Road, the Madison Mile is lined with fashionable and exclusive shops: Givenchy, Ungaro, Lanvin, Balmain, Armani, Missoni. As we mingled among the *cognoscenti* from 59th to 79th Street, the conversation was punctuated by Allan's desire to 'just pop in for a minute' at one shop or another. He stopped at Stewart Ross, Jacques Billini, D. Cenci, Verri Vomo, pointed to the shop owned by his first paramour (at age 14), and seemed proud that he was well known to the salespersons. He compared shops in New York with those elsewhere, and with deliberate carelessness mentioned the golden sablelined loden coat his lover had picked up for him at Dieter Strange-Erlenbach Pelze on Maximilanstrasse while on a trip to Munich.

It seemed important to Allan to carefully maintain the pose of studied indifference to wealth while courting it; to be able to casually buy his chocolates at Manon's, to offhandedly mention opening night – with complimentary tickets – at the most celebrated Broadway play, and to prattle on in a long monologue about the names and haunts of the famous: had he mentioned he had played golf at Treasure Cay in Abaco? That he had been skiing at Utah's posh Deer Valley ski resort? That he had stayed at the Stein Eriksen Lodge? That the king-sized tubs had gold fixtures? That he had met with this, that, or the other notable at this, that, or the other shrine? Tales of sipping thyme tea by a warming fire at Fauchon's in Paris, dancing at Regine's at the Coconut Grove in Miami, and accompanying his most current lover on a chic holiday safari to the Tree Top Lodge in Kenya were recounted as he established himself as a competent guide of where to go and what to do to oblige the demands of social snobbery.

His gilded haute circuit was more than a little at odds with his plebeian origins. The youngest son of a working-class family, he was a 'throwaway' at age 14 after telling his parents that he was gay. Although Allan's experience with sex – heterosexual or homosexual – was meagre, his father responded to his son's news by deciding it was reasonable to 'beat it out of him.' Physically abused and scorned by his father, he ran away from home. The first time, he was returned by police. The second time, apparently nobody bothered coming after him.

Allan met his first 'keeper' when he was 'picked up' while working as a street hustler and invited, along with several other youths, to attend a party. There, watching gay porno films and indulging in a broad selection of drugs, he met his first lover, a male who at the time was married with children. Kept until the age of 17 and provided with an apartment, an allowance, and gifts of clothes, drugs, and vacations, Allan was instructed in the importance of image. Although the man's friends and close colleagues were aware of the nature of the relationship, Allan was told to claim to be of the man's 'nephew' to outsiders. When asked why the affair had ended, Allan commented in a rather sarcastic tone that he grew 'too old' for his male lover. Nevertheless, he gave lavish praise to the man's generosity, his affection, and his having introduced Allan to the world of international glamour.

Since that time, Allan had been kept by numerous persons, both male and female. With a wealthy older woman he had experienced a round-the-world cruise on the luxury liner *Sagafjord*, stayed in a three-bedroom suite with the lady and her nurse at Istanbul's Hilton Hotel, and enjoyed the opulent accommodation of the Copacabana Palace while at the carnival in Rio. He had dabbled in trendy topics, explored The Way/Healthy, Happy, Holy, and Est, consulted astrologists/tea cup/taro card readers and palmists with a lover who was 'into that kind of stuff.' It was evident that Allan viewed himself as a gentleman of no small stature and prided himself on being able to introduce women – and men – to a world of glamour.

The gigolo may, on occasion, himself provide for the advancement of status claims. As such, he becomes simply a status prop with esoteric appeal that allows for the fulfilment of other desired illusions. For some of our Madames Bountiful, the point of expensive acquisitions – including their gigolos – went beyond the mere expense. For these woman, pursuing fashionable activities (such as the keeping of a preferably attractive, younger male) lent support to a positive self-image. In consequence, the society boy who could offer a background that included attendance at a posh school – be it as a youth at Eton, or as a young man at an Ivy League/Oxbridge college – could be highly sought-after even though the only remarkable or dazzling thing about his educational accomplishment was the site of his schooling. Thus, for example, one wealthy woman, who had obtained her money through a career in the media and a series of pragmatic marriages to wealthy men, selected as her gigolo a man almost thirty years her junior. Whether presenting him to her smart friends, to the first author, or to society columnists, the woman gave emphasis to the fact that he been educated in one of England's finest schools as a youth. This fact seemed important to her; first, because it suggested that he 'came from money' even though he had none himself, and, second, because it suggested that he was other than simply an adventurer with aspirations of grandeur. The woman, whose education was marginal and whose back-ground was lower-middle class, evidently saw this as attesting to both her intellectual capacities and her social status as one who was accepted within the highest echelon of society.

In her study of 'million-dollar studs,' referred to in chapter 1, the late Alice-Leone Moats drew attention to the importance of the gigolo as a status symbol for the women who married famous 'fortune hunters' in earlier decades of the twentieth century. Noting-silent screen actress Pola Negri's 'enchantment' with 'Prince' David Mdivani, Moats commented:

Pola didn't question the phoney title and accepted him at his own valuation as an almost-royal prince whom the Bolsheviks had divested of his estates and enormous holdings in the Baku oil fields. By the following year, she had a personal interest in promoting the Mdivani claims to nobility but, even at first, there was good reason to do so. Her marriage to a Count Dambski had made her a countess, and even though she was divorced when she reached Hollywood, the title set her apart – gave her a special position as the only countess in town. Gloria Swanson took care of that by marrying the Marquis Henri de la Falaise. As a marquis outranks a count, Pola was left trailing in the nobility sweepstakes. She could narrow the gap by having David as a regular visitor at her house, for a prince was several notches above a marquis.

Similarly, she suggested that the reputation of Porfirio Rubiroso as the ultimate rich woman's status symbol – acquired through his numerous marriages to heiresses and to his reputed affairs with married women such as Tina Onassis, the first wife of Aristotle Onassis, and movie stars such as Zsa Zsa Gabor – served to generate and perpetuate the legend of his appeal to numerous females. For example, she gave an example of one supposedly typical effusion by a 'news hen' who reported on his marriage to Barbara Hutton: 'Thirty pulses accelerated alarmingly, including the writer's. Friends who have seen him captivate as many as ten women at a dinner party with one sweeping glance say there is no female on earth strong-willed enough to resist a calculated approach by Rubi.' Indeed, Moats commented: 'At a party in Kitzbuehl [sic], Pierre Leygonie over-heard a lady who had met Rubi ten minutes earlier whispering to him, 'I will leave my husband for you.' This was the sort of offer he received at every party. He was so hotly pursued by women that he had very little chance to do any pursuing on his own ...'

Michael Thompson argued that what people discard and retain is an indirect way of presenting their status to others. There was a certain black humour to be observed in the conduct of women who themselves had married and remained married for money and who kept a gigolo on the side. Although the very rich are always eager to spare their interlocutors the embarrassment of knowing exactly how rich they are, it was often amusing to note the distinction these women made between the money that supports them, and could not be spoken of, and the money that was casually spent on them and by them – the expenditures on things animal, vegetable, mineral, and gigolo – and was spoken about all the time. It is wrong to suppose that such affiliations were always inspired by social snobbery and affectation, but at times their pursuits seemed ruled by little else.

Within the world of high society, much of the social behaviour of keeping gigolos seemed to approximate a rather grandiose version of musical chairs, with a chair being occupied by any of a select group of players and little seeming importance attached to who owned the chair at the time. As one well-born and monied woman rather grandly commented of the kept male, 'I never really think of a gigolo as being owned by any one person. Of course the *man* may think he's setting a trap or setting a snare for a woman, but how extraordinary! Keeping a gigolo is a *faire du foin* – something you really don't give a fig for or can snap your fingers at.'

Simultaneously, while this type of leisure-class Bountiful sank into a life of conspicuous consumption, she often took pains to limit the conspicuous presumption of the man she was involved with. Although her *nouveau riche* gigolo might have believed himself to be terribly worldly and astute in pursuing his vocation, by and large his lover did not typically transform his life into an exalted existence in any permanent sense. While the woman may have blithely picked up the tab for holidays which her husband was unable to take or indifferent about attending, or for the costs of shopping jaunts to the fashion houses in New York, Montreal, or Paris for a showing of the latest collection or to outfitt her gigolo with Giorgio Armani outfits, clothing out of *Gentleman's Quarterly*, or the best of Saville Row, most gigolos involved with such women hardly lived out the Cinderfella dream. Living expenses and the use of a leased car served to remind these men of the ephemeral and conditional nature of their relationship and their finances. As one gigolo rather theatrically moaned upon being given an BMW convertible for services well performed in the line of duty, 'That bitch. She knows I'll never be able to afford to run this thing without her and she *knows* how I love BMWs!' However, the very wealthy women seemed to stay wealthy by *not* being terribly generous; the man involved with an extremely rich married woman could receive fewer creature comforts than the man involved with one whose financial position was less opulent.

Although the term 'jet set' – 'which got its name when HCT [high-class tarts] were paid to fly around the globe by sugar daddies' – suggests that the kept relationship has been known to provide at least women with entrance into a rarefied social setting, access into the world of the wealthy is not as open as Duffy's how-to book would seem to imply. In suggesting, for example, the potentially profitable venue of the horse show, Duffy does not direct the reader as to how hanging around the paddocks is to translate into acquaintance, friendship, and/or intimacy. After all, even Cinderella did have an invitation to the prince's ball – she was not simply a gate-crashing groupie.

THE GIGOLO TRAVEL GUIDE: VISAS NECESSARY

Although four-star restaurants, grand lounges in posh hotels, and the like were pointed to by our respondents generally as potentially profitable terrain for the big-dame hunter, the private party was the one place most commonly identified as the site wherein economically advantageous introductions were most likely to take place. The reason for this? These men suggested that women were often more wary than receptive to being 'hit on' by strangers, especially in large impersonal settings. In contrast, the private party allowed for an illusion that nothing out of the ordinary was happening and that the gigolo was one 'who belonged.' By his presence, it was assumed that he was known to others within the group and positively vetted by them. In this type of setting, women were thought more likely to 'let their defences down' and not scrupulously adopt a critical or sceptical posture when the man approached.

There would seem to be a limited number of situations where admiration – real or contrived – can be expressed. Meetings on planes and the striking up of instantaneous intimacy are notable because the situation of sitting in a confined space for a long period of time allows seat mates to suspend the norm of civil inattention to a stranger and to treat the other as a temporary 'friend.' However, the chatty companion may also simply be rebuffed as a irksome pest, if not, indeed, an uncomfortably forward individual. Thus, one woman informed the first author that, on transatlantic flights, she would routinely take along a Walkman cassette player – batteries not installed – to convey the implicit message that superfluous conversation between her and her fellow passengers was unwanted. Unsolicited comments would ostensibly go unheard.

Another woman commented on the 'imprudent behaviour' of a female acquaintance who had a long history of keeping younger men:

She's a beautiful woman, looks very much the lady Ambassadress, wears gloves at cocktail parties and never takes them off. Here she is looking as if butter wouldn't melt in her mouth, looking as if she had just stepped out of *Harper's Bazaar*, roaring around having sex with people a quarter of her age ... She has become rather famous for her open-handed invitations for luncheon gatherings. She'll admit that she's terribly, terribly lonely and gives lunches to keep on seeing people ... She just approaches *anyone* it seems, the most weird mix of people, jumbles them all up, white, black, yellow. It's most amazing ... Her husband left her, her grandchildren adore her, her own children tend to be rather disapproving of her; I guess that's understandable ...

She's a gourmet cook and one would take her up on her invitations, but the things she does make it impossible really to socialize with her.

We are cautioned from childhood onwards to be wary of strangers, and are inundated with media headlines informing us that the serial killer looked like 'the boy next door': 'Perhaps because he [serial killer Ted Bundy] was so photogenic and so articulate ... many people concluded he could not have committed the crimes for which he'd been convicted. A handsome, intelligent young man who seemed to some people to have considerable sex appeal, Bundy was painted by the media as a smooth guy, respected, clean, a former law student, a Mr. Nice Guy, almost a benign killer, a good lover who would kill his victims quickly.' Daily it seems we are also reminded of the perils of casual sexual relationships and, implicitly and explicitly, entreated to regard strangers in much the same way as we would strange large dogs. The cautions issued are particularly extensive for women and, it would appear, create a typically heightened fear of the dangers that lurk for the unguarded, the naïve, or the unsophisticated. As Katha Pollitt points out, 'Fear of rape and attack, of which low-level aggravation is a reminder, plays a part in keeping women from claiming public space as their own. We are brought up to be wary – of strange men, of dark streets, of underpopulated subway cars.' Moreover, for the wealthy female, money may be seen as, somewhat paradoxically, a type of handicap inasmuch as she may perceive her assets as rendering her a more visible target for victimization.

For these reasons, the approach of the admiring stranger may be perceived as more fear-inducing than flattering. Even for women whose occupation entails frequent association with the public on a professional basis – for example, the professional actress, singer or stage performer – the behaviour of the 'stage-door Johnny' may be potentially intimidating.

John Hinkley, the would-be assassin of former president Ronald Reagan and besotted admirer of actress Jodie Foster, was to comment, 'Jodie Foster may continue to ignore me for the rest of her life, but I have made her one of the most famous actresses in the world.' Since female celebrities such as Foster, Anne Murray, Katarina Witt, and Steffi Graf have been forced to seek court injunctions to fend off their obsessive admirers, recognition of the dangers that may potentially be posed by the admiring fan or groupie may be necessary to pre-empt a threatening experience.

While Rosalind Miles has remarked that the 'attention-attack: on John Lennon, on Ronald Reagan, on Larry Hagman, may be a "new phenomenon of our times,"' a simultaneous fear of a much older phenomenon may still apply. In her study of kidnapping, Caroline Moorehead noted that the purposeful abducting of heiresses, which dates from the medieval period in England, has occurred throughout history:

In the fifteenth and sixteenth centuries, as the incomes from estates declined, so the hands of unmarried rich girls were sought, often ruthlessly, in marriage. Where a suitor was scorned he simply took. Since the abduction usually meant financial loss for the superior lord, and thus the king, the new husband had to buy his pardon after a discreet period of disgrace ... From the fourteenth century onwards abduction of wealthy heiresses was fought by legislation, and each successive statute increased the penalty for it. Henry VII ruled that accomplices were as guilty as the abductors themselves; Elizabeth I denied them the benefit of clergy. In 1707 the abduction of 'maydens that be inheritors' was made punishable by hanging ...

For the rich there is always the additional fear of literally becoming fortune's hostage.

the rich are right to fear for their fortunes. Ransom demands have grown, to keep pace with inflation, and beyond, in recent years. Kidnappers are uncannily well informed. In 1972, Pietro Torrielli broke the one milliard [billion] lire record; seven months later Paul Getty paid two milliard to get his grandson back. In 1975 Giovanni Bulgari, the Roman jeweller, is thought to have parted with ten milliards for his own release. Ottavio Rossani, a journalist with Corriere di Informazione, has calculated that over 132 milliard lire, a little under a hundred million pounds, has been paid out in ransom, most of it in the last five years. (It would have taken over 80 years to make the same amount in bank robberies.) Very little has ever been seen again. There is scarcely a prominent family who has not been hit somewhere down its family tree, a nephew, a mother-in-law, a cousin.

Perhaps the most well-known contemporary case of a heiress who was kidnapped involved Patty Hearst, the 19-year-old granddaughter of newspaper millionaire William Randolph Hearst. According to Moorehead, Hearst 'was having a shower in the flat she shared with the man she was about to marry, Steven Weed, when a white woman and two black men broke in, knocked Steven out with a bottle, and carried her off naked and struggling.' The aftermath of Hearst's kidnapping, her participation in an armed robbery at the Hibernia Bank in San Francisco with members of the Symbionese Liberation Army who had abducted her, is well known. It is interesting, however, to note that, upon receiving a presidential pardon after having served twenty-two months of a seven-year sentence for armed robbery, Hearst elected to marry her former bodyguard, not her former fiancé.

Assaults on and kidnappings of the rich and famous suggest that only the naïve would believe one can establish immediate intimacy with a wealthy Bountiful by simply riding the elevator behind/in front of her at Bloomingdale's, wandering vaguely up and down Rodeo Drive, or sitting at the juice bar at Harrod's. It is possible. Anything is possible. But it is highly unlikely.

Alice-Leone Moats noted that, prior to marrying international playboy Porfirio Rubiroso, and in reaction the cautionary advice of myriad concerned relatives and advisers, the heiress Barbara Hutton telephoned one of Rubiroso's earlier wives, heiress Doris Duke, to inquire about Duke's impressions of her ex-husband. While seeking a 'consumer satisfaction' testimonial from a lover's former wife seems a somewhat quixotic strategy, it does suggest a purposive attempt to minimize the risks of intimacy with a potential partner. Since Porfirio Rubiroso was, according to Moats, relatively undaunted by others describing him as a 'pimp' and indeed often ended an evening serenading himself while playing the song 'Just a Gigolo' on the guitar, it would appear that he appreciated that, after marrying one heiress, he had increased his chances to marry (many) others.

Given that the group one interacts with may determine whether one individual becomes involved with a princess or a pauper, or remains alone, the professional gigolo or man endeavouring to become one purposefully seeks to establish his membership in a network whose wealth is assured. Within our sample, the successful gigolo would court wealthy people or those with access to them, cajole invitations, tag along with friends or

strategically placed acquaintances, and even take seriously a passing remark from a fellow airplane passenger that he 'look me up when [he was]
in the Bay area.' Indeed, to be successful, it seemed that the aspiring gigolo
had to swallow any qualms that he may have felt about being a 'third
wheel,' intruding on other people's time/money/lives/hospitality and/or
sponging off of others. Rather, he must become polished and glib, generous in his praise and flattery, laughing easily and with as much sincerity
as he can possibly muster at both himself and those around him, and attempting in some way to make himself noteworthy and indispensable.

Alternatively, professional roles such as that of the tennis pro, the golf
pro, the personal masseur, and the personal trainer sometimes allowed a
man to acquire a new type of professional status. In all such cases it appeared that one form of sanctioned intimacy, even when circumscribed by
the nature of affiliation between customer and client, could lead to another. For example, the scope of interaction between a professional masseur and client specifically allows for intimate physical access to the client's body. Within the specialized setting of an encounter with a masseur
the patron and/or the masseur may perceive a licence to tentatively explore the boundaries of acceptable intimacy through, for example, conver-
sational frankness or the requesting/offering of the various types of extra
services available.

Similarly, a personal coach's expertise allows him to transcend temporarily the invisible status differential between himself and his patron and,
inasmuch as his patron is dependent upon him in such a context, negotiate
a desired outcome from a position of strength. Despite his relative lack of
financial means compared with his patron, the 'pro' enjoys a positional
advantage that endows him with status and prestige within the specific
context of the lesson. As the term suggests, the 'pro' is other than an undistinguished, effete lackey. Moreover, since dominance in our society is
linked with masculinity, the role of the 'pro' suggests that a type of eligibility or desirability may be attached to a man who displays competence
and expertise within a specific area, and this elevated status may be generalized into a Bountiful finding the man to be a desirable partner for
intimacy.

It is evident that not all aspiring gigolos independently command the
pedigreed background, network linkages, or occupational advantages of
the 'pro'; for this reason, strategic linkages with other society gigolos were
an important means of entrance into the social role. The importance of
networks was evident among our sample of male respondents and allowed
for an informal referral system to operate among men who were known

to each other, with men succeeding one another in their serial kept relationships, standing as a character reference for each other, and/or 'turning out' a friend or sympathetically viewed other who wished to become involved in a kept relationship. Referrals entailed a code of mutual obligations and responsibilities that solidified the man's place within a network group and allowed men to meet new patrons through their friends and/or replace their friends when their role was relinquished or terminated. In such ways, social networks of high-status individuals often seemed to have as one of their components a *demi-monde* or 'twilight world' in which flourished a somewhat incestuous system of sexual linkages with men who functioned in the roles of gigolos.

THE POWER OF KEEPING SECRETS

It is manifestly obvious that any kept relationship, be it men keeping mistresses or women keeping gigolos, is not typically given the fanfare and type of ceremonial announcement that accompanies more conventional forms of social relationships. Although not necessarily covert, information that one is keeping a lover or is being kept is generally restricted to certain people and places. Although the tabloids occasionally pose their comments as if they were the self-proclaimed representatives of a moral vigilante squad, it is unlikely that any kept relationship would be portrayed as other than the titillating event of 'so-and-so dining with her pizza boy/toy boy/happy camper.' Nevertheless, it would seem that the powerful are to a degree able to veto their indiscretions' becoming too fully explored or commented upon in the press. It often seemed that, in exchange for remaining in the continued good graces of certain Bountifuls and/or their highly placed husbands, the press had no comment to make about the kept relationship of the society *grande dame*; rather, the generosity of the woman towards the opera, the symphony, the ballet – and not towards her lover – was the focus of attention. Similarly, if the nature of their relationships was common-enough knowledge within their social network, our respondents attempted to ensure that their 'little self-indulgence' did not become a major social *faux pas*.

Thorstein Veblen commented, in his study of the leisure class, that 'if decency is observed, morals are taken for granted.' The label of respectability given to acts or behaviour is not conferred by a monolithic social judgment. The respectability of being a Madame Bountiful or a sugar daddy may be based in a logic which is only partially influenced by traditional semantic understanding of what constitutes chaste behaviour. So long as the affair was conducted with a veneer of gentility and discretion, the behaviour was thought not to be anti-social or deviant.

That our Madames Bountiful attached importance to their relationships remaining discreet behaviour became especially marked whenever the media directed reader attention to, for example, the lurid evidence of a hugely publicized divorce case or palimony suit. In 1982, when media attention was riveted on the hugely publicized divorce case of Herbert 'Peter' Pulitzer, the then 51-year-old grandson of the newspaper magnate whose name was given to the literary and newspaper prize, and his then 31-year-old wife, many of the first author's Bountifuls muttered about 'intrusive' reporting, the 'shamelessness' of reporters and so on; the participants' behaviour was judged as something that should have remained 'their own business.' They were seen as deviants only to the extent that they had willingly chosen to 'air their dirty laundry' in public.

Particularly in those cases in which the Madame Bountiful was married, the dangers of recognition by others additionally included the possibility that the woman's husband would be informed and/or that attempts would be made at blackmail. In one case within our sample, a gigolo and his wife (the latter's existence, they supposed, was unknown to the Bountiful) attempted to ensnare the Bountiful in a rendition of what, in the parlance of the confidence man, is termed the 'badger game.' Thus, the gigolo's wife proceeded to 'discover' the adulterous relationship between her husband and his Bountiful and demanded payment from the woman to both assuage her honour and prevent her disclosing the information to the woman's husband. Although in this particular case the woman was well aware of the fact that her gigolo was married to someone else and merely expressed incredulity at her would-be blackmailer's naïvety in assuming that her husband was unaware that she was keeping a lover, for others the dangers of disclosure were more considerable. Individuals who are having extramarital affairs are not generally encouraged to 'kiss and tell,' and no Bountiful, not even an unmarried one, would wish her support of a lover to be trumpeted in the popular press.

Although the Madame Bountiful may welcome media attention to the fact that she is partnered with a young/attractive/eligible male, disclosing that the relationship is being underwritten with financial support provided by her was often considered undesirable and other than flattering. Even among those women who prided themselves on their unconventionality and their self-made financial status, the issue of providing support for a male partner was seemingly construed as potentially more threatening to their publicly projected sense of self than their being partnered with a younger man and/or a man whose social-class origins were less lofty than their own.

POWER WITHIN INTIMATE RELATIONSHIPS

All interpersonal relationships, regardless of the degree of intimacy involved, contain a power dimension. Power in general refers to the ability of one person to influence the behaviour of another person, and to resist the influence of another, regardless of that other person's wishes. Relationships can vary in terms of how explicit or obvious the power dimension is, but, even in the most intimate relationship, which is supposedly of an egalitarian nature, the power dimension is present.

An individual's power is determined by a number of factors operating simultaneously.

1 / A major factor involves the amount of control, either actual or perceived, a person has over resources. We will examine types of resources shortly, but the important point here is that the greater amount of those resources one possesses, or is seen to possess, the more power one has in a relationship.

2 / A related factor is the extent to which one's partner values those resources. If the other person has no interest in the resources one controls, they will be of no consequence for the relationship.

In a fairy tale–type story by Harry Kressing called *The Cook*, a man achieves the complete takeover of a mythical kingdom by making himself indispensable through his cooking skills. Power is transferred to the cook because people will give him everything and anything to gain access to the special creations that he prepares. Similarly, if the illusion provided is intensely nourishing or compelling, one can anticipate that the playing field of Bountiful and gigolo will be less than level.

3 / The availability of alternative sources of desired resources is an important additional factor. The fewer the alternatives available to one, the greater the amount of power one's partner has. The availability of alternatives is an indicator of one person's *dependence* upon another. Simply put, the fewer the alternatives, the greater the dependence.

Clearly, would-be gigolos are dependent upon a limited number of females who possess or have access to the desired amounts of money necessary to keep these men in the manner to which they would like to become accustomed. Thus, a market is created for books such as Duffy's on where to find that limited number of women. Since it seems fair to assume that there are more gigolo than Bountiful wannabes, the males would appear to be in the more dependent position here.

4 / *Dependence* and *power* are inversely related. The lesser one's dependence upon another, the greater one's power over that person. In 1938 Willard Waller enunciated what has come to be known as 'the principle of least interest,' which states that the person who has the least interest in maintaining a relationship has the most power within that relationship. Having less or 'least' interest is attributable to a greater availability, real or perceived, of alternative sources of satisfaction or gratification. If one's needs are not being met in a current relationship, and one believes that those needs could be met in an alternative relationship, then one will be less willing to make major sacrifices to maintain the current relationship. Conversely, the more one wants or feels one needs a current partner – for what they are, or what they have, or what they can do – and the fewer the alternatives, the more dependent and the less powerful one is in that relationship.

Knowingly or unknowingly, people have adopted this 'principle' as the basis for widely held beliefs on the importance of making oneself appear to be indispensable for the happiness and life satisfaction of a partner – convincing a partner that he or she can't live without you. If successful, this strategy will result in the other person becoming dependent and doing all they can in order to maintain the relationship. In so doing, a partner loses power to control its course and shape. Therefore, the gigolo must convince his would-be Madame Bountiful that he is so special that she cannot enjoy life without him. To the extent that he is successful, she will become dependent upon him for life's enjoyment and take whatever steps are needed to keep him by her side.

5 / Power, as is true of relationships themselves, does not exist in a vacuum. The sociocultural context influences not only what will be considered as valuable resources but also who will have greater access to those resources. We have seen in earlier chapters that Western patriarchal societies traditionally granted greater power to males simply by virtue of the fact that they were male. Then, as today, power has been based upon a sex-linked share of socially valuable resources. Gigolos, in general, enjoy a certain built-in gender-based tactical advantage to which many, but not all, Madames Bountiful defer.

Many types of resources are important for the experience and expression of power in relationships. The simplest list includes the resources of money and status, love and eroticism. These resources differ in more than just the most obvious ways. Money is something which is easily 'quantified' (it can be counted, and amounts can easily be compared). As well, money can quite easily be transferred from one person or relationship to another. Finally, both money and high status can provide access to other forms of power, such as education and politics. Love, in comparison, is not easily quantified, as anyone who has ever tried to 'count the ways' can readily attest. As well, love is particularized and is not easily transferable to other persons or relationships. Finally, love cannot as easily provide access to other forms of power, although it is not incapable of doing so.

While we are easily aware that many people may want our money, it is not immediately apparent who might want our love. Similarly, while it is relatively easy to determine if another person offers more money than what we can obtain from a current partner, it is not as easy to determine if another person offers more love.

These resources are more than different, however; they are also valued unequally in most societies like ours. To state the obvious, we live in a highly materialistic society. While some people may wish to claim idealistically that love is more important than money, it is unlikely that such sentiments are widely and sincerely believed on an everyday, practical level. Love may nurture the soul, but only money can provide the necessities, as well as the luxuries, of life.

Males, both currently and historically, *generally* control the resources of money and social status, while females *generally* control the resources of love and eroticism. The stage is thus set for a bargaining or exchange of resources within intimate relationships. Within a patriarchal society, Jean Lipman-Blumen has suggested, 'in relationships between the sexes, males have a disproportionate amount of resources under their control. They could bargain their power, status, money, land, political influence, legal power, and educational and occupational resources (all usually greater than women's) against women's more limited range of resources, consisting of sexuality, [love], youth, beauty and the promise of paternity.' Since the resources themselves being exchanged are not equally valued within our society, the resulting relationships will not be egalitarian. As well, the mating gradient, discussed in an earlier chapter, further promotes the pairing of two basically unequal partners.

It is not surprising to find that economic power translates into intimate-relationship power. Research confirms that, despite the current existence of an egalitarian ideal, power is typically distributed asymmetrically or unequally in most intimate relationships. Male-dominated relationships are still the statistical norm, and the domination is supported by a combination of economics and sociocultural traditions.

The Blumstein and Schwartz research on American couple relationships found that, for heterosexual married and cohabiting couples, power within a relationship was a direct reflection of economic power acquired outside the relationship. The research confirms that males still derive a very important sense of their masculinity from their success in the market-place and use the earnings from their labours as an indicator of that success. As Robert Gould noted some years ago, men do measure their masculinity by the 'size of their paycheque.' The paycheque itself is a private and symbolic indicator of worth. It is what the paycheque translates into – a lifestyle – that provides a public indicator of worth in a materialistic society.

Blumstein and Schwartz further noted that 'these patterns have led us to conclude that it is men – who for generations have learned in the work place the equation that money equals power – who have recreated this experience in the home. Wives and cohabiting women fall prey to the logic that money talks.' However, they concluded that 'men and women feel and act differently about money. To men it represents identity and power. To women, it is security and autonomy.'

This difference is further illustrated with regard to the phenomenon of the 'pooling' of economic resources within intimate relationships. It is generally and implicitly assumed within Western marriages today that income and other financial resources will be pooled. This historical fact is something both big-dame hunters and members of old- (but temporarily-low-on-) money families have been acutely aware of. Such pooling, of and in itself, becomes a symbol of trust and of commitment to the future of the couple unit.

Many people today find both the concept and the fact of the 'prenuptial agreement' to be objectionable because it raises to the forefront the issues of trust and commitment in a relationship that is supposedly entered into 'until death us do part.' However, while the traditions of marriage make it difficult and perhaps unwise for partners to not pool their resources, cohabitation relationships lack these traditions. In the latter case, there are very few legal safeguards for protecting individual economic rights if an arrangement should fall apart, a situation which makes it difficult for partners to merge or pool their resources.

Blumstein and Schwartz found that, although married males automatically assume their income will be pooled and therefore be available for all family expenses, married women are less willing and less likely *automatically* to throw their income into the common pool. Similarly, cohabiters in general, and cohabiting females in particular, are less willing to pool their economic resources. The basic issues for these females, whether married or cohabiting, are again those of retaining an important sense of independence and autonomy through control of their own economic resources. It is this independence and autonomy that provide not only the discretionary income for things gigolo, but also a means for exerting some control within that relationship.

We did not find a single instance within our sample of a Madame Bountiful automatically and initially allowing her gigolo complete, free, and easy access to what would amount to a joint bank account. Rather, in general, money was doled out to and for the gigolo, sometimes in a miserly fashion but more often quite freely and lavishly, as the perceived need arose. It was the task of the gigolo to manipulate his Bountiful's perception of existing need.

A contributing influential factor here will be the degree to which she, and her partner, believe in the traditional male-provider philosophy. If either partner adheres to that philosophy, then the male will typical retain the greater share of power, regardless of the amount of income each brings into the relationship. Thus, as we will see in the next chapter, some Madames Bountiful may, based upon only his promise of being a provider of some sort, at some time in the future, automatically defer to their male partners. Similarly, women who have been raised to believe in male dominance will be more likely to largely turn control of their finances over to a male partner in intimacy.

At first glance, the gigolo/Bountiful relationship would appear to exist as a reversal of, or an exception to, the general form of intimate relationship. On the surface, such a relationship seems to involve a female who possesses greater amounts of money and objective status than her partner, who highly values her resources. The gigolo appears to offer 'only' love and sex to his female partners. Following the traditional model, we would have a situation wherein he is the more dependent partner and she the more powerful one.

But, does the traditional model apply? That model is based upon situations wherein males control the more highly valued resources, and therefore have power. Which is more important – gender or the resources themselves? Relationships between gigolos and Madames Bountiful provide us with a situation in which to examine the kind of variation we wrote of in the introduction as necessary for examining important issues.

It appears from what we have seen that, in general, a woman who is in a more economically dominant position will not automatically translate this into a power domination within the relationship. Rather, she is most likely to use her economic superiority to preserve her autonomy. She uses her money as a gift, but it is offered for the most part on her terms, and the terms are quite similar to those males have historically used. The giver of a gift preserves an important vestige of independence from the receiver of the gift.

Leslie, one of our Bountifuls, illustrates many of the points regarding money that were presented in the previous pages. In her own words:

I was a single mother with a daughter who was 15 at the time I met Denis, professional, ran my own successful business, lived in a professional area, with a house that was worth over half a million dollars. I was unattached at the time, and didn't really need anybody to do anything as far as the financial support and maintenance of a property, you know, were concerned. The one thing I was lacking in my life, because my life was so busy, was romance – someone who would love me for who I was not for what I had. I was very strong. I wanted someone who would love me as ... a woman.

My daughter was involved in a summer camp in North Ontario as a counsellor in training. I went up North for a weekend, armed with several books – I wasn't going on a love search meeting. I stayed at a small lakeside resort; Denis came down to see the owners of the place. He lived in the community and they were friends of his. He was 9 years younger than me; he was 26 at the time. I didn't have a problem with the age.

About a month later, he called me and said he was coming to Toronto and could we go to dinner? We did, and after that he called me a lot. On the August long weekend, we went camping. We had fun, but the plan was I'd never see him again; he was going to university and I thought this was just a nice weekend and that was the end of it.

A few days later, after I came home, my daughter told me that Denis had phoned and he was here in Toronto. A week later I saw him, we went out to a movie. When we got back to his car after the movie, his car had been broken into and he was all upset because he didn't have much money and his leather jacket had been stolen. He told me that his insurance didn't cover for the leather coat or the broken windows. We talked back and forth. I said I'd give him some money, he said he didn't want it. The next day I sent him a little card and wrote on it, 'Your better days are ahead; don't worry about it.' I wrote him a cheque for $600 and put it in the card.

[Why did you send him the money?] I really felt bad about what happened; I felt that in some way it was my fault. I also knew what it was like not to have any money. I had been a 18-year-old with a baby, and my dad wouldn't let me in the house. At the time there was a program called Birthright and you would go and live with a family and stay with them until the baby was born. They would give you a place to stay and food, and you would cook and clean, take care of their kids, whatever they asked you to do. I did everything for nothing. You were an indentured person. After Jennifer [her daughter] was born, I went back to school. Because I got a grant to go back to school – $54 a month in 1972 – the woman wanted me to give her half! I moved into a black neighbourhood – Jennifer's father was black and Spanish – and lived a very meagre life until I finished a two-year program in accounting and office management at school. I remembered that feeling of having nothing so vividly; when I met Denis, it was very close to the nerve.

I was also just very giving. Anything I had, I gave to anyone. Here was someone who now didn't have the money to have go to school full-time, living with a woman in a dirty, dirty house with cats and dirty dishes, who wanted to live out of his car. He didn't have a place to live, wasn't in school, no money or a job. By virtue of that, I felt sorry for him. I said he could stay with me until he got his act together.

I felt sorry for him. I really felt it was the quintessential lonely dog in the window that you bring home. I wasn't trying to mould him, to manipulate him into something I wanted. He had a lot of dreams and I was trying to support him. He had this dream of being this Big Important Person. A lot of dreams. About opening a different style of restaurant. He wanted to run a very elaborate graphic CADD [computer-aided design and drafting] that shows all the different elevations of lands and put all these maps on computers so people could be able to retrieve them. He had lots of ideas and he still does to this day if you give him the opportunity to tell you. He's going to change the world.

I was never looking for 'results.'

This language of gift-giving, and of using money as a form of affection and independence preservation, is a well-known part of the traditional male lovestyle. Males also recognize the implications for them of an economic imbalance within a relationship. Whether his female partner implies domination or not, it is likely that the gigolo will infer domination, for that is the only perspective readily available to him. If he is not comfortable with being in a potentially subordinate position, he must then resort to the use of techniques that will, at the very least, dilute his Bountiful's power.

This condition is reminiscent of that which has characterized females in male-dominated relationships for centuries. But even in those relationships, females have not been without their own sources of power, or without their techniques of neutralizing their male partner's domination. As Jean Lipman-Blumen has noted: 'When the dominant group controls the major institutions of society, it relies on *macromanipulation* through law, social policy, and military might, when necessary, to impose its will and ensure its rule. The less powerful become adept at *micromanipulation*, using intelligence, canniness, intuition, interpersonal charm, sexuality, deception ... to offset the control of the powerful.' (emphasis in original). These micromanipulation techniques not only can be used in an attempt to influence the balance of power within a relationship, but can, and are, used by gigolos as a means by which relationships can be initiated. As we noted a little earlier in this chapter, travelling first class on an airplane offers little assurance, in and of itself, that one will fly high as a gigolo. More is needed. It is that to which we now turn our attention.

5

Making Magic

The first gigolo the first author ever met was a 29-year-old Londoner who was introduced to her by 'Gail,' the kept mistress of an Arab oil sheik. Gail had met 'Robin,' a charming, fairly attractive man with a stunning home, in a smart West End London club in the early 1980s while her lover had been abroad. They danced, had several drinks, and arranged to go out the next day in the country. He drove up to her flat in a Mercedes, outfitted with a Fortnum and Mason's picnic hamper and rug. Dining on melon, smoked salmon, freshly roasted *poussin*, and profiteroles, washed down with a crisp white burgundy, Gail thought Robin the perfect catch. In the days immediately following, they saw each other constantly. Each was in a fool's paradise. Gail, noting Robin's availability at any time of the day, any day, his abundance of free time, and his gracious style of living, assumed he was a 'rich mama's boy' or one who was pandered to by wealthy and indulgent parents. Robin, noting her lavish jewellery, designer props, and Chelsea flat, similarly assumed that she was at least the daughter of a prosperous industrialist. Each was surprised and more than somewhat disappointed to learn that the other similarly desired to become kept.

What is involved in becoming a gigolo? While the stereotype conveyed by *American Gigolo* is suggestive, several would-be gigolos who wrote to us clearly recognized that more was undoubtedly involved, but were uncertain as to precisely what it was.

Dear Dr.,
Hi, my name is Mike but my friends call me Mikey. I found your letter on page five in the Vancouver Sun very interesting. I wrote for your professional help to learn how to become a gigolo.

Very briefly I'm a 24-year-old male in good phyisical [sic] condition, 6 feet tall, weight 170 lbs. with a dark complexion with a [sic] English background. Not bisexual.

You said in the article that women write to you who hire gigolos. Could you please explain this procedure?

Very interested in your reply.

Seriously yours,

P.S. Please use confidentiality.

Dear Dr.,

I read of your research and although I am not presently employed by a female, I have given much thought to the proposition. I have gone so far as to make up a rough draft for a personals column in search of such a woman. In the column I stated my attributes such as they are and that I wanted a financially independent female companion-partner for the good life.

I'm sure that with full communication at the outset of the relationship the affair would be totally capasetcic [sic] to both parties.

If you can do anything in the way of references or referals [sic] it would be very appreciated.

Respectfully,

Dear Madam:

I am writing to find out how an intelligent, good-natured and handsome, but unemployed, male, such as myself, might obtain more information regarding the profession of gigilo [sic]. From a recent newspaper story, I have learned that you are writing a book on the subject. When and where and at what price may it be obtained in the U.S. of A.? If it is not available here, could you please iterate, in point form, how one might go about exploring the possibility of getting into the business?

Yours truly,

Ted Peckham and Brian Ross Duffy, whose advice was presented in earlier chapters, gave exaggerated emphasis that the aspiring Cinderfella must demonstrate 'style.' However, more would seem to be involved in the role of the gigolo than being able to distinguish one end of a (polo) horse from the other, and/or recognizing that champagne as well as guns may be referred to as 'magnums.' For us, what is on display in those who successfully adopt the role of gigolo is, most simply, magic.

While the term 'making magic' most readily brings to mind David Copperfield, Paul Daniels, or the television telepathic performer who can 'read people's minds,' magic deals with the world of images and creating images; if people accept those images, what you have is magic. The hustler who attempts to disguise his manipulation of the deck of cards is engaged in magic; he purposefully creates an image that what he is doing is unexceptional and mundane, giving the illusion that nothing out of the ordinary is happening. This tactic is referred to as the 'illusion of the unexceptional.' The stage magician who creates the image that the extraordinary is happening is also 'making magic.' In this type of magic, the 'illusion of exceptional effects,' the performer places considerable emphasis on his overt control of or mastery over a given event. To the audience it seems that, 'simply' by the wave of a wand or by gentle blowing on a handkerchief, a flock of brightly coloured birds appears or disappears. The image presented by a magician may be banal and ordinary, or it may be sophisticated and extraordinary, but, in all cases, images and their manipulation are involved.

While the term 'mental magic' is commonly used by magicians themselves to refer to the practice of tricks involving ostensible ESP or telepathic abilities, such as telling the colour of a person's shirt while blindfolded or the birthdate of a person's lover, the term may also be employed in discussing the role performance of the gigolo. The gigolo is engaged in the production of magic: planning, anticipating, orchestrating, producing, and maintaining illusions and images designed to elicit or provoke the perception that he and the relationship he offers are magical, mystical, and desirable.

'Rolph,' at nearly 40 years of age, was very much a charmer, and no one seemed to appreciate this quite as much as Rolph himself. Five feet ten inches tall, with grey hair, he was attractive, with a quick-witted, high-energy intensity that served to focus attention upon himself. He had, as he termed it, 'star quality.' Rolph claimed that his father treated his mother, who left the family when he was young, like 'royalty' but that she was 'common,' disloyal to his father, and preferred to chat with lower-class café waitresses over endless cups of coffee than spend time with her children or husband. His father, in contrast, was described in almost reverent tones. According to Rolph, who was the eldest of three children, his father kept all the children happy, healthy, and mass-attending Catholics.

As the portrait painted by Rolph was at odds with the account of his family background told by Rolph's older sister – she remembered her mother as a battered wife and her father as a despot who 'farmed off' each child to a different relative following his wife's desertion – Rolph proved to be an *artiste* in the game of charades. Like Thomas Carlyle's 'The King of Liars,' Rolph 'spent his whole life in plastering together the True and the False, and therefrom manufacturing the plausible.'

Performing magic – stage magic, close-up magic, or mental magic – requires an audience; you cannot do magic without one. One can practise, do tricks, but without an audience to endorse and acknowledge that the trick is wondrous or compelling, there is no magic. To be a magician requires selectivity and presentation on the part of the performer and interpretation and appreciation on the part of the viewer. Both roles are essential for magic to be accomplished. The successful magician is not simply one who knows how the rope trick or the guessing of the correct card is accomplished, or one who simply understands the mechanics of making the elephant 'disappear.' Rather, magic is accomplished when the viewer believes the reality of the illusion the magician has created.

The first author initially met Rolph when he was the uninvited house guest of another gigolo; Rolph had been somewhat abruptly discarded by his lover for cheating on her. For three days, Rolph cried on the shoulder of anyone whose shoulder was available. 'How could she do this?' he'd wail. He had been falsely accused, he maintained. His ex-Bountiful was the only woman he had ever truly loved. He could not even think of doing such a thing. Moping about his friend's home and listening to loudly played tapes of Nana Mouskouri singing songs of feckless lovers, he created a truly doleful atmosphere. However, on the fourth day, a conversation between Rolph and his new lover (a 24-year-old heiress with whom he had been accused of being involved) seemed to lift his spirits considerably; they were off to Rome for the weekend to stay at her family's villa.

On the evening before Rolph left, he preceded to regale the first author with a story 180 degrees from the dirge he had presented the day before. His new lover was an 'angel,' so sensitive and caring, while his former lover was labelled a heartless being who simply 'toyed' with men's affections, enchanting them with what wealth could buy and then capriciously dismissing them. Both versions of 'reality' were delivered equally adamantly. And yet, still a third version emerged.

Upon his return from Rome, Rolph and his new lover visited the first author at her home. Introducing the first author as 'an old friend whom I've known for simply years' and as supposedly 'a great friend of my sister while at school,' Rolph entertained everyone with a steady stream of sparkling repartée. Quick-witted, with a knack for acerbic yet intelligent quips, Rolph conversed with seemingly spontaneous humour and brilliance; it was like listening to Mark Twain.

After an hour or so, Rolph asked to use the phone, noting that he had forgotten to return a call of some urgency. He then left the room and placed a telephone call to his ex-lover, beginning his conversation with the remark 'I've been trying to get you for the last twenty minutes solid.' Stretching the phone cord to allow him to check on his new lover's location and/or to wave and blow kisses at her, he earnestly reassured his ex-lover that he would never cheat on her, that he treasured her, needed her desperately, had lost weight, and had not been eating or sleeping in his great despair. Here was a master showman at work. The woman Rolph had telephoned seemed equally impressed; after some minutes spent in obvious acceptance of her apologies, Rolph promised to return to her that evening after he had finished some things that needed to be done. He signed off with joyful expressions and professions of undying love and, the conversation over, proceeded into the living-room, where he resumed his humorous imitations and castigation of his old lover to his new lover, issued comparisons that were markedly to the new lover's favour, and smirked like a Cheshire Cat at the first author.

What allowed Rolph to be successful as a gigolo? He did not, to the best of our knowledge, drink any special elixir, ingest tablets designed to overcome resistance in the other sex, practise mind-control or brainwashing techniques, or secrete an excess of pheromones. He had never heard of Brian Duffy or Joyce Brothers. However, he was skilled in making magic.

As Robert Prus and C.R.D. Sharper have noted, to be a successful magician, the performer must be able to create an illusion in the mind of his viewer, to co-opt his viewer into being his accomplice. He must seek to project images or convey impressions to his viewer as part of a persuasion process that attempts to foster interest, generate trust, and selectively shape the stance and receptivity of the viewer. Similarly, for a man to become a gigolo requires an audience of at least one – a female, or, on occasion, a male – who will acknowledge his performance and validate his role. Like the magic of the confidence man, the magic the gigolo practises is based on skills involving subtlety and deception.

While the stage magician is 'larger than life' and coaches his audience to await with delicious anticipation the moment of the grand illusion, illusions are by no means restricted to the realm of the stage performer. We are besieged in routine life with advertisements that direct us how we may become Somebody, eligible to fit in a *grand tableau* of other Somebodies by the consumption of the manufacturer's product. The celebrity talk show, the supermarket tabloid, the weekly entertainment magazine – all function as creators and sustainers of public personas or public identities. All direct us to become knowledgeable about the 'true' image of persons who are famous, notable, or thought worthy of admiration.

The campaign style of political figures similarly acknowledges the indispensability of images and illusions. Kissing babies; donning a hard hat, a kilt, or one's old war medals; embracing the indigent and/or the diseased; issuing warm endorsements of popular causes/concerns of the electorate – all may be seen as strategic attempts to foster and promote images of the candidate as the obvious choice for the voter. Qualities are embroidered and people recast into legends with heroic, admirable, and mythogenic features. However, such actions are not simply vainglorious or ego-gratifying testament to the individual's narcissism. While some individuals may undoubtedly come to escape into or believe in the mythomania created by themselves and/or by others acting on their behalf, there is a purpose behind the manufacture of the images. What all these manufacturers of images – public relations officers, advertisers, politicians, magicians, and gigolos – have in common is the attempt to transform an uninterested, sceptical, or cynical audience into fascinated true believers.

Although the stage magician may benefit from the aura of the stage and the ability to use larger and more elaborate props, if 'all the world's a stage,' whenever people relate to establish intimate relationships there is a little bit of magic.

MAKING MAGIC

If close-up magic is so compelling because it happens right under your nose, while the magician is engaged in performing his trick with your rings, your handkerchief, or your watch, defining things so as to make the result seem 'magical,' the performance of the gigolo enjoys a similar positional advantage. His viewer does not typically know in what form or manner illusions will appear, nor does she necessarily expect them. With the stage magician, the viewer may believe that, if only she was positioned closer to the stage, she could readily detect the deception involved; the close-up magician and the gigolo offer their audience a qualitatively different type of experience. The nearness of the magician seems to preclude the possibility of deceit, of sleight of hand; however, magic is nevertheless being performed. Moreover, he seeks to tap into his viewer's definitions of magic so that the performance, although standardized to a certain degree, can be manipulated and directed towards his viewer's specific interests or desires. It is not truly a question of employing different methods, but rather of using subtlety to assess what one's viewer defines as worthy of admiration or compelling viewing and then using this information to stylize one's presentation so as to create images as they are required.

Precisely because the image of the gigolo is so garish, be it the 'American' version or the more traditional fantasy of a swarthy 'Latin' with lacquered hair, too many gold chains, and/or too tight blacks pants, we may be unprepared for the management techniques of gigolos that we encounter. There is no insistence in routine life that people interact 'fairly' and in straightforward ways with each other, and, particularly in everyday dating situations, people may posture and pose for each other to a certain degree. It is customary for people to recall, somewhat nostalgically, the 'golden days' of their love affair, when love was new and there was a glow around their lover and the relationship. Each to the other was an unknown quantity, eager to present his or her most attractive qualities. In the early stages of a relationship, the 'Gilette stage,' one may shave away the unpleasant features of oneself as conscientiously as a man shaves his face or a woman her legs in preparation for that magical date together.

What distinguishes the close-up magic or mental magic used by the gigolo from the everyday posturing and posing that goes on within dating situations is the subtle command and contingency planning that have been considered and rehearsed. Whereas the bar hustler may employ standard lines ('What's your sign?'; 'Haven't we met before?'; 'Has anyone ever told you that you look just like Cindy Crawford/Julia Roberts/Elizabeth Taylor/Mother Teresa?'), the close-up magician/gigolo must be able to adjust to his viewer and to the setting so as to make his dialogue seem direct, meaningful, and other than preplanned or standardized. The repertoire may be the same, but the performance itself must always be different. The professional gigolo does not simply rely on circumstantial good fortune and wait, passively, for happy fate to strew his path with roses; rather, he will purposefully locate and set up opportunities for self-gain. In his performance the gigolo shows his craft and his cognizance of his role: if it looks natural and unrehearsed, spontaneous, something magical can happen.

The late Erving Goffman commented that, whenever an individual moves into a new social role, he ore she is unlikely to be fully prepared for what he or she will encounter: 'When the individual does move into a new position in society and obtains a new part to perform, he is not likely to be told in full detail how to conduct himself, nor will the facts of his new situation press sufficiently on him from the start to determine his conduct without his giving further thought to it. Ordinarily he will only be given a few cues, hints, and stage directions, and it will be assumed that he already has in his repertoire a large number of bits and pieces of performances that will be required in the new setting.'

It is the consciousness of his role tasks that defines the professional gigolo, not his level of attractiveness or the number of sexual partners he has had who have paid for services rendered. For example, it was common for male strippers to maintain that they were routinely 'picked up' by women when they performed, and then paid to perform a more specific act in a much more private setting. The male stripper may, by virtue of his profession, be seen by members of his audience as the type of man who would react other than indignantly to being propositioned with an offer of money for sex. In consequence, male respondents who were strippers were likely to estimate their female partners in the hundreds, or claim to have 'lost count.' However, promiscuity per se is not the definitive quality of the professional gigolo. Rather, the professional distinguishes himself as such by his seeking to maximize relational profits, his sensitivity to the cues of attraction evidenced on the part of potential patrons, and his knowing how to purposefully engineer a profitable relationship.

In illustration, one male escort, who worked for an agency and who ardently designed to become a society gigolo, discussed some of the difficulties he was having in finding and attracting suitable women. Bemoaning the fact that 'women lie' and 'put on false fronts,' he indignantly noted that, although he had taken to going regularly to the cocktail bar/disco of a high-priced hotel, the women who *seemed* to be wealthy were, as often or not, wearing the large portion of their income on their backs. He pondered whether or not he should let it become known that he was (or aspired to be) a gigolo. On the one hand, he commented, if his status as such became known, women who desired that form of relationship would expressly know to seek him out. On the other hand, he remarked, if he was known as a gigolo, perhaps women would seek to avoid being seen in his company, finding it 'too embarrassing' or 'intimidating' to be seen as the type who 'has to pay' for companionship. In consequence, he found himself painfully straddling the fence, uncertain as to the method by which his goals could best be achieved.

The man, 24 years old with a trendy pony-tail and a marked preference for Mondavi double-breasted suits, observed of his tribulations:

I was sitting in the bar and watched these two women – they were also working girls. One was old, but the other was young, beautiful body, nice face. The old one I think was a Madam using the young one to bring the guys in. She [the young one] would keep getting up to dance – very, very sexy dancer. Like a snake, you know? Like she had no bones at all in her body. I think the old one was fishing with a worm to get business … The old one came up to me and asked me to dance. She had these big boobs and just pinned me to the wall with them. Honest. Boobs hanging out – right under my chin. She didn't have to use her hands at all, just her boobs. She's the type who can eat you alive. I asked her, 'What do you do for a living?' She tells me, 'I help the girls to look better. I sell makeup.' I didn't want to dance with her; she was old and ugly. [How old was she?] Oh, probably, at least 30 … Anyhow, I told her 'I can't dance, I hurt my leg skiing.' She kept on talking to me anyhow, telling me how good-looking I was, 'You're a really sexy man.' And then she says, 'I do something similar to what you do. Are you a gigolo?'

I was cool and just said, 'So, do you think I'd be a good gigolo?' She told me, 'If your leg gets better' and walked away.

Now, I don't know. If she's just a hooker, it's not a big deal that maybe I made her mad at me. Maybe. Lots of really expensive hookers like to buy their sex – they're used to it and don't like the hassle. But maybe, like, I think, she's a madam and maybe she handles guys as well. I should go and talk to her. What do you think?

LEARNING THE SCRIPT: ACTING LIKE A 'GENTLEMAN'

All the gigolos we spoke to were conscious of the theatrical aspects of their work: the need for the staging and scripting of the drama they were engaged in, the need for techniques to manage a potentially unruly audience, the need to establish credibility and to deflect scepticism or disbelief, the importance of entrances and exits, and the utility and necessity of improvisational techniques that built upon past repertoires and scripts of behaviours.

Though the concept of the 'gentleman' may be antiquated as a social rank, the ideal of conduct which is part of its definition, or more accurately, its pose, was an important concern of our male respondents. In its strictest sense, the concept of the gentleman refers to a 'well-bred' man and suggests that ancestry and pedigree are all-important in the determination of moral and/or social character. While Dr Johnson defined the gentleman as 'a man of ancestry … all other dimensions seem to be whimsical,' since the time of Chaucer and his depiction of the 'very parfit gentle knight,' and perhaps before, the gentleman has been an allegorical ideal.

Although ideally the 'gentleman's code' was a pseudo-religion which would have commanded behaviour as virtuous and righteous as Job's, loopholes could always be found that made the gentleman's conduct more enigmatic than pious. For the gigolo, particularly the man who uses romance as the 'hook' in a sweetheart swindle, greater concern was often given to acting in a gentlemanly manner than to the ideal of conduct that was to distinguish the true gentleman from other men. While stressing the importance of 'acting like a gentleman,' these men were not endorsing Thackeray's view that to be a gentleman was 'to have lofty aims, to lead a pure life, to keep your honour virgin, to have the esteem of your fellow-citizens, and the love of your fireside; to bear good fortune meekly; to suffer evil with constancy; and through evil or good to maintain truth always.' Our respondents were much more likely to fashion their image of a gentleman along the lines of a Beau Brummel, or a 'dandy.' As used by them, the term gentleman simply seemed to connote a desired elegance of manner and conduct.

The comments of the following gigolo suggest the somewhat unconventional definition of gentlemanly conduct that is used by these men and how importance is attached to being able to read one's audience and respond appropriately on the basis of that unconventional knowledge.

I have carved out simple principles for getting women to respond to me. When I've got my act together I've got radar like a bat; I just know what to do and how to do it. I don't waste my time with people who don't matter; it's a waste of energy and a waste of time. Looks don't count – I look for quality people and go first class all the way. I'm not looking to get laid – that's pleasure, this is business.

Go some place second-rate and you meet second-class people. I'm too poor to go to cheap places, to not go first class. I go where the money is, where they'll be women with their husbands or by themselves, who are bored and looking for a good time. Resorts like Bendinat, Lyford Cay, St Tropez, Cannes are good because women are on holidays and looking for a good time. Besides, if they're at good places like that, they've either got lots of money or are looking to make some the same way I am. If she wants excitement I give it to her; if she just wants company and hand-holding in public, that's okay too, if she's willing to pay for it.

I approach women politely, lot of smiles but not overdone and I size them up beforehand. Very important. Like I sized you up already. You don't like offending people, you'd be afraid of making a scene – I could probably get you going if I tried to. You came in friendly but cool – that tells me you don't really trust me. But now, you've relaxed, you're sitting back in your chair, your body is more relaxed and you're aroused. [Really?] Yeah, you see, you've got your legs crossed on top of the other and you're tapping your foot in the air – that means that you're subconsciously masturbating. You're a strange lady but you know, I could get you – easy. You'd fall for a sob story. Most women do ...

I ask women things about themselves to get the ball rolling: 'What was your childhood like?'; 'Did you have a pet as a little girl?'; 'Did your father ever spank you?'; 'What did you want to be when you were little?'; 'Was your mother as beautiful as you are?'; 'Do you remember the first time you ever got kissed?' You probe their memories with questions nobody has ever asked them and get into their heads. By the time you've talked to them for an hour, you'll know their most intimate thoughts and what buttons to push. The thing to remember is: don't rush it, but don't forget there's others who'll take your chance for you if you don't have your timing right ...

Playing women is like playing any kind of game – you have to figure out if you've got any natural ability for it; if you don't, if you can learn enough to make it worth your while, and practise, always practice. Observe her carefully – is she shy? If she's sitting around in pants on a hot day you know she thinks she's fat or if she scrunches down and puts her hands over her thighs when she's sitting on the beach in her bathing suit. Tell her she has a sexy body or that she really turns you on. She knows deep down it's bullshit, but she still wants to hear it. Or, if she's a real dog – part chihuahua and part collie, and you don't know which part is which – tell her 'I just love your laugh, you have a beautiful laugh' ...

If she has a boyfriend or a husband around and she looks bored or upset, tell her 'It makes me mad to see a beautiful woman like you spending all your time alone. You have such a gorgeous walk, I bet you're a terrific dancer ... I know it really isn't my place to say this and please forgive me if I offend you, but you've got the wrong boyfriend. A woman like you should be out dancing not just sitting around ... Your boyfriend/husband seems like a very nice guy but I can't figure out what's wrong with him; why is he like that? If I could afford to, I'd be taking you shopping this minute and not letting you leave Rodeo Drive/Fifth Avenue until you had at least three complete stunning new outfits from sexy little undies to jewellery for each outfit. But that's the type of guy I am; I like to give things to people. I'm a giving sort of guy.' She'll generally be so coy by this time that it will be enough for you just to avoid woofing your cookies, but you just keep going.

You've got to be patient if you want to be successful. But that doesn't mean you spend all your time just on one woman. I have lots of women, and all think they are the 'only one' and that all the rest are simply good friends. But, if they see you with another woman you just say, 'Yes, she was coming on to me but I'm not interested in her.' She probably knows what's going on but she doesn't want to hear it ...

You can't tell me that deep down any woman who's supporting some guy doesn't know what's going on. I don't care how good her boyfriend is – that's crap. She's paying for her own good time and she *knows* it, even if she doesn't like to admit it. So you play around with her fantasy. You get her to trust you ... It's important that she doesn't catch you lying, so everything has to look true and sound true. Claude [another gigolo] nearly blew it with Diana because he told her he was fluent in French and couldn't even translate the menu in a French restaurant. I'm careful to keep the promises I make. If my lady tells me to meet her at 6 o'clock I'm there at *exactly* 6 o'clock. Not one minute before or after. When you come right down to it, she's paying for it and she expects it ...

If you follow me, you have to be a lot like a psychiatrist, always reading people, always trying to get inside their head. A lot of women I've known have been very demanding, but I recognize that they've got certain rights too. I'm not using them any more than they're using me. It's not like they're retarded cripples, that they can't pack it in if they don't like what's happening. And God knows I'm not robbing the cradle ... You have to have the right attitude.

'Alicia' [a female socialite] isn't any better than I am and look who she's married to. I could tell you stories and you'd realize that she's the biggest slut around since way back ... She's a hustler too in her own way even though she has the money not to be. For example, if she has a big party coming up what she does is go into the best shop, buy a dress – money no object – put it on her charge account, wear it, then take it back saying it was too small. It's embarrassing to go shopping with her because she does it all the time and the saleswomen don't even want to wait on her any more. Why should they? She'll come in with a bunch of her friends over lunch and buy six or seven cashmere sweaters and then, the next day, when none of her friends are around, she'll return them all. [Why does she do it?] To impress her friends. And because she's bored. You know the bumper sticker 'Born to shop'? That was made for Alicia. Fits her to a tee ... She's also cheap. Wants something for nothing. Thinks she's owed something because her old man is a big shot ... [How do you know she does this?] I've been with her. Once she bought a black crepe cocktail dress with taffeta sleeves – beautiful dress – and I *saw* her wearing it, but back it went. No shame whatsoever. When she goes into a shop you can see the old saleswomen – the ones who have been there for years – just run in the opposite direction. They work on commission, and with her it's a gamble as to whether she'll keep the dress, so why even bother? ... It's [being a gigolo] no crime and the women I go with aren't any better than I am.

Say I go up to you right now and say 'You make me really horny. I'd love to go to bed with you' – there's no harm in that, is there? You say 'yes' or 'no' and we go from there. Same thing if the woman is rich and sitting by herself having lunch or a glass of wine at the Polo Club or the Relais Plaza – wherever. I'm Adam and they're Eve and all is fair. If they go to bed with me, I didn't rape them, right? And if I tell them I don't have any money and they *offer* it to me – well I can't be blamed for that, can I? It's not like I held a gun to their heads and said 'Give me all of your money or I'm going to blow your head off.' They're free to do what they want to do – or who they want to do ...

I'm trying to make you understand that everyone is looking out for themselves. If the women were any better than we are they'd be standing on the streetcorner like the Salvation Army and handing their money out. You don't see them doing that, do you? Everyone expects something, and if she wants sex or love or thinks of marriage, good times, she's willing to pay for her fun. Why should I stop her? ...

Did you see the Woody Allen movie *Zelig*? [No, why?] Well, that's what being a gigolo is all about. It was great; he'd change his name, nationality, appearance, personality to be just like whoever he was with – so he'd fit in ... I move with the best and I'm always testing for class. I have no time for guys who sponge off a woman who is earning $30,000 a year – I'd never do that. I mean, everyone has the right to live, and women shouldn't have to pay for a guy when they're just keeping it together themselves. But a woman whose old man can't even count his money – it's another story. It has to be worth my while.

THE PROPS OF THE MAGICIAN

In the letters from our would-be gigolos presented at the beginning of this chapter, it is obvious that these gentlemen placed great emphasis on their possession of personal props or commodities (youth, height, and other physical attributes); this is perhaps to be expected of the neophyte or beginner. However, in describing the gigolo as engaged in the production of magic, a distinction must be drawn between magic that involves the use of commodities or apparatus and crafted or 'natural' magic. Just as anyone may wander into a magic store and buy a box of tricks, any man can go into a clothing store and a barber shop and emerge looking, as best he can, like Richard Gere. However, the man with a box of tricks is not necessarily skilled to perform magic, nor is the Richard Gere clone. If an aspiring gigolo seeks to attain professional status simply by relying on the gimmicks and gizmos identified as important in, for example, *American Gigolo* – the designer clothes, blow-dried hair, and workout equipment – he may not succeed; these are simply gimmicks that, in fact, may make it more difficult to create a magical impression. If the prop conveys an impression of something patently manufactured as a prop, it and not the performer becomes the target of interest. Moreover, the identification of an attribute as a common prop may destroy the illusion of magic by suggesting that anyone who possessed the prop could perform the same tricks. This is not to say that our male respondents ignored such things as grooming. They did not. However, they considered these things to be simply a part and not the totality of the role.

Even when I've been totally broke I never looked it. You've got to stay in shape and look good because that's your ticket. I've got a tuxedo that set me back almost nine hundred but it was worth it because it looks sharp each time I wear it ... Two or three excellent-quality suits, preferably a light-coloured linen or raw silk, a wool suit, a good dinner suit. A good-quality coat – I've got an excellent cashmere trench coat. Dinner shirts. You don't need a lot of clothes because if your lady has got any style she'll flesh out your wardrobe. After all, she'll probably be buying more clothes for you than you will anyhow, but you should do the basics like making sure your belt and shoes match ... I like shirts which need cufflinks – I think they look a lot smarter with a formal suit and it's a good way of getting women to spend some money ... I have a facial at least once a month and condition my skin every day. It's stupid that men think you have to be gay to have a facial – how would they like it if a woman had two big zits on the side of her neck and whiteheads from blocked pores? ... My eyebrows naturally grow together so I've had electrolysis to remove that and also the hair on my back, which can be a real turn off to some women ...

If you want a higher standard of living, you've got to look the part. You've got to make yourself at home on a tennis court, a golf course, a sailboat, a yacht. If you've got lots of money yourself it doesn't matter so much, but if you're trying to get in among a better class of people you have to pay attention to the small things because the upper classes can be total snobs. [For example?] Never wear clip-on ties. [Laughs]. Or, saying 'dinner jacket' and not tuxedo, never looking overawed at what anybody says or owns – like if you go to a party and you've always liked Liza Minnelli and she's there, you don't come on like some tourist from Milwaukee and drool all over her. You have to have style ... If you drink scotch it should be old scotch. You have to have cool and always act as if you belong and know what you're doing. (35-year-old gigolo)

As Frank Goodman observed in Melville's *The Confidence Man*, 'Life is a picnic *en costume* ... To come in plain clothes, with a long face, as a wiseacre, only makes one a discomfort to himself, and a blot upon the scene.'

DOING TRICKS

As we noted earlier, for both the professional magician and the professional gigolo, what distinguishes their role from that of the enthusiastic

amateur and hustler is not their looks or wardrobe but rather their awareness of the interpersonal skills that are essential in the production of magic
– the resourcefulness, the creativity, the role taking or attempting to gain a
sense of the other, and the use of this information to anticipate, plan, develop, and authenticate a course of action. Without some sort of effective
presentation, props are in themselves seldom mesmerizing or compelling
viewing. Rather, the magician must attempt to convey, by word, deed, or
grand design, the impression that something wondrous is occurring.

'Hustling' per se requires few of the elaborate props and relatively little
of the attention to craft that distinguishes the life of the society gigolo; it
simply requires a neat and somewhat clean apartment where a hustler and
his patron can go in relative anonymity, a man who is willing to play for
pay, and a woman able to pay for play. What the hustler typically does
not offer or desire is a sustained fantasy, a contracted and prolonged
magical performance.

Robert, 31 years old, was an aspiring amateur in Miami, Florida. A
friend of his stated that Robert was willing to talk and forwarded his telephone number. According to the friend 'Rob is the best salesman of them
all. He sells books when he's not hooking and he's taken and applied the
whole sales pitch to get women. Nothing in sales is left to chance – you say
X, he says Y, you say A, he says B. There's only so many questions or
doubts people will raise and it helps if you've got it committed to memory
like Rob has. He's done it all a thousand times ... he knows exactly what to
do and say. You'll *love* Rob.' The first author rang and heard the dulcet
tones of Robert: 'Hi. This is Rob. I'm really sorry that I'm not here to speak
with you, but if you leave your name and number, I'll get right back to you
because I'd *really* love to talk with you. Have a nice day. Ciao Bella.'

Despite his friend's build-up, Robert was not particularly charming or
attractive, but then, it turned out, he did not really desire to become a kept
man. He preferred that his time be paid for in cash and was not ill-dis-
posed to stealing from patrons, setting them up for a break and enter by
collegial professional thieves, or fencing the melted-down gold or ex-
tracted jewels from items he had himself stolen. He distinguished his role
from that of the gigolo:

Since I was little I always dreamed of being rich. I guess that isn't that uncommon
really, but for most people it doesn't go any farther than buying a lottery ticket.

I call myself a hooker, not a gigolo, even though my customers are women,
because I see a gigolo as someone who gets 100 per cent of his money from working
at it, which I don't. It's just one thing of many things that I do to earn money.

[How did you first start hooking?] I was in the military, a 'grunt,' and my sergeant's wife started coming on to me really strong. I was a young kid with a 24-hour hard-on and, at that time, I was just after whatever pussy I could get, so I didn't think too much about it ... When I got out, well, I couldn't seem to make it any place else because I had a dishonourable discharge. [For what?] You are nosy, aren't you? For getting caught getting it on with a guy. It happens all the time in the military but they just wanted to make an example with us ... I think females have it tougher hustling than guys do. No one tries to hassle me or wrestle the price down or walk out without paying. I might get a woman who went out and had a bit to drink but she's not going to be some stinking drunk ...

My worst experience as a hooker? Nothing really bad. I've had a couple of women who were straight out of *Play Misty for Me*, real fucked-up broads who wanted me, like, to marry them, you know. No fucking way. Once I had a woman throw up on me while she was giving me a blow job but that's about it ...

Ads are necessary and word-of-mouth. A street hustler can wait 50 years before a woman will drive up and pay him for a date. It just doesn't happen. Escort agencies are better, but it's still not common. Women like their little games too much. They're just not going to walk over and say 'I want to fuck you. How much?' ...

I have regulars who want to play dress up every time but that's different. [How?] Simple. We're talking an hour, couple of hours tops, each time. I can handle that. I ask how much you're willing to spend and what your trip is and if you're willing to pay what I'm looking at, then way we go. I don't have to like you. But when I'm not working – that's different. I need my own space. I don't want to be caught up in someone's trip all the time.

Matthew, an American, was interviewed on a fall afternoon in a trendy restaurant on South Moulton Street in London. Over six feet tall, with an athletic build, he was good-looking in a rugged way, with closely cropped, somewhat thinning brown hair, moustache, and a wind-burnt tan. Dressed in ironed blue jeans, with a khaki green/yellow and maroon turtleneck and beige and maroon tasselled leather loafers, Matthew was strikingly dissimilar to the somewhat prissy fastidiousness of the Richard Gere stereotype. He looked more like the stereotype of an air force officer. When this was remarked upon he laughed and replied:

That's good. That's what I want. The John Travolta three-piece suit is long out. Hell, John Travolta is long out ... I used to be able to eat like a horse. When I was younger I could eat all the time, anything I wanted, but once you hit 30 you have to watch it because you start getting the love handles and it's disgusting ... I keep myself in shape because I feel better, but it's also an investment ...

Right now, I'm sitting pretty because I landed a great old woman who is really generous but, women are fickle, you know? Today, I'm the love of her life and she's buying me everything and anything. Tomorrow, who knows? Maybe her old man finds out. Maybe the relationship becomes too hot for her. Maybe – whatever. You have to treat any relationship like any business deal. Sink some money into it, put in a lotta time, and keep your sights open for something else to come along ...

I try to get Chloe to give me cash but it's not always easy. Lots of the stuff I get from Chloe is pretty useless – it's women stuff – a silver frame to keep her picture in – tell me, is she buying that for me or for her? Like this sweater is great, right? Cost Chloe over 600 pounds, but after a while it can get like you're getting Christmas presents all the time from your mother ... The expenses are always there, and some women just don't like giving cash. Well, maybe you need cash.

Before I landed Chloe, I had to hock a set of camera equipment worth over $6,000 and all I got was not even a lousy grand. When you're selling something second-hand it's always a buyer's market. They're doing you the favour and they know it, so you get basically nothing ...

[How did you get Chloe to keep you?] Very carefully. [Laughs] That's what separates the boys from the men. Any schmuck can get a gift now and then; what I do is a full-time job. You have to make your own opportunities. You can't just sit back and wait for the women to come to you. Well, I guess you can if you want to pay someone to pimp for you but that means losing control and a big cut out of what you get. That's shit work anyhow.

I don't care what business you're in, you're never going to make any money working for someone else. Sure, you have your nine-to-five guys, but they're the ones who are punching the same clock year in, year out, until they're ready to drop. And then what happens? Golden handshake. 'Thanks very much and fuck you.' Nah, you have to make it on your own terms if you want to make big money.

One of my friends – Nadia, did you meet her? – she worked for awhile for a madam in Los Angeles. They really did a mind fuck on her. She was going to be an actress, and they told her, we'll send you to the big parties, you'll meet the hottest producers, so-and-so's wife she used to work for us – and she bought it all. I'm not saying she didn't make lots of money. She did. And she blew it all up her nose. Because she didn't have any control. She was just a puppet. Go here. Go there. Do this guy. Do this chick. It's like any big business. They don't care about the little guy. They'll try to screw you any way they can, and if they think you're weak, then they'll really screw you ...

I worked for an agency once, but only to build contacts. In and out. Its not for me. The guys that work for agencies are losers. Either they're actors looking for the big break, and think they're fucking hot, or fags. Their attitudes are crude, their tactics are crude – strictly small-time ...

If you work for an agency, all you'll ever be is small-time because any woman who hires from an agency is looking for a one-off. Let's say a woman comes in from out of town and she wants a thrill, okay, she calls an agency. That can be okay but it's not going to go anywhere because she's gone and, at best, you'll see her when she comes back into town. You get regulars but you're just a piece of meat ...

Some of these women were really into some pretty sick things. [Like?] They'd want to tie me up or have me tie them up, piss into their mouths. Some I could handle. Poking a woman up her ass doesn't turn me on, but I can handle it, or if she wants me to come between her breasts, hey, that's no problem. But the bondage crap, that's not for me ...

One woman I remember, she was into the 'Blue Angel' scene. Would dress up with this black leather James Dean jacket, leather hat, the high black boots, the whole bit, tie me up and I was supposed to play like I was helpless. She liked the real beefcake guys – the big muscles, the guys who worked out with heavy weights – to do this trip with. That's not my scene, but I could handle it ...

One woman, she hired me as a joke for one of her friends. Well that's real great, thanks a lot, now I'm a joke ... With married women you have to feel your way and test her out. A lot of married women are looking for affairs, but they don't want to be rushed.

With Chloe, I had met her a few times at parties and I thought she was interested, but I couldn't really tell at first. A few months later, I had gone skiing for a few weeks with some friends and I ran into her at a party that Victor [a friend] gave. We said hello, and she said, 'Where've you been?' so I told her. Then she says to me, 'I missed you.' Well there was my ticket. I told her, 'You have? Really?' Threw the ball back into her court, right? 'Well,' she says, 'We always have such fun together.' My turn. I tell her, 'You have a house in ——. Next time, why don't we go there together and stay there?' ...

You have to be part hustler, part public relations man, and full-time entertainer, but you have to make it all look natural.

Another male elaborated on his strategy for making his conversation compelling to his audience:

I went to a party that was hosted by —— who writes about sex and the rich, and all evening everyone was hinting that they were this character or that character in her book. The rich love celebrity stories – any celebrity will do. I met one woman, incredibly tight-assed broad that you'd think chews on iron for breakfast, and what does she start talking to me about? How she's close personal friends with the 'Happy Hooker' Xaviera Hollander and how she dated the guy who was the original Superman. [Was it true?] I doubt it, but people like her just live for celebrity stories.

When I first started, I thought I had to keep it secret who I had been with. Bullshit. I tell them, 'Oh yeah, I went for drinks with —— and grew up with —— and, did you know that ——, the big male sex symbol, used to be an escort for a fag dating service in Minneapolis?' They're mesmerized by it ... So you tell some celebrity stories, make some up and get others that you can pass along. The average person has got an attention span of about 15 minutes, but tell them stories of who you know, and who you have blowed, and they'll sit there for hours hanging on your every word. (New York, 33-year-old gigolo)

Yet another male respondent commented:

I'm a salesman. There's better looking guys and for some women that's all there is involved. What's on sale is pure fantasy, you tell me your dreams and I tell them back to you ...

In my teen years I didn't date a lot; I grew up with the idea that the only guys that could get dates were the football types. I was always the 'best friend,' the one the girl loved like the brother she never had. It taught me a lot about women, about what they were really like ...

The secret? Never tell *anyone* the full story about what you're doing. They'll be people who hate your guts – forget about them. Set your goals and know what you want out of life – five years down the road, ten years down the road – if you stay in it long enough to get a gold watch, you'll never get a gold watch. Figure out what you want, what's available and the best way to go for it. If you want to marry money, marry big money because if you've got to eat shit, you don't want to eat it in little bites. Build contacts with important people but don't waste their time with little favours – they'll get pissed off with you. (28-year-old gigolo)

MANAGING THE AUDIENCE

The gigolo, like all magicians intent on doing magic, must overcome scepticism and disbelief. It is important to stress that the magician must constantly attempt to convey, negotiate, and refurbish the apparent authenticity of his performance. Like the stage heckler, the viewer may refuse to give credibility to the images the gigolo seeks to project and/or have a potential source of knowledge which serves to unmask, uncover, or debunk the illusions projected by the would-be magician. For example, one of our respondents who was a male escort working for an agency presented himself to women as an expert in elctronics rather than as a full-time member of the world's oldest profession. While claiming a bogus professional status may be thought advantageous inasmuch as the title 'electronics expert' vicariously confers an occupational status higher than that given to 'male escort,' there are nevertheless risks involved in doing so. In the case of our escort, his attempts to embroider his accomplishments were to become somewhat more than slightly ridiculous. Eager to catapult himself into a rarefied occupational category, the man claimed to be a 'semi-conductor,' which sounds impressive but, in actuality, refers to a thing – not a profession.

Similarly, a second man was more than eager to convey the impression that he was a consummate businessman who accompanied women for 'the love of women' rather than for financial recompense. Eager to demonstrate his independent financial status, he boasted of having worked for the BBC in London and owning both a flat in Paris and a summer condo in Florida. He additionally boasted of having attended Oxford University. When the first author asked him what college at Oxford he had attended (the 'university' being composed of various colleges), he snarled and somewhat contemptuously reiterated that he had not attended a college, he had attended Oxford.

Intent on playing his role to a maximum-capacity audience, the gentleman gigolo who is homosexual or bisexual is highly unlikely to ever campaign for gay rights, act 'camp,' or draw attention to his preferred sexual partner. Homosexuality, one gigolo observed, remains a 'touchy subject' in smart society, especially in the midst of the AIDS crisis. A bisexual gigolo observed: 'No one really has time or interest in long conversations about homosexuality; everyone knows that many of the best fashion designers ... are gay, but nobody's interested in making a big deal about it. If you're smart you don't mention it [that one is gay], you don't justify it as better or worse than being straight and you don't defend it by giving a Who's Who of fagdom.'

To obtain stature as one who is kept by only the best required attention to detail and learning how to choreograph one's actions for maximum impact. A gigolo originally from Brazil, but now living in the United States, remarked:

I know many men who would call themselves 'kept men' – and with pride – but who really are not. Some can make it while others, well, just cannot. In any large city there are clubs, restaurants, hotels where one can get to know the rich. If it takes $1,000–$2,000 to join a smart sports club, it's still worth it, even if it means that you don't go drinking or buy any furniture ...

Women with me have never been a problem because I'm comfortable with myself and with my sexuality and my lifestyle and women appreciate that. I love sports –

swimming, skiing, aerobics, hiking, karate – just about any sports. If you are good at sports, it is easy to meet all kinds of tutus there. [Tutus?] Spandex. Women. Even if a man does not have much money, he can join an aerobics class, though I'd say that the number of good women there has fallen off in the last four or five years because it's not as trendy any more ...

I don't like women that much as a group. I don't like their social characters, but if you do sports, at least the women won't be fat. I hate fat women ...

I'm not a slut. I have been, but I hate myself when I am. Some men will go to bars and just pick up a girl who is easy – they're both sluts. He wants the power of the moment. That type of man will never be a gigolo. [Why not?] First of all, if you meet a woman in a cheap bar or a disco, you're already at a disadvantage because women go there with this mind-set that says, 'I'm going to just have fun and get fucked.' At the beginning of the night they think they'll find Jeremy Irons or Sting to fuck, so they aren't receptive. Later, it's 'Oh well' and they're just looking at you as last choice. That is bad, because to be a gigolo you must make a woman see you, as a winner – not as a loser.

Second, the type of woman who goes into a club and picks up a man is already a slut; she won't pay. You can take her home, screw her all night and in the morning – poof, she disappears. She can pick up men, why pay? If you meet a woman and you are skiing, or you teach her tennis – whatever – she is in a different space altogether. If you meet her at Cortina skiing, you look at her skis, her clothes – probably can't ski at all but, she's got the best equipment money can buy. That's the type of woman you want to spend time on ...

Never ask a woman for anything; let her know what you like – and wait. If she's got class, she'll know what to do ...

Style is very important. American men who try to be gigolos act like farmers; they try too hard and look phoney. They go to a good restaurant and make idiots of themselves by trying to talk with the waiter as if they're friends from school together instead of paying attention to their woman. They try to make the waiter or the waitress think that they are a great guy while the woman just sits and watches. American men are very good at picking up waitresses but not at being gigolos ...

If a man wants to be a gigolo and doesn't know someone who already is successful at it, he should find himself some smart friends who can introduce him to people who matter, seek out the people who count. If he's AC-DC this can be helpful too ... I have made close friends always with people who can help me in some ways – the fashion buyer for menswear at ——, the top hair stylist at ——, the one who does my investments – I fuck him every so often when I'm in Manhattan, but we're good friends too ...

Too many people have small-town attitudes; they think they have to please everyone. I don't bother with people who don't count and I seek out those who can be helpful to me. Smart people – that's who count (Chicago, 25-year-old gigolo)

The aspiring gigolo must not simply possess a 'bag of tricks' designed to captivate, but must solicit opportunities and people who are likely to enhance his opportunities. As a 28-year-old gigolo commented, 'everything I do is built towards recognizing me and responding to me in a positive way.' One gigolo was terribly efficient at organizing his lover's social life, another was able to convince his lover by his undivided attention and apparent rapt fascination that he truly desired to hear – for the umpteenth time – stories of her late husband's infidelities for hours at a time. If, as the man suggested, 'all of her stories have long white beards,' there was not a hint of this attitude in the posture he adopted with her.

AUDIENCE REACTIONS

Regardless of the interests, preferences, and peccadilloes of the perpetrators of illusion, the illusions themselves may captivate, enchant, and foster affection, companionship, or feelings of well-being on the part of the viewer. As the comments of various respondents suggest, there is not one singular or homogeneous audience that will uniformly evaluate the illusions magically created by the gigolo.

A close friend of an American Madame Bountiful commented:

Once she realized the situation [that she had been 'conned' out of a substantial sum of money] she then became sufficiently enraged that she wanted retaliation. There was documented evidence of about $100,000 cash outlay to the man, as well as undocumented but suspicious expenditures of about the same amount. When she realized there was only one legal recompense she could seek, for a forged check for approximately $300, she realized that it wasn't worth the cost to herself. Meanwhile, in the past year and a half she has had second thoughts. She now blames all of her other associates, including her son, for the loss of her companion, and her frequent complaint is that 'money isn't anything.' Incidentally, her physician agrees and has stated that the man 'met a great many of her needs.' She has tried every means she has to get him back; so far, he seems to be enjoying the friendship and companionship of another woman ... Perhaps male companionship is a necessary ingredient to self-perception on the part of some women; perhaps it is a cultural reliance on males and a feeling of inadequacy in meeting day-to-day demands that leads them to be willing to pay for male consideration of them as persons.

Another American woman wrote: 'Your research project may very well be trying to point up the gullibility of women and their easy exploitation. This I resent, and I would suggest to you that it may be that the sharing of resources may not be viewed by some individuals as exploitation as much as it may be a willingness to 'pay one's way' if one is able. If a widow needs plumbing replaced, she must hire a plumber; if she needs an escort to a dance and finds someone who is willing to escort her for a meal, a tank of gasoline, a new suit and provide her with the pleasure of companionship, she may very well feel that her pleasure is worth the price if she has it.'

For others, however, there was less satisfaction. In contrast to the complacent acceptance of the respondent who seemed to regard her gigolo as a 'convenience,' another woman, 49 years old and residing in London, England, was less serene. The woman, a divorced boutique owner, purchased for her lover a freehold lease on a Chelsea apartment and a Morgan sports car. To show her faith in him, she additionally acted as the financial backer for his custom woollen shop – a venture that was never to result in anything more than a pencilled business prospectus. She reacted to the illusions plied by the gigolo in a much different way than the women earlier quoted.

To me 'gigolo' conjures up impressions of an almost lovable, rascally type – irresponsible but honest in his irresponsibility. The creature I am familiar with does not fit this description. He is an evil, scheming person, literally living off the lives, the dreams of women, as well as any comforts they may provide him with. He is highly intelligent, devious to the point of brilliancy and, of course, an accomplished liar. His self-indulgence has hurt so very many people that I truly believe his past should be exposed.

I think of myself not as his past lover but as one of his victims. In fact, my entire family's life has been deeply scarred by this man. I've lost the ability to trust a man – he saw to it that I'd never be able to live with another man again. It's not the money which I can't replace, it's the trust. If a man tells me now that he loves me I just say 'Righto,' 'Super' – I can't believe a man any more.

It would seem that in reviewing the magician's performance, Bountifuls varied enormously both in the likelihood that they would see through the deceptive magic plied by the gigolo and in their satisfaction with the illusions provided. Some felt themselves seduced; others were simply amused. It would seem that the difference in assessments stemmed only partially from the professional competence of the gigolo as a magician; Bountifuls who were most scathing in their comments also seemed to be those women who most ardently wished to believe that there was such a thing as magic, who envisaged a relationship as, if not a panacea, a sought-after palliative to life's trials and burdens. They wanted – or needed – to believe that what the gigolo offered was far more than contrivance, a bag of tricks, an illusion.

Accordingly, the ability to see through the magician's performance, to simply enjoy it for what it provided, and then proceed on one's way in a light-hearted manner, seemed dependent upon the strength of the Bountiful's desire, or need, for a relationship. The stronger the need, the greater the likelihood of being seduced by the gigolo's magical line and the greater the resulting sense of bitterness and/or victimization upon realizing that the line was illusory. Conversely, the less the need, the less the commitment, and the greater the likelihood she would only be amused by what appeared, to her, to be a transparent stage presentation.

In terms that we introduced in chapter 3, Bountifuls who were characterized by a sense of 'deficiency' and the need for a love that would make them whole were more likely to be seduced by the magical performance and suffer disillusionment when the performance was over. In contrast, Bountifuls who were emotionally sufficient, of and in themselves, appeared to be able to sit back and simply enjoy the performance. Not requiring another to make them whole, they could afford to maintain a sense of emotional distance and, to the extent they became involved, enjoy a feeling of 'being' in love – or at least a reasonably acceptable facsimile. When the performance was over, disillusionment did not attend since no illusions on her part were involved in the first place.

Deconstructing the magic and the magician is always somewhat precarious without making the viewer seem somewhat gullible and hapless. This is not our intent. However, in presenting the comments of our male respondents, it is important to note that, while the Madame Bountiful may conceive of her relationship as 'unique,' signifying and attesting to a special intimacy, the gigolo commonly considers his partner as simply the viewer of his performance, as the 'interchangeable other.' As such, his comments may suggest an indifference that some could characterize as cold or unfeeling. Viewed dispassionately, however, it is simply the pragmatic voice of a magician describing his own stage performance and attests to his self-reflexivity on the topic of what he conceives to be a professional role.

THE GIGOLO AS CONFIDENCE MAN

In their book *Road Hustler*, Robert Prus and his co-author, C.R.D. Sharper, linked the roles of the magician and the 'con man' and suggested that these roles have much in common. They suggested that the magician is most basically conning his audience, and the con man is using magic to ensnare and captivate those he would seek to manipulate. According to Prus and Sharper, regardless of the type of confidence games played – of which there would appear to be an almost unlimited variety – all confidence men must successfully negotiate five basic steps. These are: (1) selecting a target for one's confidence game; (2) integrating oneself with the target and establishing trust; (3) encouraging the target to invest in the confidence man's game plan; (4) acquiring the profits of the confidence game; and (5) defusing the situation should feelings of anger, resentment, disappointment, suspicion, or hostility ensue. While this process would not be applicable to all types of gigolos, it does provide a framework in which to understand perhaps the most notorious – the Casanova Con Man or Sweetheart Swindler.

In the parlance of the confidence man, the 'sting' refers to a confidence game wherein the victim is successfully taken for a sizeable amount of money. In the history of the con, the 'matrimonial con' – wherein the victim is pledged marriage in order to have money given to the seemingly adoring paramour – is one which has successfully been played on both men and women. Because of the legacy and continuing use of the confidence game, we can briefly note the *modus operandi* used by that master magician earlier referred to, Sigmund Engel.

Sigmund Engel featured prominently in Jay Robert Nash's anecdotal history of the confidence man, *Hustlers & Con Men*, and, according to Nash, Engel's approach to his victims seldom varied. After ascertaining the wealth of the middle-aged (preferably widowed) lady, Engel would 'accidently' spy his selected target in a posh hotel or restaurant, feign a startled mien and exclaim, 'Why, you look just like my wife – I mean my former wife, God bless her, she's dead these last four years.'

The selected target, who might ordinarily have been suspicious of a strange man approaching her, would apparently feel obliged to respond to Engel's tragic comment in some appropriately sympathetic manner – at which point Sigmund would launch into his routine. Punctuating his conversation with the audible reminder to himself to telephone Hollywood – where his motion picture studio awaited his approval to continue filming the multimillion-dollar film he was making – Engel would pointedly check his watch as he launched into a conversation that typically featured fascinating personal accounts of the glamorous individuals he knew and the events he had attended.

When he would ask the woman to lunch, it was customary that she – by now intrigued and captivated by this urbane fellow who had introduced himself as the son of the man who controlled Universal Studios (or, alternatively, as a millionaire entrepreneur, an oil baron, a shipping magnate, a corporate lawyer for eastern banks) – would accept his invitation. Over time, Engel's purposeful prattle would convince her that not only did she bear an uncanny resemblance to this amazing man's dear departed wife but, as well, she could succeed to her position. The poor man! The trials those temperamental actresses and actors put him through! She could become his harbour in the storm, insulating him against the caprices of egomaniacal Hollywood types, business wranglings, and assorted thorns in the mantle of power which Engel so stoically wore.

After lavishly spending money on a whirlwind courtship, Engel generally had little difficulty in getting his targeted lady to agree to marriage within the first few days following their initial meeting. To assuage any doubts the woman might have had about ulterior motives on his part, he was always careful to allow her to 'accidentally' see his bank statements or chequebook – always from a distance – which would reveal enormous credits. Indeed, he portrayed himself as eager to share the fruits of his business acumen with his new wife; after suggesting an extended honeymoon, he would offer to take care of his bride's financial concerns. His bride, secure in the knowledge of her marital status and the seeming largesse of her husband, invariably withdrew her savings and handed them over to her ever-considerate husband.

After excusing himself to briefly attend to the opening of their joint account and the collection of various goods and luggage supposedly purchased in anticipation of their honeymoon, Engel would depart for new financial conquests and matrimonial vistas. Although pictures of Engel do not show a terribly attractive or prepossessing figure, he was undeniably successful in plying his magic; he was to 'marry' at least 200 women and acquire at least $6 million prior to finally being arrested in 1949 at the age of 80.

Upon his eventual arrest Engel informed the press that he was 'afflicted with womenmania ... Surely they can't punish me for enjoying lovely women. I go for the 57 varieties ... The age of a woman doesn't mean a thing. After all, the best tunes are played on the oldest fiddles.' Although he later attempted to justify his actions as acceptable, given that 'these women were trying to take me too,' he was convicted of grand larceny and sentenced from two to ten years in prison.

While 'celebrity lookalike' prostitutes of more recent times largely capitalize on their appearance and resemblance to such well-known actors as – who else? – Richard Gere, Burt Reynolds, and Elvis Presley to promote themselves as 'fantasy dates' for women, men, and couples, the 'star quality' possessed by Engel rested on more conventional status symbols. Whether or not Engel presented himself as 'Lord Beaverbrook' (but one of his many aliases), he consistently posed as a person of culture and wealth, a 'gentleman' who adored and worshipped women. This 'suave outlaw' with the 'aplomb of a prince,' who, according to one newspaper account, acted 'as though a red plush carpet were unrolling before him,' was highly effective as a 'sophisticated swindler.' Indeed, even after his arrest, one of his victims publicly maintained, 'Regardless of what he has done ... he is my impression of a perfect gentleman – and I have associated with some of the best society in New York.'

Many famed practitioners of the matrimonial con – for example, Nathaniel Herbert Wheeler, who cajoled 150 women over a ten-year period for $1 million; John Leonard Simmons, the Los Angeles Casanova who courted and conned more than 50 women out of approximately half a million dollars; John Levy, the Midwest American rake who defrauded women out of close to a million dollars before making the FBI's Most Wanted List; and George Ashley, who utilized his matrimonial club 'Life's Estates Ltd.' to compose not only personality and sexual profiles of his targets but financial profiles as well – used love, or its promise, as the 'pitch' or the verbal snare to induce the willing participation of the designated target. Sheathed in the gossamer veil of romance, the pragmatic nature of the man's involvement was misrepresented and disguised through artful illusions and the purposeful manipulation of images.

Earlier we noted that, for the professional, a script is modified only when circumstances dictate. That the script itself may be less than original is notable. Consider, for example, the tactics described in a 1955 article entitled 'A Way with Women,' by Robert M. Yoder, who observed:

John Leonard Simmons ... employed a favorite tactic, his remarkable resemblance gambit. The target widow was in the lobby of a Los Angeles hotel, her home. Simmons, a stout, pleasant-looking man in his fifties, hurried over. He stared: 'If ever a woman looked like my wife,' he declared, 'you do.'

There is a backspin on that shot and it is difficult to return. If the lady was offended, if she hadn't liked Simmons' looks, she could have given him an icy 'Well, I'm not!' or a haughty sniff. But she wasn't offended, and Simmons at once apologized; watch him work. 'You must pardon me for staring,' he said. 'You see, my dear wife passed on just four years ago.'

The widow's sympathies were touched ... She, too, had lost a mate, she said ... Simmons peered intently. 'Lady,' he said. 'You have just found yourself a husband' ... [H]onest folk always underestimate men like Simmons. In a matter of six weeks, he had moved on with $6300 of the widow's money ...

Simmons could make the remarkable resemblance even greater, as he did in Long Beach, the quarry this time being a widow from Iowa. It was the season of the Rose Bowl. The hotel was packed and the tingle of gala events was in the air. The stout little man hurried toward the widow with a smile that said, 'What a wonderful coincidence! Imagine running into you here.'

"Pardon me, madam,' he said happily. 'You're Mrs. Dunlap, aren't you?' His tone made it clear that Mrs. Dunlap was a fine woman to be, and the widow must have regretted having to deny it. 'No,' she said, 'I'm Mrs. Dunham.' 'The resemblance!' Simmons marveled. 'It's simply amazing. Doctor Dunlap was our family physician, back in Colorado. I always thought highly of the Dunlaps. Why, one winter night, Doctor Dunlap came through a blizzard to save one of our children.'

Touche for Simmons, obviously. Everyone is in favour of doctors' coming through blizzards to save children ... Simmons' next move was to sit down. The widow sat down too. She wasn't Mrs. Dunlap, of course. Still the names were close – Dunlap, Dunham. A small thing, but wonderfully effective in combatting the word 'stranger.' Not much trouble for Simmons either. Simply a matter of learning the lady's name from the hotel help, and choosing another with a partial overlap.

Now Simmons told the widow all about himself – about his days in the stock market – highly successful – about his five mythical married children, one adopted. In a day or two, Mrs. Dunham was referring to Simmons, archly, as her 'boyfriend.' That privilege cost her $1300. Her niece contributed $5000, two of the niece's friends, $100 more. All thrust their money on Simmons eagerly, thinking he was letting them in on a big mysterious deal in wheat, with high profits and no risks ...

Men in this line of work have to be right in their estimate of what the victims want, and they don't put too much stock in the drawing power of romance, *per se*. They promise love and devotion, of course. But they also give the lady a peek at a well-stuffed wallet and lead her to expect a cushioned life several cuts above her present circumstances. Blue Heaven with a full-time maid, plenty of charge accounts, and a generous husband.

The type of illusion conjured up by the Sweetheart Swindler is perhaps the most notorious of all the illusions created by the gigolo, for it is often accompanied with the construction of a script of romance suggesting that, once the profits from the 'Deal of a Lifetime' roll in, the ending will be of the happily-ever-after variety. In delivering even the most ridiculous of pitches to his audience, the Sweetheart Swindler uses dramatizing effects and plays the moment for optimal impact. In the case which follows, the man's delivery was neither dead-pan nor monotonous. Rather, it had considerable *élan* and flair, his voice rising and falling to add drama to what he was saying. Although our respondent found it seemingly worthwhile to extend his target audience, in this case to include the first author, more commonly this type of pitch, an appeal to greed on the part of his target, was delivered within the context of a relationship.

Do you realize there's billions and billions of dollars out there just willing to be made? ... You know what you need to make a killing? Insight! I'll let you in on my secret – do you know what's just waiting to go off like a nuclear device? Peanut butter. [Peanut butter?] Peanut butter. I have this idea you see, how I can make peanut butter the biggest seller in the world today.

Do you know that in Germany and Japan they don't have peanut butter? They don't, and I know I could make peanut butter the biggest seller in those countries. I'm letting you in on this because I know you're a smart lady and will keep this between ourselves, but I figure there's three ways we could make a fortune. Either I could present my idea to a couple of peanut butter firms here and present the ideas in Germany, get a big commission, but that wouldn't help you, would it? I could buy up one of the peanut butter companies here and export the stuff myself, but I think the best idea would be to travel to Germany, Japan, set up my own business there – you'd have to grease a few palms but it would be worth it – find out where peanuts are grown cheapest – probably some Third World country, so we could get them real cheap because of the cheap labour – and sell peanut butter with our own label.

I tell you, I know Germany and it's hot right now for peanut butter. Why? Because things are changing, people are giving up the old ways. Twenty years ago in Germany they didn't have supermarkets – you'd go to the butcher for your meat, the baker for your bread – but now, everyone goes to a supermarket. We expand out – start up our own supermarket and in the front aisles we have a big display of [peanut butter?]. You guessed it. Peanut butter. We have stalls set up to let people try it. A big toaster, so as soon as the toast comes out of the toaster, you slather lots of fresh butter all over it so it's all melted right into the toast and put your peanut butter on right away, and you stick it in someone's mouth, 'Here, sir or madam, try this.'

You can do market research to find out what time people like peanut butter best for probably as little as 20 grand. I tell you, it would go over real big in both Japan and Germany because they're into everything American. Beach Boys, Buddy Holly and [peanut butter]. Yeah, peanut butter. So, how does that sound ... We could make a fortune in it, split costs and profits 50/50 ...

One may note that in providing the choice of three options our male respondent was, in effect, using a device of the stage magician called '*équivoque*' – a technique designed to give the illusion of choice to the spectator. *Équivoque* seeks to disguise the fact that, should the spectator come to fully believe in the reality of the illusion, there are no real choices – only options that provide for their continued involvement within the illusion the gigolo as magician has created. If the viewer selects option (a), (b), or (c), there is the illusion of having chosen something freely, of having independently elected to pursue a course of action, but it's truly only action within the limited range of options provided by the magician.

However absurd the pitch might sound when one is purposefully alerted to it, the difference between the theatre of the confidence man when he is engaged in the role of the Sweetheart Swindler and that of the stage magician is that, in the latter case, the audience is cued to expect to be deceived. In the case of the Sweetheart Swindler, this is not the case. The audience that arrives at the nightclub or theatre expecting to witness magic are prepared to be dazzled, yet may still scrutinize the performance all the more closely to detect – if they can – the deception involved. However, when the Sweetheart Swindler delivers his pitch, his audience does not expect dazzling deception but rather spontaneous sincerity and, unlike the reader, is not simply exposed to written words upon a page of paper. Awareness of the context is crucial for understanding the gigolo's effectiveness.

Nigel, a 29-year-old Londoner, told the first author of his plan to construct a machine that would transport individuals from one room to another and proceeded to describe a machine straight out of the movie *The Fly*. His machine, he proclaimed, would basically break down matter and then re-create it in a new location. 'Have you mentioned this idea to anyone?' the first author queried Nigel. 'No,' he replied. 'I'm afraid that they'll steal my idea.' 'But surely,' she persisted, 'an old physics instructor?' Nigel had never taken physics, but he'd professed confidence that things would work out. He brushed aside scepticism as indicative of a lack of intelligence and/or a failure to understand the creative mind and its processes. His lover, he smugly noted, was terribly enthusiastic and encouraging of his vision. Indeed, he commented, with her financial and emotional support, he was planning to attend college and read physics. However, first he would have to take a course or two elsewhere; Nigel had neglected to mention to his Madame Bountiful that he had only one A level to his credit.

A continent away, a 32-year-old gigolo, kept by a 46-year-old woman in Vancouver, Canada, seemed to adopt a similar strategy. This gentleman, well-placed by birth but a 'society boy' who rarely performed at any role other than that of dilettante, gently but insistently persuaded his Bountiful to let him assume the role of her financial adviser for the large divorce settlement she had received from her wealthy husband. Supported by the woman prior to divorce, the man sought to increase his level of recompense beyond that which he enjoyed as the comfortable occupant of a luxurious townhouse in a posh area of the city.

In this case, the man persuaded his lover to invest substantially in a computer graphics firm that was being launched by several of his friends, assuring her that he had personally invested a large percentage of his savings in the venture and that he was confident they both would emerge from it as multimillionaires. He escorted her to his friend's house, where he and his friends pontificated in arm-chair computer lingo about the financial vistas to be conquered. They took pains to draw her attention to special features of the equipment, while the woman's lover loudly exclaimed in wonder at its efficiency and remarkable design. The man's friends/confederates rattled off the names of large companies that were supposedly bidding on the firm or were interested in amalgamating with them in business.

Lavishing praise upon the woman, the gigolo painted a scenario reminiscent of a Barbara Cartland novel as he encouraged her to buy the remaining shares in the company; she so deserved to have beautiful things, he so wanted to buy them for her, he was so abjectly humiliated to have her 'help him out' while he was 'temporarily short of funds.' With her help now, he could realize a financial windfall and take care of her in a style befitting a 'princess.' As the lovers leave the stage, dim the lights and cue the violins ...

Not unexpectedly, the company had only an ectoplasmic existence. After the woman had invested heavily in the company on behalf of both herself and her gigolo, the man dropped the one whose bank account he had just depleted for another.

When business arrangements are negotiated and consummated in a bedroom rather than in a boardroom, the contract often lacks formal documentation. Chastising herself more than a little for the greed that led her into the bogus business venture, the woman nevertheless maintained that a request for a written contract witnessed by a lawyer would have been 'all wrong, as if I didn't trust him.' Women, as feminists often tell us, may become the victims of their own wish to please. What often seems to emerge in the situation of the Sweetheart Swindler is the fusing of keeper and kept roles. Like the talking Barbie Doll whose prerecorded tape included the phrase 'Math is hard,' the woman seemed to believe that any man's financial judgment was better than her own. Although the possession of money may exercise its own kind of tyranny, the striking thing here is not the man's claim to know what is best for the woman, but the woman's willingness to slip so easily into the role of docile, helpless female.

The illusions plied are varied. Some are designed to result in marriage, some to cement a more limited relationship, others simply to divest the woman of a large amount of money or property. The stakes differ. Some of the men we interviewed were apt to boast how they had managed to acquire the life savings of a near-retirement waitress. Others would have viewed such behaviour as contemptible and beneath them. However, what was common in the tactics of the Sweetheart Swindler was the manipulation of the script of the 'true love affair' – or more commonly, its purposefully created semblance.

The Sweetheart Swindler or Casanova Con Man markets love and the prospect of an intimate relationship as his predecessors marketed spurious nostrums, elixirs, and snake oil. Each woman and each relationship is simply viewed as interchangeable with the others. Professions of undying affection, tenderness, and friendship are simply the pitch used to entice the woman into the Casanova Con Man's confidence and to promote the larger venture the man has in mind. As a 33-year-old gigolo from California commented:

Despite the pejorative connotations to the word gigolo I have decided to write you since, by strict definition, it is applicable to my present situation and in my previous relationships with women ...

I was a champion swimmer, high school body president, tall, handsome – women have always taken to me like kittens to catnip. I had several gay experiences before I turned twenty but with my masculine exterior it never made much difference. When my hand was finally tipped – no one believed it!

My present lover is an oil heiress, huge property owner. With her, I'll never have to work again. I'm going to marry this one. Sex? Oh, I'll figure something out ... She gives me clothes, the run of the house, allows me to have as many guests over as I please in her absence and pays me several thousand dollars a month – however, don't think she has the upper hand ...

Don't get me wrong, I have nothing against women, but I've always said look out for number one and I'm number one ... Most women just ask to be taken – they set themselves up ...

My present woman is insecure, really jealous of younger women (she's 57) so I just say, 'she doesn't measure up to your warm, cuddly and yielding body – not to mention your gorgeous looks, charming personality and brilliant wit. A day without you is like a day without sunshine so please don't be jealous and remove the clouds from my heart so that I may go on light-hearted once again.' Mushy enough? I tell women what they want to hear – you just have to be a good listener. It pays off in the long run.

Women will feed you clues to what they're looking for. If she says her husband was unromantic and never bought her flowers – you buy her flowers. If she says that she's always wanted to go to Rome, you say 'I'd love to go with you to Rome' and feed the fantasy about how its always been your biggest goal in life to see the Sistine Chapel ...

In the beginning if you set it up right, she'll never know that she's paying because that would hurt her pride; you have to present it right. With Ilona [the man's last lover] I really played like I wanted a relationship and that this was going somewhere. Told her that I had been shown some land right where a major cloverleaf highway would be going through and that if I could afford to buy it now, in around five years I'd have enough to settle down, we'd have a family, white picket fence, you'd make a great mother routine right? She handed over the money in no time flat. I then told her, 'Shit, the guy has upped the price' and that 'the lawyer wants more money for drawing up the deal.' More money ... Then I'm gone. What's she going to do? Tell the police? No way she's going to stand up in court and admit that she's been made a fool of. The money? What money? It was a gift, right?

Similarly, the behaviour of a Manhattan gigolo was memorable. Borrowing his Bountiful's new Jaguar, he proceeded to pick up a likely future financier at her home and take her for a stylish breakfast in 540 Park, the Regency Hotel's chandeliered breakfast room. Afterwards, he returned to find that the front of his lover's car had been damaged by a hit-and-run driver. After dropping off his latest lady prospect, the man, undaunted, stopped at a florist's, purchased three dozen long-stemmed red roses, and feigned incredulity when, upon his return, his lover asked what had happened to her car. Assuming a mien of stunned vacuity, an 'it's more than I can stand' expression, he informed her that it must have happened while the car was parked outside the florist. The man later would stress, in recounting this episode to the first author, how in his explanation to his Bountiful he had laid emphasis on the time he had spent selecting the most perfect blossoms for her. Apparently the woman had been appeased and comforted him for having been upset. Surely he could not be faulted for the careless way some people drove their cars.

The woman's easy placability was deemed favourable for the larger score her gigolo had planned. One night, after some of her friends had accompanied them to a political fund raiser for a presidential candidate, the man pouted upon their return and stated in woebegone terms that her friends had slighted him. Supposedly, whenever she had been absent from the immediate area, her friends would make catty remarks about his lack of position and his financial dependency upon her. Hastening to apologize for the supposed rudeness and insensitivity of her friends, the woman rushed to voice her confidence in him, in the man's intellectual merit, his business savvy, and his ability to achieve independent financial success. Successfully having engineered a situation wherein the woman had explicitly voiced her confidence in him, the man proceeded to launch into a contrived saga which outlined his 'lifelong dream' of opening a hydroponics company. Admittedly he had been unsuccessful at holding on to a job in the past – but only because he grew infuriated when 'incompetents' were his supervisors; admittedly, his education (a liberal arts degree in psychology) was not perhaps the ideal training for opening up this type of company, but he had worked in a greenhouse when he was 20, had a knack for raising plants, and had the drive, the initiative, and the foresight to perceive hydroponics as a growth industry. If only someone believed in him, trusted him, loved him enough to help him out ...

Confronted with the man's pathos and his florid statements of love undying, and cognizant of the man's (carefully engineered) rendition of a tragic life filled with pain (supposedly oppressed, suppressed, repressed, and depressed by all and sundry – other than his target), the woman was placed in a quandary. How could she fail this man who had been so brutalized by life's cruel inequities? The woman eventually paid for the man's play – and then he departed for newer conquests.

By viewing the woman first and foremost as a 'mark,' the Sweetheart Swindler disassociates himself from her as 'person.' Rather, he invokes the standard con's argument in forwarding his behaviour as acceptable and, not infrequently, as admirable. The Bountiful is viewed as someone who was simply asking to be taken advantage of and/or who deserved to be exploited. As a 'mark,' the target could be demeaned or exploited with little apparent cause for self-recrimination. Thus, a 26-year-old gigolo from Florida justified a con game that earned him $250,000 over an eighteen-month period from his 72-year-old lover: 'I was totally fed up with Frances' possessiveness and cheapness ... When we'd go to a restaurant the Scotch comes out in her. She's fat, ugly and cheap! She told me – 'O-o-o-o- I hate old men!' Ye, gods! I couldn't even sneak out to read a book. She wouldn't let me out of her sight. No way would I let that old buzzard use her money as a power tool, where I wasn't travelling first class, not being treated A-1 all the time. I used to kid the old gal – 'Frances, how can I compete with you? You got the money – you got the power.' This respondent claimed that the profits of his con game were 'my reward for suffering through the varicose veins and wrinkles,' while others maintained that their target had 'had it coming' for being 'so full of herself,' a 'haughty bitch,' a 'fucking career woman,' and a 'god damn feminist.' For this man and others, failing to profit from the naïvety of a woman who sought to 'play a power trip' on them or 'grab me by the balls' was thought more emasculating and cause for self-recrimination than was the perpetration of fraud, theft, or blackmail. Similarly, marked misogyny was evident in their comments, and their conversation was spiced with such epithets as 'old bitch,' 'old biddy,' 'whore bag,' 'dyke,' 'fucking snob.'

By engineering a situation wherein the woman would hand over to him large amounts of cash, property, or possessions, the con man would stress that his masculinity had been redeemed; he was, supposedly, a 'better man' for his actions than the man who would simply be contented to be kept. The term 'Sweetheart Swindler' seemed very much a euphemism in that, as a group, such men clearly viewed money as power, and their relations with Bountifuls as a zero-sum game with every gain of his being a loss of hers and vice-versa. This type of gigolo demonstrates and illustrates, in extreme form, use of the various *micromanipulation* techniques, such as canniness, intuition, charm, and deception, that were introduced at the end of the previous chapter. Thus, taking a woman seemed a competitive game designed to redress an imbalance of power.

MAGICIANS: BRIDGING ROLES AND CAREER TRAJECTORIES

Regardless of their points of entry into gigolodom, in analysing the comments of the men involved what emerged was a gigolo career which, like other careers, could evidence upward mobility – for example, rising from bar hustler to society gigolo; horizontal mobility – a shifting from one type of gigolo role to another different but equivalent type – such as from a 'lap dog' to a 'walker,' that is, from a sexual to a non-sexual relationship role; or stability within a specialized role which would involve performing the same kind of role throughout the gigolo's career with interchangeable partners, as is typically the pattern of the 'Casanova Con Man.' In the ten years we spent conducting this research, some of our male respondents have married their Madame Bountifuls, some have married women with little in the way of financial assets, some have veered off into different non-gigolo as well as gigolo roles, and some have gone to prison.

Those men who had married their very wealthy Bountifuls were extended no small degree of courtesy by society columnists; the reinterpretation and normalization of the relationship was particularly notable in those cases in which the couple had proceeded to have children or in which the man assumed an admirably paternal interest in the woman's children. 'Companions' who had been the object of derision within the press were suddenly and perhaps somewhat gratuitously given deferential and sycophantic treatment. Whereas formerly the gossip pages may have directed the reader's attention to the man being seen driving 'yet another' customized gift, wearing 'yet another' designer suit, and may have treated him with some derision, following the marriage, references were made to the tender solicitude of the loving husband, the radiance of the bride, and the blissful contentment of the happy couple.

It would seem assumed and endorsed that a husband loves his wife and that marriage makes an 'honest man' out of him. However, it does not necessarily follow that the attitude of the man had changed fundamentally as regards the conception of his role. That is, the man who is kept by his Madame Bountiful may later marry her for love, or money, or convenience, or for lack of anything better to do on a wet Saturday afternoon, and marriage may be 'just a slip of paper.' As we suggested earlier, the manipulation of images is not the singular province of the magician.

To better illustrate the range of roles that could be evidenced within a single male respondent's career as a gigolo and how the different types of roles could merge into one another, we thought it advantageous to offer some cases at somewhat greater length.

It is important to note that for the majority of our male respondents the role of the gigolo was a tertiary or service *occupation* – it consisted of making love, or manufacturing love if need be, as part of the career. They stressed the idea that a relationship consisted of a negotiated exchange, its durability dependent on the perception that both party's needs were being met. However, first and foremost, it was conceived of as a professional role.

Eric, a 27-year-old gigolo, was previously supported by a woman whose father was exceedingly wealthy and, at the time of the study, was being kept by a female executive in a large company – with the help of her company credit cards. Well-read, he was able to converse intelligently on a number of topics and throw in references to Greek literature and the heroic battles of the band of Thebes to dazzle his listeners. A high school athlete and jogging/aerobics devotee, he met his present paramour at a fashionable – and expensive – health club in Los Angeles. Between paramours, he worked as a salesman in a rather grand men's boutique and was well-groomed and garbed in a 'preppy' style. Although not overly attractive, he was exceedingly friendly and gregarious – not the type, one would surmise, that makes a comfortable living out of being attentive to middle-aged women.

When the first author asked Eric about his method of attracting financial support from women, he became somewhat defensive. Later, seemingly as an apology for his abruptness, he gave her the following note:

Women involved with: Various
Relationships began: Generally introduction by mutual friends who knew women looking for companionship. Met at dinner parties, the opera, cocktail lounges, the opening of any major play, etc. in the city.
Financial Support: Came to be given when I explained a temporary shortage of funds. Currently my lady pays my rent and most living expenses. Other friends have provided me with clothes and more recently a Porsche 924.
Support was Given: It was understood that this was the only real way to keep my attention.
Relationship with Friends: Introduced as a friend – reactions varied from envy to disgust, although the general consensus seems to be approval.
Nature of relationship: With some it was a lighthearted physical relationship, where needs were satisfied for financial remuneration. In others it was more involved on the provider's part.
Future Plans: Keep moving along – work each relationship to the mutual satisfaction of both parties.

Eric's autobiography read like a professional résumé – which, in effect, was what it was.

Case-Study: Andre

Andre, 25 years old, has been kept by various women and to different degrees since he was 15 years of age. While maintaining that he had never worked as a street hustler or turned homosexual 'tricks,' everything else seemed open for negotiation. Although his English was somewhat fractured and his conversation often wandered hither and yon, his comments do suggest his nonchalance about pursuing his career.

My dad is Persian and I was born over there in Iran. My mother is Persian/German/Russian, white skin, blonde hair, big build. My dad is from a big family; they have 450 relatives just in Southern California, lot of kids. He worked for the Iran Oil Company in public relations. He had been married before, had a son ... Mom also worked for Iran Oil in the distribution office. Because Dad did public relations we moved around a lot and it was hard for me to establish friends. I'd have to start from scratch, be on my own ... Every two years, we'd move around from one part of Iran to another, from north to east, it's a big country ...

After the revolution in Iran came up, it became really hard. Right before, Dad had been asked to go work for Iran Oil in New York, but he decided to work in the Caspian Sea. He had family in intelligence, miliary – our last name was on a blacklist and we left the country for political reasons ... It was hard to get a passport because everyone was supposed to go into the Army; my dad changed our ages to avoid military service – got us faked passports; it cost a lot of money but he did it. He sold everything we had in Iran ...

My parents and sister went to the U.S. My brother [four years older] and I were sent to Germany. I was around 15–16. Once I tried to run away; I thought I'd go around the world, just work and see the world; I was always sort of crazy that way. My brother was really good; he didn't say a word to our parents. When they called, he'd say I had just gone out or was in the washroom ... It didn't last, I came back after the week.

I went to an International high school and worked at trade shows as a security guard. One of my friends was from Holland. We'd work overnight at trade shows so no one would steal anything. It was long hours – and we'd sit down and talk. He told me he was into making home-made pornos. I was working out and had big muscles and he said that I should do one, that I'd make a lot of money. He said that no one would see my face, nothing above my belt. I did one [porn movie] and made about 2,000 Deutschmarks – about 1,500 dollars. I met people and they told me since you're working out, building your body – you should do some dancing in bars. Not like the Chippendale's here, I didn't take everything off. The ladies are sitting, not all older, 30–40 years old, drinking, you dance, talk to them a bit and get a couple hundred dollars. That is where I first got offered to go with a lady as a companion ...

[What was this first lady like?] She was divorced, 42 years old, something like that, but she knew how to make herself look younger. She was a nice lady. I liked her a lot ... Later on she gave me the idea of taking on more people; she didn't have all the time or money to spend on me. My expectations were going high – she got me her friends. She referred me to her friends. I thought she was just testing me: 'Go out with them.'

[Why did you go out with them?] Cash. Money. [How much did your main lady pay you?] At first 50 Deutschmarks a time and she'd buy me clothes. I was not her boyfriend but at first it was not a business – it was someone was just taking care of me. She told me to ask for a higher rate but I was still flexible. I asked 100 Deutsch. My brother found out – he didn't like it and said I was a prostitute.

Nobody was around to teach me certain things like how to be classy, how to sit, how to walk, what glass to grab, what wine to order. She taught me a lot of different things, and knew how to tell me things but say it in a way that wouldn't give offence. It's not that she was being a mommy to me; a mommy wasn't something that I was missing. She told me she had a son somewhere but I never met him. She never made me feel that way – she was pampering me and taking care of me but never really trying to treat me like a son ...

Maybe, I believe that these people think their money has to go somehow, you're only going to lose it somehow. She felt good paying me, without a reason. I'd tell her I wanted to buy ski equipment. She'd get out her chequebook and say, what should I make it out for? 700 Deutschmarks? I'd tell her she didn't have to, but she'd say, 'Oh, I just like to do it.' I made her happy. If you got the money, you just like to make people happy. More friendship. I learned a lot from her. She was a very nice lady.

[What did you learn?] How to try to be more mature, don't give them attitude, learned not to be a puppy. All the escorts were the same way, they'd be puppies. Not me, I'd never be their puppy. You show respect but most of them want you to be in control. They'd give you money and you spent it. 'Here's a couple of hundred, you're spending, we're going out tonight.' ...

Women aren't straight with you. They don't tell you why they want you. They never would say, 'Could we go out?' 'What do you have to offer?' 'What do you do best?' They start with the occasion, give you a good legitimate reason, bring something as a reason. 'Oh, I have to go to a wedding/the opera/a party.' Sometimes escorts are arrogant. It kills the moment. You make it a little game, a little bit different. If you push it right away they lose interest ...

I never discuss money. Not 'now it's past two hours,' that's 50 bucks. I charge a flat rate. I don't make it like 'I got to clock out of here'; my way it's like you're enjoying it too. [What did you charge as your flat rate?] 150 Deutschmarks. Do you realize this was when I was 18? That's good money for an 18-year-old. I was so like a young kid, it gave me a lot of satisfaction, not just sexually. It gave me knowledge. I was so curious how they got here, what had happened in their life, so I could learn from their mistakes. Like a psychiatrist right? You can learn from your own patients, from all the mistakes they have done; so much knowledge for free! Actually I was getting paid for it! You get close to influential, successful people – in their business not in their personal lives ...

[Is there a typical woman?] There was a lot of divorcees – most of them – not that many widows. Most of them had married young, then got a divorce and became career oriented. They'd say that their marriage was just a stupid mistake ... They had done very well, got really rich but had no one to share it with – not just sexually but psychologically also. Maybe emotionally too, though I'm not sure how they did that. I think when they do it [hire a male escort] they do it to please herself [*sic*], to show that she [*sic*] is capable, 'I could get a guy if I wanted,' 'money talks,' to show she's [*sic*] not regretting the fact that she [*sic*] got divorced.

One woman, she was 32, married, she was very jealous of me even talking on the phone to another woman. She told her husband; he said it was okay. They even threw a birthday party for me at their house. He's a totally nice guy, likes me a lot. Him and her were high school sweethearts, but she got burned off getting him off drugs and alcohol. He goes to AA meetings now, got very close to God – that's why he forgave me. That's what he said! She totally loves the guy for what he was – roller-coaster excitement, up and down all the time. It drives her crazy. Wasn't a mono relationship. Yet, she still tells me, 'If I was younger I would take you.' It's not like she's old, but most of the women where she works they're 18, 19 -- they hire a lot of young girls so she thinks she's really old. It's crazy ...

[Another woman] I got to break the ice with her just on the phone. She had really bad problems with her husband. Both of them worked for the same company, both of them were engineers. No kids. They had been married for 7–8 years. She was 33 years old.

She liked my voice on the phone. I'd make it really sexy. I would use that but be really professional. She was from Virginia, had the nice Southern voice. She liked me. All of a sudden she's faxing me letters all the time and says to me, 'Fax me a picture.' I asked her what she looked like. She told me Crystal Gayle. I didn't even know who Crystal Gayle was. I thought she was working for the same company this woman was or something. [Laughs] She told me Crystal Gayle was a singer so I went out to the record store just to see a picture of what she looked like. She had long hair below her butt, really petite person. Anyhow she really went out of control. She asks me, 'If I send you a ticket will you come and meet me in Cincinnati?' She was going there to visit her parents. I said, 'Yeah, sure.' So she sent me a ticket to meet her in Cincinnati. So I say okay, yeah, no problem.

She picked me up at this little airport in Cincinnati and we go to the hotel and she gets two beds. Two separate rooms. I tell her 'What are you doing?' She tells me, 'I promised my mother.' Right. Like, it was so crazy. We went to her room and sat on the bed and started talking. We talked for a long time, then we ordered pizza. We had a slice then, boom, we had sex. Never wound up using the other room. I told her 'You're crazy, get your money back.' 'No, I promised my mom.' She was very attractive, really nice. She got really attached to me. It got pretty crazy. She left her husband ...

I don't care what the other guys say. When you have sex with someone, good sex, bad sex, whatever – you get somewhat intimate and women just don't forget about it. You can't just turn around and be total friends. They get involved with you ...

Most of the women were between 35 and 45. Once I went with a 50-year-old woman. She told me she was 46 but I found out she was 50. [Did you ever find it hard getting aroused with an older woman?] The first time yes, but not after a while. I got used to it. I had a younger girlfriend, she was 19 and you know, after a while she wouldn't turn me on any more. It wasn't the way they [the older women] looked, it was what they do, what they know. I was respecting them for what they could teach me. It wasn't like they wanted kinky things. They just wanted normal regular sex.

[What do you consider kinky?] Ah, you know. They always just wanted plain intercourse. Sometimes, you know, they might say something but they were just joking – and even if they weren't, I just laughed it off ...

I never went down on anybody. [Why?] They're a lot of things that are intimate to you; some girls they wouldn't give every guy a blow job. To me this is intimate. I want to keep something for myself. Some girls like to give their guys blowjobs, but no sex, some girls like to have sex but wouldn't give blow jobs, some girls will give guys blow jobs but won't let them come in their mouths. You have to limit it somewhere, keep something for yourself. To me that's for somebody special. I've never even done that with a girlfriend. [How many women have you slept with?] Somewhere around 140 people – something like that. Sometimes women would push it, but they would respect you. I never would let them treat me like shit ...

It got to a point I was doing a whole bunch of women. [Did you worry about catching a disease? AIDS?] I was sleeping with these people, before I came to the U.S., without a condom. Even after I came here it was hard for me to tell them 'No, now we have to use a condom.' Fact is, I didn't like the idea myself but, they think that you're using it for *your* own safety. 'I'm paying you and you think I'm the type who has a disease?' They're rich and because they're rich they don't think that AIDS is something they would get. They think they're bullet proof. Nothing is going to hurt them. They want to feel your skin, they want to feel you, not the rubber. Feel your youth.

It's never been a goal of mine to be a golden girl, just a tool, to get to the bigger goals. I want to have my own enterprise, I'd never be happy with one business if its something you can't capitalize on, if you can't speculate. In order to get to that goal – 4 or 5 businesses – I needed faster ways to make money but at the same time, not get in trouble with, like, drugs or something. In Germany, prostitution wasn't really that illegal – it was if you went out of a certain zone – but anyway with females, it's different. It's not like you take them to a motel, screw them and then you walk. It's more classier, females want more out of it even if it's phoney, they want you to do the whole show, do the whole thing …

Females have a harder time doing this than guys. [Why is this?] It's just the way the society is. The way guys look down on girls. It's always harder for a woman, she has to work that ass off; she has to compete with the females and the males.

When I came to the U.S. I was doing some modelling too, freelance. These females were more fun to be with. That's how I met one of my women [who would keep him]. She owned a clothing chain store. She was not a designer, she just owned a chain of stores. She could have had a lot of male guys from the models, but she didn't want to have anyone from her business. I asked her for a job, but she didn't want to give me a job in her store. Maybe she wanted me to be dependent. Maybe she thought if she gave me a job I wouldn't take her out. She didn't want to mix it up, 'I'm taking you out.' You know the saying, 'never get your honey where you get your money.' Except for me. I always get my honey where I get my money. But that's different. That's work.

I didn't do it for a while, I was doing orientation. Two weeks after I got here I saw a sign 'help wanted' outside a lingerie store and walked in. I was going to college too so I filled out the application right there and asked if I could be interviewed right away. The manager, all the sales women – they were all girls. The manager didn't know what to say, didn't know how to tell me that here it's a little bit different. Females here don't even feel comfortable with the idea of going topless. What you see on TV in Germany about Americans – all the topless girls on the beach – they're afraid of even being topless, expressing themselves in any way. They're into the male bonding, female bonding, the girls 'Let's go the lunch,' the guys, 'Let's go watch football' …

Being a companion is lots easier and more comfortable in Germany than it is here. Germans are very open-minded. Because it's the centre of the world, there's a lot of traffic, so they see both sides. There's more knowledge there because everyone sees a lot of tourists. In Germany, women do not mind to be a couple with someone who doesn't even match. Everything is possible to them. In the U.S., women are afraid people will think she's the guy's 'mom' if she's with a younger guy – unless she just wants to show off. [What do you mean?] Some women they get to a certain age, flip – I want to be this age again and start to wear jeans, you know? ... Dark-haired guys are really popular in Germany. Italian-looking. Persians.

In the U.S. I started off as just a service to German ladies. I told my friends in Germany, if you know someone coming over, I'll take care of them. I did it as a translator with a German lady – she came to give a seminar for an AIDS conference. [Did she make you wear a condom?] [Laughs] After I found out what the conference was for, I thought no sex. Actually I don't think she mentioned it to me. I just put a condom on. I wasn't going to; it was a challenge to me – she's giving a paper at an AIDS seminar here – to do it without a condom, but I didn't push it ...

Later I read an ad in the paper, 'escort services.' I called up. She [the owner] asked me, 'Do you sleep with people? Our service is strictly platonic, no sex at all.' Yeah, okay. She liked my voice on the phone so I went to the interview. I was so excited – oh, I'm back in business! She [the owner] had no idea how to market her business so I tried to pick on her for not focusing on females [as patrons], just on guys only. After a while I made her a deal. I told her I want to enter into partnership with you, want to help you, get in business with you. She sounded very motivated. She's a big woman, 270 pounds, used to work for —— police department, but she got kicked out. I've seen pictures, she used to be very good looking, voluptuous, but then she got very heavy, extremely heavy. She was with a lot of guys, hundreds. She got to know a lot of guys.

She was a single mom, had a son about 9 years old, the father was a cop too but he never married her ... She was running the business out of her home where she lived with her son and her mom. She had a 3- or 4- bedroom house and had made the den into an office ...

She had 1,200 guys on paper that used her service and about 35 girls. I'd say, of the 1,200, maybe 200 were interested in a platonic service. Most just wanted to get laid. [What did the service charge?] Fifty bucks an hour, three-hour minimum, 30 bucks an hour for her. [Was it hard to find male escorts?] No! It was easy. It was hard getting the females [clients] because she [the owner] didn't know what she was doing. Even the money – there's services that charge $1,000 an hour. That sounds a lot to me, but $1,000 a night sounds about right.

I was stupid, I didn't check it [the business] like a business person. I was so confident that whatever it is, I'll turn it around. I didn't even know it wasn't even her house! It was rented. She had gone bankrupt before I met her. She didn't know how to run a business. She'd be making $8,000 a month but it would all go on old debts, not on the business. She wouldn't even pay the girls. She was hiring every week new girls for the guys. Every week fresh meat ... She didn't want to expand.

Excellent ideas but she couldn't do any money management. She was an Alice in Wonderland.

One of her girls started dating me, she didn't like it, and started acting weird at work. You can't have that in a business – it creates such an atmosphere that you can't even work in that place – it's a stressful atmosphere. She sat down one night, asked me what I want to do in my life, if I want to be married to her? She's 38. She told me she was attracted to me from day one. I didn't know what to say. I told her, 'Don't look at it now, first let's get the business going and then we'll see.'

She got so possessive of me she didn't want me to go out on dates ... I was spending 15 hours a day at her place and she thought I was just dedicating my time to her – not to her business ... Her business was like part of her body ...

I left her three months ago. It's a lot easier to start something new than to try to fix her problem.

At last contact with Andre in October 1992 he gleefully announced that he had just placed an ad in several local newspapers advertising a two-and-a-half-hour seminar on 'how to be a male companion.' He was charging $65 per person (cash only at the door) and was holding it in a restaurant ballroom owned by his cousin. 'What will you talk about?' he was asked. 'How to market yourself,' he replied. Stating that he was going to 'only do the platonic shit,' he rattled off a list of potential topics and strategic pointers such as 'never mention you're an escort unless the lady hires you direct from an agency' and general suggestions as to how to walk, how to talk, how to dress, what fork to use, what wine to order, 'what glass to grab,' 'how to be thoughtful.' 'What to do if a woman grabs your butt and how to get out of it without making offense [sic] ... ' If the guys were interested in pursuing work as a companion, he added, he would charge them $75 to join his newly started up agency.

Chortling not a little, he commented that, 'in America, the ticket to money is public speaking. To be a preacher.' Multiplying the seating capacity of the room by the specified cost of the seminar and factoring in a percentage of his audience who would wish to join his agency, Andre was confident that he'd have enough capital to finance his future plans to set up shop in Waikiki and elsewhere.

A 37-year-old gigolo *en route* from Massachusetts to London to meet his Madame Bountiful for an evening at the theatre and to then travel on to Switzerland for some skiing, commented on the skills necessary to be, in his words, a 'Great Lover':

To be the best lover a woman can have you must be better than any other man at pleasing a woman. You must be father, husband, son, Father Confessor, lover all at one time. You must be amusing and charming. You must know how to say what she wants to hear. My tongue has no bones, but it can break many hearts ...

Women with much money don't know how to amuse themselves. Ladies are not women's libbers. They do not work, take care of their own children, clean their own houses ...

A woman who desires a gigolo wants more than just sex. Sometimes she doesn't want sex at all. Dorothy just wants me to hold her till she falls asleep. We have never made love ... it's true. She ... just knows she is unhappy. So – the parties, the go-go-go ... So I baby her. I call her my little girl. I pat her and hold her. I tell her she is a bad girl when she drinks too much or when she stays out too late. [How old is she?] Dorothy will be 55, no, 56 in October ...

Her problem is not uncommon among women of her class. She is no longer young and beautiful, men do not turn to look at her now when she walks into a room and this makes her sad ... She is happy when she lets herself believe that men find her beautiful and when she thinks she is loved. But when she knows the truth – she must leave, she must go some place else – run, run, run ...

I had a little affair a year or so ago, very casual but she found out about it. Quick, quick we go to Cannes. [To break up your affair with the other woman?] No, so that she could forget. If she stays still she must think of things she does not want to very much.

In public, she smiles, she laughs, she plays the happy lady. In private, she cries, is depressed, wants to feel sorry for herself. [Do you feel sorry for her?] No, because all of us grow old ... I'll leave her soon. Being with her is too tiring. It is riding the lift, up, down, up, down.

At last contact with this man, he had retired from active life as a gigolo, although he still 'walked' his faithful Dorothy. Telling the first author that, through therapy, Dorothy had unleashed a torrent of memories of child sexual abuse, and had, in consequence, become more comfortable with sexuality, he was rather proud to note that he had pushed Dorothy towards a young man he had taken under his wing. The man himself, however, was content to live in the house that Dorothy had purchased for him early in their relationship, to receive his monthly allowance from her, to mingle as her dear friend at her numerous smart parties, and to 'walk' her and other ladies when circumstances dictated that their most current lover would not really fit in. His relationship with Dorothy, at the time of our last conversation, had exceeded the length of time of most marriages. The secret for its longevity? 'I'm a good listener.'

In watching a magician engaged in a display of his craft, the viewer often wonders precisely how the trick is accomplished. How does the magician know what card was selected? How does the magician disappear into thin air? How can he saw his confederate in half – with the confederate's toes and fingers wiggling in opposite boxes – and then magically reconstruct her? The illusions that the gigolo helps to create and sustain in interaction with his partner are not simple or uniform. However, the secret behind the magic of the gigolo is hinted at in the comment of our last respondent, who identified himself as being a good listener. This empathy component is a part of the bag of tricks that every self-respecting professional gigolo must carry with him in order to be successful.

If empathy stands for a host of relationship skills sharpened and honed by men who aspire to be provided for, thereby rejecting the good provider role for themselves, while Madames Bountiful wittingly or unwittingly assume such a role among others, it may be that our respondents are harbingers of new 'masculinities' and 'femininities' or perhaps even of the eradication of such limiting descriptors. It may be that the transgressions of the gigolo and his Madame Bountiful are expressed by their determination to locate themselves in other stereotypes. We turn now to a consideration of such possibilities.

6

Masquerades and Illusions

In the Introduction we suggested that discussions of gigolos are often mired in depictions of the sexual aspects of their relationships. The gigolo/Madame Bountiful relationship is, in the vast majority of cases, a sexual relationship, but assuredly there is more to be said. Indeed, focusing exclusively on the sexual aspect can arguably camouflage the social significance of these relationships by concentrating only on what is essentially prurient and lurid. What seemed to us to be more interesting were the ways in which the participants conceived of and accounted for their relationship and the ways in which they conceptualized their roles within it. Does the gigolo exemplify male economic liberation? Is his transgression simply that of eschewing the 'good provider' role? Does the Bountiful exemplify the truly liberated woman? Has androgyny arrived in the roles of the Bountiful and gigolo?

Before we continue with our description and analysis, we must once again note that the student of gender faces a seemingly inevitable constraint on observations, thoughts, and writings – namely, the constraint of language. In the Introduction, we referred to the Sapir-Whorf hypothesis, which suggests that language shapes our understanding of reality. We live within a linguistic reality whereby most, if not virtually all, behaviour is identified by a gender label. Applications of the terms 'masculine' and 'feminine' flow readily from the tongue and keyboard. Thus, when examining our gigolos and Bountifuls, it is easy to label behaviours as falling into one or the other category. Without the luxury, or necessity, of an available truly neutral non-gendered language, it is difficult to describe actions, thoughts, and feelings in other than stereotypical terms, regardless of whose body these reside in. As Carolyn Heilbrun acknowledged, 'so wedded are we to the conventional definition of "masculine" and "feminine" that it is impossible to write about androgyny without using these terms in their accepted, received sense.' We have scrutinized both our respondents and our descriptive terms for them to avoid, as much as possible, imposing a gendered world where none exists.

Yet, even with our cautions in place, in interviewing hundreds of gigolos and Madames Bountiful we were often struck by the ways in which the men and women constructed and reconstructed ideas of masculine and feminine behaviour. However, rather than offering a refutation and challenge to traditional conceptions of the proper roles for men and women, some of our gigolos and their Madames Bountiful seemed to incarnate gender role–defined behaviour. Instead of transcending gender socialization and the stereotyping of characteristics, behaviours, or attitudes as masculine or feminine, the liberation we witnessed at times seemed primarily to be a sexual one. Being 'a liberated woman' and a 'New Age man' could be defined by a large number of our respondents in a way that reduced the meaning of the terms to simply the perceived freedom to have sex with as many men and/or women as one wished. However, a distinction needs to be made between sexual liberation and liberation from the confinements of gender; in and of itself, sexual liberation may indicate that only a shallow type of androgyny has been attained.

Beneath the surface, the tyrannies of gender grew visible. What emerged was not a 'kinder and gentler nation' of intimate relationships but was intriguing, for, from the midst of what seemed, facilely, rather unconventional behaviour, emerged rather stereotypical so-called masculine and so-called feminine behaviour – if, at times, played out in the other-sexed body. Indeed, the caricatures of masculinity and femininity could become more obvious for their actually being played out in that other-sexed body. Under the guise of unconventionality the behaviour we witnessed was almost stereotypically gendered, with the public role performance of the gigolo suggesting artefactual femaleness, a 'she-male' deliberately fashioned and constructed out of primitive gender stereotypes. Similarly, the role of the Bountiful sometimes seemed to be composed of randomly juxtaposed portions from construct-a-gender kits. Again, the constraints of language do not provide a singular neutral term to refer to such a female that is comparable to the 'she-male' we just applied to the male. Try as we might, we drew a linguistic blank. Suffice it to say, the Bountiful role contained many elements some of which suggested artefactual maleness.

In a sex-differentiated society, rather than explore alternative ways to engage in a relationship, it may make perfect sense, at least to them, for the gigolo and his Madame Bountiful to simply exchange one set of role prescriptions for another, with the female modelling her behaviour on masculine role models and the male modelling his behaviour on characteristics more commonly associated with females.

A confounding factor in the gigolo/Bountiful relationship is that, while it might appear to be, on the surface, a role-reversal situation, with the woman in apparent control of the relationship, it really is not, with the exception of the financial-resources issues. Relationships and their management have been the responsibility of women in the past. They were and are in charge of, or responsible for, the care and nurturance of a relationship and have been expected to make the sacrifices necessary to sustain that relationship. What marks the gigolo/Bountiful relationship is the sacrifice of money to maintain the contact. However, the investment in a 'beloved' is always more than merely financial. The outlines of the traditional script in such cases have not changed that much – only certain details of the content.

Another confounding factor in the gigolo/Bountiful relationship is that while it might appear to be, on the surface, characterized by androgyny or the elimination of rigid definitions of masculinity and femininity, that appearance, in most cases, is truly only superficial in nature. As if to give support to Mary Daly's comment that the concept of androgyny suggests 'scotch-taping John Wayne and Brigitte Bardot together,' our respondents did not always so much transcend their gender as purposefully integrate imitations of the other sex into their repertoire of behaviours. They appeared to pay scrupulous attention and homage to their gendered role presentations, grafting images of archetypal masculinity and femininity together to create a whole formed from inadequate halves.

The term 'androgyny' is of ancient origin and stems from the Greek words *andros* (male) and *guné* (female). The idea of individuals having a dual nature has been recognized at least since the time of the Pythagorean myth of creation, in which individuals sought to discover and literally mate with their 'other half' to reunite and achieve wholeness. While almost all religions include beliefs that suggest similar views of dualism and reunification, masculine and feminine gender roles in contemporary Western society are often perceived in terms of mutually exclusive opposites.

The concept of androgyny sounds wonderful in theory and suggests the attainment of a 'third non-gender,' a human hybrid that, except for a few reproductively related differences, encourages and allows persons of both sexes to acknowledge 'the realization of man in woman and woman in man.' The difficulty lies in the fact that the terms 'masculine' and 'feminine' are situated within the context of male power and female subordination. Within this context of structured inequities, the stereotypes of gender define certain styles (typically associated with masculinity) as 'normal' and an admirable standard while dismissing others (typically associated with femininity) as deviant, irrational, and inferior. For example, Jimmy Breslin attempted to humorously define a 'walker' as 'a guy who has a good dinner suit and is a sensational listener [who] take[s] a woman to a charity ball as the woman talks about clothes, hair, the antique show, shoes, how old another woman is getting, clothes, hair, and interior decorating. At no time does the walker talk about anything important, for such things usually are depressing.' It is evident that Breslin conceives of a woman's vistas of concern as trivial, and the walker's role as essentially offering accommodation to a game of trivial pursuit.

While in Western society a woman may receive rewards for displaying such supposedly masculine characteristics as being assertive (versus timid), logical or rational (versus emotional or irrational), active (versus passive), a male demonstrating feminine qualities may be only psychologically benefited and not socially rewarded. Indeed, reactions from outsiders may be equivocal at best, and typically range from bemusement to ridicule and antipathy.

In the forward to *Erotica: An Anthology of Women's Writing*, Jeanette Winterson stated that the anthology 'seeks to return women to their bodies by offering a looking glass and not a distorting mirror.' The metaphor used is interesting for it presumes that such a vision is obtainable. Is it? All of us are constricted and influenced by gender socialization. Since our gender identity is always conflicted to some extent, it may be precisely within intimate relationships that the status of gender stereotypes becomes most potent and telling of social endorsement or intolerance for persons attempting to transcend these stereotypes. What exists is not very encouraging. It is apparent that people do not ignore conventional role models within intimate relationships, even though they may step outside of them. Within marriage, cohabitation, adulterous, or kept relationships, people easily and often unconsciously slip into stereotypic behaviour.

THE GIGOLO: NEGOTIATING STEREOTYPES OF GENDER

It is notable that, in his attempts to cajole his way into women's favour, the gigolo may purposefully act in ways that are stereotypically feminine, more so perhaps than the majority of biological women. In stressing his willingness to subordinate his ambitions (at least his non-financial ones) to those of his partner, to derive a social status based on his partner's position (thus becoming the 'Wife of') rather than pursuing an independent identity, to be supported by a woman, the gigolo seems to undergo a type of gender parthenogenesis through which he purposefully gives birth to a second persona – the companion, who is 'feminine.'

The man elects to fabricate his role performance during the courtship stages of a relationship along the lines of Patient Griselda, Penelope, and other self-sacrificing feminine heroines. He also becomes at least somewhat Cinderella-like in that he focuses his attentions upon achieving wealth, status, or power through affiliation rather than by a ruggedly independent masculine strategy. Rather than setting off to obtain success on his own like Horatio Alger, the self-made man, the gigolo plays at being a manipulative Blanche DuBois who 'always relies on the kindness of strangers.'

The role of the companion suggests itself as a 'shadow role,' one which draws upon another for strength, definition, and status. A shadow depends on the existence of someone or something else. By definition, a shadow is the product of the interception of light by an object and takes on whatever form is outlined by that object. If the object is removed, the shadow ceases to exist. The roles of women in conventional Western society have been crafted in the shadows of men's status and power. In many ways the gigolo may be seen simply as a caricature of what Thorstein Veblen described as the 'companion' role of the high-status wife. That is, the companion is the silent, glamorous adjunct of a high-status other who has no locus of social identity, apart from that other.

Similarly, the tactics of the gigolo may be seen as a type of 'effeminate wiles' that parody the stereotype of women's micromanipulative tactics. Being coquettish, becoming good friends with those who are thought important, and seeking to establish camaraderie within networks of socially eligible others – all suggest that the role is audience-directed. The apple-polisher performance is purposive, but it reveals the status of the companion as a subordinate, an adjunct. A person who has power on his or her own does not have to routinely adopt synthetic, sycophantic ways of interacting with others; he or she may straightforwardly express him or herself. The adjunct can only issue banal remarks and mime others' opinions precisely because of the lack of power associated with that status.

The adjunct must play the role of the 'Wife of' who seeks to ingratiate herself with others, win their admiration, and gain their friendship by acting like a chameleon, and by using hypocrisy as a social tool. The role of 'Wife of' does bestow a certain latitude; in her small pond, the 'Wife of' may be a somewhat despotic big fish. However, her power is intrinsically limited and requires that she act in accordance with stage cues set by her superiors and show deference in her dealings with them. Her power is regarded as legitimate only inasmuch as she is the recognized representative of someone or something else. For the gigolo, playing the role of 'Wife of' meant that, in the presence of the Bountiful and her friends, he was often the obsequious and fawning toady – as a way not only to appeal to the Bountiful's vanity, but also to gain recognition from others that he was a worthy person who truly cared about the Bountiful and deserved to continue in his role as her adjunct.

Nevertheless, if strategic need makes the gigolo a shadow companion, he creates this role reluctantly to fulfil a goal and, upon questioning, typically directs attention to its theatrical components. Perhaps, in part, this was why we found many men willing to identify themselves as 'gigolos'; it may be that they wished to enlarge the audience appreciative of the fact that, although they *played* the role of the adjunct, their role had more substance and required more talent and effort than might facilely be assumed to be the case.

Although the gigolo purposefully offers to his Bountiful an image of himself as the solicitous and tender lover, our respondents rarely seemed unaware of the traditional masculine role. One way of asserting one's masculinity was, for some men, to distance themselves from the designation 'gigolo' itself. Throughout this book we have noted certain male respondents who sought to offer alternatives and to negotiate semantics. Whether the term advanced was 'man about town,' 'gentleman of fortune,' or 'adventurer,' the preferred label seemed to place emphasis on the active, masculine nature of the role. To be 'kept' suggests passivity; by their selection of alternative terms these men attempted to propose that the role was more akin to that of a swashbuckling Casanova than simply to that of a dandified Caspar Milquetoast.

This pattern is evident in the comments of Mario Buatta, a Staten Island interior decorator who has walked the then Mrs Ivana Trump. In a conversation reported by Jimmy Breslin, Buatta took apparent pains to describe his role as utterly unlike that of the lowly gigolo: 'A walker is not a gigolo ... You must have some professional standing yourself. A walker is like being a Boy Scout. A Boy Scout with noble purposes. You escort a woman through the night, then take her home, but with none of this pressure to go up to her apartment. So both people can be cheery throughout the night. If the woman happens to be a bit older, you cannot mention it. Conversation? The most I've heard recently is about the women like Nan Kempner who were on television in Paris wearing $30,000 dresses. How ridiculous! But at the same time, we need the money to be spent. It serves a purpose.' In describing the role of a walker as necessitating the benign tolerance that one would afford a child or an incompetent, the distinction between 'keeper' and 'kept' in such arrangements is purposefully made obscure.

However, in the behavioural aspects or 'normalcy shows' undertaken to establish themselves as admirable, it would appear that the gigolo is stereotypically masculine and his Madame Bountiful is stereotypically feminine. They appeared reactionary individuals, willingly putting on show their embracing of stereotypical maleness or femaleness; their actions suggested a moving back towards the core culture rather than away from it. It is ironic that the rationalizations offered in support of their assumption of superficially deviant gender roles serve to align and reconcile the roles within the boundaries of conventional masculinity and femininity.

This observation may seem to contradict one we made earlier that the gigolo appears, most especially in the courtship phase of his relationships, to assume qualities that are stereotypically feminine. It is not. Even though feminism as a sociopolitical force has suggested the need to confront gender oppression on a political as well as a personal level, the roles typically assumed by men and women within the gigolo/Bountiful relationship, and the deprecation of the relational form itself by others, indicate the continued oppressiveness wrought by gender stereotyping. Exchanging a presentation of self underwritten by rigid adherence to stereotypical masculinity for one constructed to feign stereotypical femininity utilizes only opposite sides of the same coin; the result does not transcend gender as much as remain mired within it, the inevitable result of utilizing an impoverished currency.

For other gigolos, the way in which to affirm their fundamental non-deviance and assert their normalcy vis-à-vis cultural prescriptions is through the assumption of the most graphic and perhaps least attractive stereotypes of so-called masculinity. Thus, men would privately express themselves to be the dominant figure within a relationship, pointing to sexual practices like 'S & M' and/or their dominant position within the sexual act. As we noted earlier with reference to eroticism, for some men, their masculinity seemed contingent upon a strong emphasis on sex, sex, sex ...

Jessie Bernard observed that 'settling down' and providing for a family were seen as signs of maturity for men and centrally implicated in North American definitions of masculinity since at least the early 1800s. It remained so, she argued, until 1980 in the United States (and 1981 in Canada) when the Census no longer assumed that males automatically were to be considered the 'head of the household.' However, the expectation that males would be, and still could be, good providers began to decline earlier than that. In her work *The Hearts of Men*, Barbara Ehrenreich claimed that the questioning of establishment and traditional lifestyles in the 1960s changed the primacy placed on the breadwinning role as the essence of masculinity. In addition to published articles that queried whether being masculine could be hazardous to one's health, Ehrenreich suggested that the media, and most especially men's magazines such as *Playboy*, proselytized men to adopt a new definition of masculinity: being hedonistic and sexual.

Since, 'in general the 3,320,000 male single workers [in the United States] hardly earned enough to feed themselves and buy *Playboy*, let alone follow its philosophy,' men who aspire to be kept as gigolos may well endorse the redefinition of masculinity currently available to them. Especially for gigolos who are not performing for their Bountifuls many of the functions and roles currently performed by other males in our society, the seemingly undue emphasis on sex may be thought essential to presenting themselves as admirably masculine men.

For yet other gigolos, the issues of power and control were not confined to the bedroom, and these men would emphasize the feigned nature of their role, stressing the cons they had put over on the women, noting the lovers they enjoyed on the side and the large sums of money or gifts purposefully cajoled, as if these and similar features were more than admirable evidence of their potentially impugned masculinity.

This type of legitimation is indirectly illustrated in the accounts offered by such modern day Sweetheart Swindlers as Robert John Koch and Leslie Gall. Koch, a pudgy, balding 52-year-old man, had allegedly wooed 'hundreds of women' with promises of lasting relationships and even marriage, then had persuaded them to give him their money by promising to set them up in business. Somewhat ironically, Koch found himself, on Valentine's Day 1990, facing arraignment in Dallas, Texas, on charges of stealing thousands of dollars from thirteen women in ten states and facing state charges in Wisconsin, Missouri, and Virginia.

In an Associated Press release story that reported the trial, a Kenosha police detective is quoted making the bemused observation, 'If you look at this guy, you say, "What do women see?"' Clearly, the ability of a rather unattractive man to con hundreds of women out of their savings may suggest not simply individual female gullibility or naïvety but rather the social conventions and gender socialization that encourage women to endorse a view – however myopic – that men are best charged with control of a woman's finances. Leslie Gall, a short, plump, 56-year-old Sweetheart Swindler, convicted in June 1990 of stealing $54,000 worth of stock certificates from a Pico Rivera grandmother he had courted, implicitly reiterated this logic in explaining how he had come to have the woman's stocks in his possession. He maintained that he had simply taken the woman's stocks because she had once suggested that he do so for 'safekeeping.' He stated that he had 'picked them up, put them in my briefcase and forgot to tell her I took them. It's the honest truth.'

Although, when informed of his statement by a reporter, the woman accused Gall of being 'full of bull' and called his account 'absolutely a lie,' Gall's offering the statement as a supposedly reasonable explanation of what had happened is in itself suggestive. The gall of the man? At the time he also faced outstanding charges from Ft Lauderdale and Clearwater, Florida, of defrauding one elderly woman of $40,000 and forging fake identification to bigamously marry another.

A Canadian who had spent approximately eight years in Canadian prisons during the 1970s for bank fraud, Gall moved to Florida to escape an additional period of incarceration and soon left behind him a trail of forged cheques and phoney businesses and bank accounts. Using an alias, he courted and conned elderly women he would meet at seniors dances in California and Florida, obtaining money from one 69-year-old woman he had met at a seniors' dance to invest in real estate. Arrested for using a forged ID, he persuaded a Clearwater woman to bail him out of jail and married her – despite the fact that he already had a wife in Canada. Once free, Gall set off for California carrying a Thomas Bros. map book in his van with the route to every senior citizen dance in the Greater Los Angeles area highlighted in coloured ink and a briefcase laden with the newspaper obituaries of wealthy men and clippings detailing notorious con jobs. 'I've always read an awful lot,' he explained when interviewed by Shawn Hubler of the *Los Angeles Times*.

Gall claimed that he had 'never told that many lies' and that the women he had been involved with had obtained their money's worth: 'The payment the ladies received was that I made them very happy ... I made them No. 1. I sent them flowers ... I focused on them. They were wanted.' He said he loved them all.

During his interview with Hubler, Gall complained bitterly how he had been 'tricked' by a woman who had taken her suspicions about Gall's involvement with her widowed mother-in-law to the police; denying that he had planned to rob her mother-in-law, Gall portrayed the daughter-in-law as simply interested in 'protecting her inheritance' when she reported him to the police. 'She didn't care that her mother-in-law was enjoying herself and was the happiest she had ever been in her life. She was just double-dealing. She was nice to me to my face, but doing all this other stuff behind my back.' However, despite indulging in a gloss that explained his role as simply providing essential services for needy women, Gall also noted that he had chosen women as the victims of his cons because, 'put yourself in my position: If you were going to rip somebody off, you'd go opposite sex.'

At least one of Gall's women still loved him and planned to visit him in jail. The woman, a 73-year-old Redondo Beach grandmother with whom Gall had been living at the time of his arrest and whom he had talked into buying a $28,000 van 'so that the two of them could go touring,' maintained her undiminished love for Gall despite his actions. Although she noted that her family was 'aggravated' with her, the woman told the reporter,

By the time I'd heard [about Gall's past], I was so much in love with him, and I still am. You just can't turn it off. He was the most friendly person, and was so good to me. Of course, I was good to him too, and the police tell me he had big plans for me. But I didn't know that … Now, I try to pick up and go on, but I'm not doing a very good job of it. He asked me, 'Would you marry me in jail' and I think maybe I would. I love him that much. But I don't know yet what his sentence would be and it would be a terrible life being apart all the time. Lonely following the death of her husband several years earlier, the woman commented, 'I went to a psychiatrist today and I know it sounds like it didn't do much good, but it didn't, because he didn't tell me what I wanted to hear. He said just go on and forget this, and go on with your life, and then he gave me some painkillers.'

It would seem that not only Sweetheart Swindlers regard women as interchangeable and react to them in demeaning ways.

In his eagerness to assert himself as masculine, the gigolo would often willingly embrace, and offer as proof of his masculinity, blatantly manipulative and antisocial activity. Reinforcing the worst aspects of a patriarchal society through the adaptation and demonstration of its gender roles, the gigolo's actions suggest his willingness to accede to gender stereotypes. He does not reject cultural models of masculinity as much as he willingly suspends them for a period of time – with a legitimating account to sanctify his seeming lapse of conformity. For certain gigolos, such as the Sweetheart Swindler, the purposeful approximation of a feminine role of companion at the courtship stage is not so much a celebration of the feminine as it is a mockery of it. The Madame Bountiful similarly evidenced a role that is androgynous only to the extent that the woman would seem to willing embrace the patriarchal idea that masculinity is necessary for the attainment of power and status. Yet, similar to the gigolo and in counterpart fashion, she was also unwilling to ignore completely cultural models of femininity.

FEMININITY AS A MASQUERADE

In a 1929 article entitled 'Womanliness as a Masquerade,' Joan Rivière attempted 'to show that women who wish for masculinity may put on a mask of womanliness to avert anxiety and the retribution feared from men.' She commented:

Not long ago intellectual pursuits for women were associated almost exclusively with an overtly masculine type of woman, who in pronounced cases made no secret of her wish or claim to be a man. This has now changed. Of all the women engaged in professional work to-day, it would be hard to say whether the greater number are more feminine than masculine in their mode of life and character. In University life, in scientific professions and in business, one constantly meets women who seem to fulfill every criterion of complete feminine development. They are excellent wives and mothers, capable housewives; they maintain social life and assist culture; they have no lack of feminine interests, e.g. in their personal appearance, and when called upon they can still find time to play the part of devoted and disinterested mother-substitutes among a wide circle of relatives and friends. At the same time they fulfil the duties of their profession at least as well as the average man. It is really a puzzle to know how to classify this type psychologically.

For Rivière, a woman presenting this daunting role need not be as unconflicted about her femininity as one might suppose. Indeed, Rivière reported, some powerful and liberated women she observed were simply engaged in a 'masquerade of womanliness.' One of her American patients in analysis, whose occupation involved a great deal of public speaking, experienced considerable anxiety after each performance and began seeking 'reassurance' from men in the audience who were 'unmistakably father-figures': 'often not persons whose judgement on her performance would in reality carry much weight. There were clearly two types of reassurance sought from these father-figures: first, direct reassurance of the nature of compliments about her performance; secondly, and more important, indirect reassurance of the nature of sexual attentions from these men. To speak broadly, analysis of her behaviour after her performance showed that she was attempting to obtain sexual advances from the particular type of men by means of flirting and coquetting with them in a more or less veiled manner ...'

In keeping with the psychoanalytic tradition, Rivière traced this behaviour back to an unsuccessfully resolved Oedipal conflict in early childhood which ultimately led the patient to feelings of rivalry not only with her father but also with men who came to represent her father in her unconscious mind. Her acting in a seductive manner following a performance was a way of attempting to ward off criticisms and 'reprisals' for being so successful in this competition with men.

Thus the aim of the compulsion was not merely to secure reassurance by evoking friendly feelings towards her in the man; it was chiefly to make sure of safety by masquerading as guiltless and innocent. It was a compulsive reversal of her intellectual performance; ... just as her life as a whole consisted alternatively of masculine and feminine activities ... Womanliness therefore could be assumed and worn as a mask, both to hide the possession of masculinity and to avert the reprisals expected if she was found to possess it – much as a thief will turn out his pockets and ask to be searched to prove that he has not the stolen goods ...

Rivière further noted:

The reader may now ask how I define womanliness or where I draw the line between genuine womanliness and the 'masquerade.' My suggestion is not, however, that there is any such difference; ... they are the same thing.

More than sixty years later, in her 1991 book *Female Perversions*, Louise Kaplan attempted to extend and elaborate Riviere's original thesis with the claim that 'the crimes that so troubled Rivière's patient were infantile crimes based on unconscious infantile fantasies.' In support of her case, and derived from her clinical analyses with adult women, Kaplan offered a narrative of a composite case-study, 'Janet.' What emerged can most simply be phrased as 'blaming the mother':

'Janet' was born to a mother who had already given birth to two daughters. The mother this time had been especially longing for a son. When Janet was born, she took one look at her baby girl and decided that she would do nicely for the son she never had ... [I]t was altogether in keeping with the times that Janet's mother would elect a female child to fulfill her own frustrated masculine ambitions ... The problem was that Janet continued to cling to the fantasy that she could satisfy her mother's every desire, that her mother was an extension of her own self, a possession that belonged to her and to no one else. So when the time came for Janet to reckon with her father's presence in her mother's life and to recognize that she was prohibited from and furthermore incapable of possessing her mother the way the father did, she could not accept the inevitable defeat of her childhood ambitions with any grace or equanimity ... She also now desired her father and wanted him and his powers to be given to her and not to the mother ...

Janet tried to remedy this all in fantasy ... Since she envied her father for his powers, she thought she might seduce him into handing them over to her if she behaved like a perfect little princess ... [S]he began to think of her [mother] as a wicked stepmother who didn't deserve the father's love anyway ...

Unconsciously, and in keeping with traditional psychoanalytic explanations, Janet supposedly engaged in fantasies of jealous rage which involved mutilation of her father's and her mother's genitalia and eventually, at the hands of her mother, of her own. The mutilation of her parents represented a taking of their power, and the mutilation of herself represented the parents', particularly the mother's, reprisals for this theft: 'Little Janet recovered from her jealous rage by devising a clever strategy that would appease both parents and yet still allow her to triumph over them ... It was Janet's unconscious strategy for appeasing her mother that gave form and direction to her masquerade ... [S]he would act just like a powerful, protecting father to her mother ... Janet would be a proper, self-sacrificing daughter-momma and also the majestic, powerful son-daddy her mother had been wishing for.'

By adulthood, Janet had become all things to all people. She was a success in her academic career, a 'Big Daddy' to her female students in particular, a person who gave unstintingly and seemingly unselfishly of herself to her friends (especially females) as well as to her mother in times of need. All she appeared to require in turn was 'gratitude' and an acknowledgement of her 'superiority.' In addition:

At the end of a long day ... the undaunted Janet was ready and willing for sex. As much as she needed to play Big Daddy to all the helpless women in her life, the truth was that she also needed to assure herself of her femininity by having sexual intercourse as frequently as possible. It was imperative that she get more sexual pleasure than those inferior feminine women like her mother ... [U]nder the screen of ...

impeccable femininity she orchestrated the sexual scenario, essentially robbing her husband of his active masculinity ... As when baking cookies, polishing the silver, waxing the grand piano, shopping for gourmet groceries, purchasing the right books, arranging for dinner parties and theatre excursions, keeping the household accounts and paying the bills, she obligingly tended to her husband's sexual needs. She brought to the marital chamber all her practical know-how and managerial skills, making absolutely certain that everything came off without a hitch. She performed fellatio with alacrity and was an inventive bed partner ... She used her womanly arts, almost as a man would use a fetish, more as a device to avoid anxiety than as a means of obtaining sexual pleasure ... Sex was an exercise in domination and penetration.

Finally, Kaplan noted with regard to women today: 'Now at the close of the twentieth century, with all the token permission given to women to express their intellectual ambitions and erotic strivings, there is still created an atmosphere of retaliation that makes many women hold back from a full-hearted, open display of intellectual mastery and active sexual desire. A woman fears, very often justifiably, that if she challenges authority or succeeds in roles and professions that have traditionally been defined as masculine, she will be punished.'

Although Kaplan stated that she saw women like Janet 'everywhere, in my clinical practice, among my friends and colleagues,' she suggested that 'not every woman will seek refuge in a masquerade of womanliness or advertise her mind as a nonthreatening spiritual mist or display herself as a submissive or masochistic feminine type.' Rather, Kaplan suggested, 'only a Janet, who unconsciously confuses power with a rapacious theft of phallic trophies, will find it necessary to propitiate the gods by devising a strategy that employs a caricature of femininity to disguise her forbidden "masculine" strivings.' For Kaplan, femininity as a masquerade most primarily stemmed from a family constellation of 'too much mother and too little father.'

While the dynamics that Kaplan posited are certainly tortuously complicated, 'blaming the mother' is hardly a novel approach to explain any and all forms of deviation. Paula Caplan and her associates analysed 125 articles within professional scholarly journals and found mother-blaming to be widespread and a popular assumption by both clinical psychologists and family therapists. Incompetent and penis-envying mothers are held to be responsible for the genesis of practically every disorder which may conceivably befall their children including (but not limited to) enuresis or bedwetting, aggression, schizophrenia, difficulties in learning, transsexualism, homicidal transsexualism, transvestism, other assorted paraphilias, and becoming a serial murderer.

The syndrome of 'blaming the mother' is a type of psychological reductionism which restricts analysis of the issue to a very limited and superficial arena. It suggests a fetishized logic that employs ready-made Freudian precepts to treat the 'problem' of women on an individual *post-hoc* basis. As Ernest Becker has suggested, fetishization is an attempt to manage reality whereby the task becomes perceived as less unwieldy and chaotic. In the process, a fragment of reality is substituted for the whole. Thus, the process of fetishization could offer one explanation for why then vice-president Dan Quayle found it fitting to lay the cause of the Los Angeles riots squarely on the out-of-wedlock pregnancy of the television character Murphy Brown.

It is obviously easy to apply a fetishized logic to confront the problem of gender oppression and discomfort. In asserting that 'Janet' may be safely offered as a composite portrait of a 'dysfunctional woman' and then 'blaming the mother' for the origins of her pathology, we see an example of what Becker calls 'fetishizing the field.' For us, it seems that the most striking difference between the original work of Rivière and that of Kaplan is that almost seventy years separates the publication of their works. The conclusions themselves are really not all that dissimilar. In both cases 'womanliness as a masquerade' is seen as a pathological condition arising from apparent inability of the woman to negotiate successfully through an early stage of psychosexual development.

It must be stressed that, although we find the concept of femininity as a masquerade an intriguing one and useful in part in explaining the behaviour of the Madame Bountiful, we would dispute its aetiology as postulated by both Rivière and Kaplan. With due deference to the Freudians, we would argue that every daughter is likely to hate/love her mother/father, and the danger in adopting this theoretical position is that every later action in life comes to be viewed as symptomatic of the individual's parental attachments. Thus, the woman who hates her mother may really wish to (a) possess her sexually, with hatred becoming a 'classic symptom of reaction formation'; (b) possess her father sexually, with hatred being seen as the 'logical' aftermath of 'penis envy' and feelings that her mother 'castrated her' – the argument goes on and on, and all roads lead back to the nursery.

As Seymour Halleck suggested in a discussion of 'the politics of symptoms,' treatments which focus solely on symptoms rather than upon broader social or existential issues are likely to be 'efficient' but unlikely to be effective. To make the masquerade of femininity the private terrain, so to speak, of Freudians is to superficialize the depths of the questions that lie behind gender oppression. The actions of society are rendered invisible and relatively innocuous, while the 'dysfunctional' qualities of the 'patient' are stressed and validated.

We believe that to focus on intrapsychic attitudes and/or behaviours is short-sighted in that social, political, and cultural processes cannot simply be relegated to an unimportant or non-existent role. We would argue that the First Cause (that which, in an Aristotelian sense, sets all other causes in motion) of femininity as a masquerade originates most fundamentally within a society that produces, reinforces, and rewards gender stereotypes.

Case-Study: Marilyn

'Marilyn,' at the age of 45, appeared to have benefited from all the gifts the gods could bestow upon her. A successful business woman with a home and car that were testimony to her wealth, her looks were model-like. Tall and elegantly lean, with long, dark brown hair, and dressed in a brilliant red suit with fashionably short skirt and high-heeled black shoes, Marilyn looked more like the heroine of a night-time soap opera than the type of woman who, by her own admission, routinely kept her lovers. Her make-up was immaculate, her figure fine-toned by hours of aerobics and a weight-training program she adopted after seeing Linda Hamilton in *Terminator 2* (and essential, she sombrely noted, if one was going to wear sleeveless outfits), and she smelled wonderfully of expensive perfume. It seemed that this was a lady who attended to her needs and desires with meticulous care. Her hairdresser and weight trainer were mentioned with reverence; the existence and indispensability of her secretary and her child's nanny were also remarked upon, even if in a less effusive manner. Her lover, carefully outfitted in a Hugo Boss double-breasted suit, tall and sinewy, seemed similarly to convey the image of wealth and luxury.

While Marilyn's looks suggested a fastidiousness in the projection of feminine beauty, her conversation was surprising. In her language style itself, Marilyn adopted a pattern more characteristic of 'menspeech' than 'womentalk.' As sociologists and linguists note, women and men differ in their styles of speech and play different roles when talking to each other. Marilyn's pattern of speech was markedly more masculine than feminine. She dominated the conversation, shifted topics to meet her preference, and tended to bypass the questioning and hesitant tone that often characterizes female speech. The tag ending ('Don't you think so?') and child-like lead-off question ('you know what?'), the reliance on empty words ('absolutely divine') and superfluous intensifiers ('too, too, marvellous') that are said to characterize womentalk were notable only in their absence within Marilyn's conversation. While the 'don't-talk-while-I'm-trying-to-interrupt-you' syndrome is most typically a male prerogative, Marilyn's voice dominated the conversation, not infrequently interrupting and talking over someone else's discussion.

Marilyn's preferred focus of discussion on virtually all the occasions we met seemed to be two main topics: work and sex and her superior accomplishments at both. She directed attention to the fact that her business success was in an avenue typically unoccupied by females; she was, she proclaimed, a trend-setter, one who was 'paving the ground' for other women who would, someday perhaps, follow. In the interim, however, she seemed to revel in her token status, noting repeatedly the way in which she had been able to convert disbelieving male bankers and misogynistic associates into ardent fans and, at the very least, grudging admirers. She regaled her audience with the 'witty' comebacks and comments she had made in adversarial negotiations with her typically male competitors – the majority of these remarks were liberally laced with references to oral sex and intercourse. She seemed rather delighted to describe herself as an untamed 'wild child.' She would occasionally pause after referencing a man's power to the supposed size of his 'balls,' commenting on a rival's presumed competence at 'sucking' or 'blowing' other men for competitive advantage, or engaging in similar forms of sexually laced repartée to stare at the first author as if to see whether or not she was shocked or taken aback.

While her colourful descriptions did not offend, what did appear perplexing was the content of her talk. For example, within a presentation of her accomplishments that verged on the egomaniacal appeared her curious habit of reporting each designer outfit she had worn on the occasion of each and every business triumph. Such references seemed an abrupt disjuncture with the topic of conversation, and one was left to ponder why she felt it necessary to mention that she had worn clothes designed by a trendy high fashion designer on the day of her successful negotiations with a major distributor. The details of her wardrobe were almost always faithfully provided, without any prompting.

Marilyn's avowed voraciousness in things sexual was also a common theme within the majority of our conversations. She would pontificate on the superiority of one type of position or another, comment knowledgeably on the varied sensations possible through vaginal stimulation, clitoral stimulation, and the insertion of Ben-wa balls and various shaped vibrators, and direct attention to the fact that her varied lovers had all been overwhelmed and gratified by her expertise in performing fellatio. Although some of her lovers had not been as proficient or adept as she when they entered into a relationship with her, she reported that they blossomed under her tutelage and choreography. 'Gary,' she remarked, pointing an elegantly manicured fingernail at her lover, 'was a Minute Man when I met him. He isn't like that any more though. Isn't that right, darling?'

Marilyn's relations with her own family were markedly distant and abbreviated. Her mother was portrayed as an intelligent but embittered woman, the 'classic stage mother' who had projected all her thwarted desires for independence and success onto Marilyn. According to Marilyn, her mother's insistence that she be provided with extra lessons in music, French, dancing, and the like only made her feel 'pressured' and she was bitterly resentful and sceptical of her mother's seeming devotion to her. An exceptional student, Marilyn had earned somewhat mediocre grades during her college years. This fact she attributed to a 'delayed reaction' to all the years her mother had 'pushed her' into being a 'superstar.' The mother was painted as a Hydra-like figure who had verbally abused her, told her that she was 'Satan possessed' when she disagreed with her, and had subjected her to constant scrutiny. According to Marilyn, she had been allowed little privacy or opportunity to engage in independent expression as a child; she loved to write poetry but anything that did not follow the iambic metre was dismissed by her mother as 'garbage.' Only the 'Robert Louis Stevenson–style' poetry was 'acceptable' to her mother. The fact that her mother had given her perfume to use in place of deodorant when she was a teenager was mentioned by Marilyn to illustrate her mother's determination that her daughter project a feminine image.

In contrast, Marilyn stated that she had 'worshipped' her father, a hugely successful man, throughout her childhood and adult life, even though he was portrayed as largely absent within her childhood. She stated that she had been made the early and continued confidante of his dissatisfactions with his marriage and had been the only one who had 'truly loved him' and cared for him. Her claims of her loyalty to her father could become markedly petty and territorial on occasion. For example, she noted with obvious resentment that, in the later years of her life, her mother had always referred to her father as 'Daddy': 'That was *my* term for him. *I* was the one who called him Daddy.' She stressed how she had taken a protective role towards him, listening to his conversations about business – a topic her mother reportedly found boring and monotonous – making doctor's appointments for him when he seemed unwell, and buying him gifts of things he would not get for himself.

Her only sibling, a much younger brother, was portrayed as her mother's favourite. She mentioned that, as adults, they had fought often over their markedly disparate perceptions of their childhood experiences; her brother reportedly felt that she had commanded all the attention within the home and had been the mother's 'obsession,' if not the favourite, and the father's obvious 'favoured son.' Marilyn dismissed his comments; if she had been focused on by her mother, it was only as the receptor of 'pressure' and criticism. Her father's supposed favouring of her over her brother she acknowledged, without apology, as correct. However, she commented, her brother had been 'dull, dull, dull'; a follower who she had to 'order around to get him to do anything.' She repeatedly commented that she identified with her father and referred to herself as the 'son he never had.'

Marilyn's past marriage was presented as an almost inconsequential footnote in her life history. Her ex-husband was portrayed by her as rather a hapless, ineffective, creature who had risen to a position of prominence and wealth largely through her efforts. Marilyn and her husband had originally been involved in business together. Although she felt that the divorce settlement had been satisfactory, she also felt that he had benefited from the misplaced loyalty of former business associates, who, she maintained, saw him as the dominant member in their partnership 'simply because he was male.' That, after their divorce, he had become markedly more successful materially than she, was evidently grating to her. He was weak and indecisive; she was the 'doer' – decisive, forthright, the visionary. She was 'more mature' than he was. She had made him get his MBA from a prestigious university; he simply had followed her instructions by doing so. He was lacklustre and boring. She described herself as being like 'mercury' or 'quicksilver.' He was an incompetent father. She hired the best nannies. He had married a 'fat sow' of a wife; her lover was 'gorgeous' and she was 'obsessed' with ensuring that she did not get fat herself.

As if to indicate the extent of her self-discipline in this regard, she acknowledged using dieting 'aids,' including amphetamines, and to engaging episodically in the bulimic practices of purging food through self-induced vomiting after her meals and abusing Ipecac, a purgative. Rather than seeing these strategies as any cause for concern, she portrayed self-induced vomiting, for example, as simply expedient behaviour that allowed her to feast on the types of meals – like seafood pasta which she 'adored,' without damage or noticeable consequence to her figure. She laughed when she recalled that one female friend, hearing her vomiting in the bathroom of a posh restaurant after a meal, had been 'relieved' – she had thought Marilyn was 'doing coke.'

Although Marilyn acknowledged using cocaine on an 'occasional' basis in the past, she discounted any habitual use. Cocaine use, she commented, was an ''80s thing.' While she expressed some concern that her binging and purging behaviour had reportedly caused the blood vessels under her eyes to become pronounced, she mentioned that this could be deftly covered with the use of make-up or by having her eyes 'done' by a plastic surgeon. She straightforwardly acknowledged having had various cosmetic surgical procedures performed and, in a rather grand manner, pronounced this evidence of her being 'liberated' and liberal in her thinking.

Indeed, in another example of her tendency to infuse her conversation with sexual innuendos and analogies, she commented that plastic surgery was like masturbation in that: 'It's my body and I decide what feels good for me, when I want it, how I want it, and where I want it.' She mocked those 'bitter feminist types' who went around looking 'frumpy' and 'old' when 'we've got the technology' to look 'feminine' and 'attractive.' The unglamourous, the unsvelte, and the uninterested in clothes were regarded by Marilyn as suspicious 'masculine' 'feminist types' who were 'bitter' and 'jealous' of women such as herself. For Marilyn, 'feminist' was obviously a four-letter word.

While Marilyn's behaviour in public seemed purposefully crafted to portray the imagery of the 1990s Superwoman – a witty and beautiful successful businesswoman and a single mother – her relationships with her lovers, all variously kept by her in sequential fashion, seemed puzzling. Her behaviour when partnered with her lovers seemed to alternate between two principal roles – paternalistically tender and tyrannical. In the man's absence she appeared to have little inhibitions about engaging in discussions of 'the little woman' – as she termed her various men – that portrayed them as objects of ridicule. However, while she loudly disdained the importance of any one man in her life, she seemed to find it essential to be with someone who could accompany her to the right restaurants and parties, on her holidays, and to her business dinners. She was similarly consistent in describing herself as an 'independent,' 'liberated,' and 'assertive' woman, yet often seemed eager to draw attention to herself as a self-sacrificing 'feminine type,' 'long-suffering' and 'forgiving.'

Within her depictions of her relationships, men were portrayed at best as rather incompetent and purely ornamental fixtures; at worst, they were portrayed as violent creatures who would, in moments of anger, strike her, threaten her, smash her paintings, or wreck her furniture. For example, on one occasion when we were to meet for a late evening drink she was a no-show – an unusual occurrence in that Marilyn prided herself on never being late, never missing a meeting, and disdaining what she called the 'old female game of "keep 'em waiting"' as unprofessional. When we contacted her the next day to inquire if everything was all right, she sounded rather muted, her speech muffled. When asked if something was wrong, she then explained that she and her lover had had a violent fight the night before in which he had hit her; as a result, she reported, she had fallen and chipped her front tooth. She explained that she had been to the dentist early that morning and was 'just getting used to' the newness of the bonded tooth.

Marilyn commented that, her lover had been 'jealous' over not being included in her plans for the previous evening and, after spending much of the previous afternoon drinking, had become enraged and violent. She commented that when she had come home from the dentist, he had just woken up and did not have any recollection of what he had done. 'Did you tell him?' she was asked. 'Yes,' she replied, and he had been 'shocked' and had cried, begging her to forgive him. It was just that he loved her so much, she commented, and did not have the verbal ability to express himself well. 'Men are like that,' she remarked. 'It's because the other half of their brain is dominant.'

It later became apparent that she confided such intimate disclosures to many people; indeed, she was as self-advertising about her victimization and manipulation by men as she was about her triumphs and successes in the world of business. When asked if he had ever hit her before, she mentioned a time several months earlier when, under the influence of cocaine, her lover had placed a single bullet into a handgun, spun the chamber, cocked the trigger, and asked her 'Do you feel lucky?' On that occasion, she reported, he had been 'depressed' over not finding work and was feeling 'emasculated' by her wealth and success. Although the man had pointed the gun at her and pulled the trigger, the chamber had been empty. What followed seemed equally heinous; after a verbal tirade in which he reportedly accused her of being a 'haughty bitch,' a 'whore' and a 'cunt,' he had her fellate him and then told her, 'I guess this counts as an apology.' The next morning, her lover had no recollection of what he had done. 'Had you informed him?' 'No,' Marilyn replied. 'Why not?' She responded that, on that occasion, because she knew he was 'feeling so unhappy with himself already,' she had not bothered to refresh his memory.

Marilyn's lovers seemed an odd selection of men, typically at least a decade or two younger than she; less powerful; less well educated; and, if socially presentable, much less so than Marilyn herself. There was the addict whose extensive addiction she 'didn't realize' until he injured someone and smashed up her new car while driving under the drug's influence. On that occasion, after soliciting the opinions of various and sundry confidantes, Marilyn paid for the man's lawyer, gave him a 'severance package,' and bade him adieu. She grew wistful in recalling this unhappy ending: 'I loved that car.' A second lover she referred to as her 'walk on the wild side': an ex-con who could tell 'the most amazing stories,' had a host of colourful tattoos and companions, and paraded through her home a series of various comrades who flattered her while benefiting from the bountiful hospitality she was capable of providing, and from the extent of her tolerance. Another favoured and paid companion was a much younger man whom she proudly proclaimed she had 'deflowered.' All were portrayed as somewhat interchangeable and forgettable, except for the ways in which each relationship was thought to attest to her fundamental altruism.

In an early conversation, Marilyn had subdivided the world into 'givers' and 'users'; she then loudly proclaimed that she was a 'world-class giver.' Certainly the incidents she outlined suggested that she was extremely self-sacrificing and financially generous within her kept relationships. Yet, after detailing episode after episode of her lovers' callousness and insensitivity, Marilyn sighed and stated that she was destined to be 'fatally attracted' to men who were 'needy.' She commented, 'My daughter said to me a while ago, "Mom, if there's a 101 men after you, you'll pick the one psycho with the third eyeball."' While maintaining that her need for any of her male partners had been far less significant than their dependence on her, Marilyn seemed eager to assume the role of a self-suffering Madame Bountiful.

So long as the men Marilyn kept at least implicitly acknowledged her superiority and largesse with thanks and appropriate shows of gratitude, she seemed indifferent to whether or not they were employed or unemployed, ambitious or unambitious, witty or banal. Although 'addicted' to 'gorgeous blond men' with 'great asses,' she seemed equally charmed by the prospect of resurrecting and rejuvenating those whom she termed 'lost souls.' To accomplish this end Marilyn seemed almost eager to act as a Pygmalion, noting her ability to detect 'uncut diamonds' among men – especially those who were 'beautiful.' Men who appeared confident and competent did not seem to be overly appealing to her. The more eligible they seemed, the more 'boring' she maintained them to be. 'I just don't feel anything toward him,' she would invariably comment in her discussions of such a man at some later point. 'I feel like a sister to him. Strictly platonic.' Because Marilyn prided herself on 'never playing games' with the men she would date or become involved with, such associations would be brought speedily to their conclusion.

Marilyn's relationships with her kept lovers tended to be long-drawn-out affairs, ended only after numerous 'crises,' well-publicized betrayals, and much *Sturm und Drang.* Invariably, however, she would maintain that her lovers had become 'better men' for their association with her. Like an alchemist transforming raw material into something precious, she made her men her 'projects' and stressed how her various kept lovers had thrived under her tutelage and how she had been able to transform coal into diamond.

In contrast to the care and time she appeared willing to expend as the Reclamation Queen of the down and out, Marilyn seemed rather less devoted to the nurturance of her daughter. She stated that her pregnancy had been accidental and that she had not wanted a child, particularly at the stage of her life in which the child had been conceived. She commented that she would have probably opted for an abortion had her husband not been strongly opposed to the idea and she herself conscious of the fact that, 'at the time, it was not politically correct to have an abortion – it just wasn't done.' She commented that she had loathed being pregnant and found pregnant women 'repulsive,' and that, aside from enjoying the fullness of her breasts, viewed breastfeeding as something 'best left to cows.' Although she stated that she was 'unable to relate' to very small children, she maintained that she and her daughter had developed an 'incredible, best-friend relationship' that included frank discussions about sexuality and her various lovers, and stated that such discussions were 'healthy, open, and a creative force'; at the time of this conversation her daughter was under 12 years of age.

Despite her affection for her daughter, Marilyn rarely seemed preoccupied by motherhood. While a small, beautifully framed, picture of her daughter as a toddler graced a shelf behind the desk in her office, it was almost a decade old. Whether this situation resulted from a particular fondness for the picture, a desire to cultivate the impression that she was too young to have a daughter approaching her teen years, or the power of inertia is unknown. However, Marilyn was most assuredly not the type to produce 'brag books' of her daughter's photographs or comment in other than cursory fashion about her daughter's existence. Rather, in Royal fashion, she seemed to enjoy the abbreviated and scheduled outings they had together, going shopping or for lunch, but was quite content to

Masquerades and Illusions 275

have someone else assume primary care for the child. She showed little reluctance at occasionally leaving the child to be 'babysat' by her admittedly violent boyfriend when she had to work or to attend a business function and the child's nanny became ill or otherwise unavailable. She stoutly declared that her lover had never shown any sign of violence towards the child and was 'wonderful' with her.

Thus appeared a paradox more than slightly reminiscent of Louise Kaplan's 'Janet,' referred to earlier: a successful business woman who saw herself and was viewed by numerous others as masculine in her ambitiousness, her defiance of traditional norms of femininity, her eschewing the 'Mrs Cunningham [of television *Happy Days* fame] bullshit trip,' and her marked aversion for conventional feminine roles, yet engaged in many behaviours that could be seen as caricatures of femininity. At the same time as she rebelled against the bourgeois ideal of femininity, her behaviour seemed to embrace and direct attention towards her performance of stereotypical feminine behaviour, such as her fastidious concern with weight and appearance, and with monitoring and managing the relationships with her kept men. Her odd juxtaposition of work success and fashion commentary may be particularly telling. It could be argued that her strategy of presenting work accomplishment with the appendixed detailing of her wardrobe allowed her to direct attention to her masculine ambitions while still claiming proof of her essential femininity. Similarly, if her caring for psychically wounded and maimed men suggests altruistic and/or potentially self-defeating behaviour, it is also behaviour that is markedly consistent with the traditional ethos of femininity. It may also be that this presentation of self can be viewed as a tactic of accommodation to a society which, despite a veneer of gender liberation and sexual equality, still perpetuates stereotypical ideas of certain conduct for males and for females and rewards or punishes the behaviour appropriately. Marilyn's observance of certain feminine norms appears to stem less from the operation of unsuccessfully resolved Oedipal conflicts and more from an awareness of social dictates for proper role behaviour. Regardless of her underlying motivation, the resulting performance yields a complex mixture of illusions and realities.

INTIMACY MASQUERADES

While 'masquerade' has been used thus far to refer to the actions taken by individual females, it is also useful in discussing the behaviour of couples. As we have noted numerous times throughout this book, the gigolo/Bountiful relationship often takes on the appearance of an intimate relationship. Despite a frequently observable age reversal, the couple give the impression to others of conforming to the demands of the 'couples' society that we referred to in chapter 2. We have noted that some gigolo/Bountiful relationships are formed precisely in order to provide a male companion for a woman in situations where being unescorted is considered somewhat *déclassé* or even potentially dangerous. Whether it be for a single evening or for a period of years, two people 'masquerade' as a 'couple' and present themselves to the outside world as such.

We have also noted that gigolo/Bountiful liaisons are often formed for the same reasons as are other heterosexual relationships, such as to meet needs for companionship and having someone to share in the great and small events of life; needs for erotic intimacy; needs to give and receive love in its various expressions; and needs for a satisfying economic lifestyle. Just as in everyday relationships, we commonly observe that each of the partners in the liaison may bring with him or her a different set of priorities. The desired items on their lists may be the same, but the priority location of those items is different. Depending upon whether trade-offs are possible, which may be influenced by the alternatives available for each potential mate, a partnership can be formed which will meet each person's needs to a sufficiently satisfactory extent.

Case-Study: Carole and Peter

At the age of 63, Carole was both a mother of two and a grandmother of six; divorced from her executive husband since her mid-fifties, she was Madame Bountiful and Mrs Robinson to a gigolo in his early thirties. Peter was several years younger than Carole's son and looked even younger than that.

Carole had been divorced by her husband after he had a prolonged affair with, and subsequently desired to marry, a young woman in her twenties. Carole's indignation over her husband's behaviour was continuously given voice, along with her perception that men of her husband's generation could not accept 'strong women' and, in consequence, sought the fawning admiration that was 'feigned' by young 'gold-diggers.' She scoffed at her husband's seeming willingness to believe his new young wife sincere and voiced her opinion that the woman was in love with her ex-husband's bank balance not with him.

While disdaining the emotion felt by her ex-husband's new wife as – at best – 'cupboard love' (suggesting that the emotion felt, for example, by a pet towards the person who feeds it is less than 'true' love) – she directed attention to the double standard that emerged in social judgments of the younger woman/older man and the older woman/younger man relationships and rhetorically asked,

Is it all reducible to biology? I mean, just because he can still father a child – not that he was even really good at being a father to our kids – does society say that it's understandable for a man to trade a wife who is past that sort of thing for a woman who can still give him children? 'Go forth and multiply,' if you know what I mean. Maybe because a middle-aged woman can't have a baby from a young man, the whole relationship is viewed as rather pointless – I mean, using that mindset. I don't know myself but I do know that when Ben [her ex-husband] left me, I got the feeling that everyone thought it was understandable, that it was my fault. This is really being condemned without a hearing, without justice, without a trial.

It's my fault he wants a woman who tells him that everything he does is perfect? After two kids and almost thirty years of marriage, I'm supposed to pretend he's Troy Donahue? He isn't. So I got older. I can accept that. It was Ben who was having trouble with the idea that he wasn't as young anymore. Not me. I was always looking forward to getting older and doing the things that I hadn't gotten around to doing. I'm very involved in the —— Society, and am on the board of directors for the —— Foundation; I'm not some young cover girl but I'm not unattractive …

When we got divorced, I was in better shape than I am now; about two years ago I had to have eye surgery and I suffer from arthritis. When you experience pain – physical or emotional – it shows. As they say, 'experience is a series of experiences which we would rather not have had.'

[Was Peter's age a problem for you?] That's a difficult question. No. Yes. No, because after what I'd gone through, and because of my age, the men I was going out with were men that had been mutual friends when I was married. It felt strange; with them I was still Ben's wife, and so his name kept coming up. It was a civilized divorce, so people thought there was no hard feelings. This is easier said than done.

Don't forget, we had been married a long time. God knows I did all in my power to be an attentive wife; if I saw problems, I felt guilty for even entertaining the thought that Ben might have another woman. And yet, there were indications of troubling behaviour which I chose rather to attribute to the fact that there were difficulties in business and everyone has their moods. Oh, how much I went through, even now talking about it, my heart is, like, submerged in water, gasping for a beat as I remember the events, the betrayal, the trauma, the helplessness.

However, while describing herself as 'desolate,' 'ravaged,' and 'betrayed' by her husband's leaving her, Carole described herself as 'uninterested' in a relationship which included sex; sex with her husband had been an 'imposition,' a 'bother,' and she claimed to be uninterested in experiencing sex with any other man. She was quick to note that this was not attributable to menopause and went on to voice her disdain for women who 'fussed' and carried on about 'something so ridiculous.' Rather, she suggested that sex was a 'male need' and really not characteristic of women, or characteristic only of 'foolish' women who had an 'unnatural' and somewhat 'unseemly' interest in sex. Peter, she stressed, was simply a 'companion': an attractive young man ('The young are beautiful. Who can blame me for wanting to look at someone handsome and not someone ugly?') who squired her to various social events, alleviated the loneliness she found to be pervasive since her divorce, took pains to amuse her, talked with her, drove her to wherever she wished to go, and so on.

In chronicling her life, Carole presented her ex-husband as a 'good provider,' and commented that, because of the length of time they had been married, she had believed he would be her companion 'till death us do part.' However, no pretension was made that the marriage had been profoundly gratifying from a sexual or emotional perspective. She spoke repeatedly of and seemed to value highly an especially close friendship with a young woman who had died in her twenties. This woman was described as a beloved with whom she had shared intimacies, who had 'understood' her fully, and with whom she had experienced cherished memories. However, if her preference would have been, perhaps, for a female relational partner, Carole's comments suggested that this option was never one she had seriously considered, in the past or in the present.

Carole presented her marriage as simply the 'inevitable' consequence of a social imperative to be married and pressure exerted by her parents not to remain a spinster. Carole had worked only for a very brief period during her early twenties and, upon marriage, became the 'lady of the house,' true to her upper-middle-class background. She noted that, as a young woman prior to marriage, she had to have a gynaecological procedure to remove a cyst and had been issued with a 'certificate' attesting to the fact that she had been 'surgically deflowered' to present to her future husband at some later date. While despairing of the breakdown of her marriage, Carole did not seem to recognize any irony in her remarking that, on their honeymoon, she had left her husband, feeling their relationship was a 'sham' and a 'farce' that held little emotional or erotic appeal for her. However, she observed, 'there was no question' of living as a single woman. She returned to the hotel some time later on the same night.

While Carole herself often privately dismissed her younger 'companion' as a 'gigolo,' she was quick to point out that she needed a man as an escort, as a chauffer to drive her to the long-term care residential hospital where her mother was housed following a debilitating stroke, and as a companion and a largely uncritical audience for her recountings of the seemingly endless ways in which she had been 'devastated,' 'betrayed,' and 'abandoned' by ex-husband, children, and assorted friends and relatives. Moreover, if not acknowledged by her, she seemed prone to extend the prerequisite tasks incumbent upon her gigolo to include that of 'handiman,' 'gofer,' and general dog's-body. Part social secretary, part hired hand, and unofficial 'walker,' the man was charged with maintaining some semblance of order in her life as a social hostess, patron of the arts, and social luminary.

It was not infrequent that Carole's gigolo was charged with the task of acting as her agent with workmen who displeased her, caterers, travel agents, and assorted menials with whom she either disdained to bother or had recently fought. For example, upon learning that her daughter had dined with her ex-husband and his new wife, she had berated her daughter over the telephone for her 'disloyalty' and instructed her, as a dutiful daughter, loyal to her mother, to shun her father and his wife. Asked to choose between her parents by her mother, her daughter had chosen her father, and, at the time of the interview with Carole, had not spoken to her mother for a period of some months. Despite Carole's attempts to 'correct' her daughter's reasoning by writing her numerous letters, with money tucked into the envelopes, the estrangement had continued.

Indignant at her failure to convince her daughter that she should 'tell her father off' and 'have nothing to do with him,' Carole had recruited her gigolo to intervene on her behalf. When he had attempted to gently demur, murmuring that this was a 'family thing' and he did not 'feel right' becoming involved, Carole exploded at him in the first author's presence: 'Danny [her other child] says you both [her gigolo and her daughter] are both traitors and liars and he is right. If you are not a liar, then tell her what she did was wrong as I have written her. I am very hurt. I have two traitors in my life. Maybe you too are waiting for my death.'

Since Carole was lavishly generous with presents and money when her edicts were obeyed, her gigolo seemed forced to walk a fine line between the roles of dependent child, forced to accede to and indulge Carole's whims and wishes, and *paterfamilias*, charged with 'disciplining' those who displeased her. It did not seem a very enviable job description, but her gigolo seemed to negotiate it with a certain degree of *élan*. Sometime later he commented:

Carole is not that hard to figure out. She's a spoiled rich woman. That's about it. She can afford to indulge herself. And part of the way she does it is through creating her own drama out of life. Keeps her life interesting and gives herself something to talk about, you know? I never *talk* with Carole, I just listen. Stick a pair of ears on to an armchair and she probably wouldn't know the difference. She'll ask you a question and *tell* you the answer. Very one-sided.

[What do you get out of it?] She's a soft touch. If I come in with a sad song, tell her that life has really got me down, really sing the blues, she likes that. Also control, I guess. She likes to play God ...

[How did you meet her?] My former lover was the husband of one of her friends; they're all really involved in the — Foundation together. He had three boys that he was keeping at the same time and I decided I didn't like being one of a crowd. He was very, very generous. All of us had our own apartment, our own car, our own day of the week, but he could get really twisted. It's like you didn't have a right to do your own thing when he wasn't around. That's not for me. I knew Carole was looking for a companion, so I thought I could go along with it for a couple of months.

She's a strange old girl. She's not into sex. She's into everybody else's sex lives, wants to know all the details – she's kind of a pervert that way. [What do you mean?] Well, when she talks about her ex's wife, you should just hear what she says. It can start off with her just saying that she [the new wife] must know something special in bed, but it just goes downhill from there. Really dirty-minded ...

We were in the car and it came on the radio that this guy had been beaten up at a gay-rights march and had lost an eye. Well, you should have heard her. She started going on about how 'they should have pulled out the other one,' and about how he probably had oral sex with guys, was a 'cocksucker.' It was disgusting. It wasn't just what she said. It was the way she said it, going on and on about oral sex. It was just so excessive ... [Does she know that you're gay?] No!! She thinks all gays are carrying AIDS. She wouldn't sit in the same room with me if she knew I was gay. Oh she can do the social things; she does the charity banquet circuit, but that's as far as it goes. [How does that make you feel? Knowing that she hates gays?] It's not that unusual, is it? I mean, I've had to deal with it all my life. Some people want to live in the Dark Ages and that's their choice. [Does it make being with her more difficult?] It's a job. If you work with people in *any* job, you're going to find that some are nice, some are real assholes, and most are tolerable. She's somewhere between an asshole and tolerable. The difference is, I get paid well, more to deal with her than I would working somewhere else. For now.

[Is there a difference in being kept by a man or a woman?] It depends on the man or the woman! For me, obviously the sex is more enjoyable with a man. There is [*sic*] some differences of course. Like with Frank [his married ex-lover], because of who he is, there was really no question of doing things out in public, social things I mean. You have to be more careful to butch it up so nobody gets ideas ... So our relationship was pretty well limited to sex. He'd come over or I'd meet him somewhere, we'd party and have a good time, and off he'd go.

I'd say that women get a gigolo because they want to go out, show you off, more than just the sex thing, and with guys it's the opposite. Like Ari [an older, married, and bisexual friend in his fifties]; he's doing really well for himself with women and, to me, he's just an old queen. He has to pay hustlers to have sex with him, but the ladies love him. He's fat, bald, but he always gets lots of money from women ... Right now he's with a woman who's a long-time dyke who uses him so that she won't get read as a dyke. But it's the same thing like I was telling you. She's using him to protect her image. [Which is?] Respectable, rich society lady who buried her husband and wants to keep up the image of being a straight. There's lots of closet cases keeping men so that nobody finds out they're also keeping women. Like the woman who Ari walks, she isn't having sex with him or anything like that, but still, he's a guy, okay? ...

His wife and him have a pretty cool relationship. They've been together and they're friends but that's it. [Doesn't that create difficulties? That he's married and seen out with women other than his wife publicly?] Not really, because it's all part of it. Helps give him credibility as straight and gives her [the man's Bountiful] the option of playing it as 'he's just a friend' or, if she wants, like she's the 'other woman.' Throws people off, keeps them guessing, right? ... Ari makes more being a walker than most guys make in a year ...

I'd say the bigger difference is if the person is married and just having a relationship on the side or if they're in it full-time. Anytime the person's married, it's going to be more sex. When they're not married, I'd say that it's more like they're paying for emotional support, and sex is only a part of it. I figure that the emotional support I give Carole is probably far in excess of what she pays for me.

Carole is harder to take than most of the women I've been with. With other women, they want to have a good time, go places, take in the sights, but with Carole it's more. When she wants to go out, she can do herself up really nice and be the best-dressed, best-spoken, most cultured woman in the room. When she's in her 'on,' public, mode, she has this soft, pseudo-Bostonian accent. Very feminine, coquettish. A natural flirt. But on her own, it's different. Even the voice changes ...

There's no problem in going out in public; it's the private Carole that causes some problem ...

She's very competitive. Her dress has to be the most expensive. Her donation has to be the biggest. Her kids have to constantly tell her she's the best mother in the world or she tells them. She's spent her whole life playing the victim and trying to control people into doing what she wants, using money or by trying to pull a guilt trip.

She *needs* to have people dependent on her, the way a small kid would be. The only thing, she won't let her own kids grow up. Even her relationship with Danny, it's not a mature mother–son relationship. She wouldn't let it be.

With Carole, she's always going on and on about her giving her life for others, about this cross and that cross she has to bear, how she's sacrificed herself, how she 'drives herself to the bone' with all the committees she's on. The whole poor, poor, pitiful me routine. She *loves* to play the victim. I've never seen anyone who gets off on it the way she does. [Do you see her as a victim?] Are you kidding?!

Maybe in some ways she's a victim, but I doubt it. She uses the victim role for the attention it gives her. Even the break-up with her husband. Shit! Marriages fail all the time, but the way she goes on about it, you'd think she's the only one whose husband ever left her. Jesus. If I was her old man and had his money I'd be out of here like *now*. She's so into control.

[Does she try to control you?] Of course, but I'm not really involved with her so it doesn't get under my skin. I just tell myself, 'She's just blowing wind.' It's not like I have to *like* her or anything. She's my employer and she pays for what she gets. So, if she wants to spend her time bitching about her kids, fine, it's her dollar. She tries the guilt trip sometimes but it doesn't really work on me. [What does she do?] Oh, if I don't do what she wants she tells me pretty fast, 'Don't bother coming here any more. Just let me die, already. Just let me die in peace.' If that isn't control, what is? It's such a joke.

I guess some men are like that too. Some guys [gigolos] want a woman to be a mommy. They're more hooked on the emotional support the woman provides than the money end of things. They want to be taken care of and it goes far beyond her just buying them things ... That's how I see Carole. She wants the control but doesn't want it ...

I'm supposed to 'fix' things so they turn out the way she wants them to and, most of the time, there's not much I can do. You know? It would be easier if she wanted sex, but what she wants is a heavy to go off and do the dirty work. She *likes* to go on about ancient history, so I'll ask her a question or say something I know will start her off. But I have to be careful because sometimes she's good for the entire evening – gives her a chance to go into her routine, and other times, she'll do the 'What-are-you-tormenting-me-for-let-me-die-in-peace' routine.

In the comments of Carole and her gigolo are numerous illustrations of how illusions of femininity, masculinity, heterosexuality, and intimacy can be staged or purposefully contrived. Similarly, the use of micromanipulation as a tactical resource is highlighted in both the gigolo's and his Madame Bountiful's interpersonal styles.

While Carole seemed capable of assertive and controlling behaviour in myriad ways, one can notice that her energies were largely directed towards conventional feminine pursuits, whether engaging in a number of volunteer positions for assorted charitable organizations, parenting her aged and infirm parent, or monitoring the behaviour of her children and issuing sanctions when they failed to please her. However, perhaps more revealing is Carole's demand that her gigolo play the conventional role of the dominant male within a gendered relationship ('playing the heavy,' as her gigolo termed it), while rewarding him for his compliance, his passivity and obedience to her, and for his embellished representations of frailty, haplessness, and dependency – all of which may be seen as historically sanctioned elements of the feminine role. Masculinity and femininity thus become cyclic events, with the behaviour of the dependent partner reflecting neither role reversal nor androgyny as much as the individual's relative power or powerlessness.

The 'pseudo-intimacy' offered by the gigolo/Bountiful relationship in some ways dwells in the realm of fantasy. Pseudo-intimates exist in a relationship that appears on the surface to be intimate, but really is not. Interactions between the partners are essentially superficial and lack the closeness and affection that characterize a true intimate relationship. The disclosures, while seemingly of a deep and pervasive nature, are based upon fabrication far removed from honesty. Here we have the form but not the content of true intimacy. If, however, the romantic Dream or need is strong enough, the existing relationship will have to be – and can be – transformed via fantasy into a seemingly acceptable intimate partnership. Even though the specifics of the fantasy itself are variable – the hope for the spiritual (or down-to-earth), vibrant (or quiet), brilliant (or plain-spoken), exciting (or safe), ambitious (or unambitious), young (or old) partner – the idea of the Lover or Companion is both an opiate and a stimulant. If the Bountiful believes or strongly needs to believe her gigolo is a perfect specimen of humanity, she may ignore patent reality and neglect the imperfections in the story of their existing relationship. An illusion of an intimate relationship is maintained by one or both partners and also projected to the outside world.

From the case-studies we have presented, the reader may note that the women who keep men are not a single homogeneous group. If their comments arouse feelings of empathy, resentment, consternation, incredulity, or dismay in the reader, the range of reactions potentially evoked attests to the diversity of opinions on the nature of gender roles and their proper manifestation within love, sex, and relationships more generally. While the image of the 'kept' relationship in modern society continues to conjure up images of fast men, fast women, and faster cars, the reality is far richer and more complex.

MASCULINITY AS A MASQUERADE

We noted earlier that the concept of a 'masquerade' emerged from analyses of women who were successful in a masculine world and yet were attempting to assert an ultra-femininity as a form of overcompensation for their success and a form of self-protection against feared retributions for that success. However, just as the concept can be applied to women alone and to relationships, it can also be applied to men. Throughout the present and previous chapters we have noted that gigolos, in their interviews and their letters, tend to strongly stress and assert their masculinity to any and all who will give them an audience. They do so, for example, through their extraordinary emphasis upon their sexual prowess, upon their ability to manipulate and control their Madames Bountiful, and upon their ability to reap financial rewards to maintain a desired lifestyle without working, in the formal sense of that word. These presentations can be viewed as a 'mask of masculinity' which attempts to compensate for the fact that they are highly successful in performing a feminine lovestyle role.

By acting in a seemingly warm, affectionate, attentive, supportive manner, they receive financial rewards. But, at present within our society, their manner of achieving success is not positively evaluated. In part, this assessment is triggered by the essentially manipulative and fabricated nature of their endeavours. Their actions threaten to make a mockery of the form of intimate relationship extolled and desired by so many. In part, the lack of social approval is based upon a potential threat posed to conventional expectations regarding masculinity. Finally, part of the disapproval may be attributable to the fact that the financial rewards are being dispensed from female hands.

In our society, and for much of history, masculinity has been viewed as synonymous with power, and femininity with power's absence. Power, as we noted at the end of chapter 4, involves the ability to assert one's will regardless of the wishes of others. Stated another way, a powerful person is able to act independently of others – and independence has long been a central theme of the masculinity script. The assertions of masculinity found to be common among our gigolos reinforce this theme of independence and appear to constitute a reaction against the images implied in the phrase 'kept man.' To be kept suggests a loss of autonomy, will, independence, or control over one's life. It is a very debatable point as to whether one person can really 'keep' another, in the sense of assuming total and complete control over all aspects of his or her life. (In that vein, we had to constantly refrain from enclosing the word 'kept' within quotation marks throughout this book.) Our gigolos' attempts not only to assert some degree of sexual, romantic, or financial control over their Bountiful partners, but to ensure these facts were mentioned in letters and interviews, reflect a desire to maintain a public claim to power, independence, and traditionally defined, socially approved masculinity.

Just as some women attempt to reclaim a femininity when their success appears to be too threatening, many of our gigolos attempt to reclaim a masculinity to offset the threatening nature of their own success. Surrounding the efforts of the men and women is a social context which proclaims that everyone must be *either* masculine *or* feminine, but not both. Consequently, when one's claims to one side or the other are in jeopardy, it is time to put on a public mask of the socially approved gender. In this way the conventional receives apparent support, and threatening challenges are minimized for participants and observers alike. Unfortunately, this is still the essential nature of gender in our society.

Conclusion

In her article 'In Defense of the American Gigolo,' originally published anonymously in 1939, *Esquire* magazine's 'enduring First Lady,' Helen Lawrenson, suggested that the gigolo was 'the product of a world rapidly becoming feminine in every particular except, perhaps, in respect to its women. Originally a luxury, the gigolo will soon will be a necessity.' When her article was republished by *Esquire* in 1983, the magazine identified the author as 'liberated before it was fashionable' and claimed that the editors themselves 'can't help but be amused, intrigued, and provoked by Lawrenson's *prophetic* instincts' (emphasis added). They pointedly noted that the author was using the term 'gigolo' loosely to refer 'to a suitor or a lover – as distinct from a husband – and one who was in it not for the money but for the romance' and retitled the reprint 'Wanted: A New Modern Man.'

Although this cosmetic type of editing, seemingly based on the magazine's desire to disassociate itself from an endorsement of the 'gigolo,' is interesting in and of itself, the alteration seems both presumptuous and inaccurate. *Perhaps* someone on the editorial board in 1983 had access to the author's original motivations and intentions when she was writing the article back in 1939; however, the contents suggest otherwise. At times bitingly satirical, at times perceptive, at times reactionary, and at times seemingly outlandish, Lawrenson's work is worth examining if only for the fact that, in the midst of silence in relation to the subject of gigolos, Lawrenson's article was thought worthy of resurrection almost half a century after its original publication. The article is additionally interesting for *Esquire*'s 1983 suggestion that the terms 'gigolo' and 'Modern Man' could be viewed as synonyms.

Lawrenson seemed eager to invoke explicitly the spectre of the gigolo as a type of smarmy, self-protective, inevitable and necessary male response to female liberation. According to her, 'men do not become gigolos through choice, but in self-defense.' Admitting that the American gigolo was still in 'an embryo state,' Lawrenson suggested that his appearance was the 'forerunner of a new type of American man ... learning to deal with the American woman in a practical, efficient manner, in terms which she seems to understand and admire.' She suggested that the gigolo was a product of a particular social situation and that both the person and the context were poorly understood by the general population. Her ostensible purpose was to provide sketches of the essence of then modern American women, American men/husbands, and gigolos.

In a comparison between the American husband and the gigolo, Lawrenson utilized words that give a lie to the *Esquire* editorial claim that the gigolo was solely romance-motivated and not a monetary mercenary:

The gigolo, after all, boasts many qualities and advantages not possessed by the American husband. He enjoys the camaraderie, the intimate confidences, the attractive physical charms of the fair sex, to a degree seldom bestowed upon the husband; yet he is not obligated to concern himself about their general welfare or ultimate happiness. He is relieved of the weight of all home and family ties. Like a bee he may flit from flower to flower, pausing wherever he finds the honey sweetest or most profitable.

In matters of money and work – those twin threats which so heavily harass and submerge the average American husband – the gigolo is freely absolved from such aggravating duties. All this is gladly taken care of through the generosity of his feminine companions. Theatre parties, clothes, dinners, liqueurs, apartments, automobiles, even pocket money, are amply provided for him instead of by him – and without the necessity of office duties or business drudgery ... He partakes of all the benefits of husbandry, with none of its obligations or restrictions.

All in all, there is every reason to believe that the *vocation* of gigolo to American womanhood should eventually become one of the most satisfactory and *profitable* pursuits of the modern American man [emphasis added].

According to Lawrenson, American men of the time were, for the most part, not adequately prepared to become gigolos. In essence, they lacked the qualities supposedly possessed by the ultimate European gigolo role models. Among the American male deficits were a sense of fair play, even decency, and a very ungigolo-like attitude towards women.

The American man makes the mistake of having ideals. He treats his women too reverently, too respectfully; he places them on too high a pinnacle. Not only is this apt to spoil women, it makes them uncomfortable. They cannot, and do not wish to, live up to such lofty standards of conduct and virtue ... [American husbands] not only have an excessive tendency to practice strength of character and fortitude, but they attempt to meet life's battles and cares singlehanded, to shield their women folk from a cruel world.

This is most annoying to the fair sex. Women do not like strong men – that is, men who are really strong in principles and character. To begin with, a man of strength and character gives them a feeling of inferiority, one of modern woman's chief aversions. She yearns for superiority – which she calls by the name 'freedom.'

In contrast, the professional gigolo was not thought by the Modern Woman to suffer from any of these 'annoying' qualities, according to the author. In fact, 'the professional [gigolo] hampers himself with no set rules, ethics, or tenets of alleged sportsmanship. He plays only to win. He acquires effective tricks, artifices and stratagems ... He seems, in fact, ideally suited to the demands of the present-day female. He is, apparently the new modern man to match the new modern woman.' Lawrenson's depiction of the American woman appeared to reflect a combination of newly developed with enduring traits, all reflecting the social changes of the time. Once again, it is difficult for a reader to discern where the author is being serious and where satirical. She did suggest, however, that

very few modern women either like or desire marriage, especially after the ceremony has been performed. Primarily, women wish attention and affection. Matrimony is something they accept when there is no alternative ...

Basically, and contrary to general assumptions, woman is not by nature a home body. She has had this position thrust upon her by the male. Granted that woman, for her general welfare, may be better off in the home, such is not her natural inclination or desire ...

Here in the U.S.A., with women for the first time in the history of modern civilization being given full liberty and freedom to pursue her own inclinations, all feminine classes from flappers to wives, mothers to grandmothers, rich or poor, are making every effort to get away from the home as much as possible ...

The gigolo has long been aware of this, and always endeavours to make a definite appeal to this feminine yearning to get away from the home ... Neither does the modern woman primarily seek love. She craves, more than anything else, excitement, action, attention. Love is merely one of the elements which she sometimes finds useful in attaining these ends ... It will be noted that it was a misguided male poet who wrote 'Love is woman's whole existence.' Man always paints his gods after his own image.

In suggesting that gigolos attempted to appeal to women's desires for excitement and activities that took place outside the home, Lawrenson continued to portray the gigolo as someone who paid attention to what women supposedly claimed they wanted instead of what men in general (particularly American men) claimed women should want. If, as Lawrenson maintains, females (of supposedly all species) claimed to desire 'the male most resplendent in appearance,' then gigolos would dress to fit the part. If women 'place full reliance in but one of their senses – their ears,' then gigolos would develop their verbal flattery skills to accommodate this need. And, if a woman is prepared to believe the words she wishes to hear, even though she 'knows he is lying,' the gigolo would ensure those words were proffered. After all, 'the gigolo's motto is: 'The customer is always right.' He tells his female admirer anything she wishes to hear. He promises her anything, everything, if necessary. She is then quite satisfied and mentally uplifted, while he may pursue the tenor of his ways in peace.'

Both directly and indirectly Lawrenson suggested that American men had their priorities wrongly ordered when it came to serving the needs and desires of American women.

The American husband must pay less attention to ambition and success, and give more consideration to birthdays, anniversaries, the prompt lighting of milady's cigarette, the pouring of her beverages, ceremoniously helping her in and out of vehicles, etc. These, after all, are the accomplishments by which woman judges a man.

Not by his slaving ceaselessly at an office, ruining his health and personal appearance by long hours of toil, nor by self-sacrifice of his own interests and pleasures, does a woman gauge a man's love for her. Rather, it is by his close attention to trifling courtesies and chivalries in the insignificant things of life ...

The American man must decide whether he wishes to court fame and achievement in the business world, or whether he desires to be a success in matters of feminine affection. He cannot be both; not at the same time, at least. The two goals lie in different directions.

A man, for consistent popularity with the fair sex, must give a woman *all* his time, or *none* at all. She must mean *everything* to him, or *nothing*. Any middle ground is *disastrous* [emphasis added].

Lawrenson has accurately pointed to a clash of qualities that are rewarded in the work but not in the intimate relationship sphere. As we

have noted in earlier chapters, the qualities of competitiveness, independence, and hard-driving ambition that may serve well in business have,
by themselves, little to offer directly in meeting the intimacy needs of a
partner. Indeed, in this way, her suggestions that men moderate their work
emphasis and focus more upon intimate relationships would seem to anticipate many commentaries being offered fifty years later. However,
while Lawrenson would suggest it is necessary to abandon some central
tenets of traditional masculinity, such as those qualities which comprise
the provider role, her 'all or nothing' philosophy becomes grating in its
either/or emphasis. For example, her proclamations of what women 'really want' appear to trivialize women into thrill-seeking party animals fix-
ated upon trifling matters only. In the knowing or unknowing pursuit of
extremes, Lawrenson offered what appeared to be a rather ludicrous presentation of advice to the new American man/gigolo in his handling of the
Modern Woman.

One of the most subtle maneuvers, calling for the utmost of the gigolo's talent in
keeping his feminine admirer at the height of mental fullness and satisfaction, is in
mathematically striking a proper balance of appeal between her inherent inferiority
complex and her newly acquired superiority complex.

For, while the modern woman yearns acutely to display her superiority in almost
every line of endeavour, she is never quite happy or wholly contented in her contacts
with the male if she becomes firmly conscious of having achieved a completed
superiority over him ... The gigolo ... helps woman to maintain a proper equilibrium
and achieve a soul-satisfying state by skilfully, yet painlessly, deflating her ego at
certain points.

She suggested that the savvy gigolo should not direct criticism at women's attempts to develop competence in areas which would allow them
to compete with men – after all, according to Lawrenson, such endeavours
were futile anyway in that women inherently lacked ability in these areas.
Rather, men were advised to focus upon those areas of life, such as cooking and housework and style of dress, in which women claimed a degree of
superiority or expertise. These areas were to be alternately criticized and
then complimented, in all cases whether the comments were deserved or
not, in order to keep the Modern Woman on the defensive and constantly
striving to see to her man's comfort. 'Thus, by a careful blend of flattery
for those things in which she *lacks* merit, and criticism of those things for
which she *has* talent, a woman is made to maintain her balance and exist
in the idealistic feminine state of blissful discontent' (emphasis in original).

Lawrenson's prophecies of how women should or ought to be 'managed' or responded to by men within relationships clearly suggests that, although Lawrenson was a female writer, she was not a feminist writer. Directing her advice towards men's criticizing women, the author appeared to be suggesting a plan of action designed to maintain the balance of power within the hands of the 'New Man.' Tellingly, the terms 'inferiority' and 'superiority' frequently appear throughout the article; nowhere does a reader find the word 'equality.' Supposedly, by following Lawrenson's advice, the American male could hope to mitigate the problems posed by the Modern Woman. Not only would the male still retain the power of criticism and correction (i.e., social control over women's behaviour), but he would somehow ultimately be provided for in the manner of a European gigolo. How women would acquire the financial wherewithal for such provision was completely ignored by Lawrenson.

The wording of her argument suggests she was of the somewhat novel (for her time) opinion that changes in American men were required, or necessitated, as a consequence of earlier changes which occurred among American women. Indeed, 1939 marked the end of a period of intense changes in North America. The Great Depression was coming to an end. During this period, men were known to put extra effort into keeping existing jobs in order to provide for their families, or (often unsuccessfully) to seek any form of paid labour. Family survival was frequently dependent upon women's wages. The previous thirty or more years (with roots extending into the previous century) had also witnessed what came to be known as the First Wave of the feminist movement, a period of considerable agitation for women's rights in a number of domains and a limited success in bringing about actual changes in accepted female behaviour in Canada, the United States, and Great Britain. Rather than viewing these changes as liberating, Lawrenson implicitly suggested that the Age of the Modern Woman could only, and inevitably, result in the emasculation of the Modern Man.

Throughout her article one finds the premise that changes within the female gender role would ultimately lead to a complete role reversal between the sexes. Change was perceived only as extreme change, reflecting an 'all or nothing' state of mind. One may note her depiction of both the gigolo and the Modern Woman as sterile, barren creatures – themselves symbols of social collapse and disintegration.

In the suggestion that the gigolo is the antithesis of the 'normal American man' (who possessed the qualities of lofty values, honesty, hard work, and ethical behaviour), the gigolo becomes, by definition, that which is not normal. The position he occupies is one of the abnormal and perverse. Similarly, by affirming that under normal circumstances men do not ordinarily assume the role of the gigolo, Lawrenson attributed the rise of the gigolo to an abnormal social environment – one that was characterized by the rise of the new Modern Woman.

The term 'New Woman' was, from at least the late nineteenth century, often discussed in terms of 'unnatural' women – those who repudiated traditional gender roles, were politically active, pursued careers, and disdained marriage. Described as constituting an 'intermediate sex,' as 'Mannish Lesbians,' or as 'sexual perverts,' they were perceived as challenging conventional gender roles, which in turn was seen as evidence of their abnormality and perversion. We see here a fusion, and confusion, of the sexual and the social. The sexual pervert did not simply challenge the assumption of universal and 'natural' heterosexuality; perhaps more importantly, in her demands for a role beyond conventional gender, the New Woman challenged traditional boundaries of femininity and the inviolability of gender roles.

As Carroll Smith-Rosenberg observed: 'The symbolically laden phrases … "the intermediate sex," … "the Mannish Lesbian" – do not describe literal sexual acts. They are spatial and hierarchical images, concerned with issues of order, structure and difference. The term "intermediate sex" does not conjure up images of sexual passion or of physical desire. It refers, rather, to space, to the state of being in between categories – that is, outside of order. "Inversion" inverts. It turns "normal," predictable order and hierarchies upside down … [A]ll link "irregular" sexuality to challenges to social (and, of course, domestic) order … The woman who would be a man, the man who assumed the female role … symbolized social chaos and decay.'

The overall tone of Lawrenson's presentation carried this theme somewhat farther in so far as she tacitly suggested that as the Modern Woman challenges traditional roles, she 'becomes what women must not be: they become men, and turn men into women.' Modern Woman renounced the traditional feminine sphere of the home and, in consequence, begat the gigolo as the New Man. Lawrenson would appear to be in full agreement with the words of Alfred, Lord Tennyson, who wrote:

Man for the field and woman for the hearth:
Man for the sword and for the needle she:
Man with the head and woman with the heart:

Man to command and woman to obey;
All else confusion.

This legacy, in different yet not less condemnatory terms, continues into modern times and has appeared most blatantly within the rhetoric of antifeminists arguing for the maintenance of an essentially middle-class ideal of femininity, an argument which has demonstrated a depressing continuity over the past century. Resting their arguments upon a firm belief in an innate and immutable nature of gender, antifeminists past and present have argued that the traditional roles are not socially created and maintained but rather are biologically and divinely ordained. In a comparative historical analysis of American antisuffrage and anti-ERA literature, Susan Marshall noted: 'The antisuffragist view of woman's role was a reflection of middle-class values – "to be tender, loving, pure and inspiring in her home, … to raise the moral tone of every household, to refine every man, … to mitigate the harshness and cruelty and vulgarity of life everywhere" (*Anti-Suffragist*, 1908 …). The delicate female nervous system renders woman without "staying qualities, continuity of purpose, or affinity for the rough and tumble warfare in political life" (*Anti-Suffragist*, 1910 …). Moreover, "woman does not think, she feels, she does not reason, she emotionalizes," and hence a female electorate is likely to "do injury to itself without promoting the public good" (*Woman's Protest*, 1915).'

Marshall pointed to the marked similarly between these early writings of antifeminists and those of contemporary antifeminists. For example, she observed that, according to Phyllis Schlafly's *The Power of the Positive Woman*, the superiority of males intellectually and physically 'must be recognized as part of the plan of the Divine Architect for the survival of the human race through the centuries.' Decrying affirmative action as resulting in 'reverse discrimination' that denied 'the inadequacy of female qualifications,' challenges to conventional roles (such as the feminist movement and the ERA) were seen as 'opposing Mother Nature herself' and supposedly would only 'further confuse a generation already unsure about its identity.'

While in 1909 the *Anti-Suffragist* attacked suffragists as 'Amazons,' 'mannish,' 'unwomanly,' 'vulgar,' and a threat to 'Fair Womanhood,' in more recent times, the suggestion surfaces within the writings of various authors that the contemporary women's movement simply creates 'mutations' of women: 'masculine' women incalculably inferior to those who embrace 'fascinating womanhood' or who are 'REAL Women,' 'positive women,' or 'total women.' Thus, a feminist fails to understand 'that men and women are different, and that these differences provide the key to her success as a person, and fulfilment as a woman.' After all, Schlafly writes, 'marriage and motherhood give a woman new identity and the opportunity for all-round fulfilment as a woman' while the woman's movement, comprised of feminists who are 'marital misfits' and lesbian 'perverts,' 'deliberately degrades the homemaker' and would 'betray' other women for a 'brief high' or 'fix' of power.

As part of this tradition, Lawrenson's views cannot be considered as merely a quaint period piece of the 1930s. Indeed, they suggest a backlash against the First Wave of feminism, as embodied in the social presence of the liberated 'flapper' and, with the reprinting of them in the 1980s, suggest the tenacity of antifeminist ideology against the more recent Second Wave. *Plus ça change?*

Lawrenson's characterization of the Modern Man would seem to suggest that, like the road to hell, the path to becoming a gigolo is paved with good intentions on the part of men who desire only to win women's affections and to please them. Apparently, in challenging her traditional role, the Modern Woman has set the stage for men to stray from their original path and become an army of determined marching gigolos ready to advance upon the social scene. Here we find women's roles being described not of and in themselves but rather mainly in terms of their consequences for men and men's roles. And, once again, we witness a suggestion that deviation from the feminine convention will yield undesirable masculine consequences wherein women would ultimately be the losers. The old-fashioned male, with his traditional values and nobility of character, honest-spirited and hard-working, is implicitly portrayed as incalculably superior to all but the most misguided or obtuse; supposedly a female may truly expect only financial and psychological warfare to await her at the hands of a gigolo.

Lawrenson commented:

For years American women led a comparatively idle and comfortable life, allowing men to provide the home, the luxuries, the finances, and to shoulder most of the important burdens, worries and problems, as well as to set the example in gallantry and in patronage.

Now, with American women fired with a great and insatiable zeal to lead and dominate, not only in love, but in politics, business and even sports, there seems to be no convincing reason why the men should not at last sit back, relax, and enjoy some of life's carefree pleasantries ...

The gigolo's sphere is at present underestimated. As the advantages and superiority of the gigolo's position over that of the husband become more generally recognized, he will meet with as much approval from the men as he now does from the women. When that day arrives there will be a wholesale rush into the gigolo field on the part of American males ... It is the only logical solution for the rapidly declining American male.

It has been more than fifty years since Lawrenson made her 'logical solution' prophecy, which, of course, was probably made facetiously. Has the gigolo population increased since then in North America? With the increase in the numbers of women possessing more disposable income over the past fifty years, it would not be surprising if the gigolo population had indeed increased. However, a 'wholesome rush,' as Lawrenson predicted? Although it is difficult to make definitive judgments, given that, unlike McDonald's restaurants, gigolos are not blatantly recognizable nor do they advertise how many they have served, we would doubt that this is the case. While for some men, like our wannabe respondents, a fantasy tinged with a hint of envy exists for the idealized lifestyle of the high-society gigolo, both the imagery and the language popularly used to discuss the gigolo remain sheathed in disreputability.

Despite Lawrenson's predictions, the Age of the Modern Woman as yet does not seem to have arrived in other than inchoate form. The concept of 'modern' suggests an abrupt discontinuity between present and past forms of socially acceptable masculine and feminine behaviour, both outside and inside of intimate relationships; however, the existence of any such discontinuity is highly debatable. The persistence of the wage gap between male and female workers, job segregation of females within the traditionally feminine 'pink collar' labour force, and the feminization of poverty suggests that, to date, the Age of the Modern Woman, if it truly has arrived, remains, like the age of the stereotypically coquettish woman, a tightly guarded secret.

The booming economy of the 1960s and 1970s, coupled with changes that led to an expansion of the female gender role, contributed to a significant increase in female labour-force participation. During the 1980s and continuing into the 1990s, the ravages of recession and inflation added further impetus to the necessity of female employment. As a consequence, dual-income families increased in Canada from 20 per cent of all families in 1961 to just over 71 per cent in 1990. However, in 1991, the average Canadian working woman's full-time earnings were only 69.6 per cent that of the average man. Although this percentage has been increasing, it represents an increase of only slightly less than 5 per cent since the mid-1980s.

Marilyn French has noted that, in 1987, 'after fifteen years of feminist agitation begun when women earned only 59 percent of male wages,' women in the United States earned 70 per cent as much as men. She observed that 'women hold less than one-half of 1 percent of jobs in the highest echelons of corporate managers and only 3 percent of the top five jobs below CEO at all Fortune 1000 companies ... Demands for equal pay for equal work are a mockery when most people remain clustered in segregated jobs ... And male occupations *always* pay more than female occupations' (emphasis in original).

Clearly, for the vast majority of women who earn an independent income, keeping themselves may be difficult enough. For those women who are married, contributions to a dual-income family most typically represent an attempt to provide an adequate family standard of living that is otherwise unachieveable on a single provider's salary. Moreover, for other women, there is even less opportunity to indulge in the luxuries of life, such as the keeping of gigolos. In 1991, 82 per cent of almost one million lone-parent families in Canada were female-headed as were 90 per cent of all lone-parent families in the United States. The Canadian families were characterized by lower employment, higher unemployment, and an income that was just 38 per cent of the average income of two-parent families with children. American female-headed families faced comparable problems.

We have noted throughout this book that money or access to it is, by definition, central to the 'kept' relationship. If the kept woman can be used as a metaphor for the way in which women have traditionally been restrained within the confines of conventional gender roles, the emergence of the Madame Bountiful should be seen to suggest only a tempered and somewhat rarefied expansion by certain women into roles that allow them independent control of both their money and their eroticism.

Unlike Lawrenson, we do not find evidence to support the presumption that the Modern Woman is a singular type of female, and would be leery of any assertion that women constitute a monolithic group who act and react in identical ways. For example, a recent book which uses case-studies of married women having affairs offers a portrait of women as hedonists who are 'often happily married' and who, regardless of the outcome of the affair, 'feel good about doing something bad' and feel 'enriched by the affair.' Our sample of women, however, defied depiction as a homogeneous group.

The range of responses we received from women was revealing. Some did appear to be happy hedonists, content to share their fortunes with a gigolo or a series of gigolos for a variable time span. An insouciant attitude was expressed by these women towards any of their serial relationships with interchangeable men, along with a nonchalant depiction of the gigolo as simply a commodity. To extend an analogy used earlier, the gigolo became a reified equivalent of a luxury car who could be traded in at the woman's convenience when maintenance problems or boredom set in. The gigolo was, in this depiction, conceived of as primarily functional.

Other women attested to the confines of conventional gender roles. We noted in chapter 6 than many of our Madames Bountiful, while economically dominant, evidenced numerous characteristics associated with traditional femininity. First, those who were spending their husband's money on gigolos gained access to such monies through the traditional feminine pattern of marrying into it. The leisure-class wife, disdaining the discontinuity in financial status that divorce might bring about, espoused an enthusiastic preference for the 'European arrangement' wherein wives and husbands could indulge in discreet kept relationships. However, her lifestyle seemed to reflect the vestiges of stereotypically feminine roles, such as that of the historical royal mistresses, rather than a path-blazing testament to the arrival of the Modern Woman.

Second, the suggestion by various Madames Bountiful that the 'kept' relationship afforded them a degree of power within that relationship and safety from potentially predatory and/or dangerous strangers indicates that, for these women, at an abstract level, male violence against women may have as its consequence a nebulous belief that one can purchase, in keeping a gigolo, security, egalitarianism, and/or a non-abusive partner.

Third, we noted the numerous ways in which femininity could be adopted as a masquerade wherein discontinuities and deviations in stereotypically feminine behaviour are compensated for with outward signs of traditional conformity. While, for some of our female respondents, the gigolo was conceived of as simply as a peripheral adornment, for others his presence seemed more essential as a confirmation of the woman's desirability, worthiness, and social value (thus maintaining a continuity with the tradition of needing a man to affirm one's femininity).

It would be misleading to conclude from our research that Bountifuls as a group represented an abrupt departure from, and had no linkages to, traditional models of femininity. In many cases, their behaviour could not only suggest an embracing of stereotypical femininity but, perhaps, even a parody of it. Moreover, for the majority of our respondents, the difficulties which they experienced would not seem to stem from the fact that the Modern Age of the liberated woman had arrived; rather, they appeared to attest to the fact that it has not.

SUPERWOMAN AND COMMITMENT MAN: SUPERHEROES OF THE 1990S?

Numerous research studies have documented the fact that, despite the expansion of the female role to include paid labour, thus making the dual-provider marriage and family a statistical majority, women are still saddled with primary responsibility for the 'second shift' of household, family life, and/or relationship maintenance, and account on average for 75 per cent of the work done within the home. The 'Superwoman syndrome' is a well-known phrase used to describe the woman who 'has it all' in modern times – that is, all of the major responsibilities inside of the home and an equal or substantial share of responsibilities outside of the home. Nowhere yet do we see reference to an equivalent 'Superman syndrome.'

What has emerged instead is the new highly sought-after superhero of the '90s – 'Commitment Man' – that emulatory hero who is willing to commit himself to a relationship, as if this was in itself a self-sacrificial and dangerous undertaking. The imagery underlying the creation of Commitment Man somewhat inverts the traditional imagery surrounding 'men as pursuers, women as pursued' but nevertheless implies reassertion of male power. Invested in the metaphor is the suggestion that such men are in themselves scarce, invaluable, and thus to be treasured. When allied with economic and institutional power, Commitment Man embodies a potent combination of social and personal resources.

The presence of 'Superwoman,' the absence of 'Superman,' and the heralding of 'Commitment Man' give implicit testimony to the differential rates of change which have occurred within female and male spheres of social life. Throughout this century women have made significant modifications to the female gender role, while men have remained largely static. While there are certainly some individual exceptions, males in general are still performing and conforming to a role 'job description' that has been remarkably stable despite the vast changes experienced by their female counterparts. Most of our Madames Bountiful reflect these changes, with the women earning their own disposable income and dispensing it at their own discretion. Our gigolos, in contrast, still adhere for the most part to traditional notions of masculinity; their departures are only a calculated bid to achieve traditionally valued lifestyle rewards via unconventional means. As we have repeatedly noted, their innovation is not truly gender-challenging, but simply a variation on a traditional theme.

Our male respondents did not, by and large, appear as an élite army – a Delta Force, if you will – prepared to do battle against the confinements of gender roles. Rather, to extend the analogy, their actions often suggested the role of the 'double agent.' The vocabularies with which they accounted for their behaviour and the conception they held of their role indicated that their allegiance to conventional gender roles was tenacious; the challenge they theoretically posed to traditional roles seemed more apparent than real.

Certain features of the gigolo/Bountiful relationship reveal, at least superficially, a type of role reversal inasmuch as the Bountiful is evaluated by the gigolo as a 'success object' rather than as a 'sex object.' However, what readily appears as a role reversal may, paradoxically, serve to extend rather than transcend the confinements of gender within intimate relationships.

SEX OBJECTS, SUCCESS OBJECTS, AND STATUS OBJECTS

It would seem fair to say that the concept of woman as 'sex object' has become part of our common language. The castigation of men's tendency to reduce women to a body, an eroticized physical shell, surfaces repeatedly in arguments against pornography; discussions of women's portrayal within advertising, television, films, and rock videos; and analyses of social factors which are believed to contribute to both the physical and the sexual violence committed against women.

In contrast, less well known is the counter-assertion that, whereas men may trivialize women as a sex object, so too may conventional gendered expectations encourage women to trivialize men by turning them into objects of monetary success. Whereas the social injunction upon men to prove their masculinity has contributed to the development of a self-evaluative schema through which, as we mentioned in an earlier chapter, men gauge their masculinity by the 'size of their paycheques,' it has also been suggested that this type of myopia may be shared and/or endorsed by many women. The reader may recall the comments of Valerie Gibson (near the end of chapter 2) who noted the male lament that younger women were most interested in what kind of car he drove and whether he had a good job. If the desirability of an intimate partner is assessed by such a utilitarian calculus, a mental economic forecasting which seeks to predict the future standard of living or lifestyle a partner will be able to provide, the result is a negation of that partner in his full humanity. The individual becomes merely a 'success object.'

From the comments of our male respondents throughout this book, it is evident that selecting a partner on the basis of her 'success-object potential' is, in essence, the distinguishing feature of our gigolos. As we noted earlier, it is not the actual level of recompense that distinguishes the gigolo from other men; rather it is his self-identified motivation for selecting a partner, seeking to consolidate his position with her, and remaining within a profitable (for him) relationship. His ardour for his partner is directly contingent on his perception of her ability to provide him with a preferred standard of living. With some exceptions (such as the actions of certain Sweetheart Swindlers who would consider a waitress earning minimum wage to be a suitable target for their activities), gigolos typically selected their relational partners based upon the financial and/or social status of their Bountifuls and their anticipation of how bountiful they would prove to be.

The commonality of male complaints as to the age or rotundity of their female partners clearly suggested that the majority of our Bountifuls were not picked solely for their physical beauty. These women may have escaped being sought after simply as sex objects. However, the new framework for evaluation served to replace one type of reductionist framework for another.

While Helen Lawrenson claimed that the gigolo as a social being emerged in response to the changes in women's social role, there is relatively little that appears liberated in the comments of most of our male respondents. We suggested earlier how claims of voracious sexuality, rigorous heterosexual interest, financial exploitation, and psychological manipulation of their Bountifuls seemed important to these men as offering corroborative evidence of their masculinity. Domination in one form or another becomes their mechanism of gender validation. Although eager to identify themselves as gigolos, these men seemed especially desirous of proving that they were not less of a man for their association with a female who was socially and financially superior to them.

Their comments suggest a tactic of 'compensatory masculinity' in which gender characteristics associated with masculinity were brought forth and given exaggerated emphasis. If what emerged were accounts that were often sexist, infantilizing, and deprecating of women, this was apparently ignored by the men; in their eagerness to provide evidence to account for their being involved in non-traditional roles, what emerged was not very encouraging. The power dimension is never very far removed from these relationships. Implicitly and explicitly our male respondents refurbish the essential notion that male superiority and female inferiority must be maintained. Equality is clearly not within the goal structure of these men.

As their comments illustrate, our gigolos were eager to direct our attention to their manipulation of their partners and the number of ways in which, they claimed, they controlled the female's behaviour. These claims would seem important whether or not they are valid. They suggest an attempt on the part of the men to distance themselves from feminine behaviour and, in so doing, to reclaim their potentially impugned masculinity. Just as 'femininity as a masquerade' perpetuates, through women's complicity, countless acts that restrict and distort a woman's field of vision, masculinity also requires acts of obeisance. The injunction 'act like a man' reveals itself as other than a call for creative self-expression. It suggests the donning of a costume and the following of a prewritten script.

In general, men who held allegiance to the rightfulness or propriety of traditional gender roles, believing that the man should or ought to be dominant both financially and interpersonally within an intimate relationship, would evidence behaviour that had only the slightest veneer of egalitarianism. That is, the Bountiful would simply be extended permission to provide for the man, with his needs, wishes, or desires being forcefully, and occasionally forcibly, made paramount.

Our Bountifuls evidenced several orientations towards money and its use within a relationship. Some of our female respondents exemplified the conclusion of the Blumstein and Schwartz research (found in chapter 4) that money represents independence and autonomy for women. In essence, this translates into the use of money as power *for* others as opposed to the use of money as power *over* others. Instead of using money as a bargaining tool, designed to extract gratitude or indebtedness in any form, these Bountifuls would simply share their monetary resources in order to allow their gigolos to enjoy life, with recompense being a non-issue. Many Bountifuls, however, attempted to use money as either a blatant or a subtle leverage tool in order to attain any number of other different goals.

For those women who assumed that their taking on of the provider role would guarantee the sexual fidelity, loyalty and emotional support of their partner, variable degrees of satisfaction occurred. In an early case-study (chapter 2) we noted one woman's discontent with a partner who expected her to play the role of provider and wife within the relationship but had less taxing expectations for his own behaviour. Although the adage cautions us that 'money cannot buy love,' an expectation could nevertheless arise that the possession of money should allow the Bountiful to negotiate for sought-after qualities within a relationship from a position of strength. However, if she similarly succumbed to beliefs in the rightfulness of traditional gender roles within relationships, the power that money provides could become but an extremely fragile and ineffective resource.

Rather than promoting egalitarianism, financial benefits could be offered up by the Bountiful to her gigolo as a pacifier to promote peace within the relationship, dispel arguments, forestall accusations of 'haughtiness,' and/or cajole the man into good humour. Just as Sleeping Beauty was offered up to the fairies to forestall harm and win a blessing, so ceremonial exchanges could be engaged in with the hope of ensuring the well-being of a relationship which was deeply valued. Some of our female respondents evidently believed that, by creating an impression that the man was independently wealthy, and had paid for the meal, social outing, or vacation they enjoyed together, the man would welcome the convenient opportunity to ignore the good provider role. However, such actions could simply be interpreted by the man to mean that his Bountiful was conscious of the irregularity within their relationship and of his 'failure' to act as an admirably masculine companion. Like the Bad Fairy, the guest who becomes aware that others view his presence with disgust or loathing may, in turn, come to mock and curse the intended object of the proceedings.

Research conducted in the area of family violence has provided ample evidence that a negative change experienced or anticipated in a man's economic position (job loss, the impending birth of a child) may act as trigger to battering incidents. In such cases, male frustration is assumed to find an outlet in anger, with battering serving as a device to reduce tension. As feminists have noted, the batterer does not indiscriminately attack anyone and everyone in his attempts to express his hostility, frustration, and rage. Rather, he selects his intimate partner as the appropriate target of his violence. That the experience of Marilyn in chapter 6 included numerous episodes of violence should not perhaps be all that surprising. While embracing a woman's ability to earn or independently possess an income may suggest a certain receptivity among these men to non-traditional gender roles, the extent of their non-traditionality may be more apparent than real.

In noting the machinations pursued by certain women to imply the financial independence of the man, it would be misleading to suggest that such efforts were uniformly engaged in for the sole purpose of providing flattering illusions or psychic comfort for the Bountiful's male partner.

Most obviously, the comments of women who aligned the possession of a gigolo with that of other disposable purchases or status objects selected to furnish their owner with a self-flattering mirror suggests that, although the gigolo/Bountiful relationship may be seen to offer resistance to traditional gendered relationships, it may, perhaps unwittingly, merely reproduce them.

For the Bountiful who rejects the passive and submissive characteristics assigned to the feminine role only to gravitate towards those characteristics associated with masculine dominance, what may emerge within relationships may be much less than a foundation of egalitarianism and mutuality. Marilyn's humorous belittling of her gigolo as a 'Minute Man' and a 'little woman'; male strippers' reporting of the groping, pawing, and excessive manhandling by members of the audience during their performances; Carole's despotism and manipulation of her gigolo – all suggest, to varying degrees, the consequences of objectification and exploitation that can attend power. The key factor behind the differential use of power appears to be acceptance or rejection of traditional attitudes towards gender and gender relations. Today, as in the past, abuse of power appears to be associated with a rejection of the feminine and adoption of a masculine orientation.

We would hope that not all relationships characterized by female provision of economic support for male intimates would demonstrate such a depressingly superficial movement towards androgyny or at least a less gender-defined humanity. It may well be that there are many individuals in relationships who overcome the structural limitations of society and who engage in a broader repertoire of interactional patterns than did most of our respondents. However, it would appear that, for a large majority of our men and women, their relationships were characterized by, at best, a fabricated egalitarian motif.

GENDER, INTIMATE RELATIONSHIPS, AND POWER

As we have suggested in earlier chapters, the traditional and seemingly simple exchange of male money for female love and affection which has undergirded traditional forms of relationships has been and continues to be breaking down, particularly over the past twenty-five years with the emergence of a new model for intimate partnerships. The old 'male provider female caregiver' model is being replaced (not without a fight) with the expectation that intimate partners are expected to share amounts of providership and, separately, amounts of love and amounts of sexuality. In simplified terms, providership and love and sex are becoming independent bargaining stakes. The ideal relationship, whether it exists within or outside of the bonds of marriage, is still considered to be one which maximizes the amounts of providership, eroticism, and loving affection (just to mention three dimensions) experienced by both partners equitably, but none of these resources is expected to be the exclusive domain of either sex.

As we have continually noted, women in general are slowly increasing their share of economic power and, in the process, becoming less economically dependent upon men in general. Two consequences for intimate relationships appear to follow. First, as that dependency lessens, women's share of relationship power increases and, as a consequence, relationships move towards a more egalitarian arrangement. Males, as a result of their socialization, respect money and earning power, and therefore grant power to the money maker. However, since women in general do not, as we noted earlier, earn an amount equal to men, complete egalitarianism has yet to be achieved in most dual-earner relationships, and will not be achieved until earning power becomes more equitable.

The second closely related consequence of women's increased share of economic resources has, arguably, even greater implications for the future of intimate relationships between men and women. Increased economic power reduces female dependence and thereby increases their options. Once females become less dependent upon males for economic survival, women are then in a position to assert more strongly that intimate relationships become more equitable in meeting their needs. If an existing relationship fails to meet criteria for equity, the option to leave is becoming increasingly available, even if the leaving produces economic, social, and/or emotional hardship. If the possibilities for attaining equity in a potential relationship do not appear satisfactory, the option of not making that relationship permanent is now available. A woman can walk away and look elsewhere. In other words, decreased dependence provides women with an empowerment to make choices with a greater (but not yet total and complete) degree of freedom than in the past.

Official statistics and research projections would appear to reflect these freedoms. Rates of first marriage are now lower than they were during the 1960s and 1970s, while rates of remarriage since the mid-1980s have decreased in both Canada and the United States. As we mentioned in chapter 2, rates of divorce have increased dramatically since the mid-1960s. In fact, Larry Bumpass, in his 1990 presidential address to the Population Association of America, noted that, at current rates, the incidence of divorce and separation for marriages formed during the 1980s will likely reach between 60 and 67 per cent. Rates for Canada as well as England and Wales will probably be lower but still hover around the 40+ percentage rate. The reasons for these projections are many and varied but the greatest ones appear to be the increased availability of options (such as cohabitation, and a viable single lifestyle) and the increasing tendency of women in particular (since they are the most likely to seek formal dissolution of marriages) to select among those options.

The evidence clearly indicates the presence of an increasing reluctance on the part of women to either enter into, or remain within, relationships that do not offer sufficient promise of meeting their needs. We have presented evidence throughout this book of the existence of many women who are willing to fashion a relatively new form of relationship wherein they hope to exert sufficient control to have their needs met more satisfactorily. It would be both naïve and misleading to suggest that all of these changes are attributable to the one simple cause of increased female economic independence, as many conservatives, antifeminists, and other 'backlashers' are currently wont to do, thus invoking a clamour to get women out of the labour force and return them to their 'rightful place' – the home. As we have noted before, men have failed to keep up with the relatively recent changes women have undergone. This failure of men to provide the desired loving affection and egalitarian exchanges is no longer a condition to be simply accepted and endured by women who used to face a lack of attractive options. Women are now proclaiming 'with their feet' that intimate relationships are in need of important revisions and that those revisions will now most likely have to come from the efforts of men in both their personal and their social lives.

We are not suggesting that males need to renounce their currently comfortable lovestyle and adopt a solely feminine style of loving behaviours. What is essentially required is an 'in addition to' and not an 'in place of' system of changes. In other words, existing male patterns must be affirmed (something the majority of therapists and advice givers have failed to do), while additional behaviours of a more reciprocal nature are also promoted and validated. We have demonstrated throughtout this study that males are fully capable of being empathetic listeners and caring, affectionate individuals. Similarly, women are fully capable of providing money, solutions to problems, and other traditionally masculine loving behaviours. Once again, we note that females are increasingly being admired for reciprocating masculine lovestyles, but, as yet, males have not received equivalent admiration (particularly from other males) for reciprocating feminine lovestyles. Ultimately, no gendered differentiation of relationship styles, just a human differentiation, should be acknowledged.

The relationship between gigolos and Madames Bountiful constitutes only a pseudo-intimacy, as is evident from of the disclosures of the gigolos in particular. However, another factor also qualifies the nature of the intimacy being experienced here. True intimacy requires, as its most salient component, a fundamental level of equality such that there exists an egalitarian give-and-take between the participants. For this to occur, the resources of each partner, and consequently each partner her or himself, must be evaluated as essentially equal and thus each partner's contribution to the relationship honestly respected.

Of course, the major resources brought to male-female relationships are not now, nor have they ever been, accorded equivalence on a social-ranking scale. Unless social changes can be initiated and implemented which grant money and love and eroticism equal status, both partners at this point in history will have to possess nearly equivalent bases of each resource in order to achieve an equitable balance of power. We are not suggesting that intimate partners must be identical in their possession of these valued resources, just that they must be more-or-less equivalent. If such equality and mutuality between partners is absent, what emerges is simply an illusion of intimacy.

Yet, we must acknowledge that, for many of our Madames Bountiful, the illusion itself passes as an acceptable and sufficient reality. We have presented numerous case-study excerpts in which women respondents indicated that they were comfortable with the level of intimacy their relationship had attained. They appear to have analysed what they wanted and what they currently were experiencing, and decided that their important needs were being met to a sufficiently acceptable degree. Only some of our Bountifuls wished for more. These women sought a deeper level of intimacy and either tried to transform their partner or tried to paint a more intimate veneer on what actually existed. Given the current social context, true intimacy for individuals such as these will remain difficult to obtain.

SUMMARY

On the surface, gigolos, their Madames Bountiful, and the relationships between them appear to be very different from the rest of everyday society. It is on the basis of these differences, with an apparent female provider and male caregiver, that they are initially identifiable. But below the surface we found many basic similarities with the everyday world, indicating that surface appearances alone are at least partly an illusion. We have suggested that these similarities are largely attributable to the fact that, while the expectations for intimate relationships have changed, the structural features which would promote and maintain their adoption are other than firmly grounded. Consequently, relationships crafted by our respondents are bound to become lopsided attempts to build something truly new and different, being unbalanced by the very foundations on which they were laid.

We have noted repeatedly that women in general have made significant strides towards becoming empowered within relationships. However, we have also noted that, within a materialist society which has failed to validate through social or financial reward what women have traditionally done and still do as of equivalent value, males in general and the gigolo in particular recognize that masculinity and social acceptability still remain anchored to power, dominance, and privilege. The balance of the scales of power is still tipped in favour of things masculine. We have still not seen caregiving being considered one of the strengths of the male; it is still regarded by some as a weakness or a deficit to be disparaged, or by others as an activity to be acknowledged and rewarded only in private. Caregiving, and all it entails in terms of being loving and affectionate in a particular way, still suffers from the stigma of being associated with the feminine.

The search for a new male superhero, Commitment Man, seems to focus mainly upon the questions of whether he will enter into a relationship whole-heartedly and whether he will stay in a relationship over a lengthy period of time. Questions about what he will actually do within these relationships appear to fade into the background. Akin to the traditional notion that successful marriages are measured by their longevity and not by their quality, emphasis is placed upon the form rather than the content, the appearance rather than the experienced reality. Yet the emergent theme, in the era of the Pluralistic Family, is that emphasis increasingly should be placed upon the qualitative content, and less upon the form(s) it takes to achieve that desired quality.

As of yet, our respondents are not self-conscious 'pioneers' who have managed to go significantly beyond the bounds of the limitations embedded within our gendered society. It appears that they created their roles by selecting from the limited number of alternatives available to them. To create a script which transcends those limitations is very difficult. Herein lies a central paradox of intimate relationships. On the one hand, such relationships offer the greatest freedom to be whatever and whoever one wants. On the other hand, intimate relationships pose the greatest threats to that self. Being creative lays one open to an increased risk of rejection if for no other reason than one is different, and difference is often perceived as too threatening. It may be particularly difficult to be creative with a gender performance within the context of an intimate, or even pseudo-intimate, relationship wherein each partner is supposedly exposing his or her essential and whole self. In all other sectors of life, with the exception of a purely therapeutic context, we usually expose only a limited portion of our self and, if rejected, we still have the other non-exposed portions to cling to and nurture privately. But within an intimate relationship, rejection is experienced as if of the whole self and is usually devastating. To play it safe, it appears to be easiest to fall back on the more or less 'tried and true,' being basically conformist, with only a little deviation thrown in to attract attention but not immediate dismissal. Once set in motion, a self embedded within a gendered comfort zone becomes very difficult to alter in any dramatic way.

Changes that would challenge the gendered confinements of masculinity and femininity within the macrocosm of a total society or within the microcosm of an intimate relationship are difficult to achieve. For many, the relationship between Simone de Beauvoir, whose work *The Second Sex* 'dynamized the women's movement in Europe and America,' and Jean Paul Sartre was seen as 'the very emblem of the liberated couple.' Others are less convinced that this is so. Joseph Barry has argued:

There is now explosive evidence that the arrangement was tailored for Sartre; not for both; that in their 'perfect' relationship of the 'modern' couple there was the age-old pattern of dominant male-subordinate female. Whatever, one asks, led a woman who would write the basic statement for modern feminists, *The Second Sex*, to accept second place to a man? And why does she weep on every second page of her autobiographical novels? ...

Beauvoir adopted Sartre's philosophy – its ethics, metaphysics, ontology and *much of its sexism* – as her own. Paradoxically she would appropriate *macho* themes of *Being and Nothingness* – 'which ends in an orgy of sexist remarks' – in the creation of her own pioneering work, *The Second Sex* ...

Was it so successful after all ... that *pacte* [which allowed for 'contingent love affairs'] between the two from the beginning ... So often Beauvoir has remarked – as if to convince *herself* – that Sartre was not made for monogamy, nor she for children. Yet there are her incessant tears, *tristesse*, and *resentment* whenever she touches upon Sartre's liaisons ... and more than one friendly feminist has been profoundly troubled by Beauvoir's submissiveness, subordination, *wifeliness* ...

Who has spoken more harshly, more intimately, of the abusive self-centredness of Sartre? One wants to repeat Beauvoir's remark about the 'trap of love,' but one wants, at the same time, to cite the observation of Henry James that worse than the tyrant is the tyrant's victim, who is 'slave and accomplice.' (emphasis in original)

Maslow's types of love referred to earlier suggest that only where partners have already 'found themselves' can they hope to achieve satisfaction within a relationship. If the traditional feminine role has made erotic pleasure problematic and power within a relationship illusory, entrance into a relationship with a gigolo may redouble the woman's feelings of unhappiness and vulnerability. The relationship becomes burdened from the onset with the responsibility of providing a sense of self as well as some happiness, companionship, or sensual pleasure. Similarly, the man who would assume the role of financial dependent while deprecating the feminine role of one who is powerless, and who would furthermore offer only feigned courtesy rather than the respect and equality owed to his partner as a human being, ultimately offers only an illusion of intimacy. The gigolo largely forfeits an opportunity to develop his own humanity by his apparent need to validate more conventional and limited masculine gender roles. As such, the relationship is liable to become overtaxed by demands of what it can provide and what it cannot.

Equality cannot, it would seem, be achieved if only one person is operating from a position of strength. If one exists solely to draw upon the strength of the other, the result will be an inequitable relationship.

The truly egalitarian couple must necessarily leave behind conventional gendered ideologies on which they were raised. Like the fledging who leaves the nest, they must struggle on their own, uncertain of the capacities and abilities required to negotiate uncharted terrain. People who are trying to forge new intimate relationships today and 'boldly go where no one has gone before' face a lack of available role models. The actors on *Star Trek* can embark on a journey into the unknown with relative ease because they have a carefully crafted script and are professional actors who, at the end of the episode, step out of their roles and return to everyday life. Pioneering relationship fledglings have none of these luxuries; all they have is a vague set of stage directions – be equal and be intimate. Like the participants in improvisational theatre, they must, out of necessity, constantly write and rewrite their own scripts for the intimacy performances of their everyday lives. It is no easy thing for a fledgling form of relationship to establish itself within a landscape that appears settled and resistant to change. However, if they are to find a place for themselves, fledglings must assert their willingness to become autonomous foreign entities that stand apart from the parent ideologies that wet-nursed them and, if necessary, defy them.

Notes and References

The numbers below refer to page numbers throughout the book and reflect either sources for direct quotes or published and unpublished materials which directly and indirectly influenced our presentation.

INTRODUCTION

3 This work ... during the 1980s. See E. Salamon, 'Kept Women: A Contemporary Sociological study,' PhD dissertation, London School of Economics (University of London), 1983.

3 In October 1983 ... with a circulation of more than 100,000. The names of these newspapers and magazines were obtained through the '81 Ayer Directory of Publications (Bala Cynwynd, PA: Ayer Press 1981) and Ulrich's International Periodical Directory, 19th ed. (New York: R.R. Bowker/Xerox 1980).

4 Some time later ... relationship. Carl Sagan, Contact (New York: Pocket Books 1985), p. 100.

10 In 1926 ... despoiler of fair womanhood. See Edna Ferber, 'The Gigolo,' in Edna Ferber, Gigolo (Garden City, NY: Doubleday, Page 1922), pp. 69–105.

12 'Gigolos Come to TV' An expanded and revised version of this section can be found in E.D. (Adie) Nelson and B.W. Robinson, '"Reality Talk" or "Telling Tales"? The Social Construction of Sexual and Gender Deviance on a Television Talk Show,' Journal of Contemporary Ethnography 23/1 (April 1994), pp. 57–78.

12 an intelligent alternative ... issues of the day. Quoted from promotional material provided by the producers of the talk-show program, Boston 1992.

13   'para-social interaction.' See Donald Horton and R. Richard Wohl, 'Mass
     Communication and Para-Social Interaction: Observation on Intimacy at
     a Distance,' *Psychiatry* 19/3 (1956); reprinted in Gary Gumpert and
     Robert Cathcart, eds., *Inter Media: Interpersonal Communication in a
     Media World* (New York: Oxford University Press 1986), pp. 185–206.

14   'in time, the devotee - the "fan" [may] come to believe ... his [her] values
     and motives.' Ibid., p. 187.

14   'a kind of growth without development.' Ibid.

14   Just as soap-opera interaction ... 'such people.' For a discussion of the
     soap opera see Robert Cathcart, 'Our Soap Opera Friends,' in Gumpert
     and Cathcart, eds., *Inter Media: Interpersonal Communication in a Media
     World*, pp. 207–18.

14   'realistic illusion' which 'lulls the viewer ... craft of production.' Ibid., p.
     213.

18   For a discussion of the 'sex addict' see Charlotte Davis Kasl, *Women, Sex
     and Addiction: A Search for Love and Power* (New York: Ticknor and
     Fields 1989); Patrick Carnes, *The Sexual Addiction* (Minneapolis: Comp
     Care 1983); Craig Nakken, *The Addictive Personality: Roots, Rituals and
     Recovery* (Center City, MN: Hazelden Publishers 1988); Stanton Peele,
     Love and Addiction (New York: New American Library 1975).

19   Thus, the gigolo may simply be seen ... 'gerontophilia' ... parental substi-
     tute.' Edward M. Brecher and the Editors of Consumer Reports Books, in
     Love, Sex and Aging: A Consumers Union Report (Mount Vernon, NY:
     Consumers Union 1984), pp. 76–7, suggest that there may be a greater
     tendency to view the 'wife much older' union as unacceptable and, conse-
     quently, as something which 'needs' to be explained. Thus, the authors
     note that 'among our women as well as our men [respondents to the
     study], a larger proportion believe a wife-much-older marriage is a mis-
     take than believe that about a wife-much-younger marriage.'

19   'Don Juanism.' See Otto Fenichel, *The Psychoanalytic Theory of Neuro-
     ses* (New York: W.W. Norton 1945).

19   'Casanova Complex.' See S. Giora Shoham, *Sex as Bait: Eve,
     Casanova, and Don Juan* (St Lucia: University of Queensland Press 1983).

19   'Delilah Syndrome.' See Eva Margolies and Louis Genevie, *The Samson
     and Delilah Complex: Keep Your Independence without Losing Your
     Lover* (New York: Dodd, Mead 1986).

19   'Angry Woman Syndrome.' See Carol Tavris, *Anger: The Misunderstood
     Emotion*, 2d ed. (New York: Simon and Schuster/Touchstone 1989).

19   Peter Panism. See Dan Kiley, *The Peter Pan Syndrome: Men Who Have
     Never Grown Up* (New York: Dodd, Mead 1983).

19   'Peter Pan Syndrome.' Ibid.

19   'Wendy Syndrome.' Of course there are also other 'syndromes' that could be applied. Thus, in her book *Jennifer Fever: Older Men, Younger Women* (New York: Harper and Row 1988), Barbara Gordon devotes a chapter to 'Mrs. Robinsons' – named for the middle-aged female character in the film *The Graduate* – to discuss women who have affairs with younger men.

21   Anne Edwards material, excerpt from *McCall's* in *The Vancouver Sun*, 21 August 1992.

24   This strategy, known as snowball sampling ... general populace. For a discussion of the snowball-sampling technique see H.W. Smith, *Strategies of Social Research* (Englewood Cliffs, NJ: Prentice-Hall 1975), pp. 214–20.

CHAPTER 1 GIGOLOS

27   Tony Thorne, *The Dictionary of Contemporary Slang* (New York: Pantheon 1990).

27   'toy boy.' Ibid., p. 527.

27   'fancy man.' Ibid., p. 172.

27   'beard.' Ibid., p. 31.

27   'poodle-faker.' Ibid., p. 400.

28   'handbag.' Ibid., p. 230.

28   'ace of spades.' Eric Partridge, *A Dictionary of the Underworld* (London: Routledge and Kegan Paul 1949), p. 3.

28   'habitual grooves of language expression.' Andrea E. Goldsmith, 'Notes on the Tyranny of Language Usage,' *Women Studies Quarterly* 3 (1980), 179–91.

29   Simone de Beauvoir, *The Second Sex* (Harmondsworth: Penguin 1982).

30   'SWELL.' Thorne, *The Dictionary of Contemporary Slang*, p. 502.

30   'spare.' Ibid., p. 482.

30   'two different books.' Jean Lipman-Blumen, *Gender Roles and Power* (Englewood Cliffs, NJ: Prentice-Hall 1984), and Sherrill MacLaren, *Invisible Power: The Women Who Run Canada* (Toronto: Seal 1992).

31   'the gig is pronounced ... contempt.' Ferber, *Gigolo*, p. 69.

31   For discussion of backlash see Susan Faludi, *Backlash: The Undeclared War against American Women* (New York: Crown 1991) and Marilyn French, *The War against Women* (New York: Summit Books 1992).

31   'sissy boy.' Richard Green, *The 'Sissy Boy' Syndrome and the Development of Homosexuality* (New Haven, CT: Yale University Press 1987)

and *Sexual Identity Conflict in Children and Adults* (New York: Basic Books 1974); for a critical treatment of the concept see Jane Caputi and Gordene O. MacKenzie, 'Pumping Iron John,' in Kay Leigh Hagan, ed., *Women Respond to the Men's Movement: A Feminist Collection* (San Francisco: Pandora 1992), p. 77.

32 Phyllis Chesler, *Mothers on Trial: The Battle for Children and Custody* (New York: Harcourt Brace Jovanovich 1991), p. x.

32 *Peterson* v. *Peterson*. Cited in Norma J. Wikler, 'Researching Gender Bias in the Courts: Problems and Prospects,' in J. Brockman and D.E. Chunn, eds., *Investigating Gender Bias: Law, Courts, and the Legal Profession* (Toronto: Thompson Educational 1993), p. 51.

33 Margrit Eichler, 'The Prestige of Occupation Housewife,' in P. Marchak, ed., *The Working Sexes* (Vancouver: University of British Columbia Press 1977), pp. 151–75.

33 As she noted 'there is some truth ... can marry one.' Ibid., p. 163.

34 'The French ... degrees.' Lynn Ramsey, *Gigolos: The World's Best Kept Men* (Englewood Cliffs, NJ: Prentice-Hall 1976), pp. 49–50.

35 'No one in our society ... child molester.' *The Edmonton Journal,* 29 January 1994, p. B1.

35 John Lowman, 'Street Prostitution,' In V. Sacco, ed., *Deviance: Conformity and Control in Canadian Society* (Scarborough, ON: Prentice-Hall 1988), p. 62.

35 'sentences for living on the avails'. See Clayton C. Ruby, *Sentencing*, 3d ed. (Toronto: Butterworths 1987), p. 454.

36 Definitions of prostitution provided by H. Benjamin and R. Masters in *The Prostitute in Society* (New York: Julian Press 1964), p. 32.

36 E. Glover, *The Psychopathology of Prostitution* (London: LSTD 1945), p. 78.

37 M. Seymour-Smith, *Fallen Women* (London: Thomas Nelson and Sons 1969), p. 26.

38 Among the copious volumes on female prostitution see C.E. Maine, *World Famous Mistresses* (Middlesex: Odham Books 1970); A. Hardley, *The King's Mistresses* (London: Evans Brothers 1980); M. Rice-Davies and S. Black, *Mandy* (London: Sphere Books 1980); C. Hayward, *The Courtesan* (London: The Casanova Society 1926); J. Richardson, *The Courtesan* (London: Weidenfeld and Nicolson 1967); G. Masson, *Courtesan of the Italian Renaissance* (London: Secker and Warburg 1975); S. Marcus, *The Other Victorians* (London: Weidenfeld and Nicolson 1966); M. Seymour-Smith, *Fallen Women* (London: Thomas Nelson and Sons 1969); C.H. Rolph, *Women of the Street* (London: Secker and Warburg

1955); I. Scarlet, *The Professionals* (London: T. Werner Laurie 1972); Anonymous, *The Streetwalker* (London: Bodley Head 1959); J. Cordelier, *The Life* (London: Pan Books 1980); J. Sandford, *Prostitutes* (London: Secker and Warburg 1976); W. Acton, *Prostitution* (London: John Churchill 1857); F. Henriques, *Prostitution and Society* (London: MacGibbon and Kee 1962); L. Basserman, *The Oldest Profession: A History of Prostitution* (London: New English Library 1867); V.L. Bullough and B. Bullough, *Prostitution* (New York: Prometheus 1987).

38 For writings on male prostitution see, for example, M. Craft, 'Boy Prostitutes and Their Fate,' *British Journal of Psychiatry* 112/1 (1966), 111–14; K.V. Ginsburg, 'The Meat Rack: A Study of the Male Homosexual Prostitute.' *American Journal of Psychotherapy* 21 (1967), 170–85; M. Harris, *The Dilly Bos: Male Prostitution in Picadilly* (London: Croom Helm 1974); D.J. Pittman, 'A Male House of Prostitution,' *Transaction* 8 (1971), 21–7; A.J. Reis, Jr, 'The Social Integration of Queers and Peers,' *Social Problems* 9 (1961), 102–19; Jeffrey Weeks, *Against Nature: Essays on History, Sexuality and Identity* (London: Rivers Oram Press 1991), pp. 46–67.

38 'while female prostitution is almost exclusively ... (men paying men).' William Masters, Virginia Johnson, and Robert Kolodny, *Human Sexuality*, 2d ed. (Boston: Little, Brown 1985), p. 456.

38 'houses of assignation' ... 'in the fashionable West End ... parlor.' Reay Tannahill, *Sex in History* (London: Hamish Hamilton 1980), p. 362.

39 Donald Symons, *The Evolution of Human Sexuality* (New York: Oxford University Press 1979).

39 'So long as ... exist.' A.A. Sion, *Prostitution and the Law*, as cited in L.E. Rozovsky and F.A. Rozovsky, *Legal Sex* (Toronto: Doubleday Canada, 1982), p. 81.

39 'the legions ... midst.' Kingsley Davis, 'The Sociology of Prostitution,' *American Sociological Review* 2 (1937), 755.

39 Havelock Ellis, 'Studies in the Psychology of Sex,' in *Prostitution*, vol. 4 (New York: Random House 1936).

39 Mary McIntosh, 'Who needs prostitutes? The Ideology of Male Sexual Needs.' In C. Smart and B. Smart, eds., *Women, Sexuality and Social Control* (London: Routledge and Kegan Paul 1978), p. 55.

39 Interview with Madame Claude, *Penthouse*, London edition, 17/1 (April 1982).

39 Joan Wyndham, *Anything Once* (London: Sinclair-Stevenson 1992), pp. 131–43.

41 'some men are temporarily without ... prefer to buy physical sex.' See Masters, Johnson, and Kolodny, *Human Sexuality*, p. 395.

42 Ethel Person, 'Sexuality as a Mainstay of Identity: Psychoanalytic Perspectives.' *Signs* 5 (Fall 1980), 605–30.

42 'The role of gifts ... compensation.' P. Rosenblatt and R. Anderson, 'Human Sexuality in Cross-cultural Perspective,' in Mark Cook, ed., *The Bases of Human Sexual Attraction* (Toronto: Academic Press 1981), p. 242.

43 Hans Zetterburg, 'The Secret Ranking,' *Journal of Marriage and the Family* 28 (1966), 134–42.

43 'the secretly kept probability ...of the opposite sex.' Ibid., p. 134.

43 'bearer of the look.' Laura Mulvey, 'Visual Pleasure and Narrative Cinema,' *Screen* 16/3 (1975), p. 13.

46 'myth of the career women freak.' Judith Long Laws, 'Work Aspirations of Women: False Leads and New Starts,' in M. Blaxall and B. Reagen, eds., *Women and the Workplace* (Chicago: University of Chicago Press 1976), p. 35.

47 'the appearance of the cicisbeo ... husband.' William Sanger, *History of Prostitution* (New York: Medical Publishing, 1910), p. 64.

47 'her fan, her parasol, or her lapdog.' Ibid., p. 64.

47 'called in France *petit maître*, in Italy, the *cavaliere servente* ... shadow.' Egon Friedell, *A Cultural History of the Modern Age*, vol. 2 (New York: Alfred A. Knopf 1931), p. 144.

47 'originally, there can be very little question ... *cavalieri*.' William Sanger, *History of Prostitution*, p. 165.

48 'Sometimes he was a cleric ... scandalous.' Ramsey, *Gigolos*, p. 92.

48 'It is not surprising ... time.' Ibid.

48 'became the subject of immoderate raillery and satire.' Sanger, *History of Prostitution*, p. 165.

49 a series of important legal changes. See Roderick Phillips, *Untying the Knot: A Short History of Divorce* (Cambridge: Cambridge University Press 1991), ch. 9.

50 'good provider' role. See Jessie Bernard, 'The Good Provider Role: Its Rise and Fall,' *American Psychologist* 36 (1981), 1–12.

52 'one of the many zeros in the arithmetic of life.' Jim Tully, 'Rudolph Valentino: The Career of the Dead Actor Which Ended Dramatically at Thirty-One,' In Cleveland Amory and Frederic Bradlee, eds., *Vanity Fair: Selections From America's Most Memorable Magazine, A Calvalcade of the 1920s and 1930s* (New York: Viking Press 1960), pp. 112–13.

52 'The Ideal Woman.' Ibid., pp. 114–15.

53 'simply the most erotic man in the world.' A. Curtis ed., *The Rise and Fall of the Matinee Idol* (New York: St Martin's Press 1974), p. 143.

53 'the symbol of everything wild and wonderful and illicit in nature.' Ibid., p. 147.

53 When, on New Year's Day ... in the festivities. Ramsey, *Gigolos*, p. 27.

53 'for a time before he achieved career success ... patrons.' Lois Banner, *In Full Flower: Aging Women, Power and Sexuality* (New York: Alfred A. Knopf 1992), p. 28.

53 'The dance halls of the Street of the Virtues ... immoral!' M. Choisy, *A Month among the Girls* (New York: Ballantine Books 1960), pp. 88–9. See also Paul G. Cressey, *The Taxi-Dance Hall: A Sociological Study in Commercialized Recreation and City Life* (Montclair, NJ: Patterson Smith 1969).

54 'American morality could not swallow ... word.' Ramsey, *Gigolos*, p. 26.

54 'a Parisian ... "Gigolo."' Ibid., p. 29.

55 Ted Peckham, *Gentlemen for Rent* (New York: Frederick Fell 1955).

55 'well dressed women ... strangers.' Ibid., p. 21.

55 'the successful businessman ... fills it.' J.P. Getty. *How to Be a Successful Executive* (London: Wyndham 1976), p. 3.

56 'Everywhere I went ... Guide Escort Service.' Peckham, *Gentlemen for Rent,* p. 21.

56 'a dozen university men ... her own brother would.' Ibid., p. 23.

57 Peckham's rules. Ibid., pp. 28–9.

57 Peckham's additional rules. Ibid., pp. 238–9.

59 For a discussion of 'sweetheart swindlers' see Jay Robert Nash, *Hustlers & Con Men: An Anecdotal History of the Confidence Man & His Games* (New York: M. Evans 1976).

59 'American dollars began to go abroad ...supply equalled demand.' Alice-Leone Moats, *The Million Dollar Studs* (New York: Delacorte Press 1977), p. 2.

60 'It must be remembered ... his wife.' George Saintsbury, ed., *The Works of Henry Fielding, Tom Jones,* Vol. 1 (London: J.M. Dent 1893), pp. xx–xxi.

61 'You can embark ... giving.' Thomas Schnurmacher, *The Gold Diggers' Guide: How to Marry Rich* (Montreal: Eden Press 1985), p. 1.

61 For a fuller treatment of the exploits of Julian Cinquez and Allen McArthur, see Nash, *Hustlers & Con Men*, pp. 16–18 and 147–8.

61 'During the twentieth century ... demise of one set of standards.' See William J. Doherty, 'Private Lives, Public Values: The New Pluralism – A Report from the Heartland,' *Psychology Today*, May/June 1992, pp. 32–7, 82.

62 For the sexual, gender, and therapeutic revolutions, see Lillian Rubin,

Erotic Wars: What Happened to the Sexual Revolution? (New York: Farrar, Straus and Giroux 1990).

62 'This new set of ideals does not promote ...' See Doherty, 'Private Lives, Public Values.'

63 For an alternative interpretation of the therapeutic revolution see Wendy Kaminer, *I'm Dysfunctional – You're Dysfunctional* (New York: Addison-Wesley 1992).

64 'Among the unanswered questions ... Right ...' Jim O'Leary, 'Camillagate vs. Charliegate,' *The Saturday Sun* (Toronto), 16 January 1993, p. 12.

67 'beard.' Thorne, *Dictionary of Contemporary Slang*, p. 31.

69 Sue Lindsay, 'Man Gets Eight Years in Bilking: Accused Man Weeps, Then Calls Victims Names,' *Rocky Mountain News*, 26 November 1991, p. 14; Sue Lindsay, '"Ladies Man" Admits Theft from Woman,' *Rocky Mountain News*, 18 October 1991, p. 32.

69 Alfred Barakett. United Press International, 'Canuck Con Man Jailed,' *Vancouver Province*, 6 September 1992.

69 McFarlane-Grey, 'Con Man Tricked a Hundred Women,' *International Express*, 28 January 1993, p. 19.

70 'I was always eager to ... as well.' Peter Potter, *All About Love* (New Canaan, CT: William Mulvey 1988), p. 44.

70 For discussion of the lack of social validation for the 'househusband' see M. Baker and J.I. Hans Bakker, 'The Double-Bind of the Middle-Class Male: Men's Liberation and the Male Sex Role,' *Journal of Comparative Family Studies* 11 (1980), 547–61.

CHAPTER 2 THE QUEST FOR INTIMACY

73 Bernie Zilbergeld, *Male Sexuality: A Guide to Sexual Fulfillment* (Boston: Little, Brown 1978).

75 'Marriage Crunch.' Neil Bennett, David Bloom, and Patricia Craig, unpublished study, in Faludi, *Backlash*, p. 9. For a more detailed discussion of the Bennett et al. and Moorman studies, with accompanying figures, see Thomas Exter, 'How to Figure Your Chances of Getting Married,' *American Demographics*, June 1987, pp. 50–2. For a more detailed discussion of the evolution of the controversy, see Faludi, *Backlash*, pp. 9–14.

76 In fact, one sociologist has argued that North America ... 'permanent availability.' See Bernard Farber, *Family Organization and Interaction* (San Francisco: Chandler 1964).

76 C. F. Westoff and Noreen Goldman, 'Figuring the Odds In,' *Money* magazine, December 1984, pp. 32–7.

81 The 'Cinderella-Prince Charming' myth is just that ... Scott South.' See

Scott J. South, 'Sociodemographic Differentials in Mate Selection Preferences,' *Journal of Marriage and the Family* 53 (1991), 928–40.

81 E. Spreitzer and L. Riley, 'Factors Associated with Singlehood,' *Journal of Marriage and the Family* 36 (1983), 533–42.

81 According to a recent survey conducted by Britain's Institute of Management ... 8 per cent of managers. See *The Vancouver Sun*, 7 November 1992, p. C3.

81 Marshall's study of women in male-dominated professions. Katherine Marshall, 'Women in Male-Dominated Professions,' *Canadian Social Trends*, Winter 1987, 7–11.

81 'more likely ... childless.' Ibid., p. 7.

81 D. Nagnur and O. Adams, 'Tying the Knot: An Overview of Marriage Rates in Canada,' *Canadian Social Trends*, Autumn 1987, 2–6.

81 'highly educated women ... single for life.' S.J. Wilson, *Women, Families and Work*, 3d ed. (Toronto: McGraw-Hill Ryerson 1991), p. 31.

81 E. Haven, 'Women, Work and Wedlock: A Note on Female Marital Patterns in the United States,' *American Journal of Sociology* 78 (1978), 975–81.

82–3 These males comprised a very small birth cohort ... 'the marriage squeeze.' See P.C. Glick, D. Heer, and J.C. Beresford, 'Family Formation and Family Composition: Trends and Prospects,' in M.B. Sussman, ed., *Sourcebook of Marriage and the Family* (New York: Houghton Mifflin 1963), pp. 30–40.

85 John Craig, 'The Growth of the Elderly Population,' *Population Trends* 32 (Summer 1983), pp. 28–33.

85 'women with their greater life expectancy ... women.' Ibid., p. 30.

87 'our selection of a mate ... what we deserve.' Elaine Walster and G. William Walster, *A New Look at Love* (Reading, MA: Addison-Wesley 1978), p. 141.

92 Christina Onassis comment. Potter, *All About Love*, p. 195.

93 'Never ... give anyone anything, not even a kindness ...' Material on Henrietta Green in Autumn Stephens, *Wild Women: Crusaders, Curmudgeons and Completely Corsetless Ladies in the Otherwise Virtuous Victorian Era* (Berkeley, CA: Conari Press 1992), pp. 220–1.

93 F. Scott Fitzgerald, 'The Rich Boy,' in J. Cochrane, ed., *The Penguin Book of American Short Stories* (Harmondsworth: Penguin 1980), p. 312.

98 Michael Apter, *The Dangerous Edge: The Psychology of Excitement* (New York: The Free Press 1992), pp. 66–70.

102 'from dull but dutiful breadwinner ... Kevin Costner mold.' Wendy Dennis, *Hot and Bothered: Men and Women, Sex and Love in the 90s* (Toronto: Key Porter Books 1992), pp. 61–2.

102 'We dream of a world ... assholes.' Starhawk, 'A Men's Movement I Can Trust,' in Hagan, ed., *Women Respond to the Men's Movement*, pp. 27–8.

102 Whether it be in search of 'Wild Men' or 'Warriors.' See Robert Bly, *Iron John: A Book about Men* (Reading, MA: Addison-Wesley 1990).

102 'fire in their bellies.' See Sam Keen, *Fire in the Belly: On Being a Man* (New York: Bantam Books 1991).

104 M. Guttentag and P.F. Secord, *Too Many Women* (Beverly Hills, CA: Sage Publications 1983).

105 'As the sex stratification system changes ... exploited by some women.' Constantina Safilios-Rothschild, *Love, Sex and Sex Roles* (Englewood Cliffs, NJ: Prentice-Hall 1976), p. 122.

108 'Many of my own middle-aged women friends ... younger men.' Banner, *In Full Flower*, p. 5.

108 Valerie Gibson interview. Judy Crieghton, 'Older Woman, Younger Man,' *The Edmonton Journal*, 12 November 1992.

109 'nearly one-fourth of [all] brides ... in 1970.' Faludi, *Backlash*, p. 467.

109 marriage data published by Statistics Canada. 1985 calculations based on data presented in *Marriages and Divorces: Vital Statistics*, vol. 2, Catalogue 84-205 (Ottawa: Ministry of Supply and Services Canada 1986), table 3; 1989 calculations based on data presented in *Marriages: Health Reports*, vol. 2, no. 4, Catalogue 82-003S (Ottawa: Ministry of Supply and Services Canada 1991), table 4; 1991 calculations based on data presented in *Marriages, 1991*, Catalogue 84-212 (Ottawa: Minister of Industry, Science and Technology 1993), table 4.

CHAPTER 3 EROTICISM AND LOVE IN INTIMATE RELATIONSHIPS

113 'word like fuckology ... having sex.' John Money, *Gay, Straight and In-Between: The Sexology of Erotic Orientation* (New York: Oxford University Press 1988), pp. 5–6.

113 Lloyd Saxton, *The Individual, Marriage and the Family*, 6th ed. (Belmont, CA: Wadsworth 1986). See pages 112–14.

113 'We often take ... confronts.' McIntosh, 'Who Needs Prostitutes? The Ideology of Male Sexual Needs,' p. 55.

114 From the nineteenth century onwards ... See Susan Edwards, *Female Sexuality & the Law* (Oxford: Martin Robertson 1981); Barbara Ehrenreich and Deirdre English, *For Her Own Good: 150 Years of the Experts' Advice to Women* (Garden City, NY: Anchor Press/Doubleday 1978); H. Graham, 'The Social Image of Pregnancy: Pregnancy as Spirit Possession,' *Sociological Review* 24 (1976), 2; C. Smith-Rosenberg, 'Sexuality, Class

and Role in 19th Century America,' *American Quarterly* 25 (1973), 131–54; C. Smith-Rosenberg, 'The Hysterical Woman: Sex Roles and Role Conflict in Nineteenth Century America,' *Social Research* 39/4 (1972), 652–78; E. Hall, 'The Gynaecological Treatment of the Insane,' *British Gynaecological Journal*, 1900, part 63, pp. 242–51; B. Ehrenreich and D. English, *Complaints and Disorders: The Sexual Politics of Sickness* (London: Compendium 1974).

114 'nymphomania.' See Edwards, *Female Sexuality & the Law*, p. 83.

115 'They rapidly become ... common.' G.H. Savage, *Insanity and Allied Neuroses* (London, 1884), as quoted in Edwards, *Female Sexuality & the Law*, p. 85.

115 'Fliration ... number of them.' Stephens, *Wild Women*, pp. 8–9.

115 Based on their content analysis of marriage manuals ... twentieth century. Michael Gordon and Penelope J. Shankweiler. 'Different Equals Less: Female Sexuality in Recent Marriage Manuals,' *Journal of Marriage and the Family* 33 (1971), 459–66.

116 Dozens of studies, conducted mainly upon those in the vanguard of change ... with their current sexual partner. For one summary of the changes in recent times see Rubin, *Erotic Wars*.

116 'the greater the power of one gender, the greater that gender's sexual rights in that society.' See Ira L. Reiss, *Journey into Sexuality: An Exploratory Voyage* (Englewood Cliffs, NJ: Prentice-Hall 1986), p. 212.

117 Ira Robinson, K. Ziss, B. Ganza, S. Katz, and E. Robinson, 'Twenty Years of the Sexual Revolution, 1965–1985: An Update,' *Journal of Marriage and the Family* 53 (1991), 216–20.

117 'National survey data collected from American teenagers has also found ... rates of increase during the 1980s.' See S.L. Hofferth, J.R. Kahn, and W. Baldwin, 'Premarital Sexual Activity among U.S. Teenage Women Over the Past Three Decades,' *Family Planning Perspectives* 19 (1987), 46–53.

118 L. Wolfe, *The Cosmo Report* (London: Transworld 1982), pp. 251–80.

118 Kinsey surveys on sexual behaviour. A. Kinsey, W. Pomeroy, W. Martin, and C. Martin, *Sexual Behavior in the Human Female* (Philadelphia: W.B. Saunders 1953), pp. 409–45. A. Kinsey, W. Pomeroy, and C. Martin, *Sexual Behavior in the Human Male* (Philadelphia: W.B. Saunders 1948).

118 The available evidence suggests that the frequency of affairs decreases with age for husbands ... appealing in their new sexual partners. See Kathleen B. Seagraves, 'Extramarital Affairs,' *Medical Aspects of Human Sexuality* 23 (1989), 99–105.

121 'a boy's penis becomes the pole ... revolves.' See Keen, *Fire in the Belly*, p. 71.

121 Carol Tavris, 'Masculinity,' *Psychology Today* 10/1 (1977), 34–42, 82.

122 'less aggressive in bed and less aggressive in general.' See Sam Keen and Ofer Zur, 'Who Is the New Ideal Man?' *Psychology Today*, November 1989, 58.

122 'an important change in men's view ... earthshaking experience.' Bernie Zilbergeld, *The New Male Sexuality* (New York: Bantam 1992), p. 53.

123 'The classic large scale study of "American couples ...' See Philip Blumstein and Pepper Schwartz, *American Couples: Work, Money, Sex* (New York: William Morrow 1983).

123 'We have sex four times a week ... self-confidence.' Ibid., p. 207.

124 'He is ... of an older generation, where women ... overbearing.' Ibid., p. 209.

124 The recent major sex survey, *The Janus Report* ... Samuel S. Janus and Cynthia L. Janus, *The Janus Report on Sexual Behavior* (New York: John Wiley 1993).

124 'I always prefer ... activity.' Ibid., p. 85.

125 Brown and Auerback in a limited study ... male initiation predominates.' See N. Brown and A. Auerback, 'Communication Patterns in Initiation of Marital Sex,' *Medical Aspects of Human Sexuality* 15 (1981), 107–17.

125 Kathryn Kelley and Beverly Rolker-Dolinsky, 'The Psychosexuality of Female Initiation and Dominance,' in Daniel Perlman and Steve Duck, eds., *Intimate Relationships: Development, Dynamics and Deterioration* (Newbury Park, CA: Sage Publications 1987), pp. 63–87.

125 Kelley unpublished paper, cited in ibid.

125 Still, as Sharon Brehm found in her review ... male dominance.' See Sharon S. Brehm, *Intimate Relationships*, 2d ed. (New York: McGraw-Hill 1992), p. 244.

126 The most recent research on a representative sample of American women ... between 1982 and 1988. See William D. Mosher, 'Contraceptive Practice in the United States, 1982–1988,' *Family Planning Perspectives* 22 (1990), 198–205.

126 'industry estimates ... condom market'; 'whisper-thin ... carrying cases'; 'cinnamon ... choices.' Dennis, *Hot and Bothered*, pp. 140–1.

126 'you always know the bad girls ... taking it.' See Rubin, *Erotic Wars*, p. 77.

127 research of Masters and Johnson. W.H. Masters and V.E. Johnson, *Human Sexual Inadequacy* (Boston: Little, Brown 1970).

127 research by Allgeier and Fogel. E.R. Allgeier and A.F. Fogel, 'Coital Positions and Sex Roles: Responses to Cross-Sex Behaviour in Bed,' *Journal of Consulting and Clinical Psychology* 46 (1978), 588–9.

127 'dirtier ... during intercourse.' Ibid., p. 589.

127 These negative judgements may reflect ... United States. See June M. Reinisch, with Ruth Beasley, *The Kinsey Institute New Report on Sex* (New York: St Martin's Press 1990), p. 123.

127 S. Fisher, *The Female Orgasm* (New York: Basic Books 1973).

127 'spectators' of their own sexuality. See Masters, Johnson, and Kolodny, *Human Sexuality*, 2d ed.

127 Some evidence for such changes may be evident ... orgasmic most of the time. Rubin, *Erotic Wars*, p. 84.

128 'In women ... there is early appreciation of the sensual ... intense genital pleasure.' Hilary M. Lips, *Sex and Gender: An Introduction* (Mountain View, CA: Mayfield Press 1988), p. 156. See also Helen S. Kaplan, *The New Sex Therapy* (New York: Brunner/Mazel 1974).

128 research undertaken by Clark and Elaine Hatfield. R.D. Clark III and E. Hatfield, 'Gender Differences in Receptivity to Sexual Offers,' unpublished manuscript available from Dr E. Hatfield, Psychology Department, 2430 Campus Road, Honolulu, HI 96822.

128 'dominant and extroverted people.' See H. Eysenck, 'Introverts, Extroverts and Sex,' *Psychology Today* 4 (1971), 48–51, 82; H. Eysenck, 'Personality and Sexual Behavior,' *Journal of Psychosomatic Research* 16 (1972), 141–52; A. Maslow, 'Self-esteem (Dominance Feeling) and Sexuality in Women,' in M.F. DeMartino, ed., *Sexual Behavior and Personality Characteristics* (New York: Grove Press 1963), pp. 71–112.

129 'double standard of ageing.' See Susan Sontag, 'The Double Standard of Aging,' *Saturday Review* 55/38 (1972), 29–38. See also Tish Sommers, 'Aging Is a Woman's Issue,' *Response*, March 1976, pp. 12–15; Judith Possner, 'Old and Female: The Double Whammy,' *Essence* 2/1 (1977), 42; B.C. Anderson, *The Aging Game: Success, Sanity and Sex After 60* (New York: McGraw-Hill 1979); E. Fuchs, *The Second Season: Love and Sex for Women in the Middle Years* (Garden City, NY: Anchor 1978); B.D. Starr and M.B. Weiner, *The Starr–Weiner Report on Sex and Sexuality in the Maturer Years* (New York: Stein and Day 1981); Brecher and the Editors of Consumer Report Books, *Love, Sex and Aging: A Consumers Union Report*; Marilyn R. Block, Janice L. Davidson, and Jean D. Grambs, *Women Over Forty: Visions and Realities* (New York: Springer 1981)

129 'Elizabeth I of England ... not peculiar.' Banner, *In Full Flower*, p. 8.

130 Many of my friends have asked ... a little exertion.' A. Cumming, *The Love Habit: The Sexual Confessions of an Older Woman* (Indianapolis: Bobbis-Merrill 1978), 'Author's note,' unnumbered page.

132 Nice Girl rules. Nancy Friday, *Women on Top* (New York: Simon and Schuster 1991), pp. 47–9

132 Naomi Wolf, *The Beauty Myth* (Toronto: Vintage 1991), pp. 131–78.

132 'Love confirms the ... inaccessible one may have to do.' Susan Brown-miller, *Femininity* (New York: Linden Press 1984), p. 216.

132 'sex is an energy ... life.' Friday, *Women on Top*, p. 52.

132 'She suggested that ... 'sex' and 'love.' Ibid., pp. 49–56.

134 'A real man proved himself ... testing of manhood.' Keen, *Fire in the Belly*, p. 76.

135 'Contemporary romantic love is ... the other.' Saxton, *The Individual, Marriage and the Family*, p. 84.

135 Daniel Perlman and Beverley Fehr, 'The Development of Intimate Relationships,' in Perlman and Duck, eds., *Intimate Relationships*, pp. 13–42.

136 For example, while women are often believed and expected to be ... men are in fact generally more idealistic (and perhaps naïve)· than are women.' See Charles W. Hobart, 'The Incidence of Romanticism During Courtship,' *Social Forces* 36 (1958), 362–7; D.H. Knox and M. Sporakowski, 'Attitudes of College Students Towards Love,' *Journal of Marriage and the Family* 30 (1968), 638–42; S. Sprecher and S. Metts, 'Development of the "Romantic Beliefs Scale" and Examination of the Effects of Gender and Gender-Role Orientation,' *Journal of Social and Personal Relationships* 6 (1989), 387–411.

136 men typically fall in love ... until much later. See E.J. Kanin, K.D. Davidson, and S.R. Scheck, 'A Research Note on Male-Female Differentials in the Experience of Heterosexual Love,' *The Journal of Sex Research* 6 (1970), 64–72; T.L. Huston, C.A. Surra, N.M. Fitzgerald, and R.M. Cate, 'From Courtship to Marriage: Mate Selection as an Interpersonal Process,' in S. Duck and R. Gilmour, eds., *Personal Relationships: Developing Personal Relationships*, vol. 2. (New York: Academic Press 1981), pp. 53–88.

136 after the ending of marital or non-marital relationship ... for longer periods of time. See Maureen Baker, 'The Personal and Support Networks of the Separated and Divorced,' paper presented to the Annual Meetings of the Canadian Sociology and Anthropology Association, Montreal, 1980; John Money, *Love and Love Sickness: The Science of Sex, Gender Difference and Pairbonding* (Baltimore: Johns Hopkins University Press 1980).

136 Women are much more likely to closely monitor ... end the relationship.' See C.T. Hill, Z. Rubin, and L.A. Peplau, 'Breakups Before Marriage: The End of 103 Affairs,' *Journal of Social Issues* 32 (1976), 147–68.

137 Abraham Maslow ... love. Abraham H. Maslow. *Toward a Psychology of Being*, 2d ed. (New York: Van Nostrand Reinhold 1968).

137 'B-lovers ... fostering.' Ibid., p. 43.

139 In their exposition of a then new theory ... personal *myth*.' See Daniel J.

Levinson with C.N. Darrow, E.B. Klein, M.H. Levinson, B. McKee, *The Seasons of a Man's Life* (New York: Alfred A. Knopf 1978), pp. 91, 246 (emphasis in original).

139 In her book, *Women and Love*, Shere Hite ... their partners. See Shere Hite, *Women and Love* (New York: Alfred A. Knopf 1987), pp. 123–31.

139 'they have not yet found ... greatest love is yet to come.' Ibid., p. 654.

139 A number of researchers in recent years ... loving behaviours. See Francesca M. Cancian, *Love in America: Gender and Self-Development* (Cambridge: Cambridge University Press 1990); Mary Anne Fitzpatrick, *Between Husbands and Wives: Communication in Marriage* (Newbury Park, CA: Sage 1988); Lillian B. Rubin, *Just Friends: The Role of Friendship in Our Lives* (New York: Harper and Row 1985).

140 'face-to-face' and 'side-by-side' intimacy styles. See P. Wright, 'Men's Friendships, Women's Friendships and the Alleged Inferiority of the Latter,' *Sex Roles* 5 (1982), 1–20.

144 the model of courtly love. See R. Boases, *Courtly Love* (Manchester: Manchester University Press 1977); M. Foss, *Chivalry* (London: Michael Joseph 1970).

144 'the letters of Lord Chesterfield.' J. Harding, ed., *Letters to His Son* (London: The Folio Society 1973), pp. 51, 76–7.

145 Oliver Wendell Holmes, 'The Rolling Spheres of Falsehood,' in Philip Kerr, ed., *The Penguin Book of Lies* (New York: Penguin Books 1990), p. 214.

145 'mendacity is a system that ... death's the other.' Tennessee Williams, as cited in 'Introduction,' in Kerr, ed., *The Penguin Book of Lies*, p. 8.

145 Kerr, ed., *The Penguin Book of Lies*, pp. 7–8, 178.

147 'a pornography just for women.' Robert Stoller, *Observing the Erotic Imagination* (New Haven, CT: Yale University Press 1985), p. 37.

147 'male- and female-oriented erotica.' Reiss, *Journey into Sexuality*, pp. 193, 195.

147 'The success of Harlequin Enterprises, Ltd. ... of all ages.' Tania Modleski, *Loving with a Vengeance* (Hamden, CT: Anchor 1982), p. 35.

147 'If all the words of all ... sun.' *The Harlequin Story*, cited in Louise J. Kaplan, *Female Perversions* (New York: Anchor Books 1991), p. 324.

148 Reportedly Harlequin books are so popular in Japan ... Kaplan, *Female Perversions*, p. 324.

148 'clean, easy to read ... foreign places.' *The Harlequin Story*, p. 324.

148 'The basic Romance series ... a lifetime.' Ibid., p. 325.

149 'Indicative of this trend this new market.' See Jennifer Foote, 'Love Among the Ruins,' *The Globe and Mail*, 18 September 1993, n.p.

149 Carol Thurston, *The Romance Revolution* (Urbana and Chicago, IL: University of Illinois Press 1987), p. 111. See also Margaret Ann Jensen, *Love's Sweet Return: The Harlequin Story* (Toronto: Women's Educational Press 1984); Madonna Kolbenschlag, *Kiss Sleeping Beauty Goodbye* (San Francisco: Harper 1988).

149 'erotic comradeship.' Barbara Denning, *We Cannot Live Without Our Lives* (New York: Grossman 1974).

151 empathy ... non-verbal cues. See Carol Tavris, *The Mismeasure of Woman* (New York: Simon and Schuster 1992), p. 64.

151 Nancy Chodorow, *The Reproduction of Mothering* (Berkeley, CA: University of California Press 1978).

151 'with a basis for "empathy" ... feelings).' Ibid., p. 167.

151 'men who were training for ... difficult to know.' Lips, *Sex and Gender*, p. 92.

151 Tavris stressed ... power. Tavris, *The Mismeasure Woman*, p. 65.

151 Sarah Snodgrass, 'Women's Intuition: The Effect of Subordinate Role on Interpersonal Sensitivity,' *Journal of Personality and Social Psychology* 49 (1985), 146–55.

151 'Men, like Women manage ... advantage.' Tavris, *The Mismeasure of Woman*, p. 65.

CHAPTER 4 ACCESS TO POWER: CONVENTIONAL AND
UNCONVENTIONAL CHANNELS

157 'the larger portion of this book ... rich.' Schnurmacher, *The Gold Diggers' Guide*, p. 3.

157 'out of respect' Ibid., p. 23.

157 'men who want to find rich women ... breed.' Ibid., p. 3.

157 Schnurmacher on the subject of gigolos. Ibid., p. 133.

157 'a Parisian social-climber ... columns.' Ibid., p. 9.

157 'first of all, in order to marry rich ... powerful.' Ibid., p. 2.

158 'If you think that hanging around backstage ... Rod Stewart.' Ibid., p. 113.

158 Joseph Kahl suggested ... 'graceful living.' See Joseph A. Kahl, *The American Class Structure* (New York: Holt, Rinehart and Winston 1957), pp. 187–210.

159 'Every family is proud of its heritage ... either have a good family background or you don't.' See Ruth Shonle Cavan, *The American Family*, 4th ed. (New York: Thomas Y. Crowell 1969), p. 101, emphasis in original.

160 Examples of gaffes are from Henry Mayo Bateman, cited by Anne Barr and Peter York in *The Official Sloane Ranger Handbook: The First Guide to What Really Matters in Life* (London: Ebury Press 1982), p. 17.

160 'codified, archaic and a trap to the unwary.' Ibid., p. 14.

160 'The behaviour of the truly rich ... rich buy artists.' Taki, 'Living Well Is the Best Revenge,' in Taki and Jeffrey Bernard, eds., *High Life, Low Life* (London: Jay Landesman 1981), p. 68.

160 'Rangers are "we" people ... individuals.' Ibid., p. 10.

162 'Townsend was ... a divorcee ... Church of England.' Ibid., p. 79.

162 'I would like it to be known that I have decided not to marry ... before any others.' Ibid., p. 81.

162 'I've fallen in love ... divorced.' Quoted in Potter, *All About Love*, p. 72.

163 Ruth Shonle Cavan noted that ... 'types and places of education, occupation and selection of the spouse.' See Shonle Cavan, *The American Family*, p. 88.

163 'In all justice to myself ...inconsequently away!' Boni de Castellane, *How I Discovered America* (New York: Alfred A. Knopf 1924), p. 16.

164 Ramsey, *Gigolos*, p. 36.

164 marrying Mdivanis. Moats, *The Million Dollar Studs*, p. 26.

164 For discussion of Thérèse Davignac see Nash, *Hustlers & Con Men*, pp. 4–5, 299.

164 For discussion of Cassie Chadwick see John S. Crosbie, *The Incredible Mrs. Chadwick* (Toronto: McGraw-Hill Ryerson 1975).

164 For discussion of the swindle of Jay Gould see Nash, *Hustlers & Con Men*, pp. 6–15, 136, 297–9.

165 W. Stead, *The Americanization of the World*, as cited in Maureen Montgomery, *Gilded Prostitution: Status, Money and Transatlantic Marriages, 1870–1914* (London: Routledge 1989), p. 10.

165 'the absence of a love relationship ... their estates.' Ibid.

166 'Anyone who wasn't born into nobility ... their support.' 'Count Me In: How You Can Get a Royal Title of Your Very Own,' *Luxury Lifestyles: The Riches of Royalty*, 1992, p. 38.

166 'The truly rich ... wings.' Taki, 'Living Well Is the Best Revenge,' p. 67.

167 'Great wealth ... than women.' Ferdinand Lundberg, *The Rich and the Super Rich: A Study of Money and Power and Who Really Owns America* (Syracuse, NY: Lyle Stuart 1988), pp. 29–30.

167 'Take Barbara's first husband ... please!' Schnurmacher, *The Gold Diggers' Guide*, pp. 30–2.

168 'When he was finished ... sort of thing.' Quoted in William Davis, *The*

Rich: A Study of the Species (London: Sidgewick and Jackson 1982), p. 25.

168 D. Ogden Stewart, 'The Secret of Success,' *Smart Set*, March 1922.

169 Brian Ross Duffy, *The Poor Boy's Guide to Marrying a Rich Girl* (New York: Penguin 1987).

169 'explicit instruction manual for achieving health, wealth and happiness.' Steven Starker, *Oracle at the Supermarket* (Oxford: Transaction 1989), p. 2.

169 'attempts to communicate in a lively ... manner.' Ibid., pp. 8–9.

169 Our discussion of Dr Joyce Brothers is heavily influenced by Wendy Kaminer's *I'm Dysfunctional – You're Dysfunctional*, pp. 61–3.

170 'graduate of the University of Virginia ... Harvard Business School.' Duffy, *The Poor Boy's Guide to Marrying a Rich Girl*, author's biography on first (unnumbered) page.

170 'special thanks to Princess Stephanie ...;' 'other rich girls (too numerous to name).' Ibid., p. xi.

170 'was a constant ... inspiration.' Ibid., p. xi.

170 'Regrettably, I haven't found the right rich girl yet ... difficult to please.' Ibid., p. 237.

171 'whose seven husbands ... settlements.' Ibid., pp. 85–6.

171 'married twice ... playboys.' Ibid., p. 86.

171 'addicted to poor (albeit artistic) boys.' Ibid., pp. 88–9.

171 'managed ... for all.' Ibid., p. 89.

171 'the private resources ... happy.' Ibid., p. 90.

171 'led directly ... United Kingdom.' Ibid., p. 100.

171 'Mark lived by the motto ... Ibid.

171 'the rich girl's favourite diseases.' Ibid., p. 103.

171 'Jermyn Street look'; 'tailored suits ... many, many scarves.' Ibid., p. 102.

171 'never challenge Mummy ... everyone listens.' Ibid., pp. 43–4.

172 'the list is not designed to be all-inclusive ... research.' Ibid., p. 234.

174 'there's not a man alive ... woman.' Frances Kennett, *Coco: The Life and Loves of Gabrielle Chanel* (London: Gollancz 1989), p. 52.

177 'gender difference in the victim's response to victimization.' See David Finkelhor and Diana Russell, 'The Gender Gap,' in D. Russell, *Sexual Exploitation* (Beverly Hills, CA: Sage 1984), pp. 215–68.

177 'incorporating the aggressor.' See Willa Appel, *Cults in America: Programmed for Paradise* (New York: Holt, Rinehart and Winston 1983), p. 99; see also Bruno Bettelheim, *Surviving and Other Essays* (New York: Alfred A. Knopf 1979), pp. 78–81.

178   A. Nicholas Groth, with H. Jean Birnbaum, *Men Who Rape: The Psychology of the Offender* (New York: Plenum Press 1979), p. 192.

178   'no one ... mothers.' Kathy Evert, as reported in H. Vanderbilt, 'Incest,' *Lear's*, February 1992, pp. 49–77.

178   Ken Plummer, 'Paedophilia: Constructing a Sociological Baseline,' in M. Cook and K. Howells, eds., *Adult Sexual Interest in Children* (London: Academic Press 1981), pp. 221–50.

178   'because of the expectations ... women.' Ibid., p. 228.

178   Robert Merton, *Social Theory and Social Structure* (Glencoe, IL: The Free Press 1968), p. 186.

185   'You want to go out ... both cheeks.' Andy Warhol and B. Colacilo, *Andy Warhol's Exposures* (London: Hutchinson 1982), p. 15.

189   'Pola didn't question ... marquis.' Moats, *The Million Dollar Studs*, p. 17.

189   'Thirty pulses accelerated alarmingly ... Rubi.' Ibid., pp. 248–9.

189   'At a party in Kitzbuehl [*sic*] ... on his own ...' Ibid., p. 209.

189   Michael Thompson, *Rubbish Theory: The Creation and Destruction of Value* (Oxford: Oxford University Press 1979).

191   jet set - 'which got its name ... sugar daddies.' Taki, 'Endangered Species,' in Taki and Bernard, eds., *High Life, Low Life*, p. 86.

192   'Perhaps because he ... victims quickly.' Robert K. Ressler and Tom Schachtman, *Whoever Fights Monsters* (New York: St Martin's Press 1992), p. 63.

192   'Fear of rape and attack ... subway cars.' Katha Pollitt, quoted in C. Fuchs Epstein, *Deceptive Distinctions: Sex, Gender and the Social Order* (New Haven, CT: Yale University Press 1988), pp. 134–5. See also Ezzat A. Fattah, *Understanding Criminal Victimization* (Scarborough, ON: Prentice-Hall 1991), pp. 268–72.

193   'Jodie Foster ... most famous actresses in the world.' John W. Hinckley, Jr, quoted in Rosalind Miles, *The Rites of Man: Love, Sex and Death in the Making of the Male* (London: Grafton 1991), p. 5.

193   'attention attack ... "a new phenomenon of our times."' Miles, *The Rites of Man*, p. 5.

193   'In the fifteenth and sixteenth centuries ... by hanging ...' Caroline Moorhead, *Fortune's Hostages: A Study of Kidnapping in the World Today* (London: Hamish Hamilton 1980), pp. 6–7.

193   'the rich are right to fear for their fortunes ... a cousin.' Ibid., p. 88.

194   Hearst 'was having a shower ... struggling.' Ibid., p. 90.

194   Hutton telephoning Doris Duke to obtain her impressions of Rubirosa. Moats, *The Million Dollar Studs*, p. 247.

196   'If decency is observed, morals are taken for granted.' Thorstein Veblen, *The Theory of the Leisure Class* (London: Unwin 1953), p. 21.

199   'the principle of least interest.' Willard Waller, *The Family: A Dynamic Interpretation* (New York: Dryden 1938).

199   Many types of resources ... power in relationships. This section is based on E.B. Foa and U.G. Foa, 'Resource Theory: Interpersonal Behavior as Exchange,' in K.J. Gergen, M.S. Greenber, and R.H. Willis, eds., *Social Exchange: Advances in Theory and Research* (New York: Plenum 1980), pp. 79–94.

200   'in relationships between the sexes ... paternity.' J. Lipman-Blumen, 'A Homosocial Theory of Sex Roles: An Examination of the Sex Segregation of Social Institutions,' in M. Blaxall and B. Reagan, eds., *Women and the Workplace* (Chicago: University of Chicago Press 1976), pp. 16–17.

201   As Robert Gould noted ... Robert Gould, 'Measuring Masculinity by the Size of a Paycheck,' in Deborah S. David and Robert Brannon, eds., *The Forty-Nine Percent Majority* (Reading, MA: Addison-Wesley 1976), pp. 113–18.

201   'these patterns have led us to conclude ... money talks.' See Blumstein and Schwartz, *American Couples*, pp. 55–6.

201   'Men and women feel ... security and autonomy.' Ibid., p. 76.

201   Blumstein and Schwartz found that, although married male automatically assume ... control of their own economic resources. Ibid., pp. 94–111.

204   'When the dominant group ... powerful.' J. Lipman-Blumen, *Gender Roles and Power* (Englewood Cliffs, NJ: Prentice-Hall 1984), p. 8.

CHAPTER 5 MAKING MAGIC

208   'illusion of the unexceptional.' See Robert C. Prus and C.R.D. Sharper, *Road Hustler*, expanded edition (New York: Richard Kaufman and Alan Greenberg 1991), p. 212.

208   'illusion of exceptional effects.' Ibid.

208   'mental magic.' Ibid., p. 250.

208   The ideas for this section on 'mental magic' reflect the guidance provide by Robert Prus, both in his co-authored work (with C.R.D. Sharper) *Road Hustler* and in numerous conversations between Dr Prus and the first author that took place between summer 1992 and winter 1993. We are indebted to him.

209   'spent his weak life ... the plausible.' Thomas Carlyle, 'King of Liars,' in Kerr ed., *The Penguin Book of Lies*, p. 216.

211   For a discussion of close-up magic, see Prus and Sharper, *Road Hustler*; for a discussion of the differences between stage majic and close-up

magic, see particularly chapter 15, 'Magic as Interactive Theatre,' pp. 205–41.

213 'When the individual ... setting.' E. Goffman, *The Presentation of Self in Everyday Life* (Harmondsworth: Penguin 1972), p. 79.

214 'a man of ancestry ... whimsical.' See P. Mason, *The Ideal of the Gentleman* (London: Andre Deutsch 1982), p. 16.

215 'to have lofty aims ... truth always.' W.M. Thackeray, *The Four Georges* (London: Falcott Press 1948), p. 131.

219 'Life is a picnic ... himself.' H. Melville, *The Confidence-Man* (Indianapolis: Bobbs-Merrill, 1969), pp. 187–8.

224 'magician must overcome scepticism and disbelief.' See Prus and Sharper, *Road Hustler*.

230 Ibid., p. 2.

230 For a full treatment of the remarkable career and strategies of Sigmund Engel see Jay Robert Nash, *Hustlers & Con Men*, p. 159.

231 'afflicted with womanmania ... fiddles.' 'Romeo Trapped by Chicago Police,' *Newsweek*, 4 July 1949, p. 40.

232 'as though.' 'Love Racket,' *Winnipeg Free Press*, 27 June 1949, p. 1.

232 'Regardless of.' 'It Must Be Love,' *Winnipeg Free Press*, 1 July 1949, p. 1.

232 Many famed practitioners ... See Nash, *Hustlers & Con Men*, p. 151.

232 R.M. Yoder, 'A Way with Women,' *Saturday Evening Post*, 7 May 1955, pp. 36, 146.

235 '*équivoque*.' See Prus and Sharper, *Road Hustler*, p. 257.

CHAPTER 6 MASQUERADES AND ILLUSIONS OF INTIMACY

252 'so wedded are we ... received sense.' Carolyn Heilbrun, *Toward a Recognition of Androgyny* (New York: Alfred A. Knopf 1973), p. xv.

254 'scotch-taping John Wayne and Brigitte Bardot together.' Mary Daly, 'The Qualitative Leap Beyond Patriarchal Religion,' *Quest: A Feminist Quarterly* 1 (Spring 1975), 30.

254 For a discussion of androgyny see Sandra L. Bem, 'Sex-Role Adaptability: One Consequence of Psychological Androgyny,' *Journal of Personality and Social Psychology* 31 (1975), 634–43; Sandra L. Bem, Wendy Martyna, and Carol Watson, 'Sex-Typing and Androgyny: Further Explorations of the Expressive Domain,' *Journal of Personality and Social Psychology* 34 (1976), 1016–23; Sandra L. Bem, 'Beyond Androgyny: Some Presumptuous Prescriptions for a Liberated Sexual Identity,' in Julia Sherman and Florence Denmark, eds., *The Future of Women: Issues in Psy-*

chology (New York: Psychological Dimensions 1978), pp. 1–23; Sandra L. Bem and Ellen Lenney, 'Sex-Typing and the Avoidance of Cross-Sex Behavior,' *Journal of Personality and Social Psychology* 33 (1976), 48–54.

255   'guy who has ...depressing.' Jimmy Breslin, 'Walk-Around Guys: Last Hope for City?' *City Edition*, 13 February 1990, p. 2. Copyright Newsday.

255   'seeks to return women to their bodies ... mirror.' Jeanette Winterson, Foreword to *Erotica: An Anthology of Women's Writings*, Margaret Reynolds, ed. (London: Pandora 1990), p. xx.

256   'Wife of.' The term 'Wife of' is extensively discussed in Una Stannard, *Mrs Man* (San Francisco, CA: Germainbooks 1977). See also Sondra Gotlieb, *Wife of ... An Irreverent Account of Life in Washington* (Toronto: Macmillan 1985).

256   'companion.' Veblen, *The Theory of the Leisure Class*, pp. 30, 57–60, 68–72, 180.

256   For a discussion of the 'companion' role of wife see L. Iremonger, *And His Charming Lady* (London: Secker and Warburg 1961); L. Wise, *Mrs. Success* (New York: World Publishing/Garret 1970); M. Fowlkes, *Behind Every Successful Man: Wives of Medicine and Academe* (New York: Columbia University Press 1980); A. Russell Hochschild, 'The Role of the Ambassador's Wife,' *Journal of Marriage and the Family* 31 (1969), 73–87; Heather Robertson, *More Than a Rose* (Toronto: Seal Books 1991); M. MacPherson, *The Power Lovers: An Intimate Look at Politicians and Their Marriages* (New York: Putnam 1975).

257   'A walker is not a gigolo ... purpose.' *Newsday*, 13 February 1990, p. 7.

258   Jessie Bernard, 'The Good Provider Role: Its Rise and Fall,' *American Psychologist* 36/1 (January 1981), pp. 1–12.

259   Barbara Ehrenreich, *Hearts of Men: American Dreams and the Flight from Commitment* (Garden City, NY: Anchor/Doubleday 1983).

259   'in general ... philosophy.' George Guder, 'The Single Man: He's in Bigger Trouble Than You'd Ever Guess,' *Detroit Free Press*, 19 November 1974, as cited in Marie Richmond Abbott, *Masculine and Feminine: Gender Roles Over the Life Cycle*, 2d ed. (Toronto: McGraw-Hill Ryerson 1992), p. 193.

259   'If you look at this guy ... see?' 'Man Faces Federal Trial on Bank Fraud Charges,' Associated Press, 28 January 1992.

260   Material on Gall Shawn Hubler, 'Thief of Hearts,' *Los Angeles Times*, 22 June 1990, South Bay Edition. Metro Section, Part B; p. 3, column 1.

262   'to show ... men.' Joan Rivière, 'Womanliness as a Masquerade,' *International Journal of Psychoanalysis*, 8 (1927), p. 303.

262   'Not long ago ...psychologically.' Ibid.

262 'often not persons whose judgement ... manner ...' Ibid., p. 304.

263 'Thus the aim of the compulsion ... stolen goods ...' Ibid., p. 305.

263 'The reader may now ask ... same thing.' Ibid., p. 313.

263 'the crimes ... infantile fantasies.' Kaplan, *Female Perversions*, p. 271.

263 case-study, 'Janet.' Ibid., pp. 271–83.

263 'Janet' was born ... love anyway.' Ibid., pp. 271-3.

264 'Little Janet recovered ... wishing for.' Ibid., p. 276.

264 'At the end of a long day ... penetration.' Ibid., pp. 279–80.

265 'Now at the close of the twentieth century ... punished.' Ibid., p. 282.

265 'everywhere, in my clinical practice ... colleagues.' Ibid., p. 282.

265 'not every woman ... feminine type.' Ibid.

265 'only a Janet ... "masculine" strivings.' Ibid., p. 283.

265 'blaming the mother.' See Paula Caplan, *Don't Blame Mother: Mending the Mother–Daughter Relationship* (New York: Harper and Row 1989), p. 46; Paula J. Caplan and Ian Hall-McCorquodale, 'Mother-Blaming in Major Clinical Journals,' *American Journal of Orthopsychiatry* 55 (1985), 345–53; Paula J. Caplan and Ian Hall-McCorquodale, 'The Scapegoating of Mothers: A Call for Change,' *American Journal of Orthopsychiatry* 55 (1985), 610–13.

266 fetishization is an attempt ... Ernest Becker, *The Structure of Evil* (New York: George Braziller 1968), p. 297.

266 'the politics of symptoms.' Seymour L. Halleck, *The Politics of Therapy* (New York: Science House 1971).

267 For a discussion of the differences between 'male' and 'female' language styles see Deborah Tannen, *You Just Don't Understand: Women and Men in Conversation* (New York: William Morrow 1990); Barrie Thorne, Cheris Kramarae, and Nancy Henley, eds., *Language, Gender and Society* (Rowley, MA: Newbury House 1983); Barrie Thorne and Nancy Henley eds., *Language and Sex: Difference and Dominance* (Rowley, MA: Newbury Press 1975); Candace West, 'When the Doctor Is a "Lady": Power, Status and Gender in Physician-Patient Encounters,' *Symbolic Interaction* 7 (1984), 87–106; Nancy Henley and Cheris Kramarae, 'Gender, Power and Miscommunication,' in B. Giles and J.M. Wiemann, eds., *'Miscommunication' and Problematic Talk* (Newbury Park, CA: Sage 1991), pp. 18-43.

CONCLUSION

286 Helen Lawrenson, 'Wanted: A New Modern Man,' *Esquire*, June 1983, pp. 42–8.

287 'men do not become gigolos ... self-defense.' Ibid., p. 44.

287 'forerunner of a new type ... admire.' Ibid., p. 42.

287 'The gigolo, after all ... American man.' Ibid., p. 44.

288 'The American man ... "freedom."' Ibid.

288 'The professional ... new modern woman.' Ibid., p. 45.

288 'Very few modern ... his own image.' Ibid., pp. 44, 48.

289 'The gigolo's motto is ... peace.' Ibid., p. 46.

289 'The American husband ... *disastrous*.' Ibid., pp. 46, 48.

290 'One of the most subtle manuevers ... certain points.' Ibid., pp. 46, 48.

290 'Thus, by a careful blend of flattery ... discontent.' Ibid., p. 48.

292 'New Woman.' According to Carroll Smith-Rosenberg, in *Disorderly Conduct: Visions of Gender in Victorian America* (New York: Oxford University Press 1985), 'the New Woman originated as a literary phrase popularized by Henry James ... [who] used it to refer to American women of affluence and sensitivity. Young and unmarried, they rejected social conventions, especially those imposed on women' (p. 176).

292 'The symbolically laden phrases ... decay.' Ibid., pp. 286–7.

292 'becomes ... women.' Ibid., p. 283.

292 'Man ... confusion.' From Alfred Tennyson, 'The Princess,' as cited in Marie Richmond-Abbott, *Masculine & Feminine: Gender Roles Over the Life Cycle* (New York: McGraw-Hill 1992), p. 3.

293 'The antisuffragist view of women's role ... public good.' Susan E. Marshall, 'Keep Us on the Pedestal: Women against Feminism in Twentieth-Century America,' in J. Freeman, ed., *Women: A Feminist Perspective* (Palo Alto, CA: Mayfield 1984), p. 570.

293 'must be recognized ... centuries.' Phyllis Schlafly, *The Power of the Positive Woman*, cited in Marshall, 'Keep Us on the Pedestal,' p. 570.

293 'further confuse ... identity.' Ibid., p. 571.

294 'that men and women are different ... woman.' Ibid.

294 'marriage and motherhood ... woman.' Ibid.

294 'For years American women led ... American male.' Lawrenson, 'Wanted: A New Modern Man,' pp. 42, 48.

295 The booming economy ... Statistics in relation to dual-income families from Katherine Marshall, 'Dual Earners,' *Canadian Social Trends,* Winter 1993, pp. 11. See also S.J. Wilson, *Women, Families and Work*, 3d ed. (Toronto: McGraw-Hill Ryerson 1991).

295 However, in 1991, the average ... were only 69.6 per cent. *Canadian Social Trends*, Winter 1993, 31.

296 'after fifteen years ... wages'; 'women held ... female occupations.' French, *The War against Women* (New York: Summit 1992), pp. 39-40.

296 In 1991, 82 per cent of almost one million ... Information on Canadian
familes from *Lone Parent Families in Canada. Selected Highlights*
(Ottawa: Statistics Canada, Housing, Family and Social Statistics Division, December 1992), p. 1.

296 as were 90 per cent ... United States. D.S. Eitzen and M.B. Zinn, *Social
Problems*, 6th ed. (Boston: Allyn and Bacon 1994), p. 344.

296 American female-headed ... comparable problems. Ibid., pp. 343–7.

296 A recent book ...' Dalma Heyn, *The Erotic Silence of the American Wife*
(New York: Turtle Bay 1992). Quotations from Linda Kay, 'Wives Just
Wanna Have Fun,' *Chatelaine*, March 1993, pp. 91–3.

298 For a discussion of the 'Superwoman' image and reality see Wilson,
Women, Families and Work, p. 34; A. Hochschild, *The Second Shift:
Working Parents and the Revolution at Home* (New York: Viking 1989);
Myra Ferree, 'The Superwoman Syndrome,' in Christine Bose, Roslyn
Feldberg, and Natalie Sokoloff, eds., *Hidden Aspects of Women's Work*
(New York: Praeger 1987), pp. 161–80; David H. Demo and Alan C.
Acock, 'Family Diversity and the Division of Domestic Labor: How Much
Have Things Really Changed?' *Family Relations* 42 (1993), 323–31; Mar-
shall, 'Dual Earners,' pp. 11–14.

299 objects of monetary success. See William Farrell, *Why Men Are the
Way They Are* (New York: McGraw-Hill 1986), pp. 106–8. For an
earlier treatment see Safilios-Rothschild, *Love, Sex and Sex Roles*,
ch. 3.

302 Research conducted in the area of family violence ... See Del Martin, *Bat-
tered Wives* (New York: Simon and Schuster 1976); Lenore Walker, *The
Battered Woman* (New York: Harper and Row 1979); Linda MacLeod,
Battered But Not Beaten ... Preventing Wife Battering in Canada
(Ottawa: Canadian Advisory Council on the Status of Women 1987); A.
Propper, 'Patterns of Family Violence,' in M. Baker, ed., *Families: Chang-
ing Trends in Canada*, 2d ed. (Toronto: McGraw-Hill Ryerson, 1990),
pp. 272–305; Julie Blackman, *Intimate Violence* (New York: Columbia
University Press 1989); R.J. Gelles and M.A. Straus, *Intimate Violence:
The Causes and Consequences of Abuse in the American Family* (New
York: Touchstone 1988).

303 male strippers' reporting ... their performances. See D.M. Petersen and
P.L. Dressel, 'Equal Time for Women: Social Notes on the Male Strip
Show,' in E.D. Salamon and B.W. Robinson, eds., *Gender Roles: Doing
What Comes Naturally?* (Toronto: Nelson 1987), pp. 105–18.

304 at current rates, the incidence of divorce and separation ... Larry L. Bumpass, 'What's Happening to the Family,' *Demography* 27 (1990), 483–98.

See also Teresa Castro Martin and Larry L. Bumpass, 'Recent Trends in Marital Disruption,' *Demography*, 26 (1989), 37–51.

305 For a further discussion of the conservative agenda, see Constance Shehan and John Scanzoni, 'Gender Patterns in the United States: Demographic Trends and Policy Prospects,' *Family Relations* 37 (1988), 444–50. See also William Gairdner, *The War against the Family: A Parent Speaks Out* (Toronto: Stoddart 1992).

308 'There is now explosive ... "slave and accomplice."' Joseph Barry, *French Lovers: From Heloise and Abelard to Beauvoir and Sartre* (New York: Arbor House 1990), pp. xiv, 306–7, 318–19.

Index